HOW TO GO MAD
WITHOUT LOSING
YOUR MIND

D1570510

BLACK OUTDOORS INNOVATIONS
IN THE POETICS OF STUDY **A SERIES**
EDITED BY J. KAMERON CARTER
AND SARAH JANE CERVENAK

DUKE UNIVERSITY PRESS
DURHAM AND LONDON   2021

LA MARR
JURELLE
BRUCE

HOW TO GO MAD WITHOUT LOSING YOUR MIND

MADNESS
AND BLACK
RADICAL
CREATIVITY

© 2021 Duke University Press

All rights reserved

Printed in the United States of America
on acid-free paper ∞

Cover design by Courtney Leigh Richardson
Text design by Aimee C. Harrison

Typeset in Garamond Premier Pro
and Helvetica Neue LT Std by
Westchester Publishing Services

Library of Congress Cataloging-in-Publication Data
Names: Bruce, La Marr Jurelle, [date] author.
Title: How to go mad without losing your mind:
madness and Black radical creativity / La Marr
Jurelle Bruce.
Other titles: Black outdoors.
Description: Durham: Duke University Press, 2020. |
Series: Black outdoors | Includes bibliographical
references and index.
Identifiers: LCCN 2019051658 (print) |
LCCN 2019051659 (ebook)
ISBN 9781478009832 (hardcover)
ISBN 9781478010876 (paperback)
ISBN 9781478012429 (ebook)
Subjects: LCSH: African American artists. | African
Americans in the performing arts. | Racism—United
States—Psychological aspects. | Racism and the
arts—United States. | Racism in popular culture—
United States. | Eurocentrism—Psychological
aspects. | Creative ability—Psychological aspects.
Classification: LCC NX512.3. A35 B78 2020 (print) |
LCC NX512.3. A35 (ebook) | DDC 709.2/396073—dc23
LC record available at https: //lccn.loc.gov/2019051658
LC ebook record available at https: //lccn.loc.gov/2019051659

Cover art: *Inner*. 2014. © Alexis Peskine. Courtesy of
Alexis Peskine, October Gallery.

For

Eleanor Joyce Bruce (1941–2018)

and

David Anthony Hughes (1979–2020)

In love and madness, words fail—but I keep trying.

CONTENTS

ACKNOWLEDGMENTS

I am made of love. Held by love. Covered in love. Brimming with love—and praise and thanks to my family. To my niece, who is also my goddaughter, Kimberly Maria Bruce; to my mother, Kim C. Bruce; to my late grandmother, Eleanor Joyce Bruce; and to my late great-grandmother, Magnolia "Lathy" Bruce, thank you all for lifting me up, pulling me through, and carrying me over. I owe this project and my life to a mighty cohort of Bruce mothers and daughters. Thank you, also and always, to my brothers Aaron and Chazz; my aunts Carla and Cherie; my great-aunts Sissy and Betty; my great-uncle Gerald; my cousins Stacey, Carrington, Ciela, and Cassidy; my nephews Alexander and Ethan; and Rodney, who is my father.

I owe endless gratitude to my ancestors whose names I'll never know—and to my as-yet-unconceived children whose names I don't yet know: I already love you, though I've never met you; I already miss you, though I haven't left you; I don't even know you, but I can't forget you. Amen and amen.

Cheers to my editor, Ken Wissoker, and to the editorial staff at Duke University Press, especially Olivia Polk, Nina Foster, and Joshua Gutterman Tranen. I appreciate your excitement about my work, your stewardship through this process, and the kindness you've extended to me. I am also grateful to Susan Albury, project editor at Duke, who managed my many, many revisions late in the process. I am humbled and honored to publish *How to Go Mad* as part of the Black Outdoors book series, edited by J. Kameron Carter and Sarah Cervenak. Why long for a seat at the table when you can carry your meal outside? I like it out here, under open sky.

How to Go Mad originated while I was a graduate student in African American Studies and American Studies at Yale University. I am grateful to faculty mentors Elizabeth Alexander, Daphne Brooks, Joseph Roach, and Laura Wexler for their brilliance, patience, and gracious guidance. Other Yale faculty were crucial to my education, especially Emilie Townes, Robert Stepto,

Matthew Jacobson, Joanne Meyerowtiz, Jafari Sinclaire Allen, and Lisa Lowe. Shout-out to fellow students who enriched my life and learning at Yale, particularly Stephanie Greenlea, Carlos Miranda, Sara Hudson, Madison Moore, Gamal Palmer, Ana-Maurine Lara, Elizabeth Son, Calvin Warren, Charlie Veric, Brandon Terry, Deborah March, Jennifer Leath, Petra Richterova, Sarah Lewis, Darian Parker, and Karilyn Crockett.

I finished my degree while in residence at the University of Virginia as a Carter G. Woodson Predoctoral Fellow. For journeying beside me as I crossed that threshold: Thank you to UVA faculty members Deborah McDowell, Lawrie Balfour, Marlon Ross, Lisa Shutt, Eric Lott, Claudrena Harold, Sylvia Chong, and Lisa Woolfork, as well as Woodson Fellows including Z'etoile Imma, Kwame Holmes, Zakiyyah Iman Jackson, Alexandra Moffet-Bateau, and Barbara Boswell.

Many thanks to the many friends I've made through the Mellon Mays Undergraduate Fellowship, the Black Performance Theory Working Group, Interdisciplinary Performance Studies at Yale University, the Ford Foundation Fellowship, and the Summer Institute on Tenure and Professional Advancement at Duke University.

What a blessing it was to land a job at the University of Maryland, College Park. I am grateful for the indispensable support of my colleagues in UMD's Department of American Studies, especially Psyche Williams-Forson, Nancy Mirabal, Mary Sies, Sheri Parks, Jason Farman, Bayley Marquez, Jan Padios, Julia John, Dana Persaud, Asim Ali, and Betsy Yuen. The broader UMD faculty community has been fabulous to me, especially Julius Fleming Jr., Tabitha Chester, Aleia Brown, Jasmón Bailey, GerShun Avilez, Chad Infante, Faedra Carpenter, Alexis Lothian, Iván Ramos, Caitlin Marshall, Zita Nunes, I. Augustus Durham, Melissa Blanco-Borelli, Daryle Williams, and Bonnie Thornton-Dill. I've had the precious pleasure and great honor of working with current and former students at Maryland who have impacted my thinking: Tony Perry, Terrance Wooten, Ilyas Abukar, Robert Jiles, Izetta Mobley, David Chavannes, Emelia Gold, Kalima Young, Hazim Abdullah-Smith, Mark Lockwood, Dallas Donnell, Devon Betts, Nat Baldino, Sarah Scriven, Danielle Laplace, Damien Hagan, Les Gray, Otis Ramsey-Zoe, and Tara Demmy are among them.

No matter how often I receive invitations to present my research, they always fill me with giddy gratitude. I feel both wonderfully affirmed and deeply humbled when someone requests my presence on their campus (or virtual forum). Aimee Cox and Darnell Moore invited me to deliver my first ever keynote at the "Ruminations on Blackness" symposium at Rutgers University, Newark, in 2011. Curlee Holton brought me on board to present at the David Driskell Center for the Study of the Visual Arts and Culture of African Americans and the African Diaspora at UMD in 2015. Margo Crawford and C. Riley Snorton invited me to participate in "The Flesh of the Matter: A Hortense Spillers Symposium" at Cornell University in 2016. Terrell Taylor and the Department of English at Vanderbilt University appointed me as the 2018 Stirling Lecturer and hosted me for a series of wonderful events on campus. Farah Jasmine Griffin, Kellie Jones, and Shawn Mendoza welcomed me back to my undergraduate alma mater, Columbia University, for "Free to Be Anywhere in the Universe: An International Conference on New Directions in the Study of the African Diaspora" in 2018. Also in 2018, Eddie Bruce-Jones and Monish Bhatia beckoned me across the Atlantic to deliver a keynote for "Race, Mental Health, and State Violence: A Two-Day Symposium" at Birkbeck College, University of London. In 2019, Hannah Rosen and Joseph Lawless brought me to William & Mary College to participate in "On Surviving as the Object of Property: Conversations with Patricia J. Williams—A Symposium in Celebration of a Transformative Intellectual Agenda," where I met Patricia, who has since become a dear friend. In 2020, Johanna Braun and Jennifer Devere Brody invited me to "#masshysteria: Politics, Affect, and Performance Strategies," a virtual symposium hosted by Stanford University. Thunderous thanks to you all. In 2020, I was also scheduled to present with the African American Studies Speaker Series at Georgetown University and the Performance Studies Working Group at Yale University; though these talks were postponed because of campus closures, I am thankful for the invitations.

I have also presented material from this book before enthusiastic audiences in the Department of English at Cornell University, the Departments of English and American Studies at Brown University, the Department of English at Tulane University, the Department of Africana Studies at Rutgers University, New Brunswick, and the Department of English at the University of Massachusetts, Amherst. Additionally, I received excellent feedback on this research at conferences of the American Society for Theatre Research, the American Studies Association, the Black Performance Theory Working Group, the Modern Language Association, and Performance Studies International.

For reading and offering feedback on portions of this manuscript, I am immensely grateful to the anonymous readers, as well as my loving interlocutors including David Hughes, Isaiah Wooden, Soyica Colbert, Derrais Carter, Sarah Cervenak, Tim Rommen, Chad Infante, Julius Fleming Jr., and Nicole Fleetwood. Thank you to Nicole and to Patricia J. Williams for writing the breathtaking blurbs that appear on the back of this book. Many thanks to Sarah Grey for the careful copyedits and to Derek Gottlieb for the exquisite index.

I am indebted to the mentorship of Farah Jasmine Griffin, Guthrie Ramsey, E. Patrick Johnson, Soyica Colbert, Tsitsi Jaji, Margo Crawford, Herman Beavers, and Nicole Fleetwood. I have also benefited from the counsel and kindness of Marcellus Blount, Ezra Tawil, Monica Miller, Kara Keeling, Kevin Quashie, Fred Moten, Koritha Mitchell, Robin Bernstein, Lyrae Van Clief-Stefanon, Tavia Nyong'o, Joel Dinerstein, Tim Rommen, Mark Anthony Neal, Imani Perry, Christina Sharpe, Carole Boyce Davies, Hortense Spillers, Brenda LeFrançois, Tommy DeFrantz, and Therí Pickens.

I want to recite the names of a broader community of folks whose kindness, inspiration, provocation, and love were instrumental to my thinking before and beyond the writing of this book. Roughly in order of the first time I encountered each of them, this list includes Lecynia Swire, Mecca Jamilah Sullivan, Christian Pierre, Joy-Anne Mitchell, Alexander Sullivan, Marcus Mitchell, Cheryl Greene, Alexis Pauline Gumbs, David Rease, Shaun Anthony Little, Frank Leon Roberts, Malaika Adero, Martha Sullivan, Scott Poulson-Bryant, James Earl Hardy, Steven G. Fullwood, Emily Bernard, Sandy Placido, Javon Johnson, Darnell Moore, L. Lamar Wilson, Joseph Cermatori, Frederick Staidum, Kai Green, Bryan Epps, Jasmine Johnson, Aida Mbowa, Douglas Jones, Jayna Brown, Shayne Frederick, Enock Amankwah, Moses Serubiri, Aimee Meredith Cox, Wendell P. Holbrook, Don Gagnon, Tobias Spears, J. T. Roane, Evan Starling Davis, Devin Michael Brown, Kenneth Anderson, Joshua Bennett, Tina Post, Aquarius Gilmer, Jonathan Lykes, Khalid Long, Michael Robinson, Andrew Anderson, Fatima Jamal, Phanuel Antwi, Rosemary Ndubuizu, DeRon Williams, Yomaira Figueroa, Regina Bradley, Kevin Lawrence Henry Jr., Matthew Pettway, Lance Keene, Rhaisa Williams, Karen Jaime, Marquis Bey, Justin Hosbey, Ronak Kapadia, Tanja Aho, Bettina Judd, Ashanté Reese, Idris Mitchell, Chezare Warren, Antoine Crosby, Rahsaan Mahadeo, and the entire House of Fullness. I am warmed by the sheer sight of your names gathered together on these pages.

This project benefited from funding provided by the Beinecke Rare Book and Manuscript Library at Yale University, the Carter G. Woodson Institute for African-American and African Studies at the University of Virginia, the Social Science Research Council, the Mellon Foundation, the Ford Foundation, the Summer Institute on Tenure and Professional Advancement at Duke University, the Research and Scholarship Award from the University of Maryland, and the College of Arts & Humanities (Subvention Fund) from the University of Maryland.

A brief portion of chapter 1 was published as "Mad Is a Place; or, the Slave Ship Tows the Ship of Fools," in *American Quarterly* 69, no. 2 (2017): 303–8 (with gratitude to the "Mad Futures" forum coeditors, Tanja Aho, Liat Ben-Moshe, and Leon Hilton for inviting me to contribute). An early version of chapter 5 appeared as "'The People inside My Head, Too': Madness, Black Womanhood, and the Radical Performance of Lauryn Hill," in *African American Review* 45, no. 3 (2012): 371–89. An early version of chapter 7 appeared as "Interludes in Madtime: Black Music, Madness, and Metaphysical Syncopation," in *Social Text* 35, no. 4 (2017): 1–31. I am grateful to Natasha Trethewey for permitting me to include the full text of her poem "Calling His Children Home," which originally appeared in *Callaloo* 19, no. 2 (1996): 351.

I close with a litany of praise for acts of love that saved me. To Eleanor Joyce Bruce, who taught me a love that speaks when words dissolve, that knows when memory fails; to Farah Jasmine Griffin, who helped set me flowing; to Isaiah Wooden, for talking me through the night and not hanging up; to T. H. Cox, for delivering that message from the other side; to Julius Fleming Jr., for teaching and showing me patience; to Jasmón Bailey, for aspirin and prayer; to Mpho Ndaba, in praise of softness; to James Padilioni Jr., in honor of muchness; to Tsitsi Jaji, for answering when I called and even when I didn't; to Na'im Surgeon, for helping me carry my things; to Marcus Washington, for holding me steady, briefly, and letting me go; to Kondor Nunn, for picking me up from that Virginia basement, and from something lower than that; to Ahmad Washington, for picturing me more clearly and vividly than I saw myself; to Will Mosley, for reminding me to drink water and love—because weeping will dehydrate a body; to Derrais Carter, for always celebrating with me, and always being a mighty cause for celebration; to Ethan Isaiah Bruce and Alexander Mason Bruce, for making the world brand new; to Kimberly Maria Bruce, for your laughter, which is also a song, and also a prayer, and also a rally cry, and also an instruction for living; and to Kim C. Bruce, infinity times infinity—infinity times.

While this book was in production, I suffered the most violent grief and stunning sadness I have ever felt or known. David Anthony Hughes, my beloved, left this world unexpectedly and tore a hole in my chest that reached up and split the sky. David, you were and are the most extravagantly, generously, relentlessly, recklessly loving man I've ever known. You were right all along, babe. I'll spend my whole life trying to gather up and bask in this miraculous mess of love you leave behind. I now know that grief is a sort of gratitude.

God is good, life is brief, love is long, I am here, you are close, we are blessed, and it is done.

CHAPTER ONE

MAD IS A PLACE

PRELUDE: THE SLAVE
SHIP TOWS THE SHIP OF FOOLS

HOLD TIGHT. THE WAY TO GO MAD WITHOUT LOSING YOUR MIND IS SOMETIMES UNRULY. It might send you staggering across asylum hallways, heckled by disembodied voices—or shimmying over spotlit stages, greeted by loving applause. It might find you freewheeling through fever dreams, then marching toward freedom dreams, then scrambling from sleep, with blood and stars in your eyes, the whole world a waking dream.[1] But for now, we wade through a liquid void, among ominous ships, where this study begins.

The epigraphs above, supplied by the French philosopher Michel Fou-

Confined on the ship, from which there is no escape, the madman is delivered to the river with its thousand arms, the sea with its thousand roads, to the great uncertainty external to everything. He is the Passenger par excellence: that is, the prisoner of the passage. And the land he will come to is unknown—as is, once he disembarks, the land from which he comes. He has his truth and his homeland only in that *fruitless expanse* between two countries that cannot belong to him. —MICHEL FOUCAULT, *Madness and Civilization: A History of Insanity in the Age of Reason*, 1961

Those African persons in "Middle Passage" were literally suspended in the "oceanic." . . . [R]emoved from the indigenous land and culture, and not-yet "American" either, these captive persons, without names that their captors would recognize, were in movement across the Atlantic, but they were also *nowhere at all*. —HORTENSE SPILLERS, "Mama's Baby, Papa's Maybe: An American Grammar Book," 1987

cault and the black feminist theorist Hortense Spillers, are our floating signposts. They point us to the intersection of a "fruitless expanse" and "nowhere at all": an unmappable coordinate where a ship of fools crosses a slave ship, where imprisoned madness meets captive blackness in a stifling tightness through a groundless vastness. I shudder and flounder as I wonder: What vertigo does a body undergo, caught between treacherous waters below and treacherous captors above, with "nowhere" outside? How does it feel to be forcibly hauled across the sea while forcibly stagnated on the ship—to endure a cruelty in motion that is also a cruelty of stillness? What noise might ring out if the sound of a laughing "fool" joined the sound of a weeping "slave"—and would the weeper and the laugher commiserate? How does one keep time, or discern direction, or remember the way home from "nowhere at all," with no familiar beacon to behold ahead or behind? It seems to me that neither imagination nor historiography is apt to apprehend the seasickness of spirit, the existential dread, and the feverish homesickness that might menace a mad prisoner or black captive trapped at sea.

An unimaginable scene may seem a strange place to launch a study of radical imagination. Likewise, a fruitless expanse makes a bleak backdrop for pondering the fruit of mad black creativity. And furthermore, unanswerable questions may sound odd opening a work of careful inquiry. But there are lessons to learn from those who make homeland in wasteland, freedom routes to chart that start in a ship's hull, debris of mad and black life to retrieve from the sea, mad black worlds to make that rise from a ship's wake, and questions that refuse answers but rouse movements.[2] Besides, if the anticolonial psychiatrist Frantz Fanon is right, if there is "a zone of nonbeing . . . an utterly naked declivity where an authentic upheaval can be born,"[3] then "nowhere at all" may be an especially auspicious place to commence. By beginning at this curious crossing, I also hope to orient the reader—which requires that I *disorient* the reader—for the errant, erratic routes to come. Remember that the way is sometimes unruly.

Those opening epigraphs are passages of prose conjuring cataclysmic passages of persons across temporal, spatial, and metaphysical gauntlets. In the first epigraph, Foucault chases a "ship of fools" as it crisscrosses early modern Europe. To have him tell it, ships of fools were fifteenth-century nautical vessels whose lunatic occupants were deemed nuisances to their communities, expelled from home, made wards of sailors, and consigned to those ships as they drifted along European rivers and seas. When Foucault declares that the mad seafarer has "his truth and his homeland only in that fruitless expanse between two countries that cannot belong to him," the words evoke a *mad diaspora*: a scattering of captives across sovereign borders and over bodies of water; an upheaval and dispersal of persons flung far from home; and an emergence of unprecedented diasporic subjectivities, ontologies, and possibilities that transgress national and rational norms.

To a scholar of black modernity, Foucault's account may ring uncannily familiar. It brings to my mind many millions of Africans abducted from their native lands by slave traders in the fifteenth through nineteenth centuries. These stolen people were stacked in the putrid pits of slave ships; made "prisoner of the passage" called the Middle Passage; uprooted from solid "truth" and stable "homeland"; drenched, instead, in oceanic uncertainty; dragged across a "fruitless expanse"; discharged onto a land that, arguably, "cannot belong to" them; and cast into restlessness and rootlessness that persist in many of their descendants.

In the second epigraph, Spillers describes the Passage, and her words bear repeating: "Removed from the indigenous land and culture, and not-yet 'American' either, these captive persons, without names that their captors would recognize, were in movement across the Atlantic, but they were also *nowhere* at all." Some pessimists claim that the progeny of slaves are still not American, still vainly awaiting recognition as citizen and affirmation as human, still existentially captive, still suspended in that void.[4] Wherever blackness dwells—slave ship, spaceship, graveyard, garden, elsewhere, everywhere—those captives accessed what Spillers calls a "richness of *possibility*."[5] They would realize black diasporic kinesis, kinship, sociality, creativity, love, and myriad modes of being that flourish in their marvelously tenacious heirs. In a "fruitless expanse," the enslaved bore fruit. The pit held seeds, as pits sometimes do.

Both the ship of fools and the slave ship provoke historiographic dispute. Regarding the ship of fools, many historians insist that Foucault mistook an early modern literary and visual motif for a material vessel.[6] As for the slave ship, it incites crises of calculation about the number of Africans who made it to *the other side*—by which I mean *the Americas* and/or/as *the afterlife*—and about the depth of the wound that the Middle Passage inflicts on modernity.[7] Both ships defy positivist history: the ship of fools because it was likely unreal; the slave ship because it is so devastatingly real that it confounds comprehension, resists documentation, and spawns ongoing effects that belie the purported *pastness* of history. It is no wonder that when Spillers wanted to address the historical and ontological functions of the Middle Passage and its ripples across modernity, particularly black female modernity, she realized that "the language of the historian was not telling me what I needed to know."[8] (Perhaps the language of the mad methodologist, who I will introduce shortly, can better speak to Spillers's concerns.) Spillers further characterizes the Middle Passage as a "dehumanizing, ungendering, and defacing project"—and I would add *deranging* to that grave litany.[9] To *derange* is to throw off, to cast askew, "to disturb the order or arrangement of" an entity.[10] The Middle Passage literally deranged and threw millions of Africans askew across continents, oceans, centuries, and worlds.[11] I use *derange* also to signal how the Atlantic slave trade, and the antiblack modernity it inaugurated, framed black people as always already wild, subrational, pathological, mentally unsound, mad.

Although it is unlikely that a slave ship ever crossed a ship of fools in geographic space,[12] these vessels converged in the discursive domains and cultural imaginations of early Euromodernity. According to the era's emergent antiblack and antimad worldviews, both of these ships were floating graveyards of the socially dead. Both ships were imagined to haul inferior, unReasonable beings who were metaphysically adrift amid the rising tide of Reason. For the purposes of this study, I distinguish *reason* (lowercase) from *Reason* (uppercase). The former, *reason*, signifies a generic process of cognition within a given system of logic and the "mental powers concerned with forming conclusions, judgments, or inferences."[13] Meanwhile, *Reason* is a proper noun denoting a positivist, secularist, Enlightenment-rooted episteme purported to uphold objective "truth" while mapping and mastering the world. In normative Western philosophy since the Age of Enlightenment, Reason and rationality are believed essential for achieving modern personhood, joining civil society, and participating in liberal politics.[14] However, Reason has been entangled, from those very Enlightenment roots, with misogynist, colonialist, ableist, antiblack, and other pernicious ideologies. The fact is that female people, indigenous people, colonized people, neurodivergent people, and black people have been violently excluded from the edifice of Enlightenment Reason—with Reasonable doctrines justifying those exclusions.[15]

Regarding the hegemony of Reason, political theorist Achille Mbembe remarks that "it is on the basis of a distinction between reason and unreason (passion, fantasy) that late-modern criticism has been able to articulate a certain idea of the political, the community, the subject—or, more fundamentally, of what the good life is all about, how to achieve it, and, in the process, to become a fully moral agent. The exercise of reason is tantamount to the exercise of freedom."[16] While Mbembe names "passion" and "fantasy" as examples of "unreason," a third entry belongs on this list: madness itself. If those late-modern critics claim that Reason is requisite for "becoming a fully moral agent," they also imply the inverse—that unReason entails moral deficiency and ineptitude. (This is why throes of *passion*, flights of *fantasy*, and bouts of *madness* are thought inimical to one's moral sense.) Meanwhile, if "late-modern criticism" insists that "the exercise of reason is tantamount to the exercise of freedom," it also insinuates the inverse—that the condition of unReason is commensurate with the condition of unfreedom. While Mbembe's point of reference is late modernity, Enlightenment-era philosophers like David Hume, Immanuel Kant, Thomas Jefferson, and Georg Wilhelm Friedrich Hegel also asserted that unReasonable beings were suited for unfreedom, that the unReason of Africans ordained them for enslavement.[17] Within white supremacist and antiblack master narratives that calcified in the eighteenth century, to be white-*cum*-rational was to inherit modernity's pantheon and merit freedom; to be black-*cum*-subrational was to be barred from modernity's favor and primed for slavery. The Euro-modern patriarch affirmed his Reason and freedom, in part, by casting the black African as his ontological foil, his unReasonable and enslaved Other.[18]

In staging this encounter between the slave ship and ship of fools, I do not intend to imply a simplistic analogy between the two. Rather, I want to suggest that the slave ship (icon of abject blackness) commandeers the ship of fools (icon of abject madness), tows the ship of fools, helps orient Western notions of madness and Reason, and helps propel this turbulent movement we call modernity.[19]

HOW TO GO MAD:
THEORY AND METHODOLOGY

How to Go Mad without Losing Your Mind roves the intersections of madness and radical creativity in black expressive culture, particularly African American expressive culture, since the twentieth century. In the chapters that follow, I seek the mad in the literatures of August Wilson, Amiri Baraka, Gayl Jones, Ntozake Shange, Suzan-Lori Parks, and Richard Wright; in the jazz repertoires of Buddy Bolden, Sun Ra, and Charles Mingus; in the comedic performances of Richard Pryor and Dave Chappelle; and in the protest music of Nina Simone, Lauryn Hill, Kanye West, Kendrick Lamar, and Frank Ocean, among many other cultural producers and forms. In the works of these artists, madness animates—and sometimes agitates—black radical artmaking, self-making, and worldmaking. Moreover, madness becomes content, form, symbol, idiom, aesthetic, existential posture, philosophy, strategy, and energy in an enduring black radical tradition.

The *black* in this book's subtitle signifies a dynamic matrix of cultures, epistemologies, subjectivities, corporealities, socialities, and ontologies rooted in sub-Saharan African peoples and traveling in diasporic circuits and surges to the ends of the world. *Black* coalesced as a racial category amid the Atlantic slave trade and the advent of global antiblackness—but blackness contains creative and insurgent power, on display in this study, far exceeding those wretched sites of origin and those cruel conditions of coalescence.

I do not typically capitalize *black* because I do not regard it as a *proper* noun. Grammatically, the proper noun corresponds to a formal name or title assigned to an individual, closed, fixed entity. I use a lowercase *b* because I want to emphasize an *improper* blackness: a blackness that is a "critique of the proper";[20] a blackness that is collectivist rather than individualistic; a blackness that is "never closed and always under contestation";[21] a blackness that is ever-unfurling rather than rigidly fixed; a blackness that is neither capitalized nor propertized via the protocols of Western grammar; a blackness that centers those who are typically regarded as lesser and *lower cases*, as it were; a blackness that amplifies those who are treated as "minor figures," in Western modernity.[22] I appreciate that some use the big *B* to confer respect, signal gravitas, and indicate specificity. However, the impropriety of lowercase blackness suits me, and this mad black project, just fine. Besides, my minor *b* is replete with respect, gravitas, and specificity-in-collectivity, too; its smallness does not limit the infinite care it contains. As for the term *black radical creativity*, it signifies black expressive culture that imagines, manifests, and practices otherwise ways of doing and being—all while confounding dominant logics, subverting normative aesthetics, and eroding oppressive structures of power and feeling.[23]

But what of *madness*? My critical account of madness in modernity proceeds from two premises. On the one hand, madness is a floating signifier and dynamic social construction that evades stable definition. On the other hand, or maybe in the same hand, madness is a lived reality that demands sustained attention. Accounting for these exigencies, I forward a model of madness that is theoretically agile enough to chase floating signifiers while ethically rooted enough to hold deep compassion for madpersons. Thus primed, I propose that madness encompasses at least four overlapping entities in the modern West.

First is *phenomenal madness*: an intense unruliness of mind—producing fundamental crises of perception, emotion, meaning, and selfhood—as experienced in the consciousness of the mad subject. This unruliness is not necessarily painful, nor is it categorically pleasurable; it may induce distress, despair, exhilaration, euphoria, and myriad other sensations. In elaborating this mode of madness, I favor a phenomenological attitude attuned to whatever presents itself to consciousness, including hallucinations and delusions that have no material basis. Most important, phenomenal madness centers the lived experience and first-person interiority of the mad subject, rather than, say, the diagnoses imposed by medical authority.

Such diagnoses are the basis of *medicalized madness*, the second category in this schema. Medicalized madness encompasses a range of "serious mental illnesses" and psychopathologies codified by the psy sciences of psychiatry, psychology, and psychoanalysis. These "serious" conditions include schizophrenia, dissociative identity disorder, bipolar disorder, borderline personality disorder, and the antiquated diagnosis of medical "insanity," among others.[24] I label this category medical*ize*d madness—emphasizing the suffix -*ize*, meaning *to become* or *to cause to become*—to signal that mental illness is a politicized process, epistemological operation, and sociohistorical construction, rather than an ontological given. (Consider this brief example: A psychiatric patient who perceives voices, with no empirically discernable outside source, might be diagnosed with schizophrenia. Modern Western psychiatry medicalizes and pathologizes this experience as "auditory hallucination."[25] However, in another historical context or social milieu, such a sound might be regarded as, say, prophetic hearing, superhuman aurality, telepathic transmission, or merely an unremarkable sensory variation.[26] My point is that there is nothing inherently, ontologically, transhistorically pathological about hearing voices.)

Even forms of medicalized madness that are measurable in brain tissue physiology, neuroelectric currents, and other empirical criteria are infiltrated (and sometimes constituted) by sociocultural forces. The creation, standardization, collection, and interpretation of psychiatric metrics take place in the crucible of culture. Likewise, clinical procedures are designed and carried out by subjective persons embedded in webs of social relations. And furthermore, psychiatry is susceptible to ideology. Exploiting that susceptibility, various antiblack, proslavery, patriarchal, colonialist, homophobic, and transphobic regimes have wielded psychiatry as a tool of domination. Thus, acts and attributes such as insurgent blackness, slave rebellion, willful womanhood, anticolonial resistance, same-sex desire, and gender subversion have all been pathologized by Western psychiatric science.[27] Beyond these overt examples of hegemonic psychiatry, I want to emphasize that no diagnosis is innocently objective. No etiology escapes the touch and taint of ideology. No science is pure.[28]

The third mode of madness is *rage*: an affective state of intense and aggressive displeasure (which is surely phenomenal, but warrants analytic distinction from the unruliness above). Black people in the United States and elsewhere have been subjected to heinous violence and degradation, but rarely granted recourse. Consequently, as singer-songwriter Solange Knowles reminds us, black people "got the right to be mad" and "got a lot to be mad about."[29] Alas, when they articulate rage in American public spheres, black people are often criminalized as threats to public safety, lampooned as angry black caricatures, and pathologized as insane. That latter process—the conflation of black anger and black insanity—parallels the Anglophone confluence of *madness* meaning anger and *madness* meaning insanity. In short, when black people get mad (as in *angry*), antiblack logics tend to presume they've gone mad (as in *crazy*).

The fourth and most capacious category in this framework is *psychosocial madness*: radical deviation from the *normal* within a given psychosocial milieu. Any person or practice that perplexes and vexes the psychonormative status quo is liable to be labeled *crazy*. The arbiters of psychosocial madness are not elite cohorts of psychiatric experts, but rather multitudes of avowedly Reasonable people and publics who abide by psychonormative common sense. Thus, psychosocial madness reflects how avowedly sane majorities interpellate and often denigrate difference. What I have already stated about medicalized madness can also be adapted to psychosocial madness: acts and attributes such as insurgent blackness, slave rebellion, willful womanhood, anticolonial resistance, same-sex desire, and gender subversion have all been ostracized as *crazy* by sane majorities who adhere to Reasonable common sense. Whereas phenomenal madness is an *unruliness of mind*, psychosocial madness is sometimes an *unruliness of will* that resists and unsettles reigning regimes of the normal.

In its psychosocial iteration, *madness* often functions as a disparaging descriptor for any mundane phenomenon perceived to be odd and undesirable. An unconventional hairstyle, unpopular political opinion, physical tic, indecipherable utterance, eccentric outfit, dramatic flouting of etiquette, apathy toward money and wealth, or experience of spiritual ecstasy might be coded as *crazy* in psychonormative discourse. Yet it seems to me that psychosocial madness reveals more about the avowedly sane society branding an object crazy than about the object so branded. When you point at someone or something and shout *Crazy!*, you have revealed more about yourself—about your sensibility, your values, your attentions, your notion of the normal, the limits of your imagination in processing dramatic difference, the terms you use to describe the world, the reach of your pointing finger, the lilt of your accusatory voice—than you have revealed about that supposedly mad entity.[30]

These four categories are not all-encompassing and do not cover every possible permutation of madness. Furthermore, these four categories are not mutually exclusive; in fact, they often intersect and converge. *Rage*, for example, is always also *phenomenal*. Discourses of *medicalized* madness attempt to make sense of *phenomenal* symptoms and inevitably harbor *psychosocial* biases. Black people who articulate *rage* at unjust social conditions are often coded as *psychosocial* others (and sometimes diagnosed as *medically* unsound). The spillage of these categories into one another reminds us that madness is too messy to be placed in tidy boxes and too restless to hold still for rigid frameworks.

Note, also, that these modes of madness might be taken up in manifold ways for mad praxis. For example, rage might be harnessed to fuel impassioned resistance. Medicalized madness might be deconstructed to expose and address the biases in psy sciences. Phenomenal madness might be documented to teach sane majorities about the lived experience of madness. Psychosocial alterity might model otherwise ways of knowing and being, beyond entrenched status quos. In these and other ways, the protagonists in this study get mad and go mad to convey and confront the violence, chaos, strangeness, ecstasy, wonder, aporia, paradox, and danger—in short, the phenomenal madness—suffusing racial modernity.

Beyond approaching madness as an object of analysis, *How to Go Mad* adapts madness as methodology. As I propose and practice it, *mad methodology* is a mad ensemble of epistemological modes, political praxes, interpretive techniques, affective dispositions, existential orientations, and ways of life.

Mad methodology seeks, follows, and rides the unruly movements of madness. It reads and hears *idioms of madness*: those purported rants, raves, rambles, outbursts, mumbles, stammers, slurs, gibberish sounds, and unseemly silences that defy the grammars of Reason. It historicizes and contextualizes madness as a social construction and social relation vis-à-vis Reason. It ponders the sporadic violence of madness in tandem and in tension with the structural violence of Reason. It cultivates critical ambivalence[31] to reckon with the simultaneous harm and benefit that may accompany madness. It respects and sometimes harnesses "mad" feelings like obsession and rage as stimulus for radical thought and action. Whereas rationalism roundly discredits madpersons, mad methodology recognizes madpersons as critical theorists and decisive protagonists in struggles for liberation. To be clear, I am not suggesting that madpersons are always already agents of liberation. I am simply and assuredly acknowledging that they *can be*, which is a heretical admission amid antimad worlds. I propose a mad methodology that neither vilifies the madperson as evil incarnate, nor romanticizes the madperson as resistance personified, nor patronizes the madperson as helpless ward awaiting aid. Rather, mad methodology engages the complexity and variability of mad subjects.

Regarding anger, the warrior poet Audre Lorde asserts that it is "loaded with information and energy."[32] Mad methodology is rooted in the recognition that phenomenal madness, medicalized madness, and psychosocial madness, like angry madness, are all "loaded with information and energy." Mad methodology proceeds from a belief that such information can instruct black radical theory and such energy can animate black radical praxis.

Most urgently, mad methodology primes us to extend *radical compassion* to the madpersons, queer personae, ghosts, freaks, weirdos, imaginary friends, disembodied voices, unvoiced bodies, and unReasonable others, who trespass, like stowaways or fugitives, in Reasonable modernity. Radical compassion is a will to care for, a commitment to feel with, a striving to learn from, and an openness to be vulnerable before a precarious other, though they may be drastically dissimilar to yourself. Radical compassion is not an appeal to an idyllic oneness where difference is blithely effaced. Nor is it a smug projection of oneself into the position of another, thereby displacing that other.[33] Nor is it an invitation to walk a mile in someone else's shoes and amble, like a tourist, through their lifeworld, leaving them existentially barefoot all the while. Rather, radical compassion is an exhortation to ethically walk and sit and fight and build alongside another whose condition may be utterly unlike your own. Radical compassion works to impart care, exchange feeling, transmit understanding, embolden vulnerability, and fortify solidarity across circumstantial, sociocultural, phenomenological, and ontological chasms in the interest of mutual liberation. It persists even and especially toward beings who are the objects of contempt and condemnation from dominant value systems. It extends even and especially to those who discomfit one's own sense of propriety. Indeed, this book sometimes loiters in scenes and tarries with people who may trouble readers. I hope that this book also models the sort of radical compassion that persists through the trouble.

I characterize mad methodology as a parapositivist approach insofar as it resists the hegemony of positivism. (As a philosophical doctrine, positivism stipulates that meaningful assertions about the world must come from empirical observation and interpretation to generate veritable truth. However, when engaging the phenomenal, the spiritual, the aesthetic, the affective, and the mad, we must deviate from the logics of positivism.)[34] Mad methodology finds great inspiration in other cultural theorists' parapositivist approaches, including the Apostle Paul's account of "faith," Édouard Glissant's "poetics of relation," Avery Gordon's haunted and haunting sociology, Saidiya Hartman's "critical fabulation," Jack Halberstam's "scavenger methodology," Ann Cvetkovich's compilation of an "archive of feelings," Christina Sharpe's "wake work," and Patricia J. Williams's "ghost gathering."[35] These thinkers study sublime, opaque, formless, subjunctive, scarce, dead, and ghostly phenomena that thwart positivist knowing.

As a parapositivist approach, mad methodology does not attempt to wholly, transparently reveal madness.[36] How could it? Madness, after all, resists intelligibility and frustrates interpretation. Conceding that I cannot fully understand the meaning of every madness I encounter, I often precede my observations with the qualifiers *maybe*, *it might be*, and *it seems*. Between these covers, I embrace uncertainty and irresolution. I heed poet-philosopher Glissant's insistence that "the transparency of the Enlightenment is finally misleading. . . . It is not necessary to understand someone—in the verb 'to understand' [French: *comprendre*] there is the verb 'to take' [French: *prendre*]—in order to wish to live with them."[37] I want to *live with* the madpersons gathered in this study, but I do not need or want to *take* them. I strive to *pursue* madness, but not to *capture* it. Recall that I began this chapter by warning you to *hold tight*. Mad methodology also, sometimes, entails *letting go*: relinquishing the imperative to know, to take, to capture, to master, to lay bare all the world with its countless terrors and wonders. Sometimes we must hold tight to steady ourselves amid the violent tumult of this world—and sometimes we must let go to unmoor ourselves from the stifling order imposed on this world. I am describing a deft dance between release and hold, hold and release.

In short, mad methodology is how to go mad without losing your mind. At length, this book will show you.

MAD INTERVENTIONS

How to Go Mad joins a robust corpus of post-2000 black studies scholarship exploring radical imagination within black popular culture, black feminist ingenuity, black queer art, the black avant-garde, Afrofuturism, Afrosurrealism, and beyond. I want to cite just a few entries in this scholarly corpus: In *Freedom Dreams* (2002), Robin Kelley illuminates black radical imagination and freedom dreaming in black abolitionist, Marxist, surrealist, and feminist movements across the diaspora.[38] Fred Moten's *In the Break* (2003) chronicles and practices a black radical tradition—animated by a will to resistance and propelled by a "freedom drive"—in twentieth-century performance and poetics.[39] Daphne Brooks's *Bodies in Dissent* (2006) explores mid-nineteenth- through early twentieth-century circumatlantic performances that spectacularize and instrumentalize alterity to disrupt racial and sexual hegemony.[40] In his "Afrosurreal Manifesto" (2009), D. Scott Miller taps into otherworldly fantasy, mystical visions, ecstatic feeling, and aesthetic extravagance in order to defy oppressive regimes of "reality."[41] In *Wandering* (2014), Sarah Cervenak charts practices of (physical and metaphysical) wandering as black feminist strategies to evade the coercive constrictions of antiblackness, misogyny, and racial capitalism.[42] L. H. Stalling's *Funk the Erotic* (2015) theorizes black "funk" as a sensuous amalgam of erotic, ethical, and epistemological rebellion against antiblack, misogynist, capitalist, and sex-negative status quos.[43] *Radical Aesthetics and Modern Black Nationalism* (2016) is GerShun Avilez's study of the insurgent imaginations that propelled the Black Arts Movement, the fractures and ruptures that opened up within that movement, and its bustling queer afterlives and reincarnations.[44]

While *How to Go Mad* is foremost in league with such black studies scholarship, this book also speaks to—and talks back to—Western canon-dwellers from antiquity through postmodernity. Indeed, to ponder the juncture of madness and art in the West is to join a conversation with preeminent storytellers and philosophers in the Eurocentric context.[45] For example, in *Phaedrus*, the Athenian philosopher Plato (writing in the guise of Socrates) suggests that Eros, prophecy, and poetry are forms of "divine madness."[46] Throughout his dramatic oeuvre, Elizabethan playwright William Shakespeare endows characters like King Lear, Hamlet, and Ophelia with madness that begets ingenuity, cunning, and revelation; regarding Hamlet, the character Polonius opines: "Though this be madness, yet there is method in't."[47] American gothic author Edgar Allan Poe writes that "the question is not yet settled, whether madness is or is not the loftiest intelligence—whether much that is glorious—whether all that is profound—does not spring from disease of thought."[48] Nineteenth-century Eurocontinental philosopher Friedrich Nietzsche extols the revolutionary potential in madness, arguing that "almost everywhere [in Western history] it was madness which prepared the way for the new idea, which broke the spell of a venerated usage and superstition."[49] In perhaps the most influential study of madness in the West, *Madness and Civilization* (1961), Foucault details the sequestering and silencing of madness in Euromodernity. He contends that Europe's ruling classes, religious leadership, and psychiatric authorities colluded to expel madness (itself a sort of epistemology, communicative mode, and wandering way of life) into physical confinement and existential exile.[50] In *Anti-Oedipus* (1972), philosophers Gilles Deleuze and Félix Guattari find insurgent energy in schizophrenia, treating it as a locus of unruly, free-flowing desire that defies repressive incursions of capitalism and psychoanalysis.[51]

Clearly, the conjunction of madness and creativity is a common concern in Western culture writ large. However, that madness-creativity intersection is especially fraught and charged when occupied by black folks. This is because antiblack discourse constantly codes black people as savage, irrational, subrational, pathological, and effectively mad. Black artists must contend with—and also can draw upon—these associations of blackness and madness interlaid with those broader associations of artistic genius and madness.

This project owes much to disability studies.[52] Among that field's signal contributions is its interrogation of the *medical model* of disability, the dominant framework for understanding disability in the West. The medical model regards a disability as a physical or cognitive dysfunction residing in an individual body and/or mind—a dysfunction that should be corrected or cured by medical intervention. In contrast, disability studies advances a *social model*, contending that disability is a social construction: a set of social exclusions, obstructions, and derogations imposed on persons who diverge from a dominant, "abled" norm.[53] The medical and social models of disability roughly correspond to my medicalized and psychosocial iterations of madness. However, my own schema does not treat the medical and psychosocial as dichotomous; rather, I emphasize their entanglements and convergences.

Dominant discourses of "disability" tend to center the physical body, treating disabled people as "physically" feeble, infirm, *undercapacitated*. In contrast, normative notions of madness cast madpersons as dangerously *hypercapacitated*—that is, able and liable to do harm that sane persons could barely fathom, let alone act upon. Addressing such exigencies, the burgeoning field of mad studies centers the lived experience of madpersons—especially consumers, survivors, and ex-patients of psychiatric systems—and advances agendas for mad liberation. Brenda A. LeFrançois, Robert Menzies, and Geoffrey Reaume are the editors of *Mad Matters: A Critical Reader in Canadian Mad Studies* (2013), the most extensive collection of writings in mad studies to date. In an introduction articulating a comprehensive, interdisciplinary, and intersectional platform for mad studies, they write:

> To work with and within the language of madness is by no means to deny the psychic, spiritual, and material pains and privations endured by countless people with histories of encounters with the psy disciplines. To the contrary, it is to acknowledge and validate these experiences as being authentically human, while at the same time rejecting clinical labels that pathologize and degrade; challenging the reductionistic assumptions and effects of the medical model; locating psychiatry and its human subjects within wider historical, institutional, and cultural contexts; and advancing the position that mental health research, writing, and advocacy are primarily about opposing oppression and promoting human justice.[54]

I share their commitment to mad study that honors the personhood, lived experience, and agency of madpersons while recognizing the abjection that frequently haunts mad life. Like the editors of *Mad Matters*, I am invested in "promoting human justice"—alongside, I might add, relief, revelation, joy, and liberation—for madpersons and other psychosocial outcasts. However, I respectfully diverge from the editors' quest, articulated later in their introduction, for a mad studies "steadfastly arrayed against biomedical psychiatry."[55] While I decry the dire harm that biomedical psychiatry has wrought on many pathologized people, I also know that some patients and survivors find utility in it. To "validate and celebrate survivor experience and cultures," as the editors rightly intend, we might sometimes cautiously, provisionally, ambivalently, improperly, subversively take up biomedical psychiatry—all while we pursue its radical transformation.[56]

Another compendium of mad studies appears in "Mad Futures: Affect/ Theory/Violence," a 2017 special issue of the scholarly journal *American Quarterly*. Guest editors Tanja Aho, Liat Ben-Moshe, and Leon J. Hilton remark that the field of mad studies "draws on decades of scholarship and activism examining how psychiatric disabilities or differences must be understood not only as medical conditions but also as historical formations that have justified all manner of ill-treatment and disenfranchisement— even as they have also formed the basis for political identities, social movements, and cultural practices of resistance."[57] In this passage, they note the multiplicity of madness, which is at once a "medical," "historical," "political," "social," and "cultural" formation. Furthermore, they acknowledge both the abjection that may beset madness and the insurgent energy that may emanate from it. Foundational to my own study is attention to madness as a complex and dynamic process that may entail both devastating abjection and mighty agency.

This complexity is illustrated in the juxtaposition of two common figures of speech: *to snap* and *to click*. In Anglophone idiom, *to snap* is to break, to come undone, to lose control, to go crazy; *to click* is to come together, to fall into place, to make sense. Much as the sounds of physical snaps and physical clicks are sometimes indistinguishable to the ear, the processes signified in these idioms are sometimes indistinguishable to critical interpretation. As this book reveals, sometimes coming undone is precisely how one falls into place. Sometimes a breakdown doubles as a breakthrough. Sometimes a snap is a click. *Sometimes*. I recognize and reckon with occasions where madness entails pain, danger, terror, degradation, and harm for those who experience it and those in its vicinity. But I hasten to mention that Reason may entail pain, terror, abjection, and harm, too. In fact, far more modern harm has been perpetrated under the aegis of Reason—I have in mind chattel slavery, colonialism, imperialism, genocide, war, and other evils both momentous and mundane—than committed by rogue madpersons.[58]

As we work to destigmatize madness, including the medicalized madness of mental illness, it is crucial that we resist romanticizing it. Feminist bioethicist and disability studies scholar Elizabeth Donaldson warns that "the madness-as-feminist-rebellion metaphor might at first seem like a positive strategy for combating the stigma traditionally associated with mental illness. However, this metaphor indirectly diminishes the lived experience of many people disabled by mental illness."[59] Indeed, the "madness-as-feminist-rebellion metaphor" risks evacuating madness of its lived complexity in order to flatten and polish it into a shiny political badge. Whereas Donaldson admonishes against abstracting madness into a positive symbol, psychiatrist Robert Barrett critiques how madness is reduced to a negative sign. He suggests that schizophrenia is co-opted to "represent symbolically much of what has gone wrong in the modern world," forcing schizophrenic people to bear "the responsibility of representing an alienated, fragmented, meaningless, self-absorbed society—a schizophrenic society."[60] While simplistic metaphors may be rhetorically expedient, they come at grave ethical cost if they distort and objectify people. With these cautions in mind, I center representations of madness that illuminate, rather than efface, its lived experience.

No matter how carefully I qualify my mobilization of madness, and despite my work to avoid romanticizing it, this study might incite the ire of a cohort I call *rationalist readers*. Analogous to the moral reader hailed in slave narratives and sentimental novels, the rationalist reader—and more broadly, the rationalist audience—is the presumed paradigmatic consumer of psychonormative culture. Such a reader possesses psychonormative sensibilities, adheres to Reason's common sense, and shuns madness as categorically detrimental. Some rationalist readers may fear that my focus on mad blackness reinforces myths of black savagery and undermines the "respectable" project of Reasonable blackness. The latter project puts faith in Reason, a structure that I approach with well-warranted suspicion (and perhaps paranoia). Rather than integrate black people into the pantheon of Reason, or seek a place for them at its hallowed table, I want to interrogate the logics that undergird that pantheon and prop up that table. I am especially interested in artists who refuse to have a seat, but would rather flip the table and carry their meals outside.

Some of those black captives in slave ships resolved to go outside, too.[61] They leapt from the decks of those vessels and into the Atlantic Ocean, choosing biological death over the wretchedness that sociologist Orlando Patterson deems "social death."[62] Typically, psychiatry labels such leaps *suicide* and pathologizes them as the outcome of absolute self-abnegation. While the frame of psychopathology is apt for apprehending why some people take their own lives, it cannot hold all those Flying Africans. Amid the misery of the Middle Passage, suicidal ideation might be a mode of radical dreaming, an urge to escape to a distant elsewhere in an afterlife, otherworld, ancestral gathering place, heaven, or home. For the captive on the ship, suicide might be an act of radical self-care, intended to relieve and leave the hurt of the hold and expedite arrival in that elsewhere.[63] Sometimes the leap was not a plummet to doom, but a launch into flight; not an outcome of self-abnegation, but an act of self-assertion; not a bog of hopelessness, but an outburst of radical hope hurled into another world. To be clear, I do not glibly romanticize suicide; I know and ardently assert that each life is sacred, singular, precious, miraculous, and should be treated with ineffable care. At the same time, I acknowledge that there are conditions of unbearable duress where taking one's own life might be a critical and ethical act—albeit dreadful and woeful, too. *How to Go Mad* attends to people and practices who, like those Flying Africans, will not be captured by normative Reason.

By the nineteenth century, the slave ship gave way to the plantation as the paradigmatic site of black abjection and confinement in the Western Hemisphere. Meanwhile, the ship of fools, if it ever existed, was succeeded by the prison house and later the asylum as the preferred receptacle for the allegedly insane.[64] Amid these shifts, the association of blackness and madness remained. In antebellum America, that association manifested in the similar logics used to justify the plantation and the asylum. Literary and cultural historian Benjamin Reiss writes that "both institutions revoked the civil liberties of a confined population in the name of public order and the creation of an efficient labor force, and both housed a purportedly subrational population . . . with the asylum's triumph over madness paralleling the white race's subduing of the black."[65] The plantation and asylum were forums in which arbiters of antebellum Reason rehearsed methods of domination and developed logics of justification.

I want to linger at the site of the asylum to highlight the salience of space and movement in modern notions of madness. Within Anglophone idiom, subjects *go* crazy, as though mad is a place or constellation of places. The ship of fools, the insane asylum, the psychiatric hospital, the carnival, the wrong side of the supposed line between genius and madness, and even the continent of Africa are frequently mapped as mad places within Western discourse. It is as though madness is a metaphysical zone, a location outside the gentrified precincts and patrolled borders of Reason. Or maybe madness is a mode of motion occasioned in treacherous terrain: a wavering, trembling, swelling, zigzagging, brimming, bursting, shattering, or splattering movement that disrupts Reason's supposedly steady order and tidy borders. It seems to me that madness, like diaspora, is both location and locomotion. Madness, like diaspora, is both place and process.[66] Madness and diaspora transgress normative arrangements—of the sane and sovereign, in turn.

The transgressive motion of fugitive slaves was framed as madness-as-kinesis by proslavery psychiatry. In 1851, the prominent Confederate physician Samuel Cartwright coined *drapetomania*, which he described as "the disease causing Negroes to run away."[67] As formulated by Cartwright, drapetomania is a racialized diagnosis that exclusively afflicts "Negroes"-as-slaves, reflecting an antiblack antebellum insistence on conflating *blackness* and *slaveness*.[68] Of course, this discursive conflation was allied with the material, legal, and existential yoking of blackness and slaveness in chattel slavery.

Cartwright further argues that "the cause in the most of cases, that induces the negro to run away from service, is as much a disease of the mind as any other species of mental alienation, and much more curable, as a general rule." He suggests that drapetomania can be cured if the slaveholder upholds a dual role as disciplinarian master (with use of the whip, so that slaves will fearfully obey) and paternalistic protector (so that slaves will be made agreeable by bonds of affection and the incentive of protection).[69] In pathologizing black self-emancipation, Cartwright joins a proslavery, antiblack conspiracy against black freedom: antiblack slave codes criminalized black freedom; antiblack religion demonized black freedom; antiblack philosophy stigmatized black freedom; and antiblack slaveholders and vigilantes terrorized black freedom. It is no wonder, then, that antiblack medicine would pathologize black freedom. Under the obscene regime and episteme of antebellum slavery, black freedom was crime, sin, stigma, liability, and sickness, too.

Whereas drapetomania supposedly compelled black people to flee servitude, Cartwright coined another psychopathology to ail them once they found freedom. He writes that "Dysaesthesia Aethiopica is a disease peculiar to negroes, affecting both mind and body. . . . [I]t prevails among free negroes, nearly all of whom are more or less afflicted with it, that have not got some white person to direct and to take care of them." Cartwright claims that black people are constitutionally unfit for freedom, sickened by it, and that they are mentally and physically healthier when enslaved. To have Cartwright tell it, the motley symptoms of dysaesthesia aethiopica include cognitive decline, lethargy, lesions, and skin insensitivity. In a flourish of melodramatic antiblackness, he decrees that to "narrate [dysaesthesia aethiopica's] symptoms and effects among them would be to write a history of the ruins and dilapidation of Hayti, and every spot of earth they have ever had uncontrolled possession over for any length of time."[70] He names the first free black republic as ground zero in a sort of hemispheric epidemic of dysaesthesia aethiopica. If mad is a place, according to Cartwright, it might be "Hayti."[71]

The notion that slavery was salutary for black people also infused antebellum political rhetoric. John C. Calhoun, an eminent nineteenth-century politician whose career included stints as US Secretary of State and US Vice President, offered this justification for antiblack chattel slavery circa 1840: "Here is proof of the necessity of slavery. The African is incapable of self-care and sinks into lunacy under the burden of freedom. It is a mercy to him to give him the guardianship and protection from mental death."[72] Calhoun claims that freedom will careen Africans into lunacy, into a helpless and mindless oblivion that he deems "mental death." If slavery was social death and freedom was mental death, those Africans were caught in a deadly double bind—doomed one way or another. Within the wicked machinations and pernicious logics of antebellum antiblackness, black people, whether enslaved or free, were the living dead.

Beyond *discursive* conflations of blackness and madness, slavery induced *lived* convergences of blackness and madness. It perpetrated systematic trauma, induced mental distress, and ignited crises of subjectivity—which is to say, it produced phenomenal madness—in black people both enslaved and free. Regarding black women in colonial and antebellum America, for example, Nobel laureate and novelist Toni Morrison explains that "black women had to deal with post-modern problems in the nineteenth century and earlier. . . . Certain kinds of dissolution, the loss of and the need to reconstruct certain kinds of stability. Certain kinds of madness, deliberately going mad in order, as one of the characters [from the novel *Beloved*] says, 'in order not to lose your mind.' These strategies for survival made the truly modern person. They're a response to predatory Western phenomena."[73] Morrison suggests that "going mad" was sometimes a strategy to doggedly clutch hold of one's mind when Reason would steal or smash it. If Reason is benefactor of white supremacy, proponent of antiblack slavocracy, and underwriter of patriarchal dominion, an enslaved black woman might fare better by going insane instead. Rather than remain captive behind the barbed fences of slavocratic sanity, she might find refuge—however tenuous, vexed, and incomplete—in the fugitivity of madness.

Morrison fleshes out these themes in her Pulitzer Prize–winning novel *Beloved* (1987). The story is inspired by the life of Margaret Garner, a fugitive from slavery who escaped a Kentucky plantation with her family in 1856 and settled in the neighboring "free" state of Ohio. When slave catchers (authorized by the 1850 Fugitive Slave Act to legally stalk and abduct black persons living in "free" states) apprehended Garner, she attempted to kill her four children rather than see them repossessed into slavery. Like the Flying Africans, Garner preferred biological death over social death and sought the former for her children to spare them the latter. She succeeded in killing only her two-year-old daughter, Mary.

Margaret Garner is the basis for the novel's primary protagonist, Sethe, while Mary is inspiration for the novel's titular character, Beloved. As narrated in the story, Sethe goes mad in order to perform a killing that is utterly unconscionable within nearly every model of motherhood. And yet, her deed is also an astonishing, unflinching, unconditional attempt at motherly protection; she intends to save her sons and daughters from enslavement by any means, at any cost. In the moment before the killing, Sethe has a breakdown that feels like beating wings and probing beaks:

> She was squatting in the garden and when she saw them coming and recognized schoolteacher's hat, she heard wings. Little hummingbirds stuck their needle beaks right through her headcloth into her hair and beat their wings. And if she thought anything it was No. No. Nono. Nonono. Simple. She just flew. Collected every bit of life she had made, all the parts of her that were precious and fine and beautiful, and carried, pushed, dragged them through the veil, out, away, over there where no one could hurt them. Over there.[74]

Sethe originally sought sanctuary in an "over there" north of the Ohio River, but its freedom proved ephemeral and illusory. Now she seeks freedom in a more distant "over there," in an otherworldly elsewhere outside the jurisdiction of fugitive slave laws and beyond the reach of a slaveholder called "schoolteacher."[75] The man who reigns over the Kentucky plantation that Sethe fled, schoolteacher is an atrocious agent of antiblack Reason. He proposes that black people are inhuman, and he methodically tortures and dehumanizes them in order to fabricate tautological proof of his claim. He commits merciless cruelty under the auspices of Reasonable inquiry and scientific method. When he arrives in Ohio to find Sethe in a shed covered in the blood of her dead child, slain only moments before, schoolteacher resolves against re-enslaving her and her offspring. His decision does not appear to be an act of compassion upon beholding that dreadful scene. He seems, instead, to be driven by economic calculation: the family is damaged goods unworthy of repossession.[76] Schoolteacher also appears to judge infanticide as an especially base depravity, unaware or unconcerned that his own evil is what drives the mother to kill her child. After all, Sethe's infanticidal madness is a desperate attempt to escape schoolteacher's genocidal Reason.

Twenty-five years before Garner's tragedy, another enslaved person's violent defiance and alleged madness attracted far greater notoriety in the US public sphere. Nathaniel Turner was a self-avowed prophet who claimed that divine inspiration led him to organize a bloody revolt in Southampton, Virginia, in 1831. Turner and his co-conspirators massacred some sixty local white people and incited horror in countless others. After his capture, while confined in jail and awaiting execution, Turner supposedly dictated his account of the insurrection to his court-appointed counsel, Thomas Gray. In the resulting document, "The Confessions of Nat Turner: The Leader of the Late Insurrection in Southampton, VA," Turner purportedly confesses the following about the weeks before the uprising: "Many were the plans formed and rejected by us, and it affected my mind to such a degree, that I fell sick, and the time passed without our coming to any determination how to commence."[77] This unspecified sickness resulted from the anxiety of devising revolt, of plans proposed and rejected, of apocalyptic dreams deferred, which "affected" his mind. It seems that Turner is describing mental illness and distress.

If Turner's own language implies mental illness, Gray charges madness outright. He deems Turner "a gloomy fanatic" and refers to his "dark, bewildered, and overwrought mind."[78] It comes as no surprise that Gray would label Turner mad. Turner committed the most severe violations of slavery's psychosocial status quo: he rejected the subjection demanded of slaves and chose bloody insurrection instead. More curiously, Gray opines that Turner "is a complete fanatic, or plays his part most admirably. On other subjects he possesses an uncommon share of intelligence, with a mind capable of attaining any thing; but warped and perverted by the influence of early impressions."[79] The possession of "a mind capable of attaining any thing" is commensurate with modern notions of genius. Remarkably, then, the deadliest slave insurrectionist in the history of the antebellum United States was a self-proclaimed *prophet*, an alleged *madman*, and, in Gray's estimation, a perverse *genius*. The prophet, madperson, and genius all occupy epistemic alterity. Because of the prophet's access to heaven's revelations, the madperson's exile from the domain of Reason, and the genius's elevation above ordinary intelligence curves, all three of these figures inhabit spheres of mind supposedly inaccessible to normal-minded masses. As portrayed in "Confessions," Turner traverses a genius | prophet | madman triptych, partitioned by those proverbially thin lines that separate madness from genius and lunacy from prophecy.

Gray also suggests that Turner could be pretending all along, "play[ing] his part most admirably." The implication is that Turner might be feigning insanity to elicit mercy or strike fear in his punishers. Fifty years later, Nietzsche would write that those "irresistibly drawn to throw off the yoke of any kind of morality and to frame new laws had, *if they were not actually mad*, no alternative but to make themselves or pretend to be mad."[80] Whether or not this characterization applies to Turner, it alerts us to another use of madness: as equipment for dissemblance. As this study will show, some crazy persons exploit the inscrutability of madness to use it as mask, cloak, and shield.

BLACK RADICAL MADNESS IN
THE TWENTIETH CENTURY

I have surveyed several discursive conflations, historical intersections, and phenomenal convergences of madness and blackness in early modern through antebellum contexts. Now I turn to a few key expressions and theorizations of black radical madness in the twentieth century.

The figure of the "crazy nigger"[81] swaggered prominently in African American vernacular imagination at the dawn of the twentieth century, the period that historian Rayford Logan labels the "nadir" of (postslavery) US race relations.[82] The "crazy nigger" is an outlaw persona who does as he or she pleases, who is reckless, defiant, courageous, and profane, who flagrantly flouts codes of middle-class respectability and racial propriety. Whereas Reasonable people are chastened by fear of violence, stigma, and death, the "crazy nigger" seems undaunted by such concerns. He or she will fearlessly face any adversary—including powerful white racists—and thus emerges as a superlative representative of insurgent blackness.

The "crazy nigger" was a polarizing figure among black people in the nadir: a folk hero or villain depending upon the perspective of his or her beholder. He or she was a hero to those who sought a model of black defiance—providing vicarious wish fulfillment for black people who dreamed of, but never acted upon, revenge fantasies against antiblack racists. These would-be avengers might utter the phrase *crazy nigger* like an honorific. On the other hand, this mad figure would be viewed as a nuisance by those invested in placating whiteness and aligning with bourgeois respectability. To such avowedly respectable persons, the "crazy nigger" was a liability for the race, a dangerous rabble-rouser stoking racial antagonism and courting racist retribution. From the mouths of these conformists, the words *crazy nigger* might sound like an invective. What I want to emphasize is that black vernacular cultures recognized and theorized the political resonance of craziness, deploying the term *crazy nigger* to describe agents of rebellion.

At the dawn of the twentieth century, black studies trailblazer William Edward Burghardt Du Bois also theorized a sort of racialized madness. In his 1903 tome *The Souls of Black Folk*, Du Bois famously describes "double consciousness": "one ever feels his twoness—an American, a Negro; two souls, two thoughts, two unreconciled strivings; two warring ideals in one dark body, whose dogged strength alone keeps it from being torn asunder."[83] Double consciousness entails internecine "warring" in mind that might resemble the psychic unruliness and crisis I call phenomenal madness. Whereas the condition is often regarded as an existential affliction and impairment, I want to emphasize that it is also an endowment. Double consciousness grants black Americans a perceptual aptitude and epistemic access unavailable to their white counterparts. To live with this split subjectivity is to behold the spectacular scene of America's black-white racial drama while also privy to the backstage content of black life, full of complex socioracial phenomena concealed from white gazes. Thus, for all of the existential angst it entails, double consciousness might also serve as an instrument for insurgency: a scopic tool and radar technology to secretly seek black horizons of being that are hidden from white surveillance.

Other prominent antiracist and anticolonial theorists centered madness in their accounts of black suffering and black insurgency in the first half of the twentieth century. In 1941, amid world war, anticolonial foment, and Pan-African awakenings, the Négritude critic and theorist Suzanne Roussy Césaire intervened in the discourse of madness and space. In a letter to the surrealist magazine *View*, she refuses to characterize madness as a pit of abjection; rather, she imagines "the domain of the strange, the Marvelous, and the fantastic," wherein lies "the freed image, dazzling and beautiful, with a beauty that could not be more unexpected and overwhelming. Here are the poet, the painter, and the artist, presiding over the metamorphoses and the inversions of the world under the sign of hallucination and madness."[84] Césaire's domain of the Marvelous blooms at the crossroads of a surrealist rebuke of rationalism, an anticolonial rejection of colonial Reason, and Négritude's affirmation of black radical possibility. She conjures a decolonial fantasia where radical creativity begets beauty that is surreal, sublime, subversive, and *mad*.

Suzanne Césaire's collaborator and husband, Aimé Césaire, was a Martinican poet, essayist, and statesman who championed surrealism, despised colonialism, and marched at the vanguard of the Négritude movement. Furthermore, he reportedly described his poetic process as "beneficial madness."[85] His 1947 epic poem, *Notebook of a Return to the Native Land*, portrays a colonized black protagonist who endures existential despair but eventually emerges into revolutionary consciousness and embraces the ontological blackness of Négritude. The poem's speaker professes "hate" for colonial "reason" (Reason) and pledges allegiance to a living madness: "the madness that remembers, the madness that howls, the madness that sees, the madness that is unleashed."[86] This madness possesses memory, voice, vision, and agency. Thus vivified, it is a powerful ally of colonized peoples against the colonizer's pernicious Reason.

A mentee of Aimé Césaire, Frantz Fanon was a black Martinican doctor who developed a radical psychiatry that has influenced black and anticolonial freedom struggles worldwide. In *Black Skin, White Masks* (1952), Fanon describes "a massive psychoexistential complex" erected by antiblackness and colonialism.[87] That complex is a metaphysical prison house that confines black people and incites maddening crises of subjectivity, identity, humanity, and ontology. But Fanon, like both Césaires, believes that revolution can rise amid such wretched states. At the start of this chapter, I referenced Fanon's "zone of nonbeing, an extraordinarily sterile and arid region, an utterly naked declivity where an authentic upheaval can be born."[88] Fanon's declivity is so low and empty that it grants unobstructed space to gather momentum for "authentic upheaval."

The metaphorical proximity of Fanon's "zone of nonbeing" and Spillers's "*nowhere* at all" is not the only place these theorists adjoin. The two also share a commitment to adapting psychoanalysis to address the lifeworlds of Afrodiasporic peoples. In "All the Things You Could Be by Now If Sigmund Freud's Wife Was Your Mother: Psychoanalysis and Race," Spillers contends that the African American "lifeworld offers a quintessential occasion for a psychoanalytic reading, given the losses that converge on its naming. . . . The situation of the African American community is more precisely *ambivalent* than any American case we can concoct, in light of its incomplete 'Americanization' even at this late date."[89] She endorses the efficacy of psychoanalysis for interpreting the deep ambivalence that marks blackness in America. For Spillers, however, generic psychoanalysis won't do. She refashions psychoanalytic equipment to enhance its utility for black subjects—cutting, pushing, stretching, and suturing psychoanalysis in ways that Sigmund Freud and Jacques Lacan probably did not intend or foresee. For example, Spillers writes that "African persons in 'Middle Passage' were literally suspended in the 'oceanic,' if we think of the latter in its Freudian orientation as an analogy for undifferentiated identity."[90] In Spillers's custody, the oceanic is not merely a feature of infant subjectivity in a transhistorical model of psychological development. Here, the oceanic also signifies racialized subjection and subjectmaking amid the atrocity of the Middle Passage. Spillers stands among a critical mass of black cultural theorists and, more broadly, cultural theorists of color, who critically adapt psychoanalysis to address exigencies of race. Joining this cohort, I occasionally recalibrate Freudian and Lacanian psychoanalysis to engage the specificities of blackness and its antagonists.[91]

Activist-psychiatrists Price Cobbs and William Grier also retool Eurocentric psy science to address the lives of black people. Published in the immediate aftermath of Martin Luther King Jr.'s assassination and amid the righteous and riotous rage that ensued, their 1968 study *Black Rage* is a sweeping exploration of the psychosocial lives of black Americans from the colonial era through the age of Black Power. Interweaving psychiatric case studies, historiography, sociological data, and social psychology, the authors chart purportedly "pathological" features of black life as well as the psychosocial and psychocultural adaptations that black people develop for self-protection, catharsis, and healing.[92] The "black rage" announced in their book title is at once a symptom of antiblack trauma, a defense against antiblack trauma, and a mighty force in battles against antiblackness.

In fact, the shift from *Civil Rights* to *Black Power* political paradigms might be framed as a pivot from a politics of respectability to a politics of rage. Frustrated with models of passive resistance, some black activists and artists got mad—embracing rage as a powerful resource against antiblackness. The furious speeches of Kwame Ture; the incendiary, incantatory writings of Amiri Baraka; the exquisitely outraged outbursts of Nina Simone; the seething anger and schizophrenic angst surging through Adrienne Kennedy's drama; Malcolm X's status as "the angriest black man in America";[93] and the "race riots" that King described as "the language of the unheard,"[94] all reflect a politics of rage and mobilization of madness in black radical traditions of the 1960s.

The sociopolitical fervor of the 1960s also fomented the antipsychiatry movement, propelled by a motley array of psychiatric dissidents, including consumers, survivors, ex-patients, activists, academics, and radical clinicians. Members of this movement question the legitimacy of psychiatric diagnosis, alleging that mainstream psychiatry has little or no basis in objective science. Often regarded as a key figure in the movement, Thomas Szasz suggests that the very notion of *mental illness* is a sham: a system of subjective moral and ideological judgments masquerading as scientific facticity. He contends that the diagnosis of mental illness is merely an expression of social disapproval shrouded in medical jargon and granted exorbitant power. R. D. Laing, another key figure in the antipsychiatry movement, argues that schizophrenia is not an organic disease, but rather the effect of existential antagonisms and alienation from repressive family and social structures.[95]

Like antipsychiatry activists, I recognize that degradation, dispossession, disenfranchisement, dishonor, torture, murder, and other forms of harm have been inflicted on madpersons by psychiatry. Furthermore, I respect antipsychiatry's attention to racism, sexism, classism, colonialism, homophobia, transphobia, and other pernicious ideologies that have effected and affected mainstream psychiatry. And yet, I hasten to note that many psychiatric clients and consumers find healing and even empowerment through clinical intervention. Considering that psychiatry has engendered both harm and benefit for madpersons, we would be wise to approach it with critical ambivalence—rebuking its malicious modes while embracing its therapeutic and insurgent potential. In this vein, I appreciate the radical psychiatry of Fanon, Cobbs, and Grier—as well as later progressive innovations of clinicians like Alvin Poussaint and Joy DeGruy[96]—who grapple with the psychosocial exigencies of blackness.

The 1960s are the primary focus of *The Protest Psychosis: How Schizophrenia Became a Black Disease* (2010), by Jonathan Metzl, a psychiatrist and cultural critic. By the turn of the twenty-first century, African Americans were three to five times as likely as their white counterparts to be diagnosed with schizophrenia, arguably the most stigmatized mental illness.[97] Metzl traces the blackening of schizophrenia to Civil Rights–era psychiatry and the weaponization of the diagnosis against rebellious black men.[98] He culls his book title from a term that two racist psychiatrists coined in 1960s America to characterize schizophrenia. Metzl writes, "Walter Bromberg and Franck Simon described schizophrenia as a 'protest psychosis' whereby black men developed 'hostile and aggressive feelings' and 'delusional anti-whiteness' after listening to the words of Malcolm X, joining the Black Muslims, or aligning with groups that preached militant resistance to white society. According to [Bromberg and Simon], the men required psychiatric treatment because their symptoms threatened not only their own sanity, but the social order of white America."[99] I hasten to note that black women are also widely psychopathologized—as ferocious Sapphires and nymphomaniacal Jezebels—even if patriarchy presumes them incapable of posing as grave a threat as black men.[100] The fact is that black women are subject to misogynist myths of female hysteria *and* antiblack fantasies of black savagery.

Bromberg and Simon are heirs to the ignominious legacy of Samuel Cartwright. Their invention of "protest psychosis," like Cartwright's invention of "drapetomania," leverages medical authority to discredit black insurgency in an era of racial unrest. Convinced that their antiblackness is perfectly Reasonable, Bromberg and Simon denounce the "delusional anti-whiteness" of black activists. I want to linger briefly on this notion of antiwhiteness. It seems to me that when whiteness is a prized possession whose preservation is pretext for the systematic degradation of black people, antiwhiteness is a justifiable position. When whiteness is a weapon of devastating power wielded against black people, it is no wonder that some would become militant in the interest of self-defense. When whiteness is a structure of power commensurate with white supremacy and antiblackness, "hostile and aggressive feelings" strike me as neither "delusional" nor objectionable. Those "hostile and aggressive feelings" reflect a will to rise up against tyranny, an impulse to thrust the foot off your neck, a manifestation of the freedom drive. To be clear, the antiwhiteness that I am describing is not hatred for white people; rather, it is animus toward the white supremacy that is militated beneath the banner of whiteness. It is possible to care for white people while also despising and opposing the world-historical ravages of whiteness-as-domination.

Remarkably, racist psychiatrists like Cartwright, Bromberg, and Simon share an important conviction with antiracist psychiatrists like Fanon, Grier, Cobbs, Poussaint, and DeGruy. Both groups agree that black people in the West are susceptible to racialized psychopathologies. However, these camps propose dramatically different etiologies. Cartwright, Bromberg, and Simon attribute such madness to inherent defects in black psyches and black cultures. To the contrary, Fanon, Grier, Cobbs, Poussaint, and DeGruy indict antiblack racism as the cause of racialized maladies ailing black people.

Proposing such divergent etiologies and espousing such contrary ideologies, it is no wonder that these cohorts prescribe different treatments. Antiblack psychiatry has variously encouraged enslavement, colonization, institutionalization, incarceration, disenfranchisement, assimilation to whiteness, abnegation of blackness, and mind-dulling or mind-destroying medical procedures as "treatments." To the contrary, antiracist psychiatry prompts us to reckon with the pathology of white supremacy, to attend to the ongoing trauma of antiblackness, and, most ambitiously, to overturn the extant racial order.[101] Regarding that "massive psychoexistential complex" imperiling black people, for instance, Fanon writes: "I hope by analyzing it to destroy it."[102] By disclosing its sinister blueprint and exposing its corroded foundation, Fanon hopes to help demolish the complex.

A SHORT NOTE ON THE MADNESS
OF ANTIBLACKNESS

This study centers insurgent madness in black expressive cultures. However, I want to remark upon the tyrannical madness at the core of antiblackness. In an interview with journalist Charlie Rose, Morrison describes the psychopathology of antiblack racism: "The people who do this thing, who practice racism, are bereft. There is something distorted about the psyche. It's a huge waste and it's a corruption. . . . It's a profound neurosis that nobody examines for what it is. It *feels* crazy. It *is* crazy. . . . It has just as much of a deleterious effect on white people . . . as it does [on] black people."[103] Regarding the madness of "extreme racism," Poussaint puts it this way: "It is time for the American Psychiatric Association to designate extreme racism as a mental health problem by recognizing it as a delusional psychotic symptom. Persons afflicted with such psychopathology represent an immediate danger to themselves and others."[104] Both Morrison and Poussaint recognize that racism is an existential threat to its targets as well as its adherents. Appropriating psychiatric and psychoanalytic discourse, we might conceptualize any number of racist pathologies: racist neurosis, racist delusion, racist narcissism, racist melancholia, racist anxiety disorder, homicidal racist angst, and so forth.

The risk in framing antiblack racism as mental illness is that it potentially locates the problem of racism in individual psychopathology rather than deeply entrenched systems and structures. Such a maneuver might cast racism as a medical issue to be treated primarily in the psychiatric office or examination room, when, in fact, racism is a global catastrophe that must be eradicated with social, cultural, political, epistemological, and, indeed, psychic upheaval. It is worthwhile to pursue psychiatric understanding of individual racists, but this pursuit must take place within a broader project of denouncing, dismantling, and demolishing racist structures. We can and must address individual psychopathology and systemic injustice at once—recognizing how they are co-constitutive and symbiotic.

If Donald J. Trump, the forty-fifth president of the United States, is mentally ill, he offers a colossal case study in the convergence of individual psychopathology and structural violence. Trump's power as US president means that his individual mental condition can generate structural outcomes and alter global history. However, glib attempts to label Trump mentally ill are fraught with psychonormative presumptions and distortions. Trump's unpredictable behavior, astounding incompetence, extreme egotism, and profound evil have led some to conclude that he *must be* mentally ill—as though unpredictability, incompetence, egotism, and evil *must be* symptoms of mental illness. These pseudodiagnoses reflect a psychonormative tendency to cast bad behavior as mental illness and to conflate evil with madness.[105]

The term *evil* is often affixed to anything that dramatically opposes the moral codes of an avowedly good majority—much like the term *mad* is ascribed to whatever perplexes and vexes the avowedly sane majority. However, over the past thousand years, myriad atrocities have ensued when supposedly *good* majorities label outsiders *evil* and set upon combatting, correcting, or cleansing away said evil. The Crusades, the Atlantic Slave Trade, and the Holocaust, for example, all entailed leaders labeling others *evil* and stoking violence against that alleged evil. I propose a different notion of evil: I regard it as a radical will to harm, without mercy or compunction, that seeks , wreaks, and relishes said harm. This definition indicts many of the so-called good leaders and majorities I've referenced above, exposing the vicious irony that much evil is committed in the name of, and under the cover of, "good."

In short, the discourse around Trump occasions four critical reminders: not all bizarre behavior is mental illness; not all ineptitude results from psychiatric deterioration; not all egregious deeds are clinical symptoms; and madness is not synonymous with evil.

Though I caution against the haphazard use of *crazy* to describe Trumpian malfeasance, I acknowledge that Trump might be mad on some register. He might experience a chaos of mind and crisis of meaning that is phenomenal madness; he might meet diagnostic criteria for any number of mental illnesses, perhaps antisocial or narcissistic personality disorder; and he surely exploits and channels right-wing, white supremacist rage. However, I hold that Trump does not instantiate psychosocial madness. Across the broad arc of American and Western modernity, his worrisome behavior is not psychosocial alterity; instead, it is white supremacist Reason laid hideously bare. More broadly, he is a blatant extension of, rather than a rupture from, the white supremacist, antiblack, sexist, xenophobic, belligerent, and chauvinist psychosocial norms that have historically prevailed in the United States. The Afropessimist philosopher Frank Wilderson has proclaimed, citing and riffing on the work of David Marriott, that antiblack psychopathology is "supported and coordinated with all the guns in the world."[106] If Trump is crazy, his madness is literally "supported and coordinated" with more guns than the madness of any other living person as I write these words.[107]

If we are invested in black liberation, it may feel satisfying to condemn antiblackness as pathological and affirm black resistance as sane. However, such a move would reinforce the psychonormative binary that casts madness as patently bad and Reason as inherently good on opposite sides of a metaphysical wall; we would simply be swapping the occupants from one side to the other. I propose a more profound transformation: topple the wall and create liberated spaces where psychosocial variance and racial plurality (among infinite other modes of variance and plurality) can thrive in the care of radical compassion.

HOW TO GO MAD: CHAPTER BY CHAPTER

The chapters in this book span a broad range of genres and forms, from experimental fiction to hip-hop performance to stand-up comedy to poetry to memoir. Each chapter is also polyvalent, exploring madness in its phenomenal, medicalized, psychosocial, and furious forms. Furthermore, each chapter is transdisciplinary, traversing and taking up approaches including cultural studies, discourse analysis, psychoanalysis, phenomenology, black feminist theory, disability theory, performative writing, mad methodology, and beyond.

Following the present chapter's meditation on madness and modernity, chapter 2 is "'He Blew His Brains Out through the Trumpet': Buddy Bolden and the Impossible Sound of Madness." Set in New Orleans at the dawn of the twentieth century, amid the nadir of post-slavery US race relations and the rise of jazz music, chapter 2 illuminates the lifeworld and afterlifeworld of Charles "Buddy" Bolden. He was a turn-of-the-twentieth-century ragtime phenom sometimes credited as the "inventor" of jazz music; an alleged madman who spent a quarter-century in a Louisiana insane asylum; and a historical enigma and archival phantom who cannot be apprehended with positivism, but demands a mad methodology instead. I am interested in both Bolden's historical life, which leaves scant archival trace, and his mythical afterlife, which teems with activity. That mythical afterlife is an assemblage of artistic surrogations, fantasies, and recuperations—created by artists like Jelly Roll Morton, Ralph Ellison, Nina Simone, August Wilson, Michael Ondaatje, and Natasha Trethewey—inspired by Bolden and proliferating into his wake. Beyond inspiring this surge of art, Bolden also inaugurates an intriguing archetype in the pantheon of jazz: the mad jazzman. In the decades after Bolden's confinement, a number of jazz icons, including Sun Ra and Charles Mingus, would also allegedly go mad and spend time in psychiatric confinement. The chapter closes by convening Bolden, Ra, and Mingus in a mad trio.[108]

From the specter of a mad jazzman, I turn to the "soul" of a mad blueswoman in an interlude called "'No Wiggles in the Dark of Her Soul': Black Madness, Metaphor, and 'Murder!'" This section begins with a provocation from Clay, the protagonist of Amiri Baraka's 1964 play *Dutchman*. In his climactic monologue, Clay declares, "If Bessie Smith had killed some white people she wouldn't have needed that music. . . . No metaphors. No grunts. No wiggles in the dark of her soul. Crazy niggers turning their backs on sanity. When all it needs is that simple act. Murder. Just murder! Would make us all sane."[109] Amid his incendiary speech, Clay diagnoses a racialized madness afflicting black Americans and argues that it must be sated by "metaphor" or "murder!" Launching from Clay's words, this interlude carefully considers interrelations between metaphor and murder to set the scene for two subsequent chapters: one concerning a mad black woman who commits murder and the other centering a mad black woman who makes art.

Chapter 3, "The Blood-Stained Bed," surrounds the life of Eva Canada, the protagonist of Gayl Jones's 1976 novel *Eva's Man*. Since her working-class girlhood in New York City in the 1940s and 1950s, Eva's life has been overrun by sexual predation and violence. At age thirty-eight, as though unleashing decades worth of rage and vengeance, Eva murders and mutilates a man who seeks to sexually objectify her. She is quickly apprehended, deemed criminally insane, and condemned to a psychiatric prison. Carefully, I read Eva's violence as a terrible catharsis aimed at (a man who becomes proxy for) a racist-sexist world. The chapter reveals how madness animates and structures Eva's first-person narrative, how symptomology becomes narratology in the book, how an act of "murder!" and a creation of "metaphor" converge in the story. Because Eva's deeds violently violate moral norms, she pushes the limits of radical compassion.

Chapter 4 is "A Portrait of the Artist as a Mad Black Woman." Therein I read Ntozake Shange's 1994 experimental novel, *Liliane: Resurrection of the Daughter*, as a meditation on black sublimation where black madness becomes black art. Born to black elites in suburban New Jersey circa World War II, Liliane Lincoln grows to become an avant-garde performance artist, painter, sculptor, sexual adventurer, cosmopolitan world-wanderer, feminist, and faithful patient of psychoanalysis. Her peculiar madness—the product of antiblack antagonisms, misogynist traumas, and bourgeois repressions, all revealed in stylized scenes of psychoanalysis—achieves release through metaphor and art. Liliane spins neurosis into artful language and constantly sublimates fury, angst, and self-avowed "crazy" into beauty. But she is not always an exemplar of sublimation. When demeaned and imperiled by a white male lover, Liliane ponders the ethics and efficacy of killing. Alongside *Eva's Man*, *Liliane* prompts a careful meditation on artistic and violent vicissitudes of madness.

Shifting from literature to performance, but remaining in the field of black women's radical creativity, chapter 5 is "'The People Inside My Head, Too': Ms. Lauryn Hill Sings Truth to Power in the Key of Madness." At the heart of this chapter is hip-hop musician Lauryn Hill, who was twenty-three years old when her 1998 solo debut album, *The Miseducation of Lauryn Hill*, became one of the most critically and commercially successful hip-hop releases in history. Within three years, however, Hill had supposedly fallen from favor in American pop culture and had allegedly gone mad. This chapter illuminates how various pundits and publics impute madness to Hill and how Hill herself produces, activates, and brandishes madness in service of poignant protest music. Toward these aims, I chart the specter of madness in several of her performances, especially her 2001 *MTV Unplugged No. 2.0* album; I examine interviews wherein she explains her "crazy" music and conduct; and I analyze media depictions of Hill as a black woman askew. This chapter also features hip-hop musician and producer Kanye West, who cites Hill as one of his greatest influences, makes black radical music (sometimes interspersed with right-wing provocations), and endures widespread accusations of madness.

Chapter 6 considers another iconic postsoul performer supposedly gone mad: the comedian Dave Chappelle. Titled "The Joker's Wild, but That Nigga's Crazy: Dave Chappelle Laughs until It Hurts," this sixth chapter begins with an incident in 2004 on the set of his hit series *Chappelle's Show*. When he performed a satirical blackface sketch, Chappelle heard what sounded like a sinister inflection in a crewmember's laughter. The moment was both *snap* and *click* for Chappelle, who suddenly realized that his comedy might inadvertently endorse antiblackness. He became disillusioned with fame, abandoned the third season of his show, reneged on a lucrative contract, absconded from America altogether, and headed to South Africa. Remarkably, tabloid media and public discussion insinuated that he *went* crazy and *went* to Africa—as though the two were parallel journeys—evoking racist tropes of Africa as epicenter of unReason and savagery. In this chapter, I examine the specter of madness within Chappelle's performance repertoire and public persona. In particular, I read his comical threats that he might lose his mind; his satires of the madness of white supremacy and black abjection; the tabloid allegations that he had gone mad; his journey across a mad diaspora; and his affinities with the iconoclastic comedian and self-avowed "crazy nigger," Richard Pryor.

Collectively, chapters 5 and 6 investigate what I call the *maddening of black genius*, a phrase denoting the antiblack derision of blackness as "crazy," the outrage of black artists antagonized by such antiblackness, and the unruliness of mind that sometimes ensues.

The seventh and final chapter, "Songs in Madtime: Black Music, Madness, and Metaphysical Syncopation," advances a theory of madtime. As I conceive it, madtime is a transgressive temporality that coincides with phenomenologies of madness. It includes the quick time of mania; the slow time of depression; the infinite, exigent now of schizophrenia; and the spiraling now-then-now-then-now of melancholia, among other polymorphous arrangements. As a critical supplement to *colored people's time*, *queer time*, and *crip time*, madtime flouts the normative schedules of Reason, trips the lockstep of Western teleology, disobeys the dominant beat, and swerves instead into a metaphysical offbeat. I contend that some black musicians are prime practitioners of madtime, adapting it as a time signature in protest music. In order to bear out and sound out this claim, I sample the music of Buddy Bolden, Nina Simone, Charles Mingus, Lauryn Hill, Kendrick Lamar, and Frank Ocean—featuring the lyrical language of Amiri Baraka, Toni Morrison, and Suzan-Lori Parks—to stage a medley in madtime. Throughout the chapter, I consider how black protest movements might critically, ethically, radically activate madtime in pursuit of liberation.

I close with a brief afterword, "The Nutty Professor (A Confession)," which ponders the specter of madness and the figure of the black scholar. In the process, I reveal my personal investments in mad black study.

Across these chapters, I recognize and foreground madpersons as subjects and protagonists. Indeed, many of the cultural producers centered in this study are "mad," whether they have been diagnosed with serious mental illness (Bolden, Mingus, and Simone), institutionalized (Bolden, Ra, Mingus, and very briefly Jones), labeled suicidal (Ra and Shange), subject to pop culture allegations of madness (Hill and Chappelle), or known to channel spectacular outrage (Simone, Baraka, and Hill). It bears noting that, alongside these *historical persons*, my project's protagonists include *fictional characters* and *psychological phantasms*. I know better than to crudely conflate these three categories of being—so I traverse them gingerly and meticulously. Yet the most careful approach cannot guarantee a neat account of madness. Indeed, madness erodes neat epistemological and ontological taxonomies, throwing into question—and sometimes into crisis—distinctions between history, fiction, and delusion. Madness induces uncertainty over what counts as real.

Consider Buddy Bolden, for example. In the artifacts I examine, he is a historical person, a fictionalized character, and sometimes an outburst of marvelous sound that invades the senses like a voice in one's head. Then there are performers like Ra, Chappelle, Hill, and Lamar, who cultivate public personae blending biographical personhood with dramatized character. Another poignant blurring of the "real" and "unreal" occurs in Charles Mingus's memoir. He sometimes recounts historical events, sometimes crafts fabrications, and sometimes swerves into ostensibly psychotic-*cum*-fantastic reveries, often without clear indication or notice. The result is a narrative that is alternately—and sometimes simultaneously—historical, fictional, and delusional. In short, mad black study must crisscross metaphysical registers to follow the sometimes unruly flows of madness. I warned you: our passage, which began where a "fruitless expanse" joined "nowhere at all," may be dizzying.[110]

TOWARD HEALING

In "Mama's Baby, Papa's Maybe," Spillers annotates an "American Grammar Book," a complex assemblage of symbols, discourses, archetypes, themes, and recursive dramas reflecting and reproducing America's racial and sexual regimes. Following Spillers, I want to envision some contents in what we might call an American Picture Book, a repertoire of images that lately abound in American public spheres. I have in mind scenes of state-sanctioned black wounding and death that saturate our information age: black people fleeing, charging, hands up, hands clenched, battered, throttled, shot, kneeling, flailing, staggering, convulsing, slumped over, prostrate on asphalt or grass, then photographed or video-recorded, then bandied about endlessly on social media timelines and network news broadcasts. While spectacles of antiblack violence are perennial tableaux in a centuries-old American Picture Book,[111] twenty-first-century proliferation of camera technologies and social media platforms enable unprecedented capture, circulation, and consumption of such images. Then there are the terrifying sounds, which might be said to constitute an American Score: shouted commands, invectives, pleas of *Don't shoot!*, gasps, gunshots, shrieks, bloody gurgling, cries out to God, weeping, the hissing and crackling of walkie-talkies, calls for backup, and stretches of stunned silence.

Exposure to such spectacular images and strident sounds of antiblackness—compounding first-person encounters with everyday antiblackness—is enough to drive a person mad. I mean mad on multiple registers. It is enough to incite crises of selfhood and meaning that I call *phenomenal madness*; it is enough to instigate the impassioned discontent that is *rage*; it is enough to inspire rejection of extant psychonorms and an embrace of *psychosocial alterity*; and it is also enough to induce symptoms that meet diagnostic criteria for *medicalized mad-*

ness. Regarding the latter, psychologist Monnica Williams suggests that watching and listening to loops of mediatized black death inflicts "vicarious trauma": empathic secondhand trauma born of witnessing others' pain, especially others with whom one holds affinity or shares identity. According to Williams, onslaughts of vicarious trauma, as amplified in cultures of spectacle, "can lead to depression . . . and, in some cases, psychosis."[112]

But mental illness is not only a potential *outcome* of witnessing such violence; mental illness is also a *risk factor* correlated with an increased likelihood of suffering such violence. In the United States, people with untreated serious mental illness are sixteen times more likely than other civilians to be killed in encounters with law enforcement.[113] Meanwhile, black people in the US are 2.5 to 3 times more likely than their white counterparts to be murdered by police.[114] I have found no statistical data on the particular vulnerability of people who are both mentally ill and black. Nevertheless, the names Eleanor Bumpurs, Anthony Hill, Danny Ray Thomas, Isaiah Lewis, and Deborah Danner—all mentally ill black people killed in outrageous confrontations with police—testify to the tragedy of mad black death at the hands of Reasonable law enforcement.[115]

In the face of antiblack violence and trauma, theater historian and critic Harry Elam advances a theory of "racial madness" and proposes a project of "healing." Elam explains that

> within modern America, racial madness has been inextricably connected to the abuses of racism and oppression as well as to the struggle for black liberation. My point here is not to pathologize blackness. Rather, by foregrounding this concept of racial madness, I want to recognize the relationship of, and work between, the clinical, the literary, and the philosophical, between the literal and figurative symptoms and significance of this dis-ease, always conscious of the cultural and the social orientation of this condition. Racial madness was and is not simply a mental condition, not simply a social one, but one that demands nevertheless a healing.[116]

How to Go Mad is animated by deep concern for black people, mad people, and other beleaguered beings. If this project brings attention to people who have been persecuted because of their blackness and/or/as madness; if it alerts rationalist readers to the grave repercussions of demeaning the mentally ill; if it teaches techniques for practicing ethical, radical, critical, and beautiful madness; if it instigates righteous rage in the interest of social transformation; if it broadens understanding of who and what comprises a black radical tradition; if it encourages black studies to more carefully address madness; if it prompts mad studies to think more rigorously through blackness; if it urges black studies and mad studies to join forces;[117] if it testifies to the possibility of bearing fruit in a "fruitless expanse" and finding home "*nowhere* at all"; if it models radical compassion; if it urges us toward liberation; or if it simply contributes to someone's relief or healing, then, to my mind, this book succeeds.

For some, healing might mean banishing madness. For others, healing might mean harnessing madness and putting it to good use—a readiness to rally the voices inside one's head rather than silence them.[118] Now, toward the voice calling from the "deep black mouth" of jazz's "first man."[119]

CHAPTER TWO

"HE BLEW HIS BRAINS OUT THROUGH THE TRUMPET"

BUDDY BOLDEN AND THE IMPOSSIBLE
SOUND OF MADNESS

THE DEEP BLACK MOUTH

To study the mystery of Buddy Bolden—black New Orleanian born in 1877, purported "inventor" of jazz music,[1] and madman confined for twenty-four years in a Louisiana insane asylum, where he died destitute in 1931—poetry is as handy as historiography. Only a single faded photograph, several sentences in legal and medical documents, three newspaper clippings, and a few dozen testimonies endure as primary evidence of Bolden's life.[2] Historians and archivists have found no recordings, no autobiography, no interviews, no diaries, no letters, no scrapbooks,

Imagine a picture frame
that is really
a window, weathered white,
wide open. In the background,
dark arms flex
to collar a note—blow it strum it
beat it to the cut.
All you see
is the bell of a horn, or a valve,
shiny as a silver dollar.
His cornet comes toward you,
pushing through the window,
leaving the frame.
You look straight into the deep black mouth—
it is talking, loud.
Come on, it calls.
You're almost here.
—NATASHA TRETHEWEY,
"Calling His Children Home," 1996

and no sheet music generated by Bolden himself—and because he is buried in an anonymous pauper's grave, in some unknown plot in New Orleans's Holt Cemetery, there is not even an inscription to mark the place of his bodily remains.[3] Amid this dearth of documentary evidence, and into the lacuna around Bolden, there rushes the slippery and shape-shifting stuff of rumor, innuendo, legend, dream, fantasy, and art. These materials do not so much document his historical life as they constitute his mythical afterlife. Indeed, Bolden leaves little archival residue, but in the century and more since his confinement in an insane asylum, he has inspired a para-archival proliferation from an eclectic ensemble of cultural producers.

An exquisite example of Bolden's mythical afterlife is "Calling His Children Home," a 1996 poem penned by US Poet Laureate Natasha Trethewey and wholly transcribed above. Written "for Buddy Bolden" and presenting a likeness of him—a figure who carries a cornet in "dark arms," summons his children home,[4] and is noted for his loudness—the poem is an apt opening into this chapter. In fact, "Calling His Children Home" contains three openings through which we can approach Bolden. First is the "picture frame / that is really / a window, weathered white, / wide open." Second is "the cut." Third is "the deep black mouth." Each is a site of passage that conveys us nearer to him. It is worth the effort to enter all three.

1. Let's begin with the "window, weathered white, / wide open." In the metaphysics of Trethewey's poem, this window is also a wormhole bridging Bolden's lifeworld and whatever spacetime "you" inhabit. If you heed his instruction to "come on," if you climb through that world-breaching window, you might emerge in New Orleans, circa 1905, to find Bolden performing in his prime. The city was Bolden's hometown, the scene of his success, the purported birthplace of jazz, and a circum-Atlantic nexus where West Africa, Native America, the United States, the Caribbean, Western Europe, and mad—which is a place—all converge.[5] In particular, you might land in Lincoln Park, an outdoor commons where "colored" folks sought leisure and amusement, where Buddy Bolden's Band played under open sky. Legend has it that Bolden would blow his cornet with such volume and verve that he attracted and enchanted crowds from a dozen miles away. He described this practice, this ritual of playing and beckoning, as *calling his children home*.[6]

Note that the window is white. Within the racial-chromatic schema of the poem—where those "dark arms" and that "black mouth" denote racial blackness—the whiteness of this window may signify racial whiteness. If we merge this racial symbolism with a psychoanalytic sexual symbolism, the dark player's "cornet," with its "shiny" "valve," might signify a black penis or phallic object. As it "pushes through" and penetrates that white window, the latter is cast as a white sexual orifice, "weathered" and "wide" open. Meanwhile, note the sensuous exertions of those dark flexing arms as they handle, beat, and strum the music. And then he coaxes you to "come," assures you that "you're almost there," edges you toward felicitous union and completion, like a lover

2.1 Buddy Bolden (*top row, second from left*) and his band, circa 1903. This is the only known photograph of Bolden.

cheering you toward climax. This erotic emphasis is faithful to Bolden's reputation. He was, by most accounts, an emphatic lover, pleasure-seeker, and erotic adventurer amid the red-lit sexworlds that thrived in New Orleans at the turn of the twentieth century.[7] By the time the poem ends, you're close, but alas, you haven't made it yet. Seeking Bolden may inspire similar titillation and frustration in enthusiasts and historians: you may find yourself "almost there," but you never reach your destination. You approach but never arrive. Call it the *asymptotic erotic*.

2. Now, toward that "cut." The cornetist grabs hold of a musical note, synesthetically *touching a sound* in order to "blow it strum it / beat it to the cut." A polysemous signifier, "the cut" splinters into multiple meanings germane to the lifeworld of Bolden: "The cut" might signify a discrete segment of music, like many cuts that Bolden played throughout his career as cornetist

and bandleader. "The cut" might also name the musical pause or break that succeeds the blown, strummed, beaten note. Perhaps "the cut" designates a remote place, per the idiom "in the cut," like the rural Louisiana asylum where Bolden languished for a quarter century. "The cut" could also entail a tear in the skin, a metaphor for the wound that his absence opens in the corpus of jazz. Similarly, "the cut" may denote severance, and thus evoke Bolden's rupture from the incipient Jazz Age (after all, he was cut off and cast out of a blooming jazz tradition and flung into an insane asylum). This "cut" might also align with "the cut" described by another poet, Nathaniel Mackey, as "an insistent previousness evading each and every natal occasion."[8] Mackey's description is especially apt because jazz cannot be traced to an originary moment or definitive "natal occasion." Jazz was and is a diffuse, diasporic, transhistorical, rhizomatic collaboration (despite claims that one man invented it). "The cut" might also be an opening into which creative and imaginative forces rush and from which they emerge. In this respect, it is what Fred Moten, inspired by Mackey, describes as "a generative break, one wherein action becomes possible, one in which it is our duty to linger in the name of ensemble and its performance."[9]

3. Finally, we enter "the deep black mouth." It is a recess (yawning and dark), an excess (impossibly loud), and a success (effectively calling and commanding across worlds). Whereas the pane of the window is transparent, revealing precisely what lies beyond it, the "deep black mouth" is opaque and ominous. It is calling you, but also, maybe, threatening to consume you. It is poised to speak and also primed to swallow. Perhaps that mouth calls us into the grotesque, which emphasizes "the apertures or complexities, or . . . various ramifications and offshoots: *the open mouth*, the genital organs, the breasts, the phallus, the potbelly, the nose," per literary theorist Mikhail Bakhtin. Furthermore, according to Bakhtin, "the theme of madness is inherent to all grotesque forms, because madness makes men look at the world with different eyes, not dimmed by 'normal,' that is by commonplace ideas and judgments."[10] When it is shrieking, swallowing, or opening into shadow, the wide-open mouth conjures the loud, devouring, and inscrutable qualities often imputed to madness. This "theme of madness" suffuses Trethewey's Bolden; he approaches you like a dream, like an exquisite hallucination, like an unruly force that breaks the frame, like a voice inside your head inviting you into an uncanny elsewhere.

Describing "the three-sided relationship of memory, performance, and substitution," performance theorist Joseph Roach writes that "into the cavities created by loss through death or other forms of departure . . . survivors attempt to fit satisfactory alternates. Because collective memory works selectively, imaginatively, and often perversely, surrogation rarely if ever succeeds . . . the intended substitute either cannot fulfill expectations, creating a deficit, or actually exceeds them, creating a surplus."[11] I want to propose that the "window," "the cut," and "the deep black mouth" are all "cavities." Bolden's departures—through his flight from sanity, his quarter-century incarceration, his biological death, and his documentary dearth—inspire "survivors" and successors to fantasize and fabulate into those cavities. In other words, his disappearance incites artists to create into the hollow he leaves behind.[12] I call this inspiration and incitation the *Bolden effect*.

Now that we have passed through those poetic openings, the remainder of this chapter ponders Bolden's historical life before turning to his mythical afterlife. Regarding that historical life, I do not attempt an extensive biographical account of Bolden. Instead, I consider several key events and phenomena: his rise to fame, his musical innovations, his reputation for unruliness, his trademark loudness, his revelry among "the working people,"[13] his purported mental breakdown while strutting in a Labor Day parade, and his confinement to an asylum. But my true focus in this chapter is Bolden's mythical afterlife, a collection of Bolden-inspired, Bolden-incited, Bolden-infused cultural productions—the fruit of the Bolden effect. These works encompass myriad forms, including the poetry of Natasha Trethewey, the storytelling of Jelly Roll Morton, the music of Nina Simone, the drama of August Wilson, the unpublished drafts of Ralph Ellison, the fiction of Michael Ondaatje, and the mad black lives lived by jazz icons Charles Mingus and Sun Ra.[14]

Throughout this chapter, Bolden functions as a complex person and signifier. He is at once a musician who enchants nightclubs and parks, a madman who resides in an asylum, a phantom who eludes archives, a spirit who posthumously haunts the history of jazz, a soil-like residue that nourishes the efflorescence of other artists, and a sound that calls out to you from an impossible distance (like a voice in your head or a cornet song a dozen miles yonder). Musician, madman, phantom, residue, spirit, hallucination, soil, and sound, Bolden is too protean, too amorphous to be captured by positivism. He demands a mad methodology: a practice that can chase these metamorphoses through wormholes and down rabbit holes without intent to capture. As mad methodologist, I will also extend radical compassion to Bolden, across the chasm of uncertainty that separates him from me.

Charles "Buddy" Bolden was probably born on September 6, 1877, in New Orleans, Louisiana, the second of Alice and Westmore Bolden's three children. At age three, Bolden lost his six-year-old sister to encephalitis, and then, at age five, he lost his father to acute pleura-pneumonia. His mother worked, likely as a domestic, while raising him and his surviving sister, Cora, three years his junior. After a childhood and adolescence ostensibly spent in a tight-knit family unit with his mother and sister in the Central City neighborhood, Bolden emerged in his twenties as a locally renowned cornetist and band leader.[15] Although he is frequently labeled a trumpeter, Bolden's primary instrument was actually the cornet. The latter is similar to the trumpet, but shorter, with conical rather than cylindrical tubing and a slightly less piercing, mellower sound.

Bolden would gain fame for his improvisation and syncopation; for playing and living loudly; for drinking and sexing; for rubbing shoulders and bumping bellies with the city's underclass of gamblers, hustlers, pleasure-seekers, and sex workers; and for playing outside to hail those impromptu crowds he called his "children."[16] Bolden also fathered two biological children: a boy called Charles Junior (born to Bolden's longtime companion, Hattie Oliver) and later, a girl named Bernedine (born to Bolden's eventual common-law wife, Nora Bass).[17]

The charismatic cornetist eventually earned enough prominence to be anointed musical "King" in his own time and later, "inventor of jazz."[18] As jazz musician and scholar Salim Washington notes, jazz is frequently imagined within a "liberal democratic vision that valorizes the triumph of the assertive, ingenious individual," and occasionally, I might add, bestows such individuals with honorifics like "genius" and "inventor."[19] While Bolden was decisive to the popularization of jazz, to cast him as its individual originator is to efface the collaborative contributions of innumerable agents of its formation whose names are unrecorded in annals of jazz history. I have in mind West African griots, enslaved plantation musicians, Congo square drummers and dancers, recently emancipated troubadours in Reconstruction slums, masses of black common folk, and others who constituted the colossal ensemble that cocreated jazz. I tend to view Bolden's relationship to jazz the way Moten views Shakespeare's relationship to modernity. Moten muses that "I don't know that Shakespeare invents [modernity], but I think that Shakespeare—and by Shakespeare I mean this intense and absolutely emphatic radicalization of singularity that now we know under the name of Shakespeare—announces it, which is to say announces as an insistent irruption that he also enacts. By *he* I mean something much more like *they*."[20] Likewise, Bolden doesn't invent jazz, but he heralds the arrival of the Jazz Age with a clamorous cornet riff. Bolden is a *he* embedded within a *they* of countless cultural producers who precede him, whose names are rarely documented in plaques, monuments, archives, or books. Furthermore, Bolden is a *he* entwined with a *they* of artists who succeed him, who produce Bolden-inspired art into his wake.

Among Bolden's most ardent admirers was Ferdinand "Jelly Roll" Morton, fellow New Orleanian and fellow jazz iconoclast. Born circa 1885, Morton rose to fame in the 1920s as a virtuosic pianist and flashy celebrity personality. Though he crowned himself the inventor of jazz,[21] labeling Bolden a ragtime musician, Morton did grant Bolden two superlative titles: "the most powerful trumpet player I've ever heard, or ever was known," and "the blowingest man since [the angel] Gabriel."[22] In an interview with ethnomusicologist and folklorist Alan Lomax, Morton offers this earwitness account of Bolden's volume: "Yes, anytime that it was a quiet night out in the Lincoln Park—which . . . was at least about ten or twelve miles from the corner that we hung out . . . Buddy would just take his big trumpet and just turn it around towards the city and blow. . . . And the whole town would know that Buddy was there."[23] Lincoln Park was one of Bolden's legendary haunts, where carnival spectacles, sport, cuisine, and especially live music were main attractions.[24] To have Morton tell it, Bolden could play from Lincoln Park and unleash a sound that traveled a dozen miles yonder. Morton insists that Bolden boomed across the sound-absorbing and sound-obstructing buildings ascending in early twentieth-century New Orleans, so that the "whole town" could hear it. Meanwhile, the laws of physics and limits of human physiology make such feats of playing and hearing extremely unlikely.[25]

Concerning Morton's Library of Congress interviews, Lomax writes that "it has proved vain to try to check or correct Jelly's story." However, he observes that "the big outlines of his story are solid and true to life; if there is niggling about facts, there is unanimity among the feelings of Jelly and the other boys in the bands. . . . Sometimes they brag; sometimes they remember exactly what was said or how things looked; sometimes they remember it the way they wished it; but somehow out of the crossing of misty memories comes truth."[26] Lomax describes a story that cannot be captured by traditional techniques of historiography, a story that benefits from mad methodology instead. Likewise, any inquiry into Bolden's lifeworld must not merely find "facts"—it must grapple with "feelings," count "wishes," wade through "misty memories," and perhaps parse figments of imagination. Upon reading Morton's twelve mile testimony, a devout rationalist might dismiss it as deliberate fabrication, or a failure of memory, or a miscalculation of distance, or perhaps the product of delusion.

I want to linger with the specter of *delusion*, which is the psychiatric term for a belief that is adamantly held despite evidence refuting it. It seems to me that Morton's propensity for drama and embellishment, combined with his experience of the Bolden effect, yields a fabulously far-fetched account that might sound crazy (depending on who's listening). I am not attempting to diagnose Morton with any disorder; rather, I am emphasizing the likeness between an instance of the Bolden effect and the purported pathology of delusion.

Activating a mad methodology, we might seriously engage, rather than glibly dismiss, accounts that appear to be delusional, unReasonable, far-fetched, fantastical, mythical, mystical, apocryphal, improbable, or impossible. Even if Bolden's cornet call did not travel a dozen miles—even if Morton was *hearing things*, so to speak—we can still find truth in Morton's claim. The truth is that Bolden unleashed a metaphysical resonance that reverberated across the local zeitgeist of New Orleans and also echoed across epochs into the imaginations of artists convened in this chapter. The truth is that Bolden possesses an ontological loudness that surmounts asylum walls, documentary dearth, obscurity, neglect, time, and Reason, to reach me as I write these words. Twelve-mile audibility might not align with the laws of physics, but maybe it tells us something about the laws of metaphysics, about wish-worlds and dreamscapes that exceed the bounds of the physical and measurable.

We need not rely on Morton's testimony to affirm that Bolden was loud; nearly all first-person accounts of Bolden's performances emphasize his extraordinary volume.[27] I want to tune into one especially provocative description of Bolden's loudness. Upon hearing a cornet's sound bouncing through the streets of downtown New Orleans one evening at the turn of the twentieth century, a mother declared to her son, who recounted for researchers decades later, "That's Buddy Bolden. He's gonna blow his brains out one day because he plays too loud."[28] The phrase *blow his brains out* is a double entendre here, signifying both the forceful exhalation required to play a brass instrument loudly and the harm a bullet might inflict when piercing a skull. She regards Bolden as a symbol of dangerous excess and self-destruction, an object lesson within a cautionary tale.

This woman's words are uttered in a domestic sphere—and, more precisely, within the idealized scene of maternal moral instruction before tucking a child into bed. Maybe Bolden's "too loud" playing was a nuisance to domestic order: sonically breaking and entering into homes, disturbing the peace (and quiet), disrupting sleep, and prompting parental warnings. Thus characterized, Bolden seems to be at odds with family and domesticity. However, when Bolden claims to call his children home, he describes his performances with a metaphor both familial and domestic. Despite her disapproval of his loudness, the woman and Bolden have something in common: both are parents addressing their progeny. She is a mother bidding her child goodnight, while he is a father hailing his children home. But the home he cultivates is no building with walls and roof. Bolden convenes an outdoor domesticity, one that exits the edifices typically labeled domestic, and lingers in the park under open sky. Indeed, he breaks *into* homes, disturbing sleep, and also breaks *out of* home, flouting conventions of domesticity.[29]

When Lomax asks Morton, "Why did Buddy Bolden go crazy?," Morton's response reiterates the blown-brains legend: "Why, I tell you. They claim that Buddy Bolden went crazy because he really blew his brains out through the trumpet."[30] Thus described, Bolden's *too-loudness* is not merely the cause of his madness, but also an analog for his madness. Too-loudness and madness are both disruptive, both are ascribed to Bolden, and both are frequently imputed to black people in the United States as markers of (sonic and psychic) excess.

If the legend of Bolden's loudness is true, his cornet was likely audible above all the din and roar of the Labor Day parade that traversed downtown and uptown New Orleans on September 3, 1906. Bandleader and "King," Bolden had become immensely popular in the city and was a featured player in the parade. Perhaps his highness marched along the route with a kingly swagger, blowing his trademark "Funky Butt Blues," and leaving a queue of awestruck royal subjects and sideliners in his wake. And then—snap. Bolden supposedly suffered a mental breakdown and stopped marching, though there is no clear historiographic account of this incident. One wonders whether he veered suddenly off the parade route to chase an invisible phantasm or maybe slowly wandered away in a dreamy daze. Perhaps he succumbed to some mental fatigue, collapsing limply to the ground to get a bit of rest. Some have suggested that he drank one too many sips of whiskey and overflowed into alcohol-induced psychosis.[31] Others have inferred that he was overtaken by syphilitic dementia.[32] Still others claim that he was made mad by some malevolent conjurer.[33] It could be that some unbearable, ineffable sound of madness cut through the din of the parade, invaded his senses, engulfed him, drove him off the parade route, and drove him mad. Maybe it sounded like a heckler's shout, or a sonic boom, or a divine voice, or a cornet call from another world. We cannot tell for sure.

In the final chapter of this book, I will return to this scene to address how Bolden's swerve away from the parade mirrors syncopation's swerve away from the dominant beat and the madperson's swerve away from Reason. For now, I want to note that this parade was Bolden's last gig as a professional musician. According to Marquis, Bolden's condition quickly deteriorated, and he became "impoverished and incoherent, a stranger to his mother and sister and a burden they could no longer endure."[34] By spring of 1907, he would experience bouts of derangement, delusion, mania, and violent frenzy. He would drastically withdraw from family, friends, bandmates, and even his longtime brass companion. Regarding the latter, Bolden reportedly developed a fear of his cornet; perhaps a persecution complex convinced him that his instrument was booby-trapped to do him harm.[35]

Bolden's symptoms ostensibly spiked in 1906 and 1907, but it is possible that he lived and performed madly long before his parade breakdown. Thus, I wonder: If Bolden's symptoms preceded that fateful parade, how might they have impacted his music in prior months and years? Rather than propose some causal scenario that glibly credits madness as the source of Bolden's musical genius,[36] I want to speculate on the complex interrelations that might have entwined madness and music in Bolden's life. *Maybe* the stressors and intensities of being a black "King" in an antiblack world triggered a mental breakdown. *Maybe* his purported mania endowed his performances with bursts of energetic showmanship and suspensefully unpredictable swerves of sound. *Maybe* an unruly mind thwarted his planning and practice, thus pushing him to improvise instead. *Maybe* he harbored an obsessive attachment to the music, a fanatical devotion that yielded excellence. *Maybe* his musicianship was an outlet for mad energy, a container to capture and channel some of the unruly currents coursing through his mind. (In this case, the cornet might have functioned like a filter converting madness into culturally palatable music, a sort of sublimation machine. Blow mad breath in one side and hear beautiful blue notes come out the other side.) *Maybe* some combination of the preceding hypotheses is accurate, or all, or none. My point is that professional musicianship might have diminished and/or intensified his symptoms, and madness might have energized and/or impeded his music. The dearth of information about Bolden means that we may never know for sure. As mad methodologist, I am comfortable with unanswerable questions, unverifiable speculations, inexplicable wonders, and a litany of *maybes*.

Meanwhile, there is some documentary data, in the form of state-generated paperwork, confirming Bolden's admittance to the Louisiana State Asylum in Jackson on June 5, 1907. According to hospital records, he was diagnosed with manic depression and *dementia praecox*, the latter an antiquated term roughly corresponding to what is now called *schizophrenia*. Regarding Bolden's diagnosis, Marquis rightly emphasizes that antiblack bias corroded psychiatry in early twentieth-century America. He writes: "Bolden was placed in a stereotyped category of manic depressive or paranoid schizophrenic. A person in this category would have demonstrated noticeably hostile behavior toward the norms of society—the paranoid venting his frustration overtly. These characteristics were, however, true of the majority of black male patients admitted in Bolden's time. A black man could be committed if a white person complained of being upset by or the target of such hostility."[37]

While Bolden might have met "objective" diagnostic criteria for manic depression and schizophrenia, Marquis reminds us that antiblackness so deeply permeated the era's psychiatry that any such diagnosis of a black patient should be approached with suspicion. In the sordid tradition of Samuel Cartwright, doctors pathologized defiant black people in order to discredit, disenfranchise, dispossess, incarcerate, and otherwise persecute them. Any act of antiracist protest, any attempt to challenge antiblack and white supremacist status quos, any assertion of black power, or any expression of black rage might be perceived as "noticeably hostile behavior" and labeled insane. Although little is known of Bolden's racial consciousness or political sensibility, it bears emphasis that he was a working-class black man who came of age in the Jim Crow South during the "nadir" of postslavery blackness in the United States. Thus he had ample cause for hostility toward those invidious "norms of society."

There is precious little archival data about Bolden's life at the asylum. His time there is mostly mystery, referenced only obliquely in the notes and recollections of hospital staff who presided over his confinement and in the handful of terse letters they sent to his family. Amid the regimented monotony of asylum life, Bolden occasionally performed on hospital grounds. Citing statements from a ward attendant and from the widow of a doctor, Marquis reports that "Bolden would occasionally play during the twenty-four years he was at Jackson and seemingly retained traces of his old touch and mannerisms." Per the hospital attendant, "Bolden always started out quick (staccato) and would play a particular little phrase, walking around and frequently standing by the window when he played."[38] Like Trethewey's poem, this attendant's recollection locates Bolden near a window. Recall that Bolden appears in Trethewey's poem near the picture frame–*cum*–window, inviting you to "come on" through it. Here Bolden hovers near a hospital window, maybe longing to escape into the world beyond that psychiatric enclosure. Perhaps he yearned to return home to Lincoln Park with his children, to that outdoor domesticity, to those impromptu family gatherings under open sky.

In 1925, a ward doctor jotted these observations about Bolden: "Accessible and answers fairly well. Paranoid delusions, also grandiose. Auditory hallucinations and visual. Talks to self. Much reaction. . . . Insight and judgment lacking. . . . Has a string of talk that is incoherent. Hears the voices of people that bothered him before he came here."[39] I am not interested in assessing the clinical veracity of these notes; and anyway, such a task is impossible considering the sparseness of the observations, their origin in the anti-black distortions of Jim Crow psychiatry, and the lack of any corroborating data. Instead, I read these notes as accidental poetry. Briefly, I want to parse them for tropes, analogies, resonances, and evocations that speak to Bolden's broader lifeworld.

Grandiose: If Bolden ever announced his royal status, if he ever declared himself "King," an uninformed doctor might interpret his utterance as a *grandiose* delusion. Furthermore, if the doctor believed that black people were suited only for servility—a common antiblack attitude in Jim Crow Louisiana in 1925—Bolden's assertion of kingliness would've seemed all the more outlandish and outrageous.

Insight and judgment lacking: If Reason is racialized in antiblack modernity, then surely *insight and judgment* are racialized, too. I wonder how Jim Crow doctors purported to measure such *lack*, and whether they were even capable of perceiving the *insight and judgment* possessed by black patients. Indeed, black people in Jim Crow America built vast reservoirs of *insight* and systems of *judgment* that lay hidden from white gaze, protected under shrouds of opacity, and made to look like *lack*.

Talk that is incoherent: Bolden's *talk* was *incoherent* to the doctor, but might have been perfectly lucid to someone versed in the idiom of madness—in the so-called rants, raves, rambles, slurs, outbursts, unseemly silences, and gibberish sounds typically coded as crazy. Back in Lincoln Park, Bolden made his cornet *talk* to summon audiences. That *talk* exerted a compelling and even spellbinding power on the crowds who became his children and heeded his call. But in the asylum, his *talk* was unintelligible, dispossessed of the incantatory power it once held. Both the act of calling children home from twelve miles away and the act of uttering *talk that is incoherent* function to defy Reason: the former because it is improbable to Reasonable measures and the latter because it is incomprehensible to Reasonable sense.

Auditory hallucinations and *voices of people that bothered him*: Because music so deeply suffused Bolden's life, maybe melody inflected those auditory hallucinations. I wonder whether the bothersome voices in his head ever sang, whether they ever heckled him with a cacophonous or sonorous song. I hope that between and against the sounds of *people that bothered him*, he also heard voices of people comforting him with kind words or rallying him with fight songs.

Alas, Bolden would never leave the grounds of the Louisiana State Insane Asylum at Jackson. He became increasingly unresponsive, eventually failing to recognize his family.[40] He died on November 4, 1931, at age fifty-four, after twenty-four years in Jackson. The cause of death was recorded as "cerebral arteriel schlerosis [sic]," a thickening and hardening of the artery walls in the brain. Alas, he had already endured something like social death inside the thickening, hardening walls of that asylum.[41] Destitute by the time of his demise, Bolden is buried in an unmarked pauper's grave somewhere in New Orleans's Holt Cemetery; the precise location of his remains is unknown. If a graveyard is an archive of bodily residue, Bolden's unmarked gravesite performs another evasion of formal archivality, another obstruction to empiricism, a final refusal to provide documentary proof.[42]

Turning away from "the voices of people that bothered him before he came here," I move toward the clamor of people who hail him after he left here. Onward, now, to Buddy Bolden's mythical afterlife.

JELLY ROLL MORTON AND
NINA SIMONE SING BOLDEN

There are myriad variations on the lyrics of "Buddy Bolden's Blues," also known as "Funky Butt Blues." The precise origin of the song is contested. It is widely presumed that Bolden penned it, but one of his bandmembers, the trombonist Willie Cornish, also claimed credit.[43] Wherever they originated, the lyrics were handed down, revised, and reinterpreted among so many performers and audiences that it is neither practical nor especially pertinent to parse the authorship of one line or another. We would do well to regard it as a collaboration produced by an expansive ensemble.

Based on a conversation with Jelly Roll Morton, who eventually recorded the most famous version of the song, Lomax transcribed the first stanzas as follows:

> I thought I heard Buddy Bolden say
> Dirty nasty stinkin' butt, take it away
> A dirty nasty stinkin' butt, take it away
> Oh, Mister Bolden, play
>
> I thought I heard Buddy Bolden play
> Dirty nasty stinkin' butt, take it away
> A funky butt, stinky butt, take it away
> And let Mister Bolden play

A tamer version of the lyrics, expunged of scatological references, was included in Morton's 1940 commercial recording of the song:

> I thought I heard Buddy Bolden say
> You're nasty, you're dirty, take it away
> You're terrible, you're awful, take it away
> I thought I heard him say

> I thought I heard Buddy Bolden shout
> Open up that window, and let that bad air out
> Open up that window, and let the foul air out
> I thought I heard Buddy Bolden say

Reportedly based on actual events, "Funky Butt Blues" describes Bolden's reaction to a foul odor in a crowded and stifling dance hall in downtown New Orleans. The source of the odor is allegedly someone's sweaty or flatulent "funky butt."[44] The lyrics cast the source of the stench as "nasty," "dirty," "terrible," and "awful." In his definitive recording of the song, Morton barks these invectives in a gruff, unmelodic voice, as though such descriptors aren't fit for crooning.

The song's scatological content may be suited to bawdy humor—but it contains a grave inflection, too. The repeated rebuke of "bad air" and the dramatic plea that someone "take it away" suggest profound discomfort, even distress. Perhaps that "bad air" symbolizes more than just effluvium infused with funk or flatulence. Bad air might be a metaphor for any variety of foul and noxious forces lingering in the atmosphere around Bolden. Maybe bad air carries "the voices of people who bothered him," and he longs to defenestrate the sound. If, as black feminist theorist Christina Sharpe suggests, antiblackness is "the weather" permeating modernity, maybe that "foul air" is a miasma of antiblackness that he wishes he could whisk out the window.[45] (Like Trethewey's verses and the asylum attendant's recollections, these lyrics situate Bolden by a window as he longs for something to pass through it: "you" in Trethewey's poem, Bolden himself in the attendant's account, and "bad air" in this song. In all three instances, windows are portals for frustrated escape.) Or perhaps the offense was simply, literally, a rank odor. We cannot tell for sure.

The song's speaker cannot tell for sure, either, announcing, "I thought I heard Buddy Bolden say"—not "I heard Buddy Bolden say," nor "I know I heard Buddy Bolden say," nor "I am Buddy Bolden saying," but "I *thought* I heard Buddy Bolden say." This phrasing indicates the uncertainty and unreliability of the song's narrator, who may be mistaken, who might have misheard or misremembered what Bolden said. When Bolden's band performed the song at the start of the twentieth century, it was prescient, foreshadowing the mystery and uncertainty that would ensue in Bolden's wake. Recall that Trethewey's poem discharges readers before we reach Bolden, leaving us "almost there"—but not quite there. Likewise, "Buddy Bolden's Blues" leaves us guessing and wondering—but not quite sure. Both texts evoke and then elide Bolden. Even in his own blues, we encounter Bolden only indirectly and unreliably. Once again, he resists positivist knowing and invites a mad methodology instead.

Nina Simone conjures Bolden in her rendition of "Hey Buddy Bolden," a song originally composed by Duke Ellington and Billy Strayhorn. In the track, featured on *Nina Simone Sings Ellington* (1962), Simone croons,

> Buddy Bolden tunin' up
> Blowing horn was his game
> Born with a silver trumpet in his mouth
>
> He played the horn before he talked
> Born on the after beat
> He patted his foot before he walked
>
> When Buddy Bolden tuned up you could hear him
> Clean across the river
> Clean across the river
>
> He woke up the working people and kept the easy living
> . . .
> He's calling his flock now
> Here they come, here they come
> Come on Buddy Bolden
> Here they come[46]

A bodacious black protest musician who came to fame during the American Civil Rights Movement, Simone, like Bolden, was reportedly diagnosed with schizophrenia and manic depressive disorder.[47] Considering their affinities as mad black musical iconoclasts, it is especially poignant that Simone covered this ode to Bolden. Her interpretation is dramatic and incantatory. Before she begins to sing, she pounds the piano, playing dissonant chords that simulate the sometimes cacophonous sound of "tunin' up." Simone hollers the opening lyric, "Buddy Bolden tunin' up," as though meaning to project her voice across a distance. Twelve miles, maybe. Then she tells the tale of a prodigious child, "born on the afterbeat," syncopated from birth, wielding trumpet as appendage, sounding his horn before his voice, tapping his feet to the beat before walking, as though he is anointed for jazz, as though the music infuses his ontology.

Corroborating the claim that Bolden's cornet call could traverse great distances, Nina sings of its travel across the Mississippi River. According to the lyrics, Bolden "woke up the working people"—that is, he roused the black and common folk who grooved to his music in parks and dance halls. The practice of waking working people was central to Simone's own career as protest musician, where she sought to awaken revolutionary fervor in black and weary masses. In the same verse, Simone declares that "he kept the easy living." On one register, this phrase might mean that Bolden's music enhanced the "easy living," the joyful leisure, that those "working people" eked out despite being black and proletariat barely a generation after abolition. Alternately, the line might mean that his music kept those "easy" folks *alive*, that it was a life-sustaining force, a source of salvation, for the "easy" denizens of The Big Easy. An anointed child and salvific man, the Bolden of the song accrues a Christlike aura. That aura intensifies when Simone describes him "calling his flock now," likening him to a sheep herder and recalling biblical tropes of Christ as the Good Shepherd. In this song, a madman is made messianic.

THE MADMEN IN THE BASEMENT

In *Seven Guitars* (1995), playwright August Wilson portrays a group of black working people residing in Pittsburgh soon after World War II—but the living isn't easy. An entry in August Wilson's "Pittsburgh Cycle" of plays, each set in a different decade of the African American twentieth century, *Seven Guitars* takes place in 1948. The play begins just after the funeral of singer Floyd "Schoolboy" Barton and quickly rewinds to events preceding and precipitating his death. After a brief stint in jail for truancy, Barton returns to his Pittsburgh stomping grounds with dreams of moving to Chicago to make it big as a blues recording artist. He tries to recruit his sometimes-girlfriend Vera and sometimes-bandmates Canewell and Red to journey with him. Barton works desperately to make his Chicago dream materialize, but meets impassable obstacles. Meanwhile, Vera's landlady Louise, her young niece Ruby, and especially a madman named King Hedley all intervene in the ensuing drama. The play illuminates black working-class life in the thick of thwarted aspiration and repressed desire.

It's not Buddy Bolden who "wakes the working people" in *Seven Guitars*; a chicken performs that task. The play features a rowdy rooster—an incongruous sight and sound amid the Pittsburgh cityscape—whose crowing rouses the neighborhood. Considered a nuisance by most of the play's characters, that rooster is cherished and eventually slaughtered by Hedley, who is my primary concern in *Seven Guitars*. Hedley is a Jamaican-born fifty-nine-year-old madman-savant who suffers from tuberculosis, earns a living selling sandwiches made from chickens he breeds and butchers, espouses black radical beliefs, and is prone to outbursts of violence and eloquence.

The phrase "I thought I heard Buddy Bolden say" is recited eleven times during the play—eight times by Hedley himself, twice by Barton, and once by Canewell. Gone is the invocation of a foul odor banished out an open window. Hedley recasts the lyric within a story of deferred inheritance and patrimonial longing. He believes that his deceased father spoke to him in a dream to herald the coming of Bolden. According to Hedley, his dead dad has commissioned Bolden to return from the afterlife to deliver Hedley's patrimony. He explains that his father idolized Bolden: "My father play the trumpet and for him Buddy Bolden was a god. . . . He never forgot that night he heard Buddy Bolden play. Sometime he talked about it. He drink his rum, play his trumpet, and if you were lucky that night he would talk about Buddy Bolden. I say lucky cause you never see him like that with his face light up and something be driving him from inside and it was a thing he love more than my mother. That is how he named me King . . . after King Buddy Bolden."[48] The elder Hedley had a deep and intense affection for Bolden: it made him glow, drove him "from inside," exceeded even his love for his wife, and might have contained a sublimated erotic charge. To memorialize his love for King Bolden, to honor what Bolden has sown in him, the elder Hedley christens his son "King." This name turns out to be a self-fulfilling prophecy, ordaining the boy for the majesty and the madness of his namesake. As it turns out, the adult King Hedley has an imperiousness common to kings and an unruliness fit for a madman.

Hedley has "big" plans for his inheritance. He explains, "Soon I going to be a big man. You watch. Buddy Bolden give me my father's money I'm going to buy a big plantation. Then the white man not going to tell me what to do."[49] Amid a world overrun with white supremacism and black degradation, he wants to escape to a plantation of his own, to possess a home and land where he can live unbossed by whites. Hedley's madness does not distract or detach him from the reality of racial injustice; to the contrary, it seems to sharpen his focus upon it and intensify his animus against it. He opposes white supremacism and antiblackness with the audacity of a madman—a "crazy nigger"—not chastened by fear of retribution.

In an incident before the actions of the play, Hedley's animus for antiblackness erupts into terrible violence. He later recalls, "I killed a man once. A black man. I am not sorry I killed him." Queried further, Hedley explains, "He would not call me King. He laughed to think a black man could be King. I did not want to lose my name, so I told him to call me the name my father gave me, and he laugh. He would not call me King, and I beat him hard with a stick."[50] This heckler has so deeply internalized the paradigm of white dominion and black subjection that a black King seems nonsensical. Hedley continues, "After that I don't tell nobody my name is King. It is a bad thing. Everybody say Hedley crazy cause he black. Because he know the place of the black man is not at the foot of the white man's boot. Maybe it is not all right in my head sometimes. Because I don't like the world. I don't like what I see from the people. The people is too small. I always want to be a big man."[51] Hedley favors blackness that is elevated rather than debased, blackness that is kingly rather than servile, blackness that is "big" rather than "small." For the man who ridicules Hedley, the notion of elevated, kingly, or big blackness is preposterous. It *must* be crazy.[52]

The above passage reveals multiple facets of Hedley's madness: it is phenomenal, entailing the sensation that "it is not all right in my head sometimes"; it is psychosocial, bound up with his defiant blackness and his desire to subvert the existing racial order; and it is wrathful, culminating in an act of violent rage. Furthermore, if Hedley were under the supervision of a psychiatrist, he would almost certainly be diagnosed with some version of medicalized madness. When Barton and others complain about that rooster—beyond their annoyance with its noise, they also disdain the creature for reminding them of their provincial Southern roots—Hedley's madness surges again. He reprimands them for their insolence:

HEDLEY: God ain't making no more roosters. It is a thing past. Soon you mark my words when God ain't making no more niggers. They too be a done thing. This here rooster born in the barnyard. He learn to cock his doodle-do. He see the sun, he cry out so the sun don't catch you with your hand up your ass or your dick stuck in your woman. You hear this rooster you know you alive. You be glad to see the sun cause there come a time sure enough when you see your last day and this rooster you don't hear no more.

(*He takes out a knife and cuts the rooster's throat.*) That be for the living. Your black ass be dead like the rooster now. You mark what Hedley say.

(*He scatters the blood in a circle.*) This rooster too good to live for your black asses.

(*He throws the rooster on the ground.*) Now he good and right for you. (HEDLEY *exits the yard. Everyone is stunned.*)[53]

Hedley slaughters the rooster with the drama and gravitas of a worshipper performing a liturgical rite. This sacrificial ritual, alongside invocations of God, repudiations of wantonness, and allusions to coming judgment, grant his monologue a preacherly and even prophetic quality. But this is *mad* ministry and *mad* prophecy: disruptive, irreverent, punctuated by violent outburst, and stupefying onlookers.

Hedley's speech is a mad pedagogy, too. He brandishes madness in order to jolt his audience to stunned attention so that he may teach them. His lesson is that the rooster's song is a testimony. The bird bears witness to the fact that, despite the fickle ways of humans, the sun still rises, the earth still spins, and they are still alive to tread upon it—and occasionally, briefly, soar above it—just like their feathered neighbors. Hedley proposes that the rooster's fate is bound up with theirs: both roosters and "niggers" are relentlessly preyed upon, perpetually menaced by the threat of annihilation. For these people to take such a creature for granted is, per Hedley, to belittle the preciousness and precariousness of their own lives. Hedley slaughters the bird while speaking an ominous prediction, perhaps a threat: "Your black ass be dead like the rooster now. You mark what Hedley say." If the rooster's song affirms life, its silence portends death.

Whether by malicious design, cosmic accident, or fateful fulfillment, Hedley actualizes his own prophecy. In the play's tragic climax, he kills Barton and brings about the death he foretold. Here is how it unfolds: After Barton robs an insurance agency to fund his musical dreams, he busies himself burying the money in the backyard of the building where Hedley lives. Hedley sees Barton in the yard with the cash and believes he is beholding Bolden with the inheritance. When Hedley asks for his money and Barton refuses to surrender it, the madman descends into the cellar. Convinced that his birthright is being withheld, and committed to seizing it by any means necessary, "HEDLEY *comes from the cellar carrying the machete.* FLOYD, *hearing him approach, turns, and* HEDLEY *severs his windpipe with one blow.*"[54] Afterward, Hedley keeps the killing secret and assumes a cunning quiet, in sharp contrast to his candor and brashness throughout much of the play. One wonders whether he performs reckless madness to conceal a careful scheme underneath. Although his associates believe him capable of violence, none seem to believe he is capable of sophisticated duplicity and no one seems to suspect him.

In the final scene of the play, after Barton's funeral, Hedley unveils his "inheritance." According to the stage directions, he "holds up a handful of crumpled bills" that soon "slip from his fingers and fall to the ground like ashes."

The money is rendered ash-like: the residue of destruction, quickly dissipating, insubstantial, and unworthy of all the woe spawned in its pursuit. In relinquishing his inheritance and revealing his possession of the stolen cash, maybe Hedley is preparing to confess. Perhaps he will, but for now, he sings "I thought I heard Buddy Bolden say" three times before the curtain falls. All previous pronouncements of "I thought I heard Buddy Bolden say" in the play have been followed by the response "What he say?" On this last occasion, Hedley issues the call three times but receives no reply from within the play. Into the ensuing silence, the audience may long to complete the line, to respond to its call, to finally ask, "What he say?" These final words invite the audience to join in, to sing a bit of Buddy Bolden's blues.

I want to linger for a moment in Hedley's cellar. At various junctures in the play, he disappears into that cellar, which serves as his headquarters, resting place, hiding place, and storage space where he keeps a motley collection of accoutrements and equipment. He goes underground to retrieve objects including a hammer and nail, a crate of chickens, a butcher's knife, and that machete. Hedley's cellar is neither revealed nor even described—like the "deep black mouth," it is an ominous recess—and no one besides the madman ever enters it during the play.

Hedley shares this subterranean propensity with the unnamed protagonist of Ralph Ellison's 1952 novel, *Invisible Man,* who squats in an abandoned basement in Harlem. *Invisible Man* is a bildungsroman about a black man coming of age in a small Southern town and later in a Northern metropolis in 1930s and 1940s America. That man initially treads the path of respectable blackness but eventually swerves underground, where he remakes himself as a radical trickster and invisible interloper.

I want to pivot to another affinity that entwines Wilson's Hedley and Ellison's unnamed invisible man: both idolize New Orleans jazzmen. Whereas Hedley fixates on Buddy Bolden, adapting the lyrics "I thought I heard Buddy Bolden say" as a mantra, the invisible man reveres Louis Armstrong, hearing an existential query when Armstrong sings "What did I do to be so black and blue?" in the jazz standard "Black and Blue."[55] Remarkably, an early draft of *Invisible Man* featured Bolden, not Armstrong, as the protagonist's muse. Ellison biographer Lawrence Jackson explains that "Ellison decided to replace Buddy Bolden, the mysterious founder of modern jazz, with the better-known Louis Armstrong," apparently in consultation with an editor in order to bolster the book's popular appeal.[56] Thus, Bolden is never mentioned and his blues are never played in *Invisible Man.* However, Bolden is residually present insofar as he influenced Armstrong and insofar as he is a palimpsestic trace beneath the finished surface of the novel. It seems to me that Bolden is an invisible and inaudible man who lives *under* the novel's underground, who plays at a "lower frequency," so low that even a subterranean hero cannot hear it.[57]

Meanwhile, Armstrong is a fascinating foil for Bolden. Both were iconoclastic New Orleanian jazzmen who played brass instruments, but the two would chart dramatically different paths. While Bolden disappeared into obscurity and alterity, Armstrong emerged into unprecedented visibility and popularity, becoming one of the most iconic American musicians of the twentieth century. While Bolden's life bespeaks the perils of an antiblack and antimad world, Armstrong is widely remembered for proclaiming, amid global unrest in the late 1960s, that this is "a wonderful world."

"STRAY FACTS, MANIC THEORIES, AND WELL-TOLD LIES" IN *COMING THROUGH SLAUGHTER*

Michael Ondaatje's *Coming through Slaughter* devotes tens of thousands of words to imagining what Bolden might have actually said. The book is a work of historical fiction that paints New Orleans as a marvelous place peopled by eccentric and surreal characters. Ondaatje depicts the city's underclass at the turn of the twentieth century: musicians, sex workers, pimps, bohemians, addicts, outcasts, recluses, rebels, and romantics, with a madman named Buddy at its center.[58]

While walking his children to school in the mornings, Buddy entertains them with stories indiscriminately blending rumor, history, whim, wisdom, joke, and myth: "He taught them all he was thinking of or had heard, all he knew at the moment, treating them as adults, joking and teasing them with tall tales which they learned to sift down to the real."[59] Buddy's skill at storytelling and his tendency to blend real and unreal all serve him well as the editor of *The Cricket*, a local scandal sheet that he founds. At the helm of a gossip rag, he is an expert rumorist and mythmaker before he himself is enshrined in rumor and made myth. Ondaatje writes, "The Cricket existed between 1899 and 1905. It took in and published all the information Bolden could find. It respected stray facts, manic theories, and well-told lies. This information came from customers in the chair and from spiders among the whores and police that Bolden and his friends knew. Bolden took all the thick facts and dropped them into his pail of sub-history."[60] Donald Marquis's 1978 Bolden biography, published two years after *Coming through Slaughter*, claims that *The Cricket* was not a historical reality and Bolden was never an editor. Indeed, in Ondaatje's fictionalized New Orleans, *The Cricket* is purveyor of "stray facts, manic theories, and well-told lies"; in Marquis's historical New Orleans, *The Cricket* itself is a myth, made from "stray facts, manic theories, and well-told lies."

To ponder histories of radically marginalized groups—like asylum detainees or black sex workers in turn-of-the-twentieth-century New Orleans—it is crucial to investigate "stray facts, manic theories, and well-told lies." Subaltern people are typically excluded from dominant discourses and mainstream public spheres, their lives unrecorded or misrecorded by Reasonable historiography. To engage such subjects, one must mine the parapositivist, the hidden, the rumored, and the speculative; sometimes these are the only residues left behind. If official history upholds the deeds and canonizes the memories of dominant groups, then the "pail of sub-history" collects the deeds and preserves the knowledge of dispossessed peoples.

Publishing a gossip rag is fitting work for Buddy because he is categorically averse to certainty: "He was almost completely governed by fears of certainty. He distrusted it in anyone but [his wife] Nora for there it went to the spine, and yet he attacked it again and again in her, cruelly, hating it, the sure lanes of the probable. Breaking chairs and windows glass doors in fury at her certain answers."[61] If Buddy so violently despises positivism, he likely finds solace in the unfounded speculation strewn across the pages of *The Cricket* and probably takes comfort in the mystery enshrouding his life.

Buddy's evasive behavior contributes to that enigma. He is secretive about his past, presenting himself as though he sprang fully formed into the world as a twenty-two-year-old musical phenom: "Where did he come from? He was found before we knew where he had come from. Born at the age of twenty-two. Walked into a parade one day with white shoes and red shirt. Never spoke of the past. Simply about which way to go for the next 10 minutes."[62] Buddy's destination is as uncertain as his origin. He is driven by a wanderlust so powerful that it eventually dissolves his attachments to family and home and propels him to abscond from his wife and children for years. Buddy's aversion to cognitive certainty parallels his aversion to geographical fixity. He would rather let his mind and his feet wander freely into the unknown.

The climactic scene of *Coming through Slaughter* is that fateful Labor Day parade. While strutting on the parade route, Buddy spots a woman dancing in the second line:

Where the bitch came from I don't know. She moves out to us again, moving along with us. . . . Thin body and long hair . . . the girl is alone now mirroring my throat in her lonely tired dance, the street silent but for us her tired breath I can hear for she's near me. . . . Then silent. For something's fallen in my body and I can't hear the music as I play it. The notes more often now. She hitting each note with her body before it is even out so I know what I do through her. God this is what I wanted to play for, if no one else I always guessed there would be this, this mirror somewhere, she closer to me now and her eyes over mine tough and young and come from god knows where.[63]

The woman is endowed with fantastical traits that suggest she is not entirely, empirically "real." Maybe Buddy is beholding a flesh-and-blood woman who is only partially embellished in his mind. Or it could be that the woman is a full-fledged figment of his imagination, perhaps a hallucination. When he describes sudden silence on that busy street, except for the sounds of himself and the woman, the description might be hyperbole to convey his singular focus on her. That silence could also be a breach from reality: a *hysterical deafness* or psychotic break so thorough that it soundproofs him against the noisy scene around him. He then purports to hear her "tired breath" across the street, a claim that could be duplicity, fantasy, hallucination, or else a feat of superhuman hearing.

The woman's ability to anticipate his notes and rhythms precisely, "hitting each note with her body before it is even out," indicates that the two are entwined. Her dance uncannily "mirrors" his song, and then she begins to uncannily mirror him, to mimic his desire, to become his double. The expression "her eyes over mine" might mean that they are suddenly face-to-face and eye-to-eye. It might also describe a convergence of the two, as though he suddenly sees through her eyes, as though the two are telepathically conjoined. Perhaps the jazzman is experiencing a psychotic splintering, retaining his primary ego formation as Buddy while spawning a second self in the guise of this woman.

In the next instant, he plays his cornet with such ferocious force that he can "feel the blood that is real move up bringing fresh energy in its suitcase, it comes up flooding past my heart in a mad parade, it is coming through my teeth, it is into the cornet, god can't stop god can't stop it can't stop the air the red force coming up can't remove it from my mouth, no intake gasp, so deep blooming it up god I can't choke it the music still pouring in a roughness I've never hit."[64] That rush of feeling is accompanied by a rush of blood up to his head, out of his mouth, and into his instrument. Within the erotic poetics of this passage, the eruption of blood accompanies an intense climax and thus resembles an ejaculation of semen. It is later revealed that, while playing so forcefully, Buddy bursts a blood vessel in his neck. He doesn't quite *blow his brains out*, but he does unleash an explosion in his head.

Buddy announces, "This is what I wanted, always, loss of privacy in the playing, leaving the stage, the rectangle of band on the street, this hearer who can throw me in the direction and the speed she wishes like an angry shadow."[65] He surrenders to this mysterious woman and yields to the upheaval she brings. To have him tell it, she heaves him into a revolution of consciousness, thrusts him to an ecstatic and self-shattering *jouissance*, frees him from the confines of a private and discrete self.[66] It doesn't matter that the process is violent; for Buddy, it is transcendent. Alas, just pages later, Bolden is snatched down from that frenzied high and plunged into a tragic nadir between asylum walls. Ondaatje reveals that "his mind on the pinnacle of something collapsed, was arrested, put in the House of D[etention], shipped by train to Baton Rouge, then taken north by cart to a hospital for the insane." This latter passage essentially recants the claim that Buddy achieved "what he wanted," downgrading Buddy's parade transformation to an *almost, but not quite.*[67]

Coming through Slaughter closes with Buddy, listless and undone, in an asylum cell. He thinks, "I sit with this room. With the grey walls that darken into a corner. And one window with teeth in it. Sit so still you can hear your hair rustle in your shirt. Look away from the window when clouds and other things go by. Thirty-one years old. There are no prizes."[68] Once again—like in the lyrics of "Buddy Bolden's Blues," the verses of Trethewey's "Calling His Children Home," and the testimony of that attendant at the Jackson Asylum— the jazz legend is positioned near a window. This time, Buddy does not gesture toward the window or signal any desire to pass through it. Instead, he wearily turns away from it, averting his face from passing clouds. Maybe their unfettered movement mocks him and inflames his thwarted wanderlust. For most any human being, confinement in a turn-of-the-twentieth-century rural asylum would be excruciating. For Buddy, "governed by fears of certainty," this fate is especially cruel because it locks him in an utterly abject fixity and certainty. Buddy's final words are an announcement of defeat: "There are no prizes."[69]

THE MAD JAZZMEN: THE SUN RA–CHARLES MINGUS DUO

I now turn to the lifeworlds of two other mad jazz performers for whom *there are prizes*—for whom madness is a valuable material and tool for self-making. The first of these performers is the Afrofuturist, Afro(ec)centric bandleader and pianist, Sun Ra. The second is the virtuosic composer, bassist, and reputed "Angry Man of Jazz," Charles Mingus. Whereas Bolden's enigma comes from a collusion of personal misfortune, antiblackness, antimadness, and archival scarcity, both Ra and Mingus produce and perpetuate their own enigmas. Whereas Bolden is mythologized by his mourners and successors, Ra and Mingus deliberately, diligently mythologize themselves. Whereas Bolden ostensibly leaves no self-documentation, Ra and Mingus generate an abundance of self-narrative in letters, interviews, memoirs, pamphlets, manifestos, and film.[70]

Notwithstanding these distinctions, the lives of Ra and Mingus contain mad and mythical elements that harken back to Bolden. Observing these affinities, I propose that Bolden inaugurates an archetype of *the mad jazzman* that Ra and Mingus later embody in their own projects of black radical creativity. My objective is not an extensive biographical account of either musician. Instead, I illuminate the presence and power of madness in their lives and repertoires. To do so, I mobilize tools of mad methodology: reading their purported rants and raves; looking and listening for the phantoms, otherworldly beings, and disembodied voices that speak in their narratives; discerning where disclosures of pathology are also articulations of philosophy; and extending radical compassion to both men.

In Sun Ra's own words, "Me and time never got along so good—we just sort of ignore each other."[71] In *Space Is the Place: The Lives and Times of Sun Ra*, ethnomusicologist John Szwed explains that "by evading dates . . . [Ra] became ageless and timeless. 'You can't ask me to be specific about time,' he said."[72] According to a state-generated birth certificate, the being known as Sun Ra was born Herman Poole Blount on May 22, 1914, in Birmingham, Alabama. For Ra, such a certificate is bogus and worthless, an artifact of the repressive chronologies that stifle human life. He insists, "It is important to liberate oneself from the obligation to be born, because this experience doesn't help us at all . . . because whoever is born has to die."[73] In other words, to accept the premise of birth is to invite the eventuality of death. By disavowing birth—"evading each and every natal occasion," per Mackey's evocative phrase—Ra means to elude death. He casts himself as a supernatural being exempt from the biological finitude that Reason ascribes to human life. Ra practiced what we might call *radical anachronism*, refusing to conform to Western protocols of timeliness and abiding outside normative structures of time.

Szwed further writes that "Sun Ra destroyed his past. . . . Files and certificates had been destroyed or disappeared or never existed, photos vanished, and early recordings and compositions were lost in fires or deceased musicians' attics."[74] Whereas documentary dearth was Bolden's inadvertent fate, Ra deliberately destroyed evidence of his life and abetted his own erasure from "history."

Pastlessness granted Ra a clean slate, affording him opportunities for radical self-making, for "recast[ing] himself in a series of roles in a drama he spent his life creating."[75] In particular, he claimed to be a Saturnian space traveler and ancient Egyptian time traveler who knew worlds and epochs beyond earthly understanding.[76] To further theorize Ra's self-making, I briefly examine three mad proclamations he issued: a courtroom statement, a letter addressed to US military officials, and a speech in a narrative film.

Fast-forward to twenty-eight years after Ra's nonbirth. In 1942, at the height of World War II, Ra was conscripted into the US Army. He objected to the war and wanted to remain in his native Birmingham to nurture his burgeoning career as bandleader. After the draft board rejected his bid for conscientious objector status, Ra still refused to report for duty and was subsequently summoned before a Birmingham court. With awesome audacity, Ra stood before the judge and announced that "if he was forced to learn to kill, he would use that skill without prejudice, and kill one of his own captains or generals first."[77] This must have been a stunning scene: In Jim Crow Alabama, against the backdrop of World War II, a young black man addresses a powerful white official and threatens to kill other powerful white officials indiscriminately. Based on this act, the most fanatical white supremacists and devout black insurrectionists alike might have called Ra a "crazy nigger," albeit with drastically different inflections. Remember that the "crazy nigger" can be hero or bogeyman depending upon the politics of the beholder. As for the judge, staunchly on the side of white supremacy, he declared that "I've never seen a nigger like you before" and ordered Ra remanded to county jail while his case pended.[78] Considering Jim Crow's aversion to black defiance, it is a wonder that Ra did not face harsher punishment. Perhaps his presumed madness protected him; maybe the judge viewed him as a bemusing oddity rather than a serious threat.

While in jail for nearly three months, Ra wrote these words to the US marshal in charge of military conscription in Alabama: "I am so unhappy and bewildered that I am almost crazed. If ever there was a person who had reason to commit suicide, I feel that I am that person." In a subsequent letter, he confessed, "This morning I took a razor and started to slash my wrists or mutilate the one testicle I have, but I thought of the wrong of murder in any form and hesitated. Yet some things are worse than death."[79] To avoid becoming a cog in a war machine, Ra declared himself "almost crazed," threatened self-mutilation, and disclosed suicidal ideation. It is not clear whether these epistolary confessions were sincere, or whether he concocted or exaggerated them to convince his captors to free him. Whatever their sincerity, such blatant self-pathologization was a risky move. To portray himself as so troubled might have exempted him from military service but might also have landed him in some infernal prison or psychiatric ward.

Ra was labeled mentally unfit for military service after doctors diagnosed him with "psychopathic personality," "neurotic depression," and "sexual perversion."[80] The latter diagnosis refers to Ra's rumored homosexuality. It is worth emphasizing that homophobia was entrenched and enshrined in mid-twentieth-century US psychiatry. In fact, homosexuality was only fully expunged from the American Psychiatric Association's *Diagnostic and Statistical Manual* in 1987.[81]

Although Ra never publicly claimed a "homosexual," "gay," or "queer" identity, his well-known investment in homosocial and possibly homoerotic domesticity—in the all-male musicians' commune where he later insisted bandmembers live—invites queer speculation.[82] And whether or not Ra was homosexual, his spectacular flouting of racial, sartorial, familial, chronological, and cosmological norms is emphatically queer. It bears noting that queerness, like blackness and madness, is denigrated by psychonormative status quos in the West. Queerness, like blackness and madness, is a category of otherness against which Western normativity measures itself and affirms its self-coherency.

Ra went on to produce a vast catalogue of music from the mid-1950s through the 1990s, including over 150 albums traversing big band, swing, bebop, hard bop, free improvisation, funk, electronica, and other soundscapes for which there are no generic labels.[83] He founded the Sun Ra Arkestra, that band and commune whose members lived together under his leadership while receiving musical training and Afrofuturist education.[84] Disenchanted with life on earth, especially global regimes of antiblackness, Ra proposed extraterrestrial exodus for black earthlings. He was optimistic that they could find refuge on another planet, maybe Saturn. He often produced music with incantatory effect: cosmic conjure songs, theme music for intergalactic revolutions, anthems for otherworldly utopias, featuring verses like "Oh we sing this song to a great tomorrow / Oh we sing this song to abolish sorrow," repeated again and again by various vocalists.[85] He was known for his spectacular ancient Egyptian–*cum*–spaceman regalia and stage shows incorporating carnivalesque pageantry. Because of Ra's refusal of birth and death, his defiant blackness, his wartime bouts of mental illness, his ontological and possibly sexual queerness, his professed otherworldliness, and his ardent eccentricity, Ra is an overdetermined icon of black-mad-queer alterity.

That alterity is on dramatic display in Ra's 1974 surrealist film, *Space Is the Place*, for which he was both writer and star. The film depicts Ra's return to Earth, after an intergalactic journey, with plans to liberate the planet's black people and settle them in an otherworldly home. The film contains scene after scene of encounters between Ra and various incredulous or awestruck humans. One such interaction is set in Oakland, California, at a recreation center where black adolescents socialize and play. Suddenly Ra appears, as if out of thin air, and ceremoniously announces "Greetings, black youth. I am Sun Ra, Ambassador from the intergalactic regions of the council of outer space."[86]

Hearing his mystifying words and seeing his flamboyant costume, one young woman declares, "I know I'd probably take off running, I see somebody came walking down the street, coming, talking to me, all that mess to me, talking about going to outer space." Sun Ra's response is a mix of puzzling provocation and incisive commentary: "How do you know I'm real? I'm not real. I'm just like you. You don't exist—in this society. If you did, your people wouldn't be seeking equal rights. You're not real. If you were, you'd have some status among the nations of the world. So we're both myths. I do not come to you as a reality. I come to you as the myth. Because that's what black people are: myths." When Sun Ra proclaims, "You don't exist—in this society," he wedges a brief but pivotal pause between two clauses. Before the pause is a provocation in the idiom of madness: a seemingly nonsensical and unReasonable assertion of the nonexistence of his addressee. After the pause comes a trenchant clarification: Ra is referring to the negation of blackness in an antiblack society. His words allude to political nullification and social death, a predicament in which African Americans are invisibilized, silenced, mistreated as if they don't matter, disregarded as though they don't exist. But Ra knows there are vast realms outside the recognition of "this society," excluded from its "rights," unaffected by its rules, beyond its "reality," where black radical imagination and creation can flourish. He refers to this state of alterity as "myth" (others might call it *madness*) and regards it as a site of possibility unfettered by the real. It was in his role as self-avowed "myth" that Sun Ra cultivated his ingenious art practice and black radical self-making.

I have found no evidence that Sun Ra and Charles Mingus ever gigged together on earth, but their shared propensity for playing and living in the key of madness makes me dream of the two in celestial duet. Mingus was an iconoclastic jazz composer, bandleader, and bassist who innovated New Orleans–style improvisation and earned the nickname "Angry Man of Jazz" for his violent on-stage tantrums.[87] I will take up Mingus's musical performance in chapter 7, but for now I want to attend to the mad self-writing that fills his 1971 book, *Beneath the Underdog: His World as Composed by Mingus*. The volume is a polymorphous assemblage of autobiography, memoir, social realism, parody, fantasy, commentary, and confession, yielding a genre-blending, mind-bending statement on black music, macho, modernity, and madness. Before the start of the narrative proper, the metanarrative elements that frame *Beneath the Underdog* put the rationalist reader on notice. The 1991 Vintage Books edition is formally categorized as "Music/Autobiography" and is billed on its back cover as "the greatest autobiography ever written by a jazz musician." However, the main text is preceded by this disclaimer: "Some names in this work have been changed and some of the characters and incidents are fictitious."[88]

Of course, autobiographies are never wholly transparent windows into lives. All such writing contains some measure of misremembering, bias, interpolations, omissions, editorial tweaking, or self-serving embellishments, whether deliberate or inadvertent. Many autobiographies also include composite characters, combining two or more real persons in order to streamline or augment narrative. However, the outright assertion that "some of the characters and incidents are fictitious"—not imprecise, dramatized, or composite, but plainly "fictitious"—eschews the presumption of verisimilitude at the crux of conventional autobiography.

Beneath the Underdog begins with a psychotherapeutic session. In fact, the very first words are a confession Mingus utters to his therapist:

> In other words, I am three. One man stands forever in the middle, unconcerned, unmoved, watching, waiting to be allowed to express what he sees to the other two. The second man is like a frightened animal that attacks for fear of being attacked. Then there's an over-loving gentle person who lets people into the uttermost sacred temple of his being and he'll take insults and be trusting and sign contracts without reading them and get talked down to working for cheap or nothing, and when he realizes what's been done to him he feels like killing and destroying everything around him including himself for being so stupid. But he can't. He goes back inside himself.
>
> Which one is real? . . . They're all real. The man who watches and waits, the man who attacks because he's afraid, and the man who wants to trust and love but retreats everytime he finds himself betrayed. Mingus One, Two, and Three.[89]

The book begins in medias res, with the phrase "in other words," as though Mingus is rephrasing language that precedes the narrative. These opening words announce an absence, evoking but eliding something that lies before the text and beyond the reader's reach. With this gesture, Mingus forecasts the mystery and opacity that will proliferate throughout the book. Further emphasizing the unreliable narration and genre subversion to come, Mingus's therapist announces, "You're a good man, Charles, but there's a lot of fabrication and fantasy in what you say."[90]

That opening paragraph also contains Mingus's declaration that "I am three" and his description of three selves with distinct personalities. This disclosure invokes dissociative identity disorder, a condition wherein the psyche fractures into multiple personalities. Though it is not clear whether Mingus actually lived with multiple personalities, I want to explore how he conjures dissociative identity disorder within a project of mad self-fashioning. As mad methodologist, I work to cull critical theory and philosophy from purported pathology. In this spirit, I read Mingus's insistence that he is "three" as a mad revision of Hegel's dialectic.

Hegel formulates a dialectical model to describe the development of human consciousness and history—namely through the formation of a *thesis* (a proposition or condition) checked by an *antithesis* (its negation or contradiction) with the two ultimately transacting to produce a *synthesis* (a resolution). Mingus proposes a *thesis* (the hostile, explosive aggressor), its *antithesis* (the naïve, gentle pacifist), and an additional entity we might label a *parenthesis* (the aloof observer, set aside, much like the information within these parentheses) that transact to generate Charles Mingus, the *synthesis*. Whereas Hegel imagines a contest between thesis and antithesis, Mingus adds a parenthetical figure who does not do battle but rather watches and explains that struggle from a safe distance. The addition of this extra value transforms Hegelian dialectic into a new formula: "Mingus One, Two, and Three," or what we might call the Mingus trialectic, or more simply, the Mingus trio. Incorporating madness into the equation, Mingus reformulates the dialectical calculus of a prominent Enlightenment philosopher (and a prominent proponent of antiblack Reason who claimed that Africa was "no historical part of the world")[91] yielding a mad black alternative. Here, pathology is philosophy.

That parenthetical figure stands aside and watches two-year-old Charles nearly die. Mingus recounts, "When I was a child, I was knocked unconscious by a fall. A boy lay bleeding on the floor. I was that child yet I was not that child. I was someone else in the same room, yet the family couldn't see me. I was a kind of wise man as old as time. It was entirely up to me whether I let that boy lie there and walked off into infinity or breathed my conscious life into him again."[92] In this scene, physical trauma induces a breach in subjectivity; it is as though the impact of the fall knocks young Mingus out his mind. Consequently, he narrates what his two-year-old self could not have witnessed while unconscious. Mingus describes a surreal dissociation that grants him an out-of-body experience and out-of-body perspective.

According to the American Psychiatric Association, it is psychic trauma that spawns the sort of dissociative rupture evoked above. When a young mind encounters devastating hurt that it cannot process through the mechanisms of a singular ego, it might fracture into multiple personalities, as if to delegate the difficult work of coping to multiple psychic agencies.[93] Mingus recounts such trauma erupting when he peed the bed as a prepubescent boy: "Daddy would beat on his body but the child was no longer inside, he was out with me waiting till the agony was over." Mingus further confesses, "Charles asked me to take him away, out of himself, and let him die. When I refused, he no longer believed in me and began to pray to Jesus Christ to wake him up so his father wouldn't burn him or if that was impossible to take him up to heaven with the angels. So I began to watch over him."[94]

As a result of brutal abuse, the boy snaps: he splinters and dissociates from his own personality, reconstituting part of himself as a distinct being, a sort of guardian angel who keeps company with the traumatized child. In Mingus's custody, dissociation does not stifle or dissolve narration, but rather inspires and propels an alternate narrative mode. More precisely, Mingus instrumentalizes the experience of being "no longer inside" himself to produce a *dissociative narrativity*. Whereas the conventional first-person narrator is always sequestered inside their individual self, the dissociative narrator can venture elsewhere, "no longer inside" a bounded subjectivity. As a dissociative narrator, Mingus retains the intimacy and immediacy of the first-person "I," while also traversing multiple vantage points and personalities.

The specter of madness accompanies Mingus into adulthood and into the halls of Bellevue Psychiatric Hospital. In 1958—after weeks of insomnia born of frustrations in music and romance—Mingus admits himself to the hospital to get some rest. He is promptly diagnosed with paranoid schizophrenia, detained in Bellevue for weeks, and subjected to the sinister scheming of an antiblack psychiatrist he calls "Herr Doktor." The term *Herr Doktor* is a German-language honorific. In a scene thirteen years after the end of the Holocaust, the term invokes German Nazi doctors who weaponized medicine for eugenicist and genocidal evil, much like the psychiatrist Mingus encounters in Bellevue. (There are many monstrous likenesses between Jim Crow America's antiblackness and Nazi Germany's antisemitism, including the use of "medicine" for atrocious malice.)[95]

Concerning Herr Doktor, Mingus explains, "I heard him say to the other doctor 'Negroes are paranoic, unrealistic people who believe the whole world is against them.' [I asked] 'Tell me, is this paranoia we all have curable?' And he said 'Yes, this is what I am so happy to tell you. I can cure this disease with a simple operation on the frontal lobe, called a lobotomy, and then you'll be all right.'"[96] Herr Doktor joins a long tradition of antiblack psychiatry that includes Samuel Cartwright, Walter Bromberg, and Franck Simon. In order to discredit black people's existential wariness in the face of antiblackness, Herr Doktor casts them as "paranoic and unrealistic." In truth, black paranoia was an appropriate critical posture and orientation amid relentless antiblackness in the United States circa 1958. In such a context—where institutions of education, politics, medicine, law enforcement, and media colluded to denigrate black life—fears of persecution were well-founded and absolutely realistic for black people. This is still the case. Indeed an instrumental paranoia was and is valuable for unmasking the Herr Doktors of the world: erudite, genteel, insidious agents of antiblack evil.[97]

After alleging that black people are blighted by a pathological paranoia, Herr Doktor proposes lobotomy as the cure. The psychiatrist's statements discursively mutilate blackness, and his "simple operation" surgically mutilates blackness, to boot. If Herr Doktor actually existed, Mingus fortunately escaped the man's lobotomizing scalpel. Fortunately, also, Mingus managed to preserve and cultivate his creativity while at Bellevue. On his third day at the hospital, Mingus reportedly wrote "All the Things You Could Be by Now If Sigmund Freud's Wife Was Your Mother," which would appear on his 1960 album, *Charles Mingus Presents Charles Mingus*.[98] The track is a radical reinterpretation of the jubilant jazz standard "All the Things You Are," originally composed by Jerome Kern with lyrics by Oscar Hammerstein II. In chapter 7, I will take up the musical content of the song itself, but for now I want to assess the significance and signification of the track's title.

Mingus modifies the original title. From the indicative mood of "All the Things You Are," he shifts to the subjunctive "All the Things You Could Be by Now If Sigmund Freud's Wife Was Your Mother." This titular invocation of Freud bespeaks the bassist's preoccupation with psychiatric authority while in that mental hospital. Significantly, the title is not "All the Things You Could Be by Now If Sigmund Freud Was Your Father," which would indicate your direct relation to the doctor. Based upon this phrasing, your relationship to Martha Freud (Sigmund's wife) is evident, but your relationship to Sigmund himself is ambiguous. It is unclear whether he is your biological father, your devoted stepfather, or merely your mother's spouse with whom you lack any filial bond. *Mama's baby, papa's maybe*, indeed.[99] Mingus conjures a scenario of uncertain paternity involving the iconic "father" of psychoanalysis, a man known for systematizing the study of family secrets.

But what, after all, could you be by now if Martha Freud were your mother? If you were white, male, and Sigmund's offspring, maybe you'd be heir to his vast epistemological estate, a primary beneficiary of one of modernity's most influential theories of subjectivity. But what if you were black? What if Mingus, a black man reared in an antiblack and white supremacist society, imagined himself or another black person in this titular provocation?[100] A black child born of Martha Freud would ostensibly have a black father, and therefore would not be Sigmund Freud's offspring. If you were Martha Freud's black child, you might be branded a scandalous "black bastard" son or "tragic mulatta" daughter, conceived in an interracial extramarital tryst, the outcome of miscegenation. Maybe you'd be omitted, overlooked, disinherited, banished, disavowed—the repressed child waiting to return. If Sigmund Freud's wife were your mother, maybe you'd make a *miscegenated psychoanalysis*, a psychoanalytic hermeneutic that inherits something from Freud's *body* of knowledge but isn't from his *flesh*.[101] Maybe you'd bring about a psychoanalysis informed by the "afterlife of slavery,"[102] colored by the exigencies of blackness, mindful of the trauma of antiblackness, and attuned to the mad creativity that black people have honed to keep their minds.

Remarkably, other jazz icons including Lester Young, Bud Powell, Thelonious Monk, and Charlie Parker were all institutionalized for severe mental illness at some point in their lives.[103] Alongside Bolden, I choose to highlight Sun Ra and Charles Mingus because of their extensive self-writing—in contrast and complement to Bolden's archival reticence—but all these performers belong to a curious fraternity of mad jazzmen.[104]

Why this seeming preponderance of mental illness among early and mid-twentieth-century jazz icons? It could be that the intensity, volatility, and exigency of a showbusiness life in Jim Crow America incited unruliness in mind or activated otherwise latent mental illness in these men. Or perhaps the very same iconoclastic temperament that made them jazz innovators also made them renegades against psychonormative status quos, thus earning them the label *crazy*. There may be merit in either of these hypotheses, but I am most intrigued by a third possibility.

I suspect that these performers were not exceptional, compared to their black working-class contemporaries, in experiencing psychic unruliness or clashing with Reason. What made these jazz performers exceptional was their access to financial resources, support networks, and the cachet of celebrity—privileges that gave them and their families leverage to pursue treatment in psychiatric care instead of punishment in jail or prison. In short, I hypothesize that these jazz performers were not more likely to be mad. They were more likely to be hospitalized as mentally ill—rather than imprisoned as criminal, the likely fate of countless other black people—for their alleged madness.[105]

THE AFTERBEAT

In *Madness: The Invention of an Idea* (1962), Foucault pens a phenomenological account of schizophrenic "subjects suffering from hallucinations." To have Foucault tell it, they "hear . . . voices, not in the objective space in which sound sources are situated, but in a mythical space, in a sort of quasi space in which the axes of reference are fluid and mobile: they hear next to them, around them, within them, the voices of persecutors, which at the same time, they situate beyond the walls, beyond the city, beyond all frontiers."[106]

Laws of physics and limits of physiology govern human hearing. Distance, obstruction, and auditory threshold may impede sound from registering for a given listener. But Foucault describes a schizophrenic sense of "sound" unmoored from those laws and capable of perceiving persecutorial voices across every expanse and through any barrier. According to Foucault, the schizophrenic person experiences the impression of boundless aurality—a sense that their hearing extends "beyond all frontiers" and into infinity. Below I interpolate Foucault's passage, replacing "voices" with "Bolden's cornet" and referring to Bolden's children rather than "schizophrenics." They

> hear [Bolden's cornet], not in the objective space in which sound sources are situated, but in a mythical space, in a sort of quasi space in which the axes of reference are fluid and mobile: they hear next to them, around them, within them, [Bolden's cornet], which at the same time, they situate beyond the walls, beyond the city, beyond all frontiers.

Thus modified, Foucault's passage might describe the sensation of hearing a cornet twelve miles away. Perhaps Jelly Roll Morton heard Bolden "not in the objective space in which sound sources are situated," but in a "mythical space" fit for the mythical man Morton believed Bolden to be. Bolden's cornet call transgresses conventional physics and physiology to achieve a metaphysical loudness that resonates "beyond the walls" of the asylum, "beyond the city" of New Orleans, beyond the Mississippi River, "beyond all frontiers," beyond biological death, beyond documentary dearth, and across a fantastic distance to reach his other children, including the motley ensemble of cultural producers in this chapter. This, again, is the Bolden effect: a force swerving away from Reason into parapositivist realms of the mythical, dreamy, imaginary, improbable, irrational, maybe even impossible, across twelve miles, over one hundred years, and farther still.

Blackness, like Bolden, is often omitted from formal archives, coded as crazy, held in captivity, and kept under duress—while nonetheless thriving in the downbeat, performing mighty feats of genius, and producing surges of creativity that overflow the lack imposed upon it. Maybe, after all, the *Bolden effect* is another way to say *black radical creativity* and *black sociality*.

Compelled by that Bolden effect, we lean longingly into picture frames to find him; we hear him across endless distance; we await the inheritance he brings; and we follow him to the "pinnacle of something" to witness him collapse there. He leaves us *not quite, not yet, not sure.* He comes through the window, into the cut, out the mouth, along the parade route, in the dancehall, in the asylum, in the basement, at the park, after the beat, calling his children, home with his children, carrying treasure, earning no prizes, blowing his brains out, whiskey-soaked, blood-soaked, a wellspring, a lacuna, a void, a plenitude, imposing, evading, unbearably loud, irresistibly loud, impossibly loud, undeniably loud, yet still, somehow, difficult to discern: "I thought I heard Buddy Bolden say," but I can't tell for sure. *I might just be hearing things.*

Now that we've heard the sound of madness in the rise of jazz, it's time to listen out for the sound of madness at the onset of the blues. The first known commercial recording of a black person singing the blues was Mamie Smith's 1920 "Crazy Blues," about a woman's despair and vengeance in the wake of a hurtful man.[107] In the following interlude, I turn from the specter of a mad jazzman to the soul of a mad blueswoman.

"NO WIGGLES IN THE DARK OF HER SOUL"
BLACK MADNESS, METAPHOR, AND "MURDER!"

These words are prelude to murder. In a scene sweltering with summer heat and racial animus—set entirely aboard a New York City subway car circa 1964—a black man named Clay spews this speech at his antagonist, a white woman called Lula. She approaches him on the moving train and starts a conversation that spans matters of race, sex, violence, revolution, art, and madness. Initially flirtatious, increasingly pugnacious, and

A whole people of neurotics, struggling to keep from being sane. And the only thing that would cure the neurotics would be your murder. Simple as that. I mean if I murdered you, then other white people would begin to understand me. You understand? No. I guess not. If Bessie Smith had killed some white people she wouldn't have needed that music. She could have talked very straight and plain about the world. No metaphors. No grunts. No wiggles in the dark of her soul. . . . Crazy niggers turning their backs on sanity. When all it needs is that simple act. Murder. Just murder! Would make us all sane. —CLAY, from Amiri Baraka (né LeRoi Jones), *Dutchman*, 1964

finally murderous, their exchange is the central event of Amiri Baraka's one-act tragedy, *Dutchman*.[1] The play debuted in 1964, amid an American public sphere teeming with myths of brutish, monstrous black men.[2] Exploiting such fantasies, Baraka places the above words in Clay's mouth as a cunning red herring. Upon hearing Clay's speech, many viewers and readers—especially those who harbor the belief that black men are constitutionally violent—will presume that Clay is bound to kill Lula. However, in a dramatic reversal of such pernicious presumption, *Lula murders Clay*. After he rebuffs her advances and delivers that diatribe, she thrusts a knife into his chest. In *Dutchman*, a white woman is aggressor and murderer while a black man lays prostrate and penetrated.[3]

Clay's climactic speech is concerned with the subject of madness and delivered in an *idiom of madness*: an outburst of outrage, a series of incendiary phrases, an unruly exclamation that flouts codes of Reasonable, respectable speech in the era of Civil Rights. He pronounces a grim diagnosis of black America, labeling its ranks "a whole people of neurotics." According to Clay, this madness is the result of black agony boiling beneath the surface, longing to erupt, but channeled instead into acceptable forms like blue notes and jazz riffs.[4] He cites Bessie Smith, Empress of the Blues, as a case study in this racial madness. He suggests that the malady can achieve catharsis through "metaphor" or "murder!," through art-making or death-dealing. However, he clarifies that the two processes are unequal means of relief. Metaphor merely alleviates this madness; murder, the more potent treatment, can cure it.

Clay's claim about the therapeutic efficacy of violence for black people echoes Frantz Fanon's assertion about the therapeutic efficacy of violence for colonized peoples broadly. In *Wretched of the Earth*, translated into English just one year before the debut of *Dutchman*, Fanon writes that "at the level of individuals, violence is a cleansing force. It frees the native from his inferiority complex and from his despair and inaction; it makes him fearless and restores his self-respect."[5] According to Fanon, anticolonial violence does not merely negate colonial rule; it has positive effects, too, elevating the esteem, rousing the courage, and propelling the self-actualization of colonized peoples. Maybe Clay has read Fanon. It could be that *Wretched of the Earth* is among the books that Clay gathers up, as he collects his belongings and prepares to exit the train, just before Lula murders him.

RACING SUBLIMATION

Maybe Sigmund Freud's *Civilization and Its Discontents* is in Clay's collection too. Insofar as Clay theorizes interrelations between madness and art, he has a prominent predecessor in Freud. The founder of psychoanalysis coined the term *sublimation* to denote the displacement or conversion of socially objectionable impulses, including erotic and aggressive drives, into socially acceptable and culturally valued activities. Politics, religion, scholarship, athletics, industry, and art are among those satisfactory outlets and outputs. Furthermore, Freud suggests that the sublimation of humankind's baser urges is vital to the formation and preservation of civilization.[6] Because sublimation upholds prevailing codes of propriety, it is inevitably shaped by sociocultural norms and constrained by reigning structures of power. Depending upon one's subject position, their perceived and actual amenability to dominant norms, their access to culturally valued activities, their subjection to scrutiny, and their vulnerability to punishment for transgressing norms, they will be urged to perform sublimation to greater or lesser extents and via various methods.

Since the sixteenth century, African-descended people in the Americas have had to sublimate under the duress of antiblack terror, violence, and surveillance. In the United States, where *Dutchman* is set, black people need not exhibit explosive aggression or brazen sexuality to be judged improper and uncivil. They are enmeshed in a racist symbolic order that constantly casts them as pathological, irrational, violent, and perverse—and then punishes them for those imputed traits.

Whereas Freud theorizes sublimation as an unconscious process, the situation of black people in antiblack contexts demands a revised theory and modified model. Toward this aim, we would do well to turn to Fanon's miscegenated and blackened psychoanalysis. Writing in *Black Skin, White Masks*, Fanon claims that "since the racial drama is played out in the open, the black man has no time to 'make it unconscious.' . . . The negro's inferiority or superiority complex or his feeling of equality are conscious. These feelings forever chill him. They make his drama. In him there is none of the affective amnesia."[7] Fanon claims that black people are forced to remain relentlessly aware of their racial precarity; thus, they do not have the chance to submerge their racial complexes and defense mechanisms into the unconscious. The ubiquity of antiblackness demands that black people remain *hyper*conscious instead.

Following Fanon astray from Freud, I propose that a conscious and ritual practice of sublimation has served as a critical sociopolitical and psychosocial strategy for countless African Americans and other black diasporans. In zones of racist surveillance, many black people have deliberately practiced rituals of sublimation, converting raw materials of spirit, passion, sex, and aggression into the socioculturally acceptable goods of religiosity, industry, respectability, and art. Who knows how often black slaves swung axes into firewood instead of the flesh of masters, sublimating murderous rage into labor? Who knows how frequently "respectable" ladies at the height of the black women's club movement deliberately displaced erotic energies into ecstatic worship, sublimating sexuality into religiosity?[8] Who knows how many black howls of despair have been converted to soul or blues riffs, sublimating anguish into art? Meanwhile, some African Americans have not earnestly performed sublimation, but have merely pretended it: publicly displaying respectable veneers while secretly harboring and privately indulging transgressive sexual and aggressive drives. Others have refused to ever take part, neither sincerely nor duplicitously, in rituals of sublimation.[9]

Clay suggests a provocative counterpoint to sublimation, a process we might call *exclamation*. Quintessentially performed by oppressed persons against oppressive figures and structures, exclamation channels political and artistic energies into violent outburst to achieve psychosocial catharsis. Where *sub*limation thrusts unseemly impulses down into the unconscious (per the prefix *sub-*, meaning *down* or *below*), *ex*clamation hurls such unseemliness out into the social world (per the prefix *ex-*, meaning *out* or *outside*). Clay would trade the corrosive neurosis that eats away the insides of the black body politic for an explosive madness that spews into a racist public sphere, deforming that sphere and subverting its structure.

Exclamation can manifest in both physical/material and discursive/representational forms. Although Clay endorses the *physical* act of murder, what he actually accomplishes is the *discursive* utterance of "murder!" hurled at Lula. (I leave "murder!" in quotation marks and appended by that exclamation point to emphasize its rhetoricity.) The thrust of a knife might be an act of exclamation, but so too is the thrust of ferocious invectives and shocking phrases. Exclamation might entail the blast of bullets from a pistol, and it might also mean the menacing shout of "murder!" Exclamation might manifest as physical violence done to a body, but it might also take shape as discursive violence: a devastating speech aimed at an antagonist in a play and rippling outward to theatergoing publics who read and behold that play.

In his incendiary Black Arts writings, Baraka endorses both discursive and physical violence as weapons against antiblackness. On the discursive register, he champions crafting language as "a weapon to help in the slaughter of these dim-witted fatbellied white guys who somehow believe that the rest of the world is here for them to slobber on,"[10] and touts "'poems that kill.' / Assassin poems, Poems that shoot / Guns."[11] These passages do not merely describe violence, they *do* discursive violence through their capacity to disturb. On the physical register, Baraka claimed, "We want *actual* explosions and *actual* brutality."[12] He spearheaded an insurgent Black Arts Movement in tandem with militant factions of the Black Power Movement, the former prepared to shoot discursive bullets, and the latter prepared to shoot lead bullets in mortal battle with antiblackness.

Protest musician Nina Simone also expressed a desire to deploy both physical and representational violence for revolutionary aims. Regarding her desire to do physical violence amid the turmoil of the Civil Rights era, Simone confessed, "If I'd had my way, I'd have been a killer. . . . I would have had guns, and I would have gone to the South and gave them violence for violence, shotgun for shotgun . . . but my husband told me I didn't know anything about guns, and he refused to teach me, and the only thing I had was music, so I obeyed him."[13] Concerning representational violence, she declared a desire to inflict it with her performances: "I want to shake people up so bad that when they leave a nightclub where I've performed, I just want them to be to pieces. . . . I want to go in that den of those elegant people with their old ideas, smugness, and just drive them insane."[14]

Skeptics may suggest that any conversion of rage into performance art is sublimation because it avoids *real* violence—where *real* violence is narrowly understood as physical. I insist that discursive violence is *real*, too, and can inflict real harm on psychic and affective registers. Hortense Spillers also reminds us that discursive violence engenders real effects when she declares, "Sticks and stones *might* break our bones but words will most certainly *kill* us."[15] Baraka and Simone know this too; they recognize the devastation discursive violence has wrought upon black people and want to return "violence for violence" in pursuit of black liberation.

I want to emphasize the symbiotic interrelation between material and discursive violence. *Material/physical* violence often *represents* social relations, and *representational/discursive* violence produces *material* effects. By way of example, consider this: The body of a black person physically lynched from a tree or stabbed dead on a subway car also represents and relays the ongoing atrocity of antiblack violence. Meanwhile, the representation of lynching on, say, a perversely jovial postcard generates material harms; I'm thinking, for example, of how such representations embolden further acts of physical violence and can even induce physiologically adverse stress in people beholding said lynching photograph. In short, physical violence and representational violence are symbiotic, co-constitutive, and both are terribly *real*.

SUBLIMATION AND EXCLAMATION

Clay names blues genius Bessie Smith as a prime practitioner of sublimation and suggests that she redirected murderous feeling into music.[16] To further probe the relationship between the musical and the homicidal, I pivot toward another blueswoman surnamed Smith. In 1920, vaudeville queen Mamie Smith released the first blues recording performed by a black vocalist and the first hit "race record." Written by Percy Bradford, "Crazy Blues" describes the malaise and murderous angst of a heartbroken woman.[17] It is worth pausing over the fact that the very first blues record performed by a black singer is a "crazy" blues—not *brokenhearted* blues, not *down-and-out* blues, not *lonely* blues, but *crazy* blues. The fact that madness figures so prominently in this musical milestone is fitting; after all, unruliness of mind and heart are perennial concerns of the blues.

It is a telling coincidence that both jazz and blues are ushered to widespread popularity by mad musicians: a "mad" jazzman named Bolden and a "crazy" blueswoman named Smith. The social upheaval and turmoil of black life at the turn of the twentieth century—the fresh trauma of slavery, the intense dissonance of double consciousness, the failure of Reconstruction, the unpredictability of migration, the depth of the nadir—engendered psychic upheaval and turmoil that surely felt *crazy* for many. During this same period, a series of cultural and technological developments meant unprecedented music-making opportunities for black artists: a Great Migration worth of black people arrived in cosmopolitan city centers, sparking cultural renaissance and artistic awakening; technological advances meant unprecedented possibilities for media recording and reproduction; and white mainstream music consumers developed ravenous appetites for black music. In short, that mad jazzman and crazy blueswoman arrived amid a deeply mad and increasingly commercialized zeitgeist.

Returning now to "Crazy Blues," Smith sings madness and sorrow as follows:

> I can't sleep at night
> I can't eat a bite
> 'Cause the man I love
> He don't treat me right
>
> . . .
>
> Now I've got the crazy blues
> Since my baby went away
> I ain't got no time to lose
> I must find him today
> Now the doctor's gonna do all that he can,
> But what you gonna need is a undertaker man!
> I ain't had nothin' but bad news
> Now I got the crazy blues
>
> . . .
>
> I'm gonna do like a Chinaman, go and get some hop
> Get myself a gun, and shoot myself a cop!
> I ain't had nothin' but bad news
> Now I've got the crazy blues

Abandoned by her lover, the song's protagonist is bereft. Soon hunger and sleep desert her, too. She is overtaken by a wild longing, a crazy blues, for her lost beloved. When Smith sings "What you gonna need is a undertaker man," the lyrics warn that death may be the outcome of these blues—but *whose* death is being foretold? Whose funeral will that "undertaker man" officiate? It could be that the speaker is foretelling her own death, imagining herself wasted away by grief or driven to suicide. On the other hand, she might be referring to the death of her flighty lover, implying that she will kill him.

Remarkably, the singer also threatens to shoot a cop, as though it will bring her a bit of catharsis. Considering that police officers in the United States in 1920 were overwhelmingly white men, Mamie Smith's "Crazy Blues" persona might be the blueswoman Clay conjured—finding solace in killing white people. In short, it seems that the protagonist of the song is a woman for whom "murder!"—of her lover, herself, or a (white) cop—could bring some relief.[18]

I propose that the blues can serve for sublimation *and* exclamation. During the height of its popularity in the mid-twentieth century, blues music potentially functioned as a codified and conscious system of black sublimation, transforming black rage, lust, and despair into palatable metaphors and catchy tunes. Paradoxically, blues music may entail quite the opposite effect insofar as it does not disappear rage, lust, and despair; rather, it retains these affects as its primary themes. Furthermore, it can intensify these feelings depending on the disposition of the singer and listener. Indeed, blues songs sometimes *cheer* black lust, *threaten* black violence, *promise* to "shoot"—thus *exclaiming* black madness.

Clay's speech and Mamie Smith's verses are provocative entrées into the next two chapters, which form a diptych on black madness in relation to "metaphor" and "murder!" In particular, I explore the lifeworlds of two fictional mad black women. The first of these women is Eva Medina Canada, the embattled protagonist and eventual murderer at the center of Gayl Jones's *Eva's Man* (1976). Second is Liliane Lincoln, prodigal daughter of the black bourgeoisie, cosmopolitan artist, and heroine of Ntozake Shange's *Liliane: Resurrection of the Daughter* (1994).

Though their lives are dramatically different on registers of class, personality, and life trajectory, the two share many affinities: Both are black American women born circa 1940 (making them Clay's contemporaries);[19] both confront antiblackness and misogyny on interpersonal and structural registers; both are only children shaped by the infidelity of their mothers and the abuse their fathers perpetrate against those mothers; both are wandering women who eschew the heteronormative protocols of conjugal-maternal domesticity; both are "treated" by psychiatric authority in stylized scenes of analysis; and both are haunted by madness. It is useful to view the two in chiastic relation: Eva commits murder, but she also makes poetic language and metaphor. Liliane makes art, but she also articulates and nearly acts upon murderous rage.

Through a synthesis of close reading, sociocultural contextualization, black feminist intervention, psychoanalytic inquiry, and mad methodology, the next two chapters center mad black women in antimad, antiblack, misogynist worlds. I will chart transformations of violent angst into art—and artful inclination into physical violence—as they occur in acts of sublimation and exclamation. When regarding murder, I will treat it not merely as a symptom of individual pathology and interpersonal malice, but also as the outcome of social ills and structural evils. My analysis is always attentive to the precarious preciousness of life and the gravity of its theft and loss. All the while, I know that moralist sanctimony cannot grasp the existential agony—or the murderous rage—that sometimes springs from the wretched and dispossessed.

Carefully, now, I turn to Eva.

CHAPTER THREE

THE BLOOD-STAINED BED

HOW WOULD YOU FEEL?

When Eva Canada asks "How would you feel?" in the passage above, she dares "you" to perform a formidable feat of empathy. After unfurling a gruesome account of murder and mutilation—of killing a man by poison, castrating him by bite in bed, lingering in his tenement bedroom, blood on the sheets, blood on her teeth—Eva urges you to project yourself into her predicament. She prompts you to predict the feelings that might visit you on that blood-stained bed: maybe some amalgamation of terror, wonder, pleasure, remorse, revulsion, relief, sadness, numbness, and sensations for which there are no words. I want to amplify Eva's question, to hear its reverberations beyond the blood-stained bed, beyond the tenement room, beyond the scene of the crime, beyond the horizon of Eva's fictional world, and into the material and historical worlds that you and I inhabit. I want to take up Eva's query as a political provocation, an ethical challenge, and a petition for radical compassion: *How would you feel* to endure a life so rife with violence that murder is its dreadful culmination?

Gayl Jones's 1976 novel, *Eva's Man*, is a grim story of precarity, violence, madness, and dogged agency amid it all. Told entirely from Eva's perspective, the novel entails both an impressionistic depiction of her psychic life and a stark chronicle of her social world. Born in rural Georgia in 1937 and raised in New York City in the 1940s and 1950s, Eva is beset by abuse from childhood

A red swollen plum in my mouth. A milkweed full of blood. A soft milkweed full of blood. What would you do if you bit down and your teeth raised blood from an apple? What would you do? Flesh and blood from an apple. What would you do with an apple? How would you feel? —EVA CANADA, from Gayl Jones, *Eva's Man*, 1976 onward. Her task at every turn from young girlhood to middle age is to evade or else endure sexual violence and exploitation from a parade of predatory men and boys. As a child and adolescent, Eva must beware Mr. Logan, the elderly man and pederast lurking in the hallways of the building where she and her family live; she must confront Freddy Smoot, the boy bully who penetrates her with "a dirty popsicle stick";[1] she must evade Tyrone, her married mother's boyfriend, who molests her, stalks her, and tries to snatch her beneath a stairwell to violate her further; she must thwart her scheming cousin Alfonso, who attempts to seduce and sexually assault her between beatings of his wife; she must fend off Moses Tripp, who attempts to buy her sex on the street and thrusts his hands between her legs to seize it; and she suffers conjugal rape at the hands of James Hunn, to whom she is married briefly beginning when she is eighteen years old and he is fifty-two. Adulthood does nothing to mitigate this constant predation.

At age thirty-eight, while lounging in a blues club in upstate New York, Eva meets a man named Davis Carter. He invites her to his home and pressures her to remain there for a few days; the two plan to have sex once her period subsides. Soon after they have sex, and with no warning or explanation, Eva lethally poisons him, maims him, and leaves his lifeless body on the bed. Although they take precautions to keep menstruation from staining the sheets, mutilation bloodies the bed after all. In naming this chapter after that *blood-stained bed*, I mean to evoke and echo Frederick Douglass's description of the "blood-stained gate" in his 1845 *Narrative of the Life of Frederick Douglass*. After recounting the torture of his Aunt Hester by a slaveholder, Douglass discloses that "it was the first of a long series of such outrages, of which I was doomed to be a witness and a participant. It struck me with awful force. It was the blood-stained gate, the entrance to the hell of slavery, through which I was about to pass."[2] Such ghastly cruelty was a crucible where enslaved subjectivity was forged.

If the blood-stained gate signifies the violent subjection and subjectification of enslaved people, this blood-stained bed evokes the sexual violence central to the subject formation of the enslaved and many among their descendants. There is a trail of blood running from the gate to the bed, from the brutality of chattel slavery to the brutality of its afterlives and reincarnations. In foregrounding the blood-stained bed, I reiterate what feminist theorists and historians like Hazel Carby, Darlene Clark Hine, Saidiya Hartman, and Danielle McGuire have revealed: the fact of sexual violence, the fear of sexual violence, and the aftermath of sexual violence have terrorized and galvanized the political subjectivities of black girls and women.[3]

Numerous critics take for granted that Eva is mad and that her madness is the outcome of racial and sexual traumas. Several scholars have generated incisive analyses of Eva's purported insanity—but mostly as a secondary or ancillary concern in discussions of trauma, misogyny, sexual violence, and language formation within the novel.[4] I center and prioritize Eva's madness, which traverses all four categories in my schema: it is a *phenomenal* unruliness of mind that sometimes seems to scramble time and collapse space; it is a suppressed and then explosive *rage* against decades of degradation; it is a *medicalized* and pathologized set of behaviors that land her in a psychiatric prison; and it is a shocking rejection of *psychosocial* norms.

The principal assertion of this chapter is that Eva's madness is not merely a site of abjection but also a locus of beleaguered agency. Pushing against the grain of scholarship that suggests madness is a failure or impossibility of communication—scholarship epitomized by literary critic Marta Caminero-Santangelo's insistence that "the madwoman can't speak"—this chapter emphasizes the expressive and narrative efficacy in Eva's madness.[5] As I will explore in turn, Eva's experience of madness shapes the book's unreliable narration, its repetitive-compulsive structure, its mad idiom, its strategic silence, its deliberate incoherence, its "crazy blues" aesthetic, and its monstrous poetics. The result is a mad and maddening narrativity that Eva marshals for self-protection and self-assertion amid dire danger.

Because Eva's bloody deed is repugnant to the vast majority of moral and ethical codes, she pushes and tests the limits of radical compassion. Remember that radical compassion, the heart of mad methodology, endures even and especially in the face of deeds that disturb. If radical compassion were easy, it would not need to be radical at all. Remember, also, that radical compassion is a mode of care—not celebration, not romanticization, not endorsement, not enjoyment. I extend such care to Eva, and to the abjected humanity she represents, even as I lament the dreadful harm she commits.

Another vital function of mad methodology is to contextualize the sporadic violence of madness amid the structural violence of Reason. Throughout this chapter, I locate Eva's mad crime within a broader web of Reasonable crimes that are perpetrated by antiblack, misogynist, racial capitalist, carceral, and necropolitical regimes surrounding her. In other words, if we are to conduct an ethical forensics of Eva's deed, our investigation must center her while also panning outward to survey her surroundings. Indeed, the scene of the crime does not end with that blood-stained bed and tenement room. There are violent geopolitical and world-historical systems, structures, and other murderers implicated in this horror. There is culpability that seeps in and spreads out—like scarlet liquid through pale sheets—to the end of the world.

"HOW MUCH IS TRUE?"
THE UNRELIABLE NARRATOR

Within the first few pages of the novel, Eva identifies herself as an unreliable narrator. She warns the reader of her potential for fantastical and delusional misrememberings as well as deliberate dissemblance. When questioned by prison psychiatrists, Eva explains that a deceitful memory is to blame for the lies she sometimes tells: "Sometimes they think I'm lying to them. . . . I tell them it ain't me lying, it's memory lying." To her reader, however, she divulges that the latter explanation is also untrue: "I don't believe that, because the past is still as hard on me as the present, but I tell them that anyway."[6]

Memory is typically a mind's intermediary between *right now* and *back then*, a mnemonic bridge or vehicle that grants cognitive access from the present to the past. If memory fails or deceives us, if "it's memory lying," we might unknowingly utter untruths about the past. However, Eva's past does not require a mnemonic bridge for access because it is always already here, pressing "hard," weighing heavily, bypassing the mediation of memory, and impacting her with the same force and immediacy as her present. The severity of Eva's trauma erodes any partition between (a traumatic) *then* and (a traumatized) *now*.

To analyze this incessant intrusion of past upon Eva's present, I turn to Freud's notion of repetition compulsion. In short, repetition compulsion is the rehearsal of traumatic past events via obsessions, dreams, flashbacks, fantasies, hallucinations, or behaviors—a complex of symptoms overlapping with what modern psychiatry calls post-traumatic stress disorder (PTSD).[7] In thought and/or action, the repetitive-compulsive subject returns again and again to the scene of trauma. Freud conjectures that a desire for "mastery" might animate repetition compulsion. What he means is that the repetitive-compulsive subject revisits a traumatic event driven by an unconscious urge for a *do-over*. The subject wants to confront the trauma again, but with a different outcome, a more desirable outcome, a mastery over that trauma.[8]

Freud also proposes a second, more radical, hypothesis for the origins of repetition compulsion. He speculates that it might emanate from a primal and unconscious "death instinct, the task of which is to lead organic life back into the inanimate state,"[9] "from which the living entity has at one time or other departed and to which it is striving to return."[10] Freud claims that the psyche is driven toward death as the most perfect state of equilibrium and calm. He further wonders whether "sadism is in fact a death instinct which, under the influence of the narcissistic libido, has been forced away from the ego and has consequently emerged only in relation to the object."[11] If Freud were to analyze Eva, He might conclude that her "death instinct" is aimed at Davis and unleashed into his flesh. Whether in pursuit of mastery, driven toward death, projected sadistically, or otherwise propelled, repetition compulsion often permeates Eva's consciousness and structures her first-person narration. In the novel a narrative technique emerges from a purported psychiatric symptom; thus, in my analysis, the project of narratology resembles symptomology.

On numerous occasions in Eva's story, people appear to commit violent deeds and speak wounding words that are uncannily similar to other people's deeds and words years before. Furthermore, the narrative juxtaposes or fuses traumatic events across time and space so that incidents decades and miles apart become indistinguishable from one another. The effect is a frequently dizzying text in which distinctions between then and now, between here and there, between interior fantasy and exterior event, between subject and object often merge into a mishmash of constant hurt.

In the following exemplary passage, Eva weaves together memories of sexual encounters: "Davis squeezed my ankles, I squeezed the boy's [Freddy's] dick. It was like squeezing a soft milkweed. . . . The musician [Tyrone] made me put my hand down between his legs."[12] When Eva invokes incidents of childhood molestation perpetrated by Freddy and Tyrone alongside an adult liaison with Davis, these three persons converge in her stream of consciousness as fungible agents of sexual predation. She describes a montage of flesh—penis, hands, legs—like one chimerical being pressed ominously against her. This passage epitomizes repetitive-compulsive narrative because it entangles and condenses memories of trauma across time. In the process, such narration illustrates and dramatizes the material persistence of sexual violence in Eva's lifeworld.[13] Perhaps a vision of multiple hurtful men flashes across Eva's mind when she murders Davis. Maybe, in her homicidal imagination, she does not merely kill one man, but rather slays a monstrous fusion of many men.

Another poignant example of Eva's repetitive-compulsive narration involves two passages—separated by over one hundred pages and narrating incidents nearly twenty years apart—that are bound by an uncanny resemblance and a traumatic confluence. The first incident occurs as follows: During Eva's girlhood, her mother, Marie, has a prolonged extramarital affair. While John (Marie's husband and Eva's father) is at work, Tyrone (Marie's blues musician boyfriend who eventually molests Eva) regularly visits their apartment and carelessly leaves evidence of his presence. John discovers the affair and learns who the other man is, but does not confront Marie for months. After a long period of silence and apparent serenity, John suddenly erupts into vengeful violence in their apartment. He snatches Marie into their bedroom and sweetly asks Eva to close the door. Then, through the walls, the young girl hears her father snarl these words to her mother:

> "Act like a whore, I'm gonna fuck you like a whore. You act like a whore, I'm gonna fuck you like a whore."
>
> He kept saying that over and over. I was so scared. I kept feeling that after he tore all her clothes off, and there wasn't anymore to tear, he'd start tearing her flesh.[14]

It is worth noting that Eva has no room of her own. She resides in her parents' living room, just on the other side of their bedroom door, without a private space for absconding, without her own bed, without her own door to shut. From that living room, through those tenement walls, Eva hears her father's cruelty but cannot see or hear her mother's response. All Eva perceives is the sound of her father's sinister refrain, the noise of tearing clothing, and the prelude to marital rape. The girl is left to imagine her mother suffering awful violence, torn bare of clothing, agency, dignity, and flesh.

Nearly a decade later, Eva's possessive husband, James, suspects she cheated on him. Eva claims she is innocent, but he is intractable and brutal. He berates and ostensibly rapes her:

> "You think you a whore, I'll treat you like a whore. You think you a whore, I'll treat you like a whore."
>
> Naw, he didn't slap me, he pulled up my dress and got between my legs.
> "Think I can't do nothing. Fuck you like a damn whore."
>
> Naw, I'm not lying. He said, "Act like a whore, I'll fuck you like a whore."[15]

Do these events actually occur with such uncanny similarity? Does Eva unwittingly fantasize their likeness? Or else, is she deliberately embellishing? Anticipating that a reader will doubt her story, Eva explains, "Naw, I'm not lying." Black feminist literary critic Candice Jenkins asserts that "while the representation of this sex act—or of the specific words that accompany it—may relate to Eva's mental instability, their inclusion does reiterate the notion that in this novel, sex and violence are interchangeable."[16] Indeed, these incidents typify the entanglement of intimacy and brutality throughout *Eva's Man*. Whether these two scenes of conjugal abuse physically took place as such, or whether Eva misremembers, hallucinates, or falsifies them, they are bound together by a powerful repetitive-compulsive affinity. Whether in mind or matter, whether fantastically or materially, the second incident entails Eva reliving the trauma of the first. As a child, she is a terrified witness to conjugal rape; as an adult, she becomes (or imagines herself to become) the primary object of such harm. In so becoming, Eva inherits a matrilineal legacy of what Christina Sharpe calls "transgenerational trauma."[17]

Improbable coincidences, like the passages above, or glaring inconsistencies, like the passage below, may incite skepticism about Eva's narrative integrity. *Integrity* is a doubly useful word here, since it signifies wholeness and honesty, both of which Eva refuses to grant her reader. Consider the following exchange between Eva and her prison psychiatrist:

> Why did you think you bit it all off?
>> I did.
>> The police report says you didn't.
>> I did . . . I wanted to.[18]

The ellipsis between "I did" and "I wanted to" marks a shift from the indicative mood to the subjunctive mood, from the grammar of memory to the grammar of fantasy. Furthermore, this exchange differs from most of the novel's dialogue in that it is not bounded by quotation marks. Typically, quotation marks indicate the verbatim transcription of speech set apart from a narrative voice. Without quotation marks, the above dialogue seems subsumed into Eva's unreliable narrative voice. The words accrue a dreamlike quality, as though they are not the content of an external conversation, as though they may be fragments and figments of Eva's imagination.

Gayl Jones deliberately injects equivocation and ambiguity into the text. By her own admission, she wants to incite confusion over what is "real" and what is "fantastic." In an interview with black feminist literary scholar Claudia Tate, Jones discloses, "I was trying to dramatize a sense of the 'real' and the 'fantastic,' or fancied and real episodes, coexisting together in Eva's narrative. The question that the listener would continually hear would be: How much of Eva's story is true and how much is deliberately not true; that is, how much of a game is she playing with her listeners/psychiatrists/others?"[19] Tate concurs, suggesting that Eva "refused to divulge something that would give coherence to her story."[20] Clinical psychiatry might diagnose Eva with some combination of antisocial disorder, post-traumatic stress disorder, and schizophrenia—framing her deceptive "games" as symptoms of antisocial disorder, her traumatic fixations as evidence of PTSD, and her seeming ruptures from reality as signs of schizophrenic psychosis. However, Jones claims that such narrative instability is not merely dysfunctional or pathological, but that it is an effective strategy of opacity and self-defense. Eva is guarding herself against predators, doctors, police officers, lawyers, readers, and anyone else who may be intent upon *laying her bare* (in all the menacing meanings of the latter phrase).

Conversing with critic and editor Charles Rowell, Jones further elaborates that "though [*Eva's Man*] is written in the manner and language of social reality (social realism) it might not be—it might be more psychological realism."[21] *Eva's Man* forgoes the linearity, reliability, clarity, verisimilitude, and appeals to Reason that are standard features of social realist protest novels. It is repetitive (and repetitive-compulsive) rather than linear, mercurial rather than reliable, opaque rather than clear, fantastical rather than verisimilar, mad rather than Reasonable. And yet, no matter its departure from social realism, *Eva's Man* is still a devastating account of social evils. It dramatizes the mind-bending effects of those evils; yields a haunting phenomenology of a life amid those evils; testifies to the recursive, relentless action of social violence; and assembles a narrative apparatus from the wreckage of that violence. The madwoman can speak after all, though her utterances may baffle, disturb, and revolt.

"SOME KIND OF BLUES RITUAL": EVA AS BLUESWOMAN

I have already introduced Mamie Smith and Sigmund Freud separately, but now I want to summon them together to reveal an intriguing coincidence between the two. Recall that 1920 was the year Smith released "Crazy Blues," the first vocal blues track recorded by a black singer. That same year, Freud also published "Beyond the Pleasure Principle," his essay introducing repetition compulsion. I propose that her record and his essay are both trenchant commentaries about trauma and its aftermaths, especially apt for a globe still reeling from the atrocities of World War I. Moreover, the content of her historic blues and his monumental theory are uncannily similar. The blues, as she practices it, fixes upon a traumatic event and builds a repeating and riffing musical refrain around it. Repetition compulsion, as he theorizes it, fixes upon a traumatic event and amasses a repeating psychosyndrome around it. With this affinity in mind, I contend that the repetitive-compulsive quality of *Eva's Man* might also be read and heard as a *blues* quality. I want to emphasize the efficacy of the blues, as musical genre and cultural ritual, for conveying and chronicling black madness.[22] Indeed, the blues tradition is apt for articulating the unruliness of mind that sometimes ensues amid poverty, heartbreak, loneliness, and antiblackness.

The title of Jones's novel emulates blues idiom. The phrase *Eva's Man* is a proclamation of heterosexual possessiveness, like the mentions of *my man, my gal,* and *my baby* that abound in blues lyrics. The people referenced in these possessive phrases are often the cause of deep hurt; it is usually the case that *my man done left me* or else *my gal don't treat me right* or, in Mamie Smith's "Crazy Blues," "my baby went away." Within this blues idiom, Davis is *Eva's man*: the object of her affection and cause of her vexation.

Meanwhile, blues music plays at pivotal scenes in the novel. For example, a blues medley scores the first interaction between Eva and Davis. As she sits in "the darkest corner" of a blues club "eating cabbage and sausage, drinking beer and listening," he greets her and takes a seat. Together, the two watch and hear a blueswoman sing "The Evil Mama Blues," "Stingaree Man," and "Wild Women Don't Get the Blues."[23] Another song on the setlist that night is "See See Rider." In Ma Rainey's definitive version of the song, she sings of heartbreak, grief, madness, and a murderous vendetta against an unfaithful man: "I'm gonna buy me a pistol just as long as I am tall . . . Gonna kill my man and catch the Cannonball." Pondering black women's blues lyrics, black radical philosopher Angela Davis reminds us that "the most frequent stance assumed by the women in these songs is independence and assertiveness—indeed defiance—bordering on and sometimes erupting into violence."[24]

When that blues singer croons "Gonna kill my man" in the backdrop of Davis and Eva's initial encounter, she foretells the doom to come. Like Eva, the song's protagonist is a beleaguered blueswoman capable of killing a man who crosses her. Here I use the term *blueswoman* capaciously, to denote a broad constituency of mostly black and working-class women who possess profound wisdom born of great hardship, who forge exquisite beauty from terrible pain.[25] Eva is a sort of blueswoman insofar as she is black, working-class, a gifted storyteller, and a passionate lover wounded by a hurtful man. What's more, she is given to violent vengeance that fulfills the threats crooned in Smith's and Rainey's songs. Played at this pivotal point in the narrative, "See See Rider" hails Eva as blueswoman and foreshadows Eva as murderer.

Beyond the novel's blues title and its narrative depictions of blues singing, *Eva's Man* also portrays and theorizes "blues ritual." Much prose is devoted to the travails of Eva's cousin Alfonso, his wife Jean, and his brother Otis, who all move from Kansas City to New York City during Eva's adolescence. Alfonso and Jean are embroiled in a bizarre, recurring ritual of violence. Eva explains:

He'd keep getting mad at something Jean did—we never did know what it was she did. . . . Every time Alfonso got mad at Jean—it was like a spell or something that come over him—every time he got mad at Jean, he would take her down to this hotel and start beating her out in front of it. He wouldn't take her inside, he'd beat her outside. Couldn't nobody do nothing with him, and they would send for Otis. Otis was the only one that could do anything with him.[26]

Alfonso never discloses a motive for this brutality. As for Jean, she confesses that she does not understand why she remains with a man who repeatedly batters her. As though entranced, the two rehearse this public scene of violence over and over again, only halted by Otis's interventions. Eva recounts that "Otis said it was like they were working some kind of blues ritual. He said he couldn't stop watching."[27] We might think of a "blues ritual" as a repetitive performance of trauma that achieves aesthetic resonance even as it retains its traumatic force.[28] That aesthetic power might be rooted in sadism. It might be intermixed with *schadenfreude* (that is, pleasure in another's misfortune). It might result from a desire to vicariously behold and purge one's own violent impulses. It might emerge from a desire to ponder one's own fears and vulnerabilities via the spectacle of someone else's pain—a version of morbid curiosity.[29]

Otis is not merely audience to this brutal blues ritual: he is a player in their ensemble, one-third of their trio. Eva recalls, "[My parents] told me that Alfonso and Jean were still going at it, and that Otis couldn't be talked into making his own life, because he still felt that they were his 'mission.' Daddy said Otis was just as crazy as them and that the three of them belonged together."[30] It seems that Otis finds purpose and pleasure in saving his sister-in-law and placating his brother, purpose and pleasure that can persist only if that abuse persists. Otis is caught between a desire to prevent this violence and a desire to preserve it.

Blues aesthetics also infuse the rumors, legends, and myths passed down ritualistically among characters in the novel. Themes of heartbreak, hard luck, loneliness, waywardness, poverty, star-crossed sex, and death all recur in these blues tales. For example, Eva's cellmate Elvira tells a story of love, madness, and death—a crazy blues in prose form:

"I knew a man once," Elvira said. "He drove every woman he had crazy. I don't mean easy crazy. I mean hard crazy. Had some of em committing suicide and stuff, and even when these women knew how he'd done all these other women, they still wonted [sic] him. I guess they figured he won't get them, figured they was different or something. He was good-looking, too. But every one of em that went with him just got plain messed up. He messed up every woman he went with. That's the way I think of that nigger you had."[31]

A prison intellectual, Elvira theorizes "easy crazy" and "hard crazy." The former is a mild and manageable experience of madness, while the latter is so severe, so agonizing, that it might make life unbearable. Knowing that this man will drive them "hard crazy," women continue to pursue him, as though compelled by an irresistible force.

This crazy-making man has a female counterpart, the Queen Bee, who is also the subject of ominous lore. A friend of Eva's mother explains that "every man [the Queen Bee] had end up dying. I don't mean natural dying, I mean something happen to them. Other mens know it too, but they still come."[32] It turns out that the Queen Bee is an accidental *femme fatale*; she does not intend to cause harm, but is the accursed conduit of men's deaths. Like her male counterpart, she has a long queue of suitors who pursue her, like moths to the flame, despite the doom she brings. These *homme fatale* and *femme fatale* fables are likely variations on the same story, differently gendered and variously disseminated through lore and rumor. The key difference is that the man survives his own deadliness while the Queen Bee is eventually a casualty of her death-dealing curse. You see, when she is overcome by a love so intense that she cannot bear the thought of causing her lover's death, she takes her own life in order to spare his. Despite the gender difference that distinguishes these two versions of myth, both culminate with female death. In this vernacular milieu, black women find no reprieve.

Eva's husband James imparts another crazy blues. He describes "this man who owned this store and these people wanted to take the store so they could tear it down and make a branch of the State Mental Hospital there, but in order to get it they had to prove the man was insane. They ended up proving the man was insane, but in a few years ended up moving him back out there on the same ground where his store had been. He said that was a true story."[33] These are bitter, bleak blues: a man is victim of a sinister conspiracy, pillaged and dispossessed, cast into abjection, and left with the tragic irony of imprisonment on the very same ground where he once prospered. In this blues tale, psychiatry becomes a devastating weapon for persecution. While the man's race and location are never revealed, such evil would be especially easy to accomplish in Jim Crow America at the expense of a black person. White supremacists used intimidation, terror, murder, and also, as above, trickery and perjury, to steal black property. We may never know how many black people were deemed "insane" in rigged courtrooms and examination rooms, under Jim Crow and beyond it, their possessions confiscated by their persecutors.[34] Such incidents remind us that clinical or juridical "proof" is not necessarily commensurate with truth. In these cases, proof is falsehood fabricated to uphold an antiblack, white supremacist, profiteering status quo. Regarding Eva, I wonder whether bogus proof was marshaled against her. How many antiblack, white supremacist, avaricious, and misogynist doctors and lawyers had a hand in Eva's fate?

James relays one more tale of crazy blues, but this time he is the proverbial bluesman beating back sorrow: "'A man talks to himself when he's lonely,' James said. 'I go out to restaurants sometimes, but I sit way over in the corner by myself. People see me and think I'm crazy because I just be sitting over there laughing and talking to myself. Or either somebody ask, "What's that nigger talking about?" and somebody answer, "Probably talking some shit." A man's lonely and he laughs and talks to himself. He ain't crazy, he's lonely.'"[35] James's confession of loneliness and degradation positions him within the novel's cohort of people living, singing, recalling, and confessing the blues. Remarkably, both loneliness and psychosis might compel a man to "talk to himself": a lonesome man might "talk to himself" because he longs to hear the sound of any voice, if only his own; a psychotic man might seem to "talk to himself" while keeping company with imaginary friends or voices in his head. For uttering wayward words without apparent audience or interlocutor, for speaking in an idiom of madness, for issuing unseemly speech, James is labeled a *crazy nigger*.

Sometimes unseemly silence is coded as crazy, too. Such is the case with Eva, whose silence I study below.

"I SAID NOTHING": ON SILENCE AND VIOLENCE

In the previous chapter, I pondered the "deep black mouth" of Buddy Bolden: shouting, opening into darkness, and threatening to swallow. I now return to the trope of the mad mouth, but now the mouth is Eva's and it is shut. Her closed mouth is a matrix of silence and of violence: the former epitomized by lips sealed tight, the latter epitomized by teeth biting hard. In this section, I assess Eva's persistent silence and climactic violence.

In her own words, Jones is fascinated by "the psychology of language as a means of getting to the psychological reality of patients." Moreover, the author is invested in exploring "the extremes of psychological and linguistic deviation, and at the same time using the things I'd learned about language here (rhythmical flexibility, syntactical dislocation, forms of linguistic tensions) as a means of getting to the basic reality of people in general."[36] Eva's most remarkable "linguistic deviation" is her extraordinary propensity for silence. Consider the following three passages in which Eva is asked to describe how the murder and mutilation felt:

"How did it feel in your mouth?" Elvira asked.

I didn't answer.[37]

The psychiatrist said he didn't just want to know about the killing, he said he wanted to know about what happened after the killing. Did it come in my mind when I saw him lying there dead or had I planned it all along. His voice was soft. It was like cotton candy. He said he wanted to know how it felt, what I did, how did it make me feel. I didn't want him looking at me. I had my hands on my knees. My knees were open, I closed my knees.

"I want to help you, Eva."

I said nothing.[38]

"How did it feel, Eva?" the psychiatrist asked.

My mother got an obscene telephone call one day. A man wanted to know how did it feel when my daddy fucked her.

"How did it feel?" Elvira asked.

"They told me you wouldn't talk. They said I wouldn't get one word out of you," the psychiatrist said. "Did you feel you had any cause to mutilate him afterwards? Why did you feel killing him wasn't enough?"

"How did it feel?" Elvira asked.

"How do it feel, Mizz Canada?" the man asked my mama. She slammed the telephone down.

"Eva. Eva. Eva," Davis said . . .

I don't want to tell my story.[39]

Again and again, Eva's inquisitors urge her to confess what motivated her deed and describe the sensations it stirred. She regularly responds to their questions, as above, with silence or elision. Even Eva's internal commentary is sparse in these passages. She thinks to herself, "I didn't answer," "I said nothing," and "I don't want to tell my story." Eva similarly refuses to explain an incident in her teens when a man sexually assaults her on the street before she stabs him in retaliation. When her parents and investigators ask for her side of the story, she later admits "I didn't tell anybody . . . I just let the man tell his side."[40] Eva forgoes the chance to defend herself in court and is sentenced to three months in reformatory school and three months in jail. When interrogated by police about the murder of Davis, she initially responds with the same impervious quiet. Even her internal voice is reticent, offering little clarification of her motives. Thus, to call Eva *unsound* is to activate a double entendre. First, her unsoundness is a literal refusal to make a sound—a withholding of audible and decipherable answer—when she is questioned. Second, her unsoundness might be a condition of pathology or instability, as presumed by that psychiatrist.

Eva chooses silence rather than rehearse the scripts or participate in the discursive milieus typically designated for self-interested, Reasonable subjects. She does not seek reprieve through juridical testimony, psychiatric talking cure, forensic deposition, public confession, pleas for penitence, or liberal rights discourse—genres of speech often uttered by the accused seeking mercy or favor.[41] In the racial history of the United States, such discursive repertoires and speech acts have not proven reliable tools of remedy for black people. In fact, such state-solicited and state-mandated speech is frequently weaponized to vilify, pathologize, condemn, and exploit black people. It is no wonder, then, that many black people approach courtrooms, examination rooms, interrogation rooms, classrooms, and liberal public spheres with deep caution and suspicion.[42] I want to suggest that Eva is among these suspicious black folks, that her reticence is informed by individual and cultural memory of malicious "incitements to discourse."[43] Rather than read Eva's silence as an inability to speak or a failure of language, we might interpret it as a critical refusal of speech informed by the expectation that her words can and will be used against her.

Regarding strategic silence, Foucault insists that "silence itself . . . is less the absolute limit of discourse, the other side from which it is separated by a strict boundary, than an element that functions alongside the things said, with them and in relation to them within over-all strategies. . . . There is not one but many silences, and they are an integral part of the strategies that underlie and permeate discourses."[44] He contends that silence is not the outside or absence of discourse, but rather is its own mode of discourse with a range of complexly communicative grammars, idioms, and contents. Indeed, silence speaks on various registers.

Also touting the potential efficacy of silence, black feminist theorist and literary critic Aliyyah Abdur-Rahman ponders the "strategic silence" around sexual violence in slave narratives, contending that "slaves incorporated and managed silence as a trope and narrative technique to call attention to what language could not directly relate."[45] Slave narratives use silence to signal the unspeakable horror of chattel slavery. Silence constitutes a negative space and narrative aperture that the reader might fill with her own dreadful visions.

Regarding Holocaust testimony, psychiatrist and trauma theorist Dori Laub suggests that recounting such brutality may induce an "impossibility of speaking, and in fact of listening, otherwise than through silence" and cautions interlocutors to "respect . . . the silence out of which this testimony [speaks]."[46] Abdur-Rahman and Laub teach us that words may fail and language may shatter under the weight of atrocity. It may become necessary to speak through silence and listen to it, to seek recourse in an ethical and critical wordlessness.

Foucault, Abdur-Rahman, Laub, and Eva all admonish against any facile equation of silence with absence. They encourage us to critically engage silence, to recognize its density, variety, multiplicity, and potentiality. In the process, they complicate Audre Lorde's admonition that "your silence will not protect you."[47] To be clear, Lorde's claim is absolutely apt in many contexts. Silence will not protect subjugated peoples when it precludes them from bearing witness to one another, commiserating with one another, soliciting help from one another, comforting one another, imparting wisdom to one another, declaring love for one another, strategizing together, organizing together, warning one another of danger, or speaking truth to power. If silence categorically obstructs these modes of address, it may prove devastating and debilitating.

However, when oppressed peoples are urged to recite pernicious lies, parrot master's speech, confess sacred secrets, pledge allegiance to their oppressors, tattle on their comrades, renounce their friends, or berate themselves—then silence can be a mode of self-protection, if only tenuous and provisional.[48] For dispossessed people, neither a categorical allegiance to (free) speech nor a categorical faith in (protective) silence will suffice alone. A counterhegemonic repertoire must strategically deploy both speech and silence, both clamor and hush, both brazen declaration of political demands and soundproof pursuit of clandestine goals. Like signifying, silence is a critical element of black vernacular, literary, and political cultures.[49] Like signifying, silence is characterized by ambiguity, which makes it difficult for outsiders to decipher. It is because of this elusive quality that silence, like signifying, has served as an effective tool for black subterfuge in the face of antebellum slaveholders, corrupt prosecutors, tyrannical cops, and other agents of antiblack inquisition.

"A SWOLLEN PLUM":
METAPHORS AND MURDER

Along with silence, Eva displays an eerie calm that perplexes and vexes those around her. Elvira observes, "You too serene. When a woman done something like you done and serene like that, no wonder they think you crazy,"[50] and

Davis similarly comments on Eva's unseemly serenity.[51] In clinical contexts, impervious calm in the face of tragic or terrifying events may be interpreted as "flat affect," a potential symptom of depression, schizophrenia, or post-traumatic stress disorder. Beyond the clinical context, proverbial wisdom suggests that, in matters of weather and human behavior, uncanny serenity may be the calm before the storm. Eva's father exemplifies this proposition with his sedate behavior before he finally snatches his wife into their bedroom to brutalize her. Along with mendacity and silence, Eva's placid façade is a technology of disguise that she uses to conceal her psychic interior. Her tranquility precedes Davis's murder, too. Hidden behind her cloak of calm, she shows no signs of murderous intent.

Eva's motives for killing are manifold. For now, I will focus on the two that appear most obvious: displaced rage and amorous jealousy. Regarding displaced rage, it seems that Davis is the object of wrath that has amassed in Eva over dozens of years—a rage felt for countless men who have violated and abused her since girlhood. Eva's prison psychiatrist opines, "You know what I think . . . I think he came to represent all the men you'd known in your life." When Eva breaks from her characteristic reticence to ask, "Who?," the psychiatrist retorts, "I got something out of you," and Eva thinks, "He was proud of himself."[52]

The above passage is significant not only because it presents a plausible hypothesis of Eva's motive, but also because it exposes the doctor's smugness and acquisitiveness. Regarding this passage—and the likeness between the psychiatrist's attitude and the disposition of many men in the novel—literary scholar Casey Clabough notes that "transcending race, education, and social standing, the male impulse to exploit, to 'get something out of' women, constitutes an important defining visceral and philosophical dimension among Jones' male characters."[53] When the psychiatrist refers to "all the men" Eva has known, he is describing himself, too. Like the others, he treats Eva as object: a vessel into which he can project his desires and presumptions; an instrument that he can wield to accomplish his own agenda; or else a raw material from which he can extract "something," if only distortive misapprehensions. When Eva announces, "He was proud of himself," she mocks his arrogant presumptuousness. I read this exchange as an admonition for the rationalist reader, too: Beware, lest you also become smugly "proud" of yourself with glib and reductive interpretations of Eva.

Regarding amorous jealousy, a usual suspect in the lineup of murder motives is the jealousy of a jilted lover perpetrating a crime of passion. The following proclamation appears near the conclusion of the novel, without specific attribution or clear context: *I submit the insanity of Eva Medina Canada, a woman who loved a man who did not return that love.*[54] Ostensibly the words of a court-appointed defense attorney entering a plea before a judge, this statement aligns with the crime of passion framework frequently invoked in criminological and popular discourse. Supporting the jilted-lover hypothesis is Eva's response when Davis reveals he is married—just as she begins to feel tenderness for him. In uncharacteristically melodramatic and emotive prose, Eva admits that Davis's disclosure feels like "big rusty nails sticking out of [her] palms."[55] With this stigmatic image, Eva renders herself curiously Christlike. Like the biblical Christ, Eva suffers terrible violence; however, her hurt does not generate the redemptive, transcendent effect attributed to Christ's suffering.

Eva alludes again to the Bible when she eventually explains how it felt. Remarkably, she does not utter her confession aloud to any of her in-text inquisitors; she discloses it within a narrative stream of consciousness available only to readers. Now, I finally return to the phenomenology of the bite:

> I opened his trousers and played with his penis. My mouth, my teeth, my tongue went inside his trousers. I raised blood, slime from cabbage, blood sausage. Blood from an apple. I slid my hands around his back and dug my fingers up his ass, then I knelt down on the wooden floor, burning my knees. I got back on the bed and squeezed his dick in my teeth. I bit down hard. My teeth in an apple. A swollen plum in my mouth.
>
> "How did it feel?"
>
> A red swollen plum in my mouth. A milkweed full of blood. A soft milkweed full of blood. What would you do if you bit down and your teeth raised blood from an apple? What would you do? Flesh and blood from an apple. What would you do with an apple? How would you feel?[56]

Slimy cabbage, "blood sausage," "an apple," and "a red swollen plum" are spread at the center of this grotesque meal. Foodstuffs are poignant analogs for the grotesque body, which, per Mikhail Bakhtin, "is not a closed, completed unit; it is unfinished, outgrows itself, transgresses its own limits."[57] The tearing, slicing, leaking, spilling, biting, and swallowing that take place in the preparation and consumption of food all dramatize the properties of grotesquerie.

Eva's Man contains several profane transubstantiations wherein human bodies are figuratively cannibalized by human predators and scavengers. When Eva's cousin Alfonso begins to prey on her, for instance, he makes a pass with a metaphor of food. After she reveals to him that she is sexually inactive at seventeen years old, he replies, "And ain't had the meat? Most girls your age had the meat *and* the gravy,"[58] where "meat" apparently signifies a penis and "gravy" seems to mean semen. Another figurative fusion of human flesh and meat takes place when a man without thumbs, an acquaintance of Alfonso, plops down at their table and begins to eat pigs' feet. The man openly ogles the teenaged girl and calls her "sweetmeat," as though he would like to add her to his meal.

But there is another register in which the stranger evokes human flesh as meat: his own body manifests such a convergence. Eva recounts, "The man sucked on a piece of pigfoot. I kept looking at his thumbless hand." The pig-foot and thumbless hand—both appendages, both dismembered—seem to merge over his dinner plate. As Eva glances at him, the man is rendered meat-like, a monstrous chimera of human and pork. Another figurative convergence of human flesh and foodstuff occurs later while Eva and Davis lounge in his apartment. As he eats lukewarm eggs, Davis announces that "'egg's the same thing a woman's got inside her,' . . . That's why it smells that way. It smells like fuck."[59] Davis likens hen's eggs to women's reproductive systems and suggests that both smell like "fuck." In one fell swoop, he animalizes and metaphorically cannibalizes women.

Within Eva's grotesque poetics, Davis's penis is *figuratively reconstituted* as cabbage, sausage, apple, and plum. Between Eva's teeth, Davis's penis is *physically reconstituted*, left mutilated and possibly excised. Note that the cabbage and sausage are imported from the meal the two originally ate together at that blues club. The sausage's cylindrical shape might resemble a penis, and the cabbage's slime may approximate the semen and blood that come from Davis's penis. The apple hails the forbidden fruit of Eden, and "blood from an apple" invokes the spilling of blood and dawn of death that afflicted the world, according to the Old Testament, when Eve and Adam ate the fruit. Finally, the fleshy but firm texture of a "swollen plum" simulates the taut tactility of an erect penis.

Eva's life has abounded with domineering men who would reduce her to raw material and bare flesh for their unlimited use and consumption.[60] At the scene of the murder, she turns the tables, accessing an utterly inert male body for her own use and consumption. She ponders it, handles it, plays with it, takes it in, tastes it, bites it, and then muses poetically over it. Literary scholar Carol Davison proposes that "Eva is driven by a type of 'ritual logic' in her castrating act. Although this logic may be deemed incoherent by the official culture, a coherence subtends it." According to Davison, Eva's crime uncannily emulates ancient religious rites. She writes that "Eva's act partakes of an ancient ritual sensibility wherein catharsis and purgation play central roles."[61] Indeed, Eva's molestation and mutilation of Davis's dead body have the dramatic, meticulous, ornate, and protracted character of ritual. Considered in conjunction with Freud's notion of sublimation—which may manifest as religious rites and rituals—Eva might be said to perform a ghastly parody of those rites, an extreme act of exclamation.

That ritualistic property also characterizes Eva's description of the deed. She unfurls a stylized account of the murder, in stark contrast to the descriptive minimalism throughout much of her narration. That description entails a gruesome mess of violence and artfulness, a creative flourish to describe a destructive outburst, a perverse poetics whose preferred idioms are the monstrous and grotesque. Notably, though, the artfulness of Eva's figurative language does not disguise its terrifying meaning. That terror remains fully visible—highlighted rather than obscured, exclaimed instead of quieted—by its poetic recounting. In short, Eva's deed is a shocking act of exclamation: an outburst of violent agency and cruel creativity militated against a cruel world. Furthermore, her narration of that deed is also an act of exclamation, inflicting rhetorical and aesthetic violence upon many readers. Maybe that shocking narrative will shake some readers to the core, shattering their complacency in the process.

Following her account of the murder, Eva asks the questions that open this chapter: "What would you do?" and "How would you feel?" After she has finally explained the bloody deed, she refuses to let readers nonchalantly turn the page. Eva seeks reciprocity. She has revealed to us what she did and how she felt, and now it is our turn to confront what *we* might do and how *we* might feel. After a lifetime of being solicited, propositioned, interrogated, and interpellated, Eva turns the tables and poses questions of her own. In other words, Eva's shocking exclamation—a physical murder and narrative "murder!"—opens up into an incisive interrogation. And what would you do, after all? Would you collapse and weep on the blood-stained bed? Would you linger, stunned and transfixed, at the scene of the crime? Would you turn the poison upon yourself? Would you flee to fugitivity? Would you surrender to law enforcement? Would you retreat into impervious silence?

If Eva's crimes have alienated rationalist readers, if her deeds have opened up an ethical chasm between rational audience and mad protagonist, her questions call across that expanse to solicit radical compassion. Surely, that distance will be a bridge too far for many readers, rationalist and otherwise. Many will be unreceptive to empathetic entreaties from a woman who has committed, and just finished ornately describing, such dreadful acts. In her review of the novel, Lorde writes, "Repeated like a depraved slide show rather than the terrible acts of brutalized people, the human destructiveness within *Eva's Man* erupts without feeling nor [*sic*] understanding, without context. And so it can exist safely separate from ourselves and our own angers. Eva Canada has no quest nor self, only unsatisfied hunger, hurt, and mute revenge."[62] I agree with Lorde on two accounts: first, the phrase "repeated slide show of depravity" is a trenchant description of the traumatic visions that repeatedly invade Eva's consciousness; second, the book frequently thwarts and refuses "understanding."

But I want to linger with Lorde's assertion that "the human destructiveness" in the book "can exist safely separate from ourselves and our own angers." If this safe separation exists, it should not be naturalized and accepted as a foregone conclusion. Instead, such a separation should be actively surmounted. I propose a mad methodology that disallows easy distancing of Eva from our lives, that emphasizes context and activates compassion to reveal the nearness of Eva to us all.

Concerning context, mad methodology locates sporadic eruptions of mad violence within unrelenting systems of Reasonable violence. Accordingly, Eva's *individual act* of human destructiveness must be framed within the *vast and world-historical regimes* of human destructiveness that undergird modernity. I have in mind the mundane antiblackness, misogyny, sexual violence, poverty, and carcerality that pervade Eva's lifeworld as well as the ongoing histories of slavery, genocide, extractive colonialism, settler colonialism, racial capitalism, and war that delimit her lifeworld. Perhaps Eva's eruption is an attempted attack on such regimes of violence; her victim is a domineering man who might, in her mind, stand in for the structural misogyny besieging her. Perhaps Eva's outburst is an extension of those regimes of violence—a pathological imitation, writ small, of the cruelty done to her. However we interpret the motivation and implication of Eva's crime, we must not interpret that crime in isolation.

Here is the bloody heart of the matter: Whether native, settler, enslaved, slaver, colonizer, colonized, capitalist, commodity, consumer, consumed, or their descendants, we are all heirs to this world-historical "human destructiveness." But we do not all receive the same parcel of inheritance. Some of us inherit a heightened susceptibility to being destroyed, while some of us stand to inherit the spoils of such destruction. As a poor black girl and woman, Eva is especially vulnerable to those structural collusions of antiblackness, misogyny, sexual violence, racial capitalism, and carcerality.[63] It is critical to attend to such peculiar precarity even as we acknowledge that this human destructiveness imperils and/or implicates every person on earth. Ultimately, *all of us are bound to Eva by blood: blood on our hands, blood in our veins, blood from our wounds, "blood at the root,"*[64] *blood on the gate, or blood on the bed*. No one is clean. By this accounting, none of us "can exist safely separate" from Eva Canada.

My hope is that these contextual insights invigorate radical compassion: profound care and abiding existential entanglement, even and especially with the most debased among us. One may wonder whether I am overgenerous or extending too much benefit of the doubt to Eva. It bears repeating that I am not describing *moderate* compassion, *ordinary* compassion, or *easy* compassion; I am touting something *radical*. Motivated by radical compassion, our primary impulse must not be to discard Eva or retaliate against her—but rather to abolish the structures that erect and uphold the blood-stained bed.

LOOKING

When Lorde likens *Eva's Man* to a depraved "slide show," she uses a decidedly visual trope. After probing matters of speaking and listening, of sound and soundlessness, I now turn to practices of looking and visuality in the novel. I am concerned both with *looking like* (seeming or resembling) and *looking at* (directing one's gaze) as they manifest in Eva's lifeworld.

To ponder visuality in *Eva's Man*, we would do well to highlight the book's repeated evocations of Medusa, a mythical monster who is cursed to kill all who look directly into her eyes. It is worth noting that themes of monstrosity are salient across Jones's oeuvre. Sharpe has examined "monstrous intimacies"—racialized and sexualized "horrors, desires, and positions"[65] and "everyday intimate brutalities"[66] inherited from chattel slavery and suffusing modern social relations—in Jones's first novel, *Corregidora*. *Eva's Man* is also teeming with monstrous intimacies, not merely in the mundane brutality it depicts, but also in its attachment to Medusa.

As told by the Roman poet Ovid, the story of Medusa is rife with misogynist violence and indignity. Erstwhile a beautiful maiden, Medusa is raped by the sea god Neptune in the temple of the war goddess Minerva. Enraged by the desecration of her temple, and clearly driven by a victim-blaming logic, Minerva curses Medusa.[67] The war goddess transforms the young woman into a supernaturally hideous monster with writhing snakes for hair. Moreover, all who look upon Medusa's face are instantly turned to stone. Medusa's victims, aspiring heroes come to slay the creature, become instant monuments to their own shocked deaths. The monster's lair must have resembled a sinister sculpture garden arrayed with would-be conquerors made stone effigies.

Medusa is doubly violated; she is raped and then she is punished for being raped. She finds no solace, no recourse, no justice through the aegis of authority—only intensified violation and degradation. In this respect, Medusa shares a tragic likeness with countless women and girls who suffer sexual violence and then find their pain compounded by victim-blaming from hostile communities and authorities.[68] The popular version of the Medusa myth perpetrates a third violence, a sort of representational violence, against the snake-haired being. She is flattened into a crude symbol of evil, her suffering effaced, her plight ignored across millenia of retellings.

Just as evil is imputed to Medusa, so too is it ascribed to Eva—beginning decades before the latter commits murder. When twelve-year-old Eva resists Tyrone's advances, he calls her a "little evil devil bitch." When, as a young woman, she refuses another man's sexual propositions, he replies, "You a evil ole bitch. Your name ain't Eva, it's Evil."[69] The latter man exploits the phonetic similarity of "Eva" and "Evil" to debase her. He acts as though he has a right to access and possess her body, as though her refusal is the immoral offense in their encounter.

Eva's hair becomes another basis for comparison with Medusa. After Davis confiscates her comb, refusing to let her tend to her hair, she eventually asks, "My hair looks like snakes, doesn't it?" Her question evokes the cluster of serpents, instead of hair, that sprouts from Medusa's head.[70] While Eva initially seems embarrassed about this Medusa-like quality, she later embraces the resemblance. From her prison cell, Eva muses, "I'm Medusa. . . . Men look at me and get hard-ons. I turn their dicks to stone. I laughed."[71] In a rare moment of jest, Eva announces solidarity with Medusa. They both cause men to harden—and for both, this stiffening is a curse. In Medusa's case, the curse is a supernatural malediction that petrifies men into stone and causes their deaths. For Eva, the curse is a plague of sexual predation often attached to hard dicks.

When a psychiatrist inquires about Eva's motive, she replies (in another passage of dreamlike dialogue without quotation marks) that Davis was looking at her:

> Did he frighten you?
> He was sitting on the bed looking at me.
> What did he do to you, Eva?
> I wasn't like that. I was just sitting over there. And then he came and sat down and then went back to his room, but I wasn't like that. And he was looking at me. He wouldn't let me comb my hair or nothing.[72]

Pages later, Eva confesses that "every man could look at me the way he was looking. They all would. Even when I. He thought I was his."[73] In each of the three preceding passages, Eva suggests that Davis's glance provokes her, that her violence is self-defense or else retribution against his intrusive, acquisitive look.

Medusa's victims look at Medusa and die. Eva's victim looks at Eva and dies. In both scenarios, to exercise male gaze is to incur death.[74] Usually an assertion of domination, Eva and Medusa reconstitute male gaze as liability, vulnerability, and exposure to annihilation.

Whereas Eva decapitates the head of a man's penis, Medusa is eventually decapitated by a named Perseus. In order to aim his deathblow (without gazing directly at her) he uses the surface of his shield as a mirror and stalks her reflection. He prevails by viewing a mediated, indirect vision of her. When Freud analyzes the Medusa myth, he similarly seems to regard her only indirectly and reflected off his own masculinist equipments. In "Medusa's Head," Freud offers a stubbornly phallocentric reading of the myth, interpreting it as a parable for castration anxiety. He concludes that Medusa's decapitation is an analogy for castration; that the snakes of Medusa's hair mollify this anxiety by signifying surrogate phalli; and that the hardening of Medusa's victim represents the penis erecting and asserting its presence in the castration-anxious male subject.[75] Freud's reading of the myth occludes female subjectivity and fails to explore how the subject without a penis might process and possess the Medusa myth.[76] Such indirection parallels many characters' encounters with Eva. They do not see her straightforward; they only behold refracted, distorted images of her that are bounced off the surfaces of their own weapons and shields. And sometimes they treat her as a reflective surface on which they can regard themselves.

Agents of state-sanctioned surveillance and inquest also aim their gazes at Eva. A forensic psychiatrist is one among several white men who lurk at the perimeters of *Eva's Man*, invariably occupying positions of official authority. In addition to Eva's psychiatrist, the other white men who appear in the novel are police officers. They monitor Eva, interrogate her, and utter snide, racist-sexist remarks about her crime and uncombed hair. As she sits in her waiting cell with disheveled hair, a detective asks his colleague, "She looks dangerous, too, doesn't she?" and his colleague responds, "They all look dangerous."[77] This exchange exemplifies a practice of antiblack looking that "sees" black people as categorically dangerous, criminal, crazy, and thus requiring social control. Looking at blackness through this antiblack lens, white supremacists endorse tyrannical policing practices, severe sentencing codes, bloodthirsty vigilantism, and the proliferation of prisons.

Men frequently remark upon how Eva looks—both how she *appears* and how she *directs her gaze*. I turn now to the latter. Consider, for example, Davis's account of the moment when he first noticed Eva in a dark corner of that blues club:

"I can read your eyes."

"Can you?"

"Yeah, that's why I came over."

"You couldn't see my eyes then."

He nodded. "Yes I could."[78]

Davis would have us believe that Eva's eyes glow in the dark. It is more likely that he fantasizes a vision of beckoning eyes. Like so many men before him, he treats Eva as a mere receptacle for his desire, a drawing board on which he can plot his own fantasies. He stubbornly sticks to his story, no matter that darkness and distance would have obstructed his vision. Davis later recounts when first he saw her face up close: "I could tell by your eyes how you felt. I could smell you wanted me." Eva responds, "I couldn't help looking."[79] To have Davis tell it, Eva's eyes emanate a desire so strong that it induces synesthesia. He suggests that the *sight* of her eyes *smells* like desire, as though her yearning is so intense that it bursts the limits of visuality and invades his olfactory sense, too. Davis practices looking with an air of authority, insisting that what he sees is truth. In contrast, Eva seems passive in the exchange, conceding and confessing that she "couldn't help looking" at him. In this encounter, Davis's male gaze seems to overpower Eva, amounting to another act of male domination in Eva's lifeworld. (Of course, she eventually exacts revenge on him for his pernicious looking.)

Tyrone claims to see the same sort of brazen desire in Eva's twelve-year-old eyes. As the two sit in her mother's living room, Eva's gaze lingers on Tyrone's crotch. When he later attempts to rape her, he claims that her gaze was an invitation. He projects his predatory will onto Eva's young eyes, casting blame on the child. For her part, Eva confesses, "I don't know what made me look where I was looking. When I first started looking there, I didn't realize that's where I was looking, and then when I realized, I kept watching down between his legs. I don't know how long he saw me watching there, but all of a sudden he took my hand and put it on him."[80] Once again, Eva expresses helplessness and haplessness about her own gaze. Whereas she claims she "couldn't help" looking at Davis, she claims not to "know what made [her] look where [she] was looking" when her gaze landed between Tyrone's legs. Perhaps she truly does not know, or perhaps she knows and chooses to withhold. As a result, the only available descriptions of Eva's eyes—in the living room and in the blues club—come from chauvinistic and predatory men. I suspect that Tyrone and Davis perceive Eva's eyes as mere mirrors. Therein, they see their own desires flattened and thrown back at themselves.

Freddy imagines a very different affect emanating from young Eva's eyes. After the incident with the popsicle stick, he accosts her in an alleyway and proclaims, "I'ma put [my penis] in you like Mama's men put it in her." Eva recalls, "I didn't try to run. I just stayed with him. He still had my arm. He held my arm and unzipped his pants and took his thing out. Then he kept looking from my eyes to his thing. And then all of a sudden he pushed me away from him, and turned and zipped his pants back up, and went upstairs. I didn't know what he'd seen in my eyes, because I didn't know what was there."[81] Freddy retreats as though the young girl has brandished a weapon. His own gaze darts back and forth from her eyes to "his thing" before he flees, as though he is calculating the damage she might do, as though he is overtaken by castration anxiety.

Perhaps there is something flashing from Eva's eyes that signals her capacity for vengeful violence, to do harm to the "things" that accost and assail her. Decades later, her eyes transmit an ominous warning to Davis, too. He confesses, "*I never seen a woman look at me like that. The way you were looking when you told me not to look at you. . . . Like you could kill me. Like you could just kill me, baby.*"[82] Considering the sexual and racial predation that overruns Eva's world, eyes that glint like polished knives might come in handy to stave off would-be predators. Such ominous eyes would dispense with the need to speak threats, convenient for such a reticent woman. Alas, it seems that Eva never wholly masters nor completely comprehends the power in her gaze—or else she cunningly feigns ignorance.

I want to zoom in upon one last occasion of looking in *Eva's Man*. During her wanderlustful adult years, on a leg of an interstate bus trip to Wheeling, West Virginia, in search of itinerant work, Eva meets an unnamed Denver-bound man. He also claims to see intense affect in Eva's eyes, but of a different shade: "He said when he first saw those eyes of mine, he knew I could love a man."[83] Perhaps he actually perceives a capacity for a deep and abiding affection in her eyes. However, in a narrative so bereft of the beneficence traditionally associated with love, I wonder whether his invocation of "love" is merely another technique of predation, another projection from another man who views her as vessel for his fantasies and desires.

Whatever the Denver-bound man's motivation, Eva refuses his advances and he calmly relents. Their encounter is insignificant to the plot of *Eva's Man*, but it is still remarkable for its benignity and levity. In any case, theirs is a brief exchange between two people who cross paths while heading toward different destinations: he to Denver, then somewhere in California, and then "maybe" Mexico; she to Wheeling and then, who knows? The two part ways when he transfers buses at a crossroads somewhere in the Midwest.[84]

In its final scene, *Eva's Man* returns to the image of consumed genitalia. The novel concludes as Elvira, after much pleading and prodding for Eva's affection, finally performs cunnilingus on her cellmate. Elvira entreats, "Tell me when it feels sweet, Eva. Tell me when it feels sweet, honey." Recalling her reply, Eva utters the final sentence of *Eva's Man*: "I leaned back, squeezing her face between my legs, and told her, 'Now.'"[85] Literary scholar Biman Basu asserts that "Eva's culminating 'Now' has to be read as an affirmation, even if made in prison. Far from being passive acquiescence, Eva's participation represents affirmation."[86] Whereas much of the novel is preoccupied with sealed lips, clamped jaws, and silent withholding, this final scene beholds the *open* mouth of a woman performing cunnilingus and the *open* mouth of another woman announcing that it finally feels sweet. This encounter might be read as a revision of that gruesome incident with Davis. Then, on the blood-stained bed, clenched teeth inflicted genital mutilation; now, in a prison cell, an outstretched tongue provides genital pleasure.

After amassing tens of thousands of words to describe past pain, Eva's last word declares present pleasure, summons readers into that sweet now, and leaves us to linger there as we close the book. After raising blood from an apple and consuming many bitter crops, this moment beholds Eva finding a dollop of sweetness.[87] I do not mean to romanticize Eva's final word or to invest it with transcendent power. A spoonful of sweet cannot erase a tongue's memory of blood—and "Now" is no magical incantation to erase Eva's trauma or spirit her away from that prison. Maybe this sweetness is an anomalous feeling or maybe, just maybe, it marks a new phase where Eva's pleasure will be affirmed.

Jones returns to the site of psychiatric confinement in "Asylum." Published in her 1977 short story collection *White Rat*, "Asylum" is a pithy parable of madness, confinement, resistance, and refusal. The story serves as a powerful companion piece to *Eva's Man*. At the center of "Asylum" is an unnamed black woman detained in a psychiatric hospital for urinating in a first grade classroom in front of a teacher and her own grandnephew. The plot entails a series of antagonistic exchanges between the woman and the hospital personnel who hold her captive.

Within those asylum walls, the protagonist's primary concern is the concealment and protection of her genitalia from the invasive gaze and probe of doctors. She explains: "I know one thing. [The hospital physician] ain't examining me down there. He can examine me anywhere else he wants to, but he ain't touching me down there. . . . I take my clothes off but I leave my bloomers on cause he ain't examining me down there."[88] One wonders whether this unnamed protagonist has experienced sexual violence in the past, whether she comports herself with a vigilance born of trauma.

When she earlier urinates in the classroom, she transgresses prevailing codes of modesty and decency; the result is an act of *indecent exposure*. Later, when she refuses to fully disrobe in the doctor's office, she defies clinical protocols for patient conduct; the result is an act of *insurgent enclosure*, obstructing his access to her body. This woman's "craziness" lies, in part, in her reversal of normative codes of bodily visibility. She exposes herself when expected to remain covered and remains covered when instructed to expose herself.

The woman repeatedly responds to nurses, orderlies, and doctors with acts of refusal and withholding. Just as she denies the physician access to her genitals, she denies hospital personnel access to her inner thoughts. When escorted by a black woman orderly, the protagonist thinks, "You know, I don't belong here, I start to say, but I don't."[89] Recall teenage Eva's refusal to speak in her own defense after stabbing a man who assailed her. Both Eva and this unnamed woman decline opportunities to defend themselves. Perhaps young Eva forgoes proclaiming her innocence because she knows she is presumed criminal. Likewise, this woman may forgo proclaiming her sanity because she knows she is presumed crazy. It seems that the latter is so suspicious of authority that even an assertion of innocence is too great a disclosure.

Hospital personnel practice their own strategic refusal and withholding, repeatedly demurring to explain what they have in store for her. For example, at the start of the story the woman asks the nurses, "When the doctor coming? When I'm getting examined?" but they do not answer or even acknowledge her. She observes, "They don't say nothing all these white nurses."[90] After the woman concedes that her grandnephew was present to witness her urination in the classroom, the doctor

> doesn't comment. He just writes it all down. He says tomorrow they are going to have me write words down, but now they are going to let me go to bed early because I have had a long day.
>
> It ain't as long as it could have been.
>
> What do you mean?
>
> I look at his blue eyes. I say nothing. He acts nervous.[91]

In this brief passage, silences are exchanged in a battle of wills. He silently transcribes her, and then she silently ignores his question. That the doctor "acts" nervous suggests that she might have won this skirmish. Alas, she faces formidable odds because his silence leverages the colossal power of psychiatric authority and hegemonic Reason in an antiblack, antimad world. I have already discussed the insurgent potential within silence. The above passages remind us that the practice of silence can serve as a tool of hegemony, as a technique to withhold recognition and information from subjugated people.

The protagonist eventually complains of a strange ailment: "My niece comes to visit me. I have been here a week. She acts nervous and asks me how I'm feeling. I say I'm feeling real fine except everytime I go sit down on the toilet this long black rubbery thing comes out a my bowls [sic]. It looks like a snake and it scares me. I think it's something they give me in my food."[92] She implies that the "long black rubbery thing" is some parasitic worm exiting her body, introduced into her system by the hospital food. Considered in relation to histories of racist medicine perpetrated against black people, she has cause for paranoia.[93] To put this paranoia in historical perspective, the infamous Tuskegee syphilis experiments were still in process while Jones composed some of the stories included in *White Rat*.[94]

That black rubbery object also appears in a dream, where the doctor "pulled this big black rubbery thing look like a snake out of my pussy and I broke the stirrups and jumped right off the table."[95] This phallic object is lodged within her—but she dreams of expelling it. Using a Freudian dream hermeneutic, we might read that "thing" as a phallic object erupting from inside her, suggesting an ambivalent amalgam of internalization and repulsion regarding male genitalia and the phallic power accorded to men.

When the doctor believes she has made enough progress to warrant less supervision, he and the woman have the following exchange:

> We think you're sociable and won't hurt anybody so we're going to put you on this floor. You can walk around and go to the sun room without too much supervision. You'll have your sessions every week. You'll mostly talk to me, and I'll have you write things down every day. We'll discuss that.
> I'll be in school.

Her announcement that "I'll be in school" might contain a double entendre. Perhaps she likens those daily writing assignments and weekly discussion sessions to (infantilizing) grade school tasks. Perhaps, on another frequency, she tauntingly proposes a return to the scene of her indecency. After all, her conduct in an elementary school classroom was the grounds for her confinement.

She explains that in response, "He says nothing," another weaponization of silence. The woman continues, "I watch him write something down in a book. He thinks I cant [sic] read upside down. He writes about my sexual amorality because I wouldn't let the other doctor see my pussy."[96] When she will not submit to a genital examination, the doctor concludes that her noncompliance indicates "sexual amorality"—possibly, though not necessarily, the doctor's or detainee's malapropism for "sexual immorality." Though her refusal is an act of self-defense, he believes that it is a symptom of shame from a wanton woman afraid of being exposed. If the doctor adheres to the heteropatriarchal, anti-black, sex-negative attitudes prevalent in mid-twentieth-century medicine, his notion of sexual immorality likely encompasses extramarital sex, homosexuality, female sexual autonomy, and any expression of black sexuality.

In addition to these presumptions about her sexuality and morality, the doctor also presumes she is incapable of reading upside down. There is resonant symbolism in this reference to inverted literacy. While reading upside down literally describes her glance at the doctor's paperwork, it might also signify a practice of counterreading—akin to what Walter Benjamin calls reading "against the grain," similar to Jacques Derrida's "deconstruction," in league with bell hooks's "oppositional gaze," and commensurate with my own practice of reading for mad idiom.[97] To read upside down, I propose, is to turn hegemonic logic on its head, to expose its underbelly, to deliberately misread its terms and disobey its instructions, to scramble its syntax, to imagine its top on bottom and its bottom on top, to search for its subversive subtexts, to discover counterdiscourses in its gaps. Indeed, reading upside down, as articulated by this mad black woman in a psychiatric hospital, belongs in the toolkit of mad methodology.

POSTSCRIPT: THE SCENE OF THE CRIME

In a 1979 conversation with Gayl Jones, Claudia Tate notes that the author "refuses to divulge [much] biographical information, contending that her work must live independently of its creator, that it must sustain its own character and artistic autonomy."[98] Adamant about securing the boundary between biographical and fictional matters, Jones explains that "there are some critics who can't separate or don't want to separate the 'persona,' the character's neurosis/psychosis, from the author's psychological autonomy. They feel that the character's preoccupations are those of the author."[99] Such "critics" are liable to view black literature as a sociological window opening into the biographies of black writers, rather than an artistic window opening out toward infinite expanses of black creativity.[100] Heeding these cautions from Tate and Jones—and critically aware that Gayl Jones is *not* Eva Canada and that no confluence should be presumed between the two—I want briefly to touch upon an incident in Jones's life that is pertinent to the matter of madness and black radical subjectivity.

Lucille Jones, mother of Gayl Jones, died in a Kentucky hospital in March 1997. According to hospital officials, cancer was the cause of her death—but

Jones and her husband Bob Jones insisted that Lucille was murdered by hospital personnel in an antiblack conspiracy. Consequently, the wife and husband initiated a series of confrontations and antagonisms with local medical and police authorities. On the morning of February 20, 1998, those clashes reached fever pitch when police arrived at the couple's home under the auspices of serving Bob Jones a fourteen-year-old warrant. (He was charged in 1983 with brandishing a weapon and threatening participants in a Michigan gay pride rally. A warrant had been issued for his arrest, but husband and wife evaded capture by fleeing to France for five years.) According to published reports, the couple barricaded themselves in their house with their gas turned on for a three-hour showdown.[101] By the time the confrontation was over, Bob Jones had allegedly slit his own throat, dying within a day. Gayl Jones was remanded to a psychiatric facility for two weeks, after she reportedly threatened to do harm to herself and others.

What follows is an excerpt from Jones's call to 911 as a police SWAT team assembled outside her home: "If you try to do anything they will have to kill me because I will try to destroy this whole country. . . . I hope the spirit of my mother and the spirit of my African ancestors destroy you, and I hope the spirit of my mother's ancestors and people of color all around the world decide that America is the contemptible and obscene place and destroy every American."[102] Jones speaks a searing malediction. She invokes ancestral spirits and multitudes of people of color worldwide, threatening the dispatcher, the police, all Americans with annihilation. Jones utters a damning exclamation to convey outrage at the racial status quo. She does not describe precisely what makes America so "contemptible" and "obscene," but she may have in mind any number of travesties and atrocities: settler colonialism, chattel slavery, genocide of indigenous peoples, Jim Crow, coup-conspiracies, warmongering, mass incarceration, and so forth, committed under the auspices of American progress and Reason.

Jones's sweeping indictment of American malice returns our attention to the broad systems and structures of violence surrounding Eva. I want to conclude this chapter with an emphatic reminder that Eva's violence cannot be viewed in isolation. There are other murderers stalking the scene of the crime, other "obscene" deeds that demand reckoning. In fact, the modern West is the site of relentless murder, whose conspirators do not fear capture or prosecution; whose perpetrators are unlikely to receive psychotic or psychopathic diagnoses; whose victims are treated with indifference or contempt in mainstream public spheres.

Hortense Spillers describes a strain of symbolic and discursive violence on display in slave ship manifests, plantation ledgers, Civil Rights–era policy recommendations, legal codes, and perennial stereotypes that mutilate blackness. Spillers writes, "Even though the captive flesh/body has been 'liberated,' . . . dominant symbolic activity . . . remains grounded in the originating metaphors of captivity and mutilation so that it is as if neither time nor history . . . shows movement, as the human subject is 'murdered' over and over again."[103] This murderous conspiracy has been perpetrated by other murderers including colonialists, slaveholders, moderate politicians, jurists, philosophers, law enforcement agents, and violent mobs, among others.

Antiblack discursive violence and material violence are constant co-conspirators. Such discourse works to incite, teach, normalize, and justify the state-sanctioned death-dealing at the heart of modern governance, which Achille Mbembe calls *necropolitics*.[104] Mbembe's formulation indicts a massive array of modern technologies of necropower including warfare, slow genocides, prison-industrial complexes, militarized policing, capital punishment, forced sterilization, infrastructural neglect, medical malfeasance, environmental racism, and systemic poverty. In the exercise of necropower, "weapons are deployed in the interest of maximum destruction of persons and the creation of *death-worlds*,"[105] producing a massive underclass of the dispossessed and disposable living dead. Eva treads over terrain "grounded in the original metaphors of captivity and mutilation" and traverses "death-worlds." In order to attend to Eva, it is not enough to isolate an individual *pathology of murder*; we must trace a vast *ecology of death*.

When Eva Canada clamps her jaws to excise some portion of Davis's penis, she commits an act of violence that both manifests and resists the hideous malice that has harmed her for thirty years and more. Her castrating teeth are cut and trained on a steady diet of cruelty—mundane and monumental, intimate and public, symbolic and material, local and global, misogynist and antiblack, profiteering and colonizing, lifelong and death-bound, physical and metaphysical—that has been forced upon her since her youth. Those violent and murderous systems are far more menacing than Eva's awful bite. No intellectual intervention, no public policy, no advocacy platform, no criminal justice agenda, no psychoanalytic diagnostic, no ethico-theological appeal, and no revolutionary upheaval can sufficiently address the murder Eva commits without gazing intently at the murderous regimes above and beneath her. Nor will any such effort succeed unless its agents confront Eva's question, her provocation, her challenge: *How would you feel? What would you do?* And furthermore, if you take up the work of radical compassion, *What* will *you do*?

CHAPTER FOUR

A PORTRAIT OF THE ARTIST
AS A MAD BLACK WOMAN

A ROOM AND A GARDEN

This is all designed for Liliane . . . [She] can come here for the rest of her life and know herself to be one of the most ravishing creatures on earth.

—BLISS LINCOLN, from Ntozake Shange, *Liliane: Resurrection of the Daughter* (1994)

Virginia Woolf, the famed feminist novelist, essayist, and madwoman, proposed in 1929 that every woman writer should have a room of her own: a private space to abscond, dream, and draft in peace.[1] In 1983, the iconoclastic womanist writer Alice Walker urged black women to venture beyond private rooms, search outside for their mothers' gardens, and behold the unsung beauty planted there.[2]

Realizing both Woolf's and Walker's visions, Liliane Lincoln has a room of her own—and her mother's garden, too. The titular heroine of Ntozake Shange's 1994 novel, *Liliane: Resurrection of the Daughter*, she is the only child of an eminent black judge and resplendent black homemaker. Her parents are ostensible models of black respectability who strive to provide her a cloistered girlhood in 1940s and 1950s America. Liliane's father, Judge Parnell Lincoln, carefully presides over his daughter, obliging her to live respectably and become an exemplary race woman. Her mother, Mrs. Sunday Bliss Lincoln, nourishes a free-spirited, starry-eyed dreaminess in the child; Bliss seems to believe that the greatest racial uplift rises on the wings of sublime beauty and lofty imagination. Liliane's room sits in the family's plush home in suburban New Jersey. Meanwhile, her garden blooms in the estate's backyard, a verdant sanctuary where she can return to be reminded of her own beauty and bounty as "one of the most ravishing creatures on earth."[3] If the garden signifies Liliane's youth, her mother tends the flowers (the "Lili" most precious among them) while her father keeps watch at the fence around it.

No matter her class privilege and parental protection, Liliane is vulnerable to racist-sexist forces that menace black girlhood, whether in the form of state-sanctioned antiblack violence in public or misogynist vitriol she sees her father hurl at her mother in private. Furthermore, the pressures of respectability on a black girl in the 1940s and 1950s—Liliane confesses, "We were never children, we were the future of the race"—incite elaborate rites of repression and sublimation.[4] Heir to her mother's whimsical dreaminess and her father's neurotic intensity, Liliane grows up to become a painter, sculptor, performance artist, world traveler, rapturous lover, adamant defender of black and feminine dignity, psychoanalytic patient, and exquisite sublimator. Her madness is an *unruliness* of mind, which she variously describes as a "roar" inside her head, a feeling of existential vertigo, and a sensation of strangulation. It is also an intense *rage* against misogynist and antiblack antagonisms; a *medicalized* process entailing regular visits to a mental health clinician; and the psychosocial *alterity* of brazen black female sexuality that unabashedly flouts respectable psychonorms.

If Liliane's madness supplies much of the novel's *substance*, her effort to manage madness shapes the novel's *structure*. Regarding that structure, the book's episodic configuration mimics patterns in Liliane's life: She embarks on a series of grand adventures interspersed with visits to her analyst; likewise, the book is a series of epic chapters partitioned by scenes of psychoanalysis. Those psychoanalytic scenes serve to sort, frame, and orient the novel much like analysis serves to sort, frame, and orient Liliane's marvelously unruly self. Meanwhile, the *style* of the book—especially the prose-poetry of chapters written from Liliane's perspective—might be read as the fruit of sublimation, madness made gorgeous language art. More broadly, the novel portrays a series of sublimations performed by Liliane's jurist father, her epicurean mother, her macho lover Victor-Jésus, and her mad friend Hyacinthe Malveaux, among others. The book is populated by black folks performing various rituals of sublimation, consciously and unconsciously, with intense intentionality and oblivious roteness, with great ease and fierce struggle. Throughout the world of the novel, madness is raw material that is carved, stroked, strewn, tuned, burnished, finessed, and alchemized into goods like art, etiquette, capital, and respectability.[5]

In this chapter, my missions are to elaborate how madness infuses *Liliane*'s substance, structure, and style; to chart complex interrelations of crazy and creativity in the novel; and examine its kaleidoscopic portrait of the artist as a mad black woman.

The author of at least nineteen collections of poetry, six novels, five children's books, and sixteen plays, Ntozake Shange is most widely known for her Obie Award–winning choreopoem, *for colored girls who have considered suicide / when the rainbow is enuf*. Shange's writings, including *for colored girls* and *Liliane*, frequently foreground the creative, sexual, and political milieus of black artist-heroines.[6] *Liliane* was published in 1994, eighteen years after Gayl Jones published *Eva's Man*. Both novels should be counted among a remarkable efflorescence of US black women's literature from the 1970s through the 1990s. In this period, black women novelists in the United States achieved unprecedented critical and commercial success, while black feminist literary critics generated a paradigm-shifting corpus of scholarship interpreting those novels.[7] Also during this era, the "feminist sex wars" were waged with especial fervor. Contingents of "sex-positive" feminists and "antipornography" feminists debated the merits of pleasure-centric politics, pornography, sex work, and bondage, discipline, dominance, submission, and sadomasochism (BDSM), questioning whether these could be woman-empowering in the late twentieth century.[8]

While writing *Liliane*—and impacted by the light and heat generated by those critical frictions and conflagrations—Shange described the book's protagonist as "an existential feminist," "politically committed," and "very sensually alive." According to Shange, Liliane is "so vitally committed to experiencing herself and having those experiences impact on the world around her that she doesn't really leave us thinking that she is wanting for too much or that she's unable to fend for herself. She's a real challenge to write about and, on the other hand, real gratifying, because more often than not she gets what she wants."[9] In Liliane's lifeworld, the personal process of "experiencing herself" is also the politicized and public work of "impact[ing] the world around her." Existentially feminist, she embodies and blackens the feminist axiom that the personal, including the sexual, is always political.

Liliane's existential feminism contrasts with Eva's ambiguity and aloofness vis-à-vis many feminisms.[10] I invoke Eva here, and will occasionally reinvoke her in this chapter, to juxtapose these two fictional women. For now, I want to elaborate a few stark distinctions between them. Whereas Eva's agency is rooted in instrumental silence, Liliane dreads silence and finds empowerment in bountiful, lyrical language. Whereas Eva is withdrawn and withholding, a defensive disposition amid constant predation, Liliane's exuberance emanates into her world, often changing its atmospheres and charming its inhabitants.

Eva's Man—which frequently entwines sex with hurtful violence, male sexuality with predatory sadism, and female sexuality with victimization—might be treated as evidence in an antipornography or sex-negative agenda. Meanwhile, *Liliane*'s portrait of avowedly liberated, pleasurable sexuality lends itself to a sex-positive ethos and manifests femme and feminist sexual agency. When Liliane proclaims, "I look at men and take some home or leave the country, borders have never intimidated me," her words read like a slogan of sexual autonomy, diasporic and cosmopolitan praxis, and joyfully wayward womanhood.[11]

In delineating these disparities between Eva and Liliane, I do not mean to pit them against each other as ontological foils or ideological adversaries. Rather, I view the two as representational complements who collectively cover an expansive ground to reveal vicissitudes of mad black womanhood between metaphor and murder. And besides, there are many affinities between the two. Both are black women, born circa 1940, who are structurally vulnerable to antiblackness and misogyny. Both are driven by wanderlust that keeps them from settling down into heteronormative domesticity. Both refuse to comply with respectable womanhood and are consequently marked as "crazy" in the milieus they inhabit.

More provocatively, I want to propose that both share an antagonistic relationship to the *P/phallus*: Eva mutilates a *literal penis*, while Liliane subverts the matrix of patriarchal power, subject-formation, language regulation, and hegemonic social relations that Lacanian psychoanalysis associates with the (Symbolic) *Phallus*. Of course, Eva's dental castration of the penis of a man she just murdered is a long, far cry from Liliane's sexually adventurous womanhood.[12] I do not intend to conflate these drastically different deeds. Rather, I mean to emphasize that both acts—biting off a section of a penis and having the gall to be woman and fuck whomever you please—are regarded, in the gendered worlds these women occupy, as symptoms of pathology. More pointedly, both acts might be said to mark the end of the P/phallus, where "end" signifies *its fleshly tip*, *its political limit*, and *the thought of its abolition*.

THE THEATER OF HER UNCONSCIOUS

Ntozake Shange was an enthusiastic advocate of psychoanalysis who believed that it helped her become a "finer writer and a fuller person."[13] It is no wonder, then, that talk therapy informs key aspects of *Liliane*. The novel stages scenes of psychoanalysis and invites psychoanalytic readings of its contents. Twelve such scenes—each entitled "A Room in the Dark" and preceded by a Roman numeral, "I" through "XII"—stand like pillars between chapters, scaffolding and partitioning the novel. Whereas the plot trots the globe and traverses decades, these dark scenes always occupy the same undisclosed space in hour-long sessions during Liliane's adulthood. The sessions are a stabilizing routine amid the flux of Liliane's lifeworld. No matter how far she journeys, she faithfully returns to that darkened room; it is a pit stop for rumination and revelation between adventures.

Depicted only in that darkened room, Liliane's analyst is enigmatic. Scant information is revealed about him beyond his profession and his maleness. His name is never disclosed, his history is never illuminated, his visage is always shrouded in shadow, and his appearance is hardly described. The single description of his corporeality comes during a session when Liliane muses on what it might be like to marry him. She decides that he's "too dark" to garner her family's approval, hinting at the blackness of her analyst while divulging the colorism that governs matrimony among her kin.

Liliane's remark about the analyst's marriageability is one of many occasions when she regards him as an object of romantic and erotic intrigue. Perhaps the dimness of the room conjures romance for Liliane and inspires amorous transference during their sessions. She often professes attraction to the analyst and flirts with him. In response, he deftly redirects each come-on into an opportunity to probe the psychoanalytic significance of her attraction. With great subtlety and care, he assists her in excavating childhood trauma, reckoning with family drama, unpacking her romantic baggage, assessing her friendships, critiquing her own art, and coming to terms with her wonderful, terrible unruliness. This "dark" man in a "darkened" room doubly evokes opacity, even as he helps Liliane achieve clarity. He inhabits and engenders a *radiant dark*, reminding us that a scene of opacity can be a site and source of clarity, that revelation can emerge in shadowy spaces, that some subtle truths are easier to behold under the cover of night than in a blaze of sunshine. Insofar as the analyst is enigmatic, appears exclusively in that shadowy room, and interacts with no one but Liliane, he sometimes resembles a (genial) phantom.

These dark scenes are transcribed as lines of dialogue without quotation marks, without narrative rumination, but interspersed with bracketed descriptions of physical actions, the latter like stage directions. Consequently, the therapy passages resemble scripts, a format that emphasizes their theatricality and the general drama of the Freudian model. Indeed, psychoanalysis is aptly captioned with theatrical metaphors: it generates *scripts* of inquiry and disclosure; it *stages* dramatic revelations; it induces transference, which *casts* the analyst in *roles* of various figures in the patient's life; it hinges upon the analyst's perception of symptomatic *cues* that reveal the patient's hidden impulses; it positions the latent contents of the unconscious as *backstage* events; and it erects special *scenery* (like a darkened room or an office with a comfortable couch) for its purposes.[14]

In these dialogues, long dashes appear to indicate a switch in speaker as the two exchange questions and answers about Liliane's psychic life. Sometimes a dash appears with no language thereafter, signaling an instant of silence, or what theatrical parlance might label as a beat-length pause. On occasion, several dashes appear consecutively, one above the other, as pauses are exchanged. The first seven lines of the novel all entail silence, each containing either an emptiness *performing* silence or a verbal statement *describing* silence. They appear as follows:

—

—

—Maybe it's not the silences.

—

—Not the silences that bother me.

—

—It's just the noise like a roar inside my head takes over when it's silent.[15]

The very first line of the book, Liliane's, is a dash followed by a blank space that indicates silence. The second line, her analyst's, contains yet another marker of silence. In the third line, Liliane speaks the first words of the novel, "Maybe it's not the silences," referencing something that might or might not be caused by silence. The next quartet of lines are as follows: another beat of silence from her analyst, then another comment concerning silence from Liliane, then another marker of the analyst's silence, then another statement on silence from Liliane.[16] By staging these expressions of and about silence, Shange prompts the reader to pay closer attention to wordless spaces and soundless intervals—to ponder their meanings, uses, and effects.

Liliane's analyst touts the therapeutic efficacy of silence and the communicative potential in wordlessness. In these opening lines of the book, each of his silent responses prompts Liliane to continue, challenges her to finish her thought without answer or affirmation from him, and allows her to build conversational momentum on her own. Soon after, the analyst imparts that "sometimes our work is talking. Sometimes our work is simply being, experiencing feelings and thoughts we've put so far away we have no words for them."[17] He understands that some sensations resist verbalization, but can still be processed in silent and meditative presence. Guided by such principles, he conducts a psychoanalytic practice that honors silence, accommodates it, lingers in it, encourages it, and indexes it within a glossary of communicative tools.

After affirming the power of "simply being" with "no words," he continues, "Then, the silence and our breathing allow these feelings to find the shapes and sounds of the words we need."[18] For all his insistence upon the importance of silence, he finally positions it as vestibular to speech: a space of preparation before the reinstatement of language, before the all-important arrival of "the words we need." The analyst endorses a *silent treatment*, so to speak, but ultimately places faith in a *talking cure*. However, there are some silences that cannot ever be shaped and sounded into resonant words. In the previous chapter, Dori Laub, Aliyyah Abdur-Rahman, and Eva Canada all highlighted occasions of traumatized silence that refuses to give way to speech. Some silences are the effect of events so utterly traumatic, or strange, or sublime that they dissolve discourse, elude language, and refuse translation. There are occasions when words are not needed, words are not adequate, words are not possible, and words simply fail.

Liliane also knows how unyielding silence can be. She confesses that "I can't breathe in silence" because silence "presses down on me like a man who doesn't know his own weight can fuck me to death cause literally he's also blocking my esophagus."[19] Liliane personifies silence as a hulking man who not only ties her tongue but blocks her esophagus, who could inadvertently suffocate her under the massive weight of his body, who could be a lover suddenly turned killer, who could "fuck [her] to death."

It turns out that her association of silence with suffocation originates in an event of violent trauma, an incident when an ex-lover strangled her on the street. Silence is a trigger, thrusting her back in time to this terrible scene:

> The bastard tried to choke me right at Sheridan Square the night my show opened, he spit on the sidewalk, turned round, and wrapped his fingers bout my neck like I was a magnum of Perrier & Jouet. . . . Now, whenever a melody ends, I feel his fingers on my throat. . . . People walked past, went across the street to the park. And nobody said anything. Did anything. The traffic kept comin', cars to New Jersey and cabs with medallions kept movin'. I heard the downtown IRT and all. Outta nowhere I heard him screamin', "Who do you think you are?" and . . . I couldn't breathe. So I couldn't answer. . . . I couldn't answer.[20]

The assault takes place just after the debut of one of her art exhibitions. When he chokes her, he stifles her breath, her voice, and her joy in artistic achievement. Later, the unnamed assailant becomes a malicious apparition conjured whenever melodies end. Significantly, the silence in this scene is not merely Liliane's asphyxiated wordlessness. It is also the apathetic or fearful silence of passersby who neither speak nor act in her defense.

Liliane also admits that "when it's really silent, I can't feel anything. I mean, I start to lose where the floor is. Why a flower is different from a rug, you know to feel, or even that walls don't curl under themselves like cats."[21] To have her tell it, sound grounds her; it is an anchor that moors her to the world and its objects. Put otherwise, sound binds Liliane into a familiar and stable Symbolic Order, where flowers bloom and walls stand stiff. Absolute silence sends Liliane into a dreamy chaos, hurls her into a Symbolic *Disorder*, where a flower might flatten and spread like a rug or a wall might purr and saunter like a kitten. Gently, the analyst invites Liliane to embrace the unstable sensation that overtakes her in silence. She might grope and flounder and stumble, but these acts can be processes of discovery. He seems confident that she will eventually get her bearings, orient herself, catch her breath, speak needed words, and find her way.

But if silence makes walls "curl under themselves," it might prove useful to linger in absolute quiet for a while. Perhaps, in the absence of sound, some especially oppressive wall will curl under itself and fall, thus clearing the way for Liliane's next discovery or adventure. Because this Symbolic Disorder deviates so drastically from the Reasonable world, it might be rich ground to cultivate radical creativity—to imagine liberated futures utterly unlike the present reign of Reason.

RESURRECTION OF THE MOTHER: DEATH, BLISS, AND MADNESS

The most formative trauma in Liliane's life is likely the "death" of her mother, Sunday Bliss Lincoln, commonly called Bliss. Her mother's name is a trilogy of cheery signifiers in the Lincoln lifeworld: "Sunday" evokes the hallowed relaxation of the Sabbath, especially salient in their respectable black church milieu; "Bliss" signifies intense joy; and "Lincoln" is the surname of the sixteenth president of the United States, commonly overpraised as emancipator of enslaved black people in 1864. In so naming Bliss, Shange makes the mere mention of her name an overdetermined announcement of good tidings.[22]

Bliss displays enough bohemian eccentricity and nonconformity to ruffle the feathers of her black bourgeois peers, but also enough charm and finesse to smooth them over. As Liliane's best friend Roxie divulges, "S. Bliss did as she pleased and she seemed to please most folks most of the time."[23] Liliane's early rapport with her mother is exemplified by the following rendezvous over breakfast during Liliane's childhood: "Liliane and S. Bliss exchanged flowers at the breakfast table. Lili handed her mother drawings of the blossoms Bliss groomed. And then Bliss laid a flower in Lili's palm. . . . When their eyes met, Bliss giggled like a precocious child, raised her left eyebrow a bit, hugged Lili, and turned jauntily to Parnell, saying: 'What a delight to the eye you are this mornin' my sweet darlin.'"[24] The two coo pretty, giddy words to one another and perform courtly rites of affection. The effects of their florid words are redoubled when they exchange drawings of flowers and actual flowers. The latter are plucked from that mother's garden, that patch of soil meant to grow her daughter's imagination and nourish her self-esteem.

A matrilineal garden is invoked in Alice Walker's monumental 1974 essay, "In Search of Our Mothers' Gardens," referenced at the start of this chapter. Walker sketches a brief biographical account of her own mother, Minnie Lou Tallulah Grant Walker, and explains that "my mother adorned with flowers whatever shabby house we were forced to live in. . . . Because of her creativity with her flowers, even my memories of poverty are seen through a screen of blooms—sunflowers, petunias, roses, dahlias, forsythia, spirea, delphiniums, verbena. . . . And I remember people coming to my mother's yard to be given cuttings from her flowers. . . . whatever rocky soil she landed on, she turned into a garden."[25] Beyond her genius for horticulture, Minnie Walker was a black woman born in Georgia in 1912, a domestic worker, the wife of a sharecropper, and the mother of eight children. Sunday Bliss Lincoln's lot in life would seem far easier to till, since she is married to a New Jersey judge with only one child to raise and access to rarefied bourgeois privilege and wealth. Still, Mrs. Walker and Mrs. Lincoln are both black women navigating antiblack, patriarchal worlds, black women who make gardens on those lots to inspire their artist daughters.

Bliss instills in her daughter an idyllic, utopic sensibility when others believe she should be training Liliane in the pragmatic logistics of respectable black girlhood. Bliss's worldlier sister Aurelia laments, "You can't build all this for no child, especially in this day and age. Why she can't even drink water some places. Plus, hear me now, if she carries on like you, she'll be dead before either one of us: me or you. How's that sit with your fancy ways and dreamin's?"[26]

Behind her bouquets of ornate words and gestures, Bliss secretly resents all the pageantry and disdains Liliane. Strolling through the garden she has grown for her daughter, Bliss confesses to her sister, "I'm sick of it. I'm sick of all of it. The posturin', and frontin', the fuckin' grandeur of it. I'm sick. Sick and tired of it all." She continues, "And dammit, look at her. She doesn't even look like a LaFontaine [Bliss's maiden name]. Look at her, dammit. I can't even imagine how she's related to me. I can't. I can't explain how she happened. I can't I just can't."[27] She feels so alienated from her daughter that she imagines the girl to be a stranger, a baffling accident of mismatched progeny. Bliss's melodramatic mothering is an elaborate ruse to conceal motherly contempt. Bliss has sublimated her angst to build castles in the sky and gardens in the backyard as buffers between herself and Liliane.

Bliss resembles the image of the black middle class described by sociologist E. Franklin Frazier in his 1957 polemic *Black Bourgeoisie*. Bliss's garden confession likely took place in the mid-to-late 1950s, around the time that Frazier's tome was published. In a searing critique of America's black middle class, Frazier writes that "despite the tinsel, glitter and gaiety of the world of make-believe in which middle-class Negroes take refuge, they are still beset by feelings of insecurity, frustration and guilt. As a consequence, the free and easy life which they appear to lead is a mask for their unhappy existence."[28] He argues that a peculiar madness ails the black bourgeoisie: a breach from reality that keeps them from confronting their staggering self-doubt and insecurity; a sort of delusional disorder inducing elaborate rites of "make-believe." For all of Frazier's totalizing hyperbole about black middle class, he describes Bliss with uncanny accuracy. Her "fancy ways and dreamin's" closely resemble Frazier's "make-believe." Furthermore, her revelation in the garden is the removal of "a mask of [her] unhappy existence" to reveal a "sick and tired" scowl underneath.

When Bliss leaves Parnell for a white man, her community deems it far more egregious than mundane adultery. Liliane and her analyst discuss how:

> my mommy, S. Bliss, knew it was better for us to see her dead than to see her with a white man.
> —How is that, Lili?
> —Cause you could forgive someone for dying, but not for runnin' off with one of them. I would have been, oh my God, I would have been "blacklisted," of all things. It's like having a baby out of wedlock. The black bourgeoisie takes these things very seriously.
> —Are you saying a whole community would have turned against a child?
> —We were never children, we were the future of the race.[29]

According to the moral codes of that community, Bliss's interracial infidelity is an act of racial treason, an unforgivable crime against respectable blackness.[30] Liliane also ponders the scandal from her father's perspective, proclaiming that "white people made my father kill off my mother, take my mother away from me. It was such an affront to his 'manhood,' his 'dignity,' that he couldn't allow my mother to live in the house with a white man in her heart."[31] Invested in patriarchal "manhood"—but never wholly allowed to possess it or exercise its prerogatives because of his blackness—Parnell's masculinity is always already agonized. The notion of a white man stealing his wife, confiscating what patriarchy insists is his conjugal property, is unbearable for the judge. He would rather see her "dead."

This death is not biological. Instead, it is an irrevocable expulsion from the family and community where Bliss once held high status. Liliane recounts her father's vitriol and her own sorrow when Bliss leaves: "Daddy said she had to go and to forget she ever had a daughter. Forget she had me, or he'd see her rot in jail. Unfit! Slut! Tramp! Whore! Rot in jail! She's going to Hell. Mommy, Mommy, why didn't you take me? Mommy, Mommy, come get me, Mommy. Daddy said she's dead, she's dead. Better. Sluts can't raise children. Sluts run off with their lovers and die. They die and they can't take their children. I can't go with Mommy. She's dead."[32] In a sinister parody of the judicial process, Parnell charges his wife with being "Unfit! Slut! Tramp! Whore!" He prosecutes her, arguing that "sluts can't raise children." He finally sentences her to "death" for her alleged transgressions against race, respectability, patriarchy, matrimony, and maternity. Bliss seems to accept this sentence and promptly disappears, perhaps relieved to leave behind all the trappings of grandeur—including her only daughter. Notably, Parnell does not attempt to physically assault Bliss. Maybe the judge is too savvy about the law—and too invested in his persona as a righteous, respectable, Reasonable man—to commit prosecutable violence. Instead, he assaults her verbally and murders her symbolically.

Parnell is a fascinating case study in sublimation in his own right. Although this chapter is primarily concerned with art as sublimation's output, it is important to emphasize that politics, athletics, religiosity, and, in this case, *the law* are also frequent fruits of sublimation. Who knows what murderous contempt Parnell has alchemized into judicial authority? Who knows what furious energy animates his arm when he slams down a gavel, and whether that arm longs to pummel and throttle instead? Especially telling is the judge's use of the term *unfit*, with its legalistic connotations, to curse his wife. His word choice suggests convergences of professional duty and personal fury.

Consider Parnell's screed alongside that formative scene from Eva's childhood when her father attacks her mother:

"Act like a whore, I'm gonna fuck you like a whore. You act like a whore, I'm gonna fuck you like a whore."

He kept saying that over and over. I was so scared. I kept feeling that after he tore all her clothes off, and there wasn't anymore to tear, he'd start tearing her flesh.[33]

Both of these scenes depict rituals of punitive misogyny punctuated by the invective "whore." Eva's father violently draws his wife *near*, into their bedroom and against his body in vicious closeness. In contrast, Liliane's father pronounces his wife "dead" to eject her *away* from home and community. By the time Eva hears her mother abused, she has already become accustomed to ruthless abuse of women and girls; it is disturbing and dreadful, but doesn't produce the peculiar terror of the unfamiliar. For Liliane, whose family unit had erstwhile seemed so picture perfect, her father "kill[ing] off" her mother inflicts unprecedented shock and devastation. It also initiates her motherless adolescence.

As an adult artist, Liliane attempts to sublimate orphanly anguish into beautiful art. In a talk therapy session centering on her absent mother, Liliane "pulls out a small book" and confesses, "This is our book, me and Mommy, I mean, Sunday Bliss. She wrote me some letters that I never told you about cause I wanted to make them something, anything I could hold, before I shared her with anybody. She's my mother. I love her. I want some of her for myself, that's all . . . See, these are parts of the letters Mommy sent me that I glued onto pages here and then drew or painted around them my feelings. That's why I figured we'd have a book of our own, something we made together."[34] Liliane creates a scrapbook-*cum*-art journal: a palimpsestic assemblage of her mother's letters ornamented by Liliane's own loving doodles. Everything is pressed in place and held together with glue, the paper and paint adhering, though mother and daughter do not. The scrapbook is an aesthetic representation of the communion that Liliane longs to share with her mother. If only the scrapbook held enough stickiness to seal a mother-daughter bond, or enough beauty to lure her Bliss back home, or the power to resurrect her mother from the "dead." *Liliane: resurrection of the mother*.

HER IRREPRESSIBLE GLOW

The phrase *go out of one's mind* implies that the mind is an enclosure or container. Presumably, to stray outside the enclosure is to enter a mad wilderness; to spill from the container is to be mired in a mad mess. Presently, I want to ponder Liliane's propensity to breach and overflow the enclosures of domesticity, nation, propriety, body, and sanity erected around her.

Like Eva, Liliane is a peripatetic woman who refuses to plant deep roots in any particular locale. Both Eva and Liliane eschew conjugal-maternal domesticity and move outside the heteronormative home sphere. Eva's roaming seems propelled by economic necessity (she works as an itinerant laborer), alienated rootlessness, and post-traumatic restlessness (after so much predation, she prefers to be a moving target rather than a stationary one). Liliane is driven by a diasporic impulse, a bohemian search for beauty, a cosmopolitan commitment to worldwide belonging, and her own post-traumatic restlessness in search of a lost mother. Liliane's waywardness breaks the white picket fence that respectable patriarchy would enclose around her. She muses, and I repeat, "I travel a lot. I look at men and take some home or leave the country, borders have never intimidated me. My passport is in order and I carry lines of credit, perfume, four fancy dresses and six nightgowns. I always sleep naked alone at least once a week. I pray and say hail marys by some window at dusk."[35]

Literary theorist Brent Hayes Edwards theorizes diaspora as a dynamic range of practices and ways of being that do not respect borders but rather roves across national, continental, oceanic, and other thresholds. Liliane is an especially artful practitioner of diaspora who embodies what Edwards calls "vagabond internationalism": a diasporic life that is "'loose' and joyous," "inherently . . . open and wandering,"[36] and a "vibrant resistance" to the rigid structures, like the nation-state and the picket fence, that partition modernity.[37]

Edwards's notion is influenced by Claude McKay's description of "the vagabond lover of life" in the 1929 novel *Banjo*: "The vagabond lover of life finds individuals and things to love in many places and not in any one nation. . . . Man loves place and no one place, for the earth, like a beautiful wanton, puts on a new dress to fascinate him wherever he may go."[38] In the world McKay depicts, the "vagabond lover" is a man, while the earth beneath him is feminine and "wearing many dresses." Liliane subverts the gendered essentialism of McKay's construction. On the one hand, with her own "four fancy dresses" in tow, Liliane favors that feminized earth. On the other hand, insofar as she "finds individuals and things to love in many places and not in one nation," she also resembles that masculinized vagabond.[39] Thus Liliane breaches and dissolves the patriarchal dichotomy that opposes the feminine-passive-earth with the masculine-assertive-explorer.

On one of those diasporic jaunts, Liliane finds herself in Paris, at a fast-food eatery next to the Moulin Rouge, where she meets a Guadeloupean called Jean-Rene. She will take him as a lover. Of their initial encounter, Liliane muses, "I always assume people can smell how happy I am, how full of love I can be. That's how Jean-Rene found me in Paris at that fast-food souvlaki place. He could smell my joy, he said."[40] No matter the aromas of seasoned meats floating through the restaurant, Liliane's scent prevails and pulls Jean-Rene toward her. Liliane's joy and love generate a scent, like an enchanted emission of pheromones. Recall that in *Eva's Man*, Davis announced to Eva, "I could smell you wanted me."[41] His claim was part of an invidious pattern of men projecting desire onto Eva (most citing her gaze; Davis citing her gaze and smell) to justify their aggression. Eva's supposed scent might have been the fabrication of a predatory man, but Liliane claims her fragrant joy and love as elements of her own ontology.

Not only does Liliane's "love" exude a fragrance, it radiates a light, too. In one of her talk therapy sessions, she describes a dream of a fancy ball: "I was having a wonderful time, sort of like Scarlett O'Hara at that first party at Seven Oaks. Well, I felt unbearably gorgeous, when suddenly I realized my clit was glowing, I mean like silver neon lights in Las Vegas, my pussy was beaming artificial light all over this very delicate and elegant fête. No matter how I held myself, what contortions I forced my body into. The glow was irrepressible."[42] I read this dream as an allegory for an intense feminine and feminist desire that resists concealment, bursts beyond interiority, and permeates the space and people around it. This scene epitomizes Shange's description of the character: Here, Liliane is "experiencing herself [including her radiant vagina] and having those experiences impact the world [including partygoers bathed in neon light] around her."

I want to emphasize that Liliane's sex generates an "irrepressible glow" in this dream sequence. The word *irrepressible* brings to mind the Freudian notion of repression, a process that thrusts unruly memories, thoughts, and emotions into the unconscious. Liliane's sex will not be repressed in a darkened basement of the unconscious; it will shine in fancy ballrooms. Note that Liliane likens herself to Scarlett O'Hara, the protagonist of Margaret Mitchell's plantation fantasy novel-*cum*-blockbuster film, *Gone with the Wind*.[43] Scarlett is arguably the most famous representation of a "Southern belle" and slave mistress in the history of American popular culture—an icon of aristocratic, antebellum, ornately gowned, tightly corseted white femininity. Shange lampoons that iconography by overwhelming it with the bling of a clitoris. Liliane's shining sex becomes a metonym for brazen sexuality, disrupting the bourgeois and patriarchal repressions and niceties that governed her youth. Liliane's female sexuality is neither a site of lack nor a cause for (penis) envy, as Freud might aver. To the contrary, Liliane's "pussy" is a pleasurable and irrepressible plenitude. *Her sex is not dearth—it is abundance.*

Liliane ponders that irrepressible sex during her escapade with Jean-Rene: "If only my mother could see me now: Jean-Rene meticulously placing strawberries, blueberries, kiwis, grapes, melon balls in a crescent around my vulva. Oh dear. Oh dear. Oh dear. My cat has yellow eyes. Now my pussy has lime-green ones, amber pupils, slits."[44] Remember that *Eva's Man* figuratively fused female reproductive organs with scrambled eggs, a man's disfigured thumb with pigs' feet, and a mutilated penis with bitten fruit, all in a matrix of grotesque transubstantiations. But sex and fruit meet joyfully in this scene: Liliane's vulva is the cornucopia in a merry feast.

Liliane and Jean-Rene make their way to Casablanca and make love atop a cliff. While painting a watercolor tableau "using wine as water to moisten [her] paints" and drifting down from an orgasmic high, Liliane announces, "I feel a sharp pain in my groin, my heart is racing, I am losing my breath. I see Jean-Rene. His eyes are glazed over as if in a trance. I swoon. My blood has come. The forces of this sacred earth have drawn menses from my body. The sun sets. I use this last liquid to highlight the figures in my painting."[45] Menstrual blood is rife with symbolism for both Eva and Liliane. Whereas Eva's menses made her "nasty" in Davis's judgment and "not good" by her own account, Liliane's menstrual blood is regarded reverently, a substance summoned from her body by the "sacred earth," and a material for artmaking. Liliane describes a series of liquids—wine, water, blood, and paint—variously surrogated for one another. When Liliane replaces paint with menstrual blood, she intermingles the stuff of artistic creation and the material of biological procreation. When Liliane replaces water with wine to wet her paints, she evokes Christ's miracle of changing water to wine at a wedding party, per the Christian gospels. For Liliane, menses is both sacred and aesthetic. In the New Testament, the word becomes flesh.[46] In *Liliane*, (menstrual) blood becomes picture.

Notwithstanding her joyful emissions of fragrant love, clitoral light, and sacred menses, Liliane's effusive quality is not always fun. It sometimes leaves her depleted and distressed. In another dark room session, a panicked Liliane confesses that "I'm coming out of my body. . . . Parts of me, my feelings are streaming out of my hands and thighs. I sense when I am walking that my thoughts are dripping down my calves from behind my knees. I am leaving puddles of myself underneath me and I can't pick myself back up, put myself back together."[47] Whereas the glow that radiated from her sex seemed inexhaustible, here she describes an emanation that is utterly exhausting.

Liliane's complaint of this "streaming" sensation precedes her confession that she once terminated a pregnancy. Her analyst interprets those dripping and streaming dreams to be repetitive-compulsive invocations of the abortion, asking, "Are the puddles of yourselves mixed up with the lost baby?"[48] In answering his question, Liliane decries the pressure to mother that interpellates and inundates many women. She replies, "I never did like to see women with babies. They looked so beat-down, covered with baby equipment, just mommy, not a woman with a name or feelings, like a pack animal or something. I don't have any place to put a baby."[49] Liliane views motherhood (or at least motherhood with small children) as a series of burdens, indignities, and diminutions of a woman's humanity. Ironically, Liliane seems to inherit this disdain for mothering from her very own mother. It appears to be part of their mother-daughter resemblance.

Foregrounding the "crazy" quality of Liliane's angst, her analyst replies, "You brought your crazy selves, that were falling away from you here. Maybe, this is their home. The slipping parts of you may need to be somewhere puddles of feelings aren't out of place."[50] He designates their psychoanalytic jurisdiction as a refuge where her "crazy selves" can dwell peacefully. He promises to maneuver the psychoanalytic apparatus like a receptacle to catch that dissolution, but it might be futile. The smell of Liliane's joy, the glow of her pussy, the blood-made-pigment from her womb, the parts of herself slipping down her legs, and the unruliness of her mind: these are all occasions in which Liliane overflows containers meant to hold her. A portrait of the artist as a mad black woman won't be kept in a tidy frame.

"SHOULDA CUT THE MUTHAFUCKAH": HURTING LOVE

Liliane's most passionate love affair is with Victor-Jésus María, an Afro-Latino photographer who takes literal portraits of the artist as a young woman and attempts to metaphysically frame and crop who he sees. In the novel, Victor-Jésus is the most prominently featured of Liliane's lovers and the only male narrator.

The two first meet on the streets of the Lower East Side of Manhattan when he suddenly begins to snap pictures of her without permission. Victor-Jésus is a charismatic man who garners Liliane's intense and abiding affection. He is also a brazen sexist chauvinist and antagonist who incites her madness—both anger and unruliness. Victor-Jésus would like to subjugate Liliane, including on the registers of language and speech. He proclaims, "Now I'm a nice fella but I had to get her to where she spoke my language; I had to get her to where she knew wasn't anybody could understand her but me. Nobody could insist that particular tongue but me. Ever. Not a soul."[51] In Lacanian psychoanalysis, the "Name of the Father" is a patriarchal regime composed of "laws and restrictions that control both your desire and the rules of communication."[52] It would seem that Victor-Jésus is a self-deputized enforcer of his own version of these laws. He would like to render Liliane illegible to others so that he can be her sole confidant and have exclusive access to her inner self.

He'd like to control her vision, too—to crop her worldview like he crops the borders of a photograph—but he realizes that his efforts are futile. He admits, "She saw the most pristine forms, dazzling color in anythin'. She felt the texture of stuff: rice, skin, water, the ringlets of black naps on my chest. I couldn't have forced her vision to be any less, but I tried til it was no more use."[53] He is bound to fail because of Liliane's extraordinary propensity for bursting through containers and frames. If he ever *has* Liliane, it is because she willfully and provisionally gives in to him. He recalls, "I used to have her, regular, wild, relentless and soft as a tropical surf. My Liliane, she said she couldn't keep giving in like that. . . . She called it giving in. I called it being mine. She said it was ontologically impossible."[54] The sheer force of Liliane's ontology—especially her will to freedom and urge to wander—cannot be possessed by Victor-Jésus, no matter his schemes.

When Victor-Jésus's machismo incites Liliane's "existential feminist" rage, the outcome is explosive. He explains, "She'd jump up and call me every lowdown exploitative muthafuckah in the world. It was '*chingathis*' and '*chingathat.*' 'I'll be damned if it ain't some sick-assed voyeuristic photographer thinks his art is nourished by a woman's tears.' 'Suck it, niggah,' she'd scream, or sometimes she'd say, 'Suck it, spic,' when she was really mad. . . . She'd go stormin' out saying, 'My art is not dependent on fuckin' you or hurtin' you.'"[55] Antagonized by Victor-Jésus's chauvinism, Liliane snaps. She goes mad (as in crazy) and gets mad (as in angry). If Audre Lorde were to witness this outburst, she might remind us that "anger is loaded with information and energy."[56] Indeed, Liliane's anger informs and energizes a scathing rebuke of misogyny. She mobilizes mad idiom—here, a series of furious phrases and shouted obscenities— to condemn a sadistic, scopophilic male gaze that feeds upon female pain. She frames Victor-Jésus's art as failed sublimation because its malice has not been converted to anything like innocuous art; rather, his "sick-assed voyeuristic" photography is its own act of violence. To wit, both Liliane and Victor-Jésus are mad in this scene. His madness perpetrates misogynist injury while her madness animates feminist insurgency.

Victor-Jésus's outrageous bids for dominance are cushioned between palliative expressions of fondness and passion. During one of their peaceable periods, Liliane and Victor-Jésus collaborate in guerrilla performance art alongside a California highway. He explains:

> Here we are working on Lili's new project: being the living tissue of lost ancestors in graves she digs along the Coast Highway where passing automobiles are flagged down to come to our funeral services which Lili

officiates. We've got these feathers and cowries tied round our necks, faces painted, sometimes teeth, too.... Anyway people get out of their cars and come to our funeral. Our spirits are nourished by their visits and the ghosts of the New World get up and dance with gringo enthusiasts: That is until we reveal ourselves as the not-so-well-off folks of color from the Mission that we are. *Tu m'entiende* that dead Aztecs are so less threatening than a live *cholo*.[57]

They perform a spectacular mix of elegy and parody. That elegy, a funeral to mourn and honor "lost ancestors," gives way to parody, a spoof of how settler "gringo enthusiasts" picture indigeneity. Those enthusiasts seem to prefer caricatures of mythical, noble, ghostly savages over the mundane reality of living, breathing, contemporary people of color.

Their performance is a critique of the brutal distortions that permeate settler colonial imagination. Such critique pleases Victor-Jésus, who rails against the evils of settler colonialism and racism even as he endorses and upholds the evils of sexism and misogyny. When Liliane meets a white, hippy biker named Zoom on the side of that highway, Victor-Jésus's response merges his critique of white settler colonialism and his complicity with patriarchy. He declares that "Lili rode off on that bike with that white boy and what had been territory as yet undiscovered by European 'explorers' was swept away on the wheels of a 750 Harley-Davidson."[58] He objectifies Liliane as the soil beneath men, colonialist and indigenous, who wage battle to claim and possess it. At the heart of Victor-Jésus's avowed anticolonial zeal is a desire to assert patriarchal prerogative over a black woman. In this respect, he resembles Judge Parnell Lincoln: intent on possessing a black woman and defending said possession against the encroachment of white men.

To Victor-Jésus's delight, Liliane and Zoom are swiftly undone by racial and sexual antagonisms. Probably recalling the scandal of her mother's affair with a white man, Liliane decides to conceal Zoom's whiteness from her family. She plans to present him as a light-skinned black man and alters a photo to make his skin appear darker. Zoom responds bitterly:

He screamed at me. "Nobody has the right to be ashamed of me. You have no right to make me dark or light or less white. Who do you think you are, you bitch."

Then, I don't know how I got there. I was in the kitchen with a butcher knife. I was looking at my Zoom, saying "You get out of my house now. Get out right now." He looked bewildered. I said "Zoom, get out now before I try to hurt you. Get out." I screamed. I started to cry but my hand didn't waver. I held the knife in front of me toward the door til I heard him start the bike. Then I knew how primitive I am. Victor, I couldn't have a white man, not even Zoom, raise his voice to me in my house. I just couldn't.[59]

Note that Zoom shouts, "Who do you think you are[?]"—the same words that Liliane's unnamed assailant roared while choking her in a memory recounted to her analyst. In the book's depiction of Zoom and Liliane's time together, there is no mention of him battering her; in fact, she describes him as characteristically "gentle."[60] Thus, it is unclear whether Zoom is the culprit for that strangulation on the street or whether another man, in another violent rage, poses the same question to Liliane. Embedded in the words *Who do you think you are?* is the suggestion that *you* have overstepped a boundary, that *you* have mistakenly judged yourself to be more powerful, more capable, more authorized, more deserving than *you* truly are. Such a question can be weaponized to diminish one's sense of self-regard and self-esteem.[61] Whether or not Zoom and the unnamed assailant are one and the same, the sameness of their words points to a similarity between the two: both men do Liliane harm and cause her lasting trauma.

When Zoom calls Liliane a "bitch," he inadvertently hails her into a radical bitchiness: a readiness to do battle, to be unruly and unruled, to express fury, to disrupt the propriety of demure womanhood. Liliane claims and mobilizes a praxis of bitchiness in her own self-defense; she declares, "He musta lost his mind. If a niggah bitch is what he was after, a niggah bitch gone fuckin' crazy is what he muthafuckin' got."[62] Here Liliane also claims the mantle of the "crazy nigger"—and more precisely, the crazy "niggah bitch"—as an intrepid, insurgent agent of black vengeance. Notably, Zoom never calls her "niggah" in their argument as it is transcribed in the novel. Perhaps she has unconsciously suspected, all along, that naked antiblackness hides beneath his veneer of white liberalism. Such suspicion might interpolate her memory of the scene.

Liliane further proclaims that "white people can't just walk in and turn everything upside down, make me not belong to me again."[63] She fears an imperious, insidious whiteness that could topple her life and undermine her freedom, so she responds with the ferocity of a woman in grave danger. Put otherwise, Liliane feels her safety and dignity imperiled by the raised voice of a white man, so she gets mad and goes mad. She announces herself "primitive," signifying on the racist trope of the violent savage—the menacing counterpart to the "noble savage" she performed near that highway. According to Liliane, some primal and "primitive" impulse (perhaps the rush that fills a body when *fight-or-flight* tips toward *fight*) carries her into her kitchen and toward that knife. Suddenly lucid and wielding a weapon, held steady despite her shouting and sobbing, Liliane considers choosing *murder* over *metaphor*. Ultimately, Liliane does not stab or otherwise assault Zoom; she watches him retreat from her home and her life on his motorbike. By way of postscript, she later wishes she had wounded Zoom, confiding to Victor-Jésus that she "shoulda cut the muthafuckah, made him bleed."[64] Remarkably, in Liliane's explosive encounters with both Victor-Jésus and Zoom, madness is a source of violent frenzy *and* a manifestation of antisexist, antiracist tenacity.

I want to consider one final example of Liliane's wrath. Liliane is undone when her dearest friend since childhood, Roxie Golightly, is murdered by her husband, a "white Latin" named Tony. When Roxie earlier confides to Liliane about a pattern of marital abuse and terror, Liliane begs her friend to leave. Alas, Tony murders Roxie just before her planned escape. Feeling guilty and outraged, Liliane tells her analyst that her friend's murderer "needs his eyes pulled from their sockets. I want to beat his skull with a baseball bat until there's nothing left but a pile of his filthy mean demented brain that long-haul trucks run over again and again so we can't even tell he was human."[65] She fantasizes a grisly killing that would render its victim not only dead, but mutilated, overkilled, unrecognizable as human, hardly even identifiable as organic matter. Liliane exclaims gruesome rhetorical violence—but as with Zoom, she resists the urge to do physical violence.

Instead, Liliane sublimates homicidal angst into responsible acts of bereavement and estate administration for her deceased friend: "I have a lot of things to do. A memorial service, an inventory of paintings and sculptures, bank account."[66] That "memorial service" is a *ritual* of remembrance; that "inventory of paintings and sculptures" is a procedure to preserve *art*; that "bank account" holds and transmits *capital*. When Liliane channels murderous rage into socially acceptable processes of *ritual*, *art*, and *capital*, she reluctantly models sublimation.

A MAD BLACK GIRL STANDING GUARD

Roxie Golightly is not Liliane's only murdered friend. Sawyer Malveaux, one of Liliane's adolescent sweethearts, is also violently killed. Coming of age in the 1950s, Sawyer is "a rich colored boy who'd been thrown out of Morehouse, Tufts, Fisk, and finally St. Louis University, who'd wrecked a TR 6, a hard-top Ford, and a vintage Jag, all replaced by Daddy. This faun in the thick and thin silk socks, who wiped his brow with silk handkerchiefs and would arrange an abortion for anybody for $1,500."[67] He is a prodigal son and prince of the black bourgeoisie whose prosperity is the priority of his family and community. A spoiled and reckless adolescent, Sawyer swaggers about committing spectacular indiscretions with impunity. His deeds are routinely overlooked by his family, as though discipline is too harsh for his highness, as though admonition might disrupt his ascent.

He is a heartbreaker, too: a beautiful, joyful, charismatic, enchanting young man who leaves a queue of starry-eyed young women—not least Liliane—in his wake. He is young Liliane's ideal amalgamation of rough rebel surface and precious bourgeois core, "a courageous colored man with enough niggah in him to make any niggah at ease and enough class to make them wonder about theirs."[68] Liliane perceives in Sawyer the same sort of effusiveness that she possesses. Looking back years later, she rejoices, "My drawings of Sawyer reveal such splendor, such irrepressible fervor to burst open, shower the planet with his scent."[69] Notice that Liliane's description of Sawyer contains the word "irrepressible," which she also used to explain her own clitoral glow. According to Liliane, he exudes a lifeforce that will not be restrained or repressed. It is vibrant and abundant and potent enough to cover the entire earth, to impact the whole world around him, much like Liliane exerts her "impact on the world around her." Notwithstanding the power and vastness of his aura, Sawyer is still mortal. In his twenties, he is shot four times in the head, killed in the streets of East St. Louis, the details of his murder left a mystery.

Sawyer leaves behind a sister, Hyacinthe, whose life is undone by violence of another kind. The harm done to her is a conspiracy of antiblackness, patriarchy, respectability politics, and Reason that does not physically kill her, but casts her into a social death entombed in a mental institution. According to Liliane, "The Malveaux family had [Hyacinthe] committed when she returned from Cornell one summer with a twelve-inch Creole Afro."[70] Hyacinthe's Afro is an expression of black beauty in step with burgeoning Black Pride and consciousness movements in 1960s America. She prefers unstraightened hair that wanders along kinky and curly routes unruled by chemical straightener or Eurocentric aesthetics. Alas, her parents believe that her hairdo is symptom of an unruly mind and unruly will, so they have her confined to a psychiatric ward. To be clear, Hyacinthe self-identifies as mentally disturbed before her hospitalization; however, it appears that the Malveauxs are less concerned with their daughter's mental health than with exacting punishment and exercising control. Indeed, kinky hair has long been a site of contestation in black intimate spheres and in broader American public spheres—often met with disapproval and targeted for cropping, straightening, or concealment. Likewise, antiblackness endeavors constantly to crop, straighten, and conceal blackness itself.

Whereas Sawyer's transgressions land him in prestigious university after university, Hyacinthe's hair lands her in a mental institution. Of course, this disparity is gendered. Patriarchal politics of respectability hold women to higher and stricter standards of propriety—often inflicting harsher punishment on women, especially black women, who break the rules. This double standard applies to sexual behavior, interpersonal etiquette, filial duty, and physical appearance, including hair.[71]

Beyond approaching Hyacinthe as target of harm or object of analysis, I want to center her as a critical theorist who generates analysis through and about madness. Along with Eva and Elvira in Gayl Jones's *Eva's Man* and the unnamed protagonist of Gayl Jones's "Asylum," Hyacinthe is an institutionalized mad black woman whose insights are mocked, ignored, or condemned. As a young woman, from within that psychiatric ward, she discloses murderous impulses: "I could never stand white folks, let alone how they treat us. That's why I'm here. That's why they say crazy cause I want to fuck white folks up, break they necks. But I'm a girl."[72] Hyacinthe has a mortal gripe with "white folks," and "how they treat us." She is probably referring to centuries of structural antiblackness working to manipulate, violate, denigrate, and annihilate black life, perpetrated under the banner of "whiteness" and in the name of "white folks." Hyacinthe also includes the caveat that she is "a girl." Within the patriarchal logics of 1950s America, women were presumed inept in both noble and nefarious endeavors. If she were a man, a professed desire to "fuck white folks up" might seem more menacing; but because she is "a girl," she is probably presumed to pose less threat. Hyacinthe suggests that her feminized madness has "protected" her—perhaps from harsher punishment that would be meted against a black man with homicidal wishes against whiteness.[73] Of course, Hyacinthe's confinement in a mental institution is not a truly "protected" condition; she is a mad black young woman, vulnerable to sundry racial, sexual, and medical persecutions behind those hospital walls.

Hyacinthe shows no signs of resentment toward her brother, no bitterness about the unfair favor and privilege the family affords him. After she acknowledges, "but I'm a girl," she does not describe the structural dangers that threaten (mad) black girlhood and womanhood. Instead, she pivots into a litany of doting praise for her brother: "Well, hell, I've always been a girl and my brother was more beautiful than me, lovelier, smooth, soft, delicate, brown, long, limber, suave, warm, kissable, kissing, kisses, kiss me, Sawyer. No. No. Stop."[74] She stops her reverie for two reasons. First, she seems to recognize the incestuous energy gathering in her words; those repeated, lingering "kisses" seem to contain a sexual charge, hinting that Hyacinthe is not immune to her brother's allure.

The other reason for her sudden stop is that she has begun to recite a list, a compulsion she's trying to curb. She earlier frets, "I cannot make lists. No lists. They will not let me outta here if I make lists."[75] Hyacinthe slips into another list recitation when she describes the matter of her hair: "That's another reason why I'm here. I let my hair go back, get nappy, turn back, wrinkle, crinkle, twist, curl, swirl, oh shit. I've gotta stop these lists."[76]

In these passages and many others, Hyacinthe exhibits an obsessive compulsion to recite lists, to string together sometimes redundant, sometimes cumulative, sometimes revisionary chains of signifiers. During the chapter she narrates, Hyacinthe sometimes fixates on emotionally charged moments and lodges herself there, overloading narration with exhaustive lists that appear to distress her, even as they seem to satisfy a neurotic compulsion. These list recitations constitute a distressing hypernarrativity, distinct from Liliane's joyful narrative abundance. Hyacinthe's lists could be said to dramatize authorial labor: the author's task is to compose language, to proliferate it, to revise it, sometimes again and again. Hyacinthe's neurosis generates a superabundance of words and revisions that, in another time and world, might make her a prolific writer.

Years earlier, at a sleepover celebrating Liliane's sixteenth birthday, adolescent Hyacinthe announces her madness. Addressing Liliane's friend Bernadette, Hyacinthe asks: "Do you know where they send us to get our eyes to glow in the dark, Bernadette, I want to know. Bernadette, is that your real name or your slave name? Where is the school for niggahs where they show us how to roll our eyes like this and then like that? Am I getting it right? How's this?" Liliane's cousin Lollie interjects: "Listen, Bernadette, Hyacinthe has problems. . . . Hyacinthe has episodes of, what shall we call it? Ah, times when bein' a Negro scares her to death. She starts talkin' all that strange slavery talk about glows, and eyes, and big teeth, sometimes, too."[77] Lollie glibly dismisses Hyacinthe's questions, but I want to mine them for critical insights.

Those glow-in-the-dark rolling eyes bring to mind grotesque eyeball contortions common in blackface minstrelsy. Perhaps that "school for niggahs" is a training site where black people are taught to perform spectacular abjection and submit to dramatic degradation. I am not thinking of a physical edifice but rather a diffuse ideological apparatus interpellating black people into abject subjecthood.[78] By sighting/citing/siting the specter of wretched blackness in that plush home, among the respectable daughters of the black bourgeoisie, Hyacinthe reminds us that money and prestige cannot insulate black people from the history and persistence of antiblackness.

In another haunted passage, Hyacinthe describes dreams of "mad, anguished niggahs" crowding her consciousness: "I'd wake to blood and torn human organs every morning until I learned to take the moans of the folks who were dying in my body. Then, when I screamed it was 10,000 mad, anguished niggahs who've seen the bottom of the Mississippi River, the floor of ravines outside Springfield, hid behind stalactites and stalagmites in coves near Jeff City, holed up in corrals by the Kentucky border."[79] Hyacinthe's scream channels the sound of ten thousand souls in staggering pain. These persons are fugitive slaves: wild-eyed and paranoid, lurking and darting into hiding places, frantic with fear of capture, apprehended and punished, wounded and bleeding, flying and vanishing, dying and haunting—and maybe, eventually, *free*. In this passage, the presence of death, anguish, and madness does not impair Hyacinthe; to the contrary, it strengthens and emboldens her. Though she initially tries to resist these "anguished niggahs," Hyacinthe ultimately allies herself with them and speaks on their behalf. Those nameless thousands are a community of witnesses, a ghostly counterpublic beseeching her to testify to the relentlessness of antiblackness.

Literary critic Wolfgang Karrer asserts that "beneath the asylum tale lies the slave narrative."[80] Hyacinthe seems to agree. Regarding the psychiatric ward where she is confined, she explains that "there are two-way mirrors and microphones in here, I'm sure. It's a teaching hospital and whatever they didn't find out about us during slavery and circus tours, they gonna find out now."[81] Hyacinthe connects the plantation, the circus, and the asylum as sites where black people have been spectacularly undone. The black slave (captive on the plantation), the black freak (enclosed in the circus tent), and the black madperson (confined to the asylum) are all made objects to be picked apart for white comfort, pleasure, and edification.

Hyacinthe further recounts, "Lollie says it's not the worst thing in the world that I imagine I'm cutting white folks' throats during pleasant banter at the lunch table."[82] Just as she smuggles "strange slavery talk" into Liliane's slumber party, Hyacinthe harbors dreams of murder amid lunchtime niceties. Pristine scenes of bourgeois domesticity are disrupted by her mad presence and the ghastly visions she carries with her. Hyacinthe knows that sometimes a plantation is the soil underneath a well-appointed bedroom or fancy dining room; sometimes the ghosts of enslaved ancestors crash slumber parties; and sometimes the murmurs of the dead compete with "pleasant banter." Lest others be lulled into complacency, Hyacinthe remains vigilant: a mad black girl standing guard and ready to remind them.

Later, from her hospital room, gazing at pictures of Liliane's coterie, Hyacinthe declares, "See, looky here. There's Rose Lynne, Roxie, Lollie, Bernadette. . . . We remarkable, ain't we? Look at us. Just as fine as we can be. Just as . . . susceptible to murder as anybody else."[83] "Susceptible to murder" is a provocative double-entendre. Considering that two members of Liliane's circle have been murdered, we might interpret Hyacinthe's statement to mean *susceptible to being murdered.* Alternately, we may read her statement as commentary on the angst that plagues these black bourgeois folks, angst that could compel someone to "cut [a] muthafuckah." This latter interpretation would translate her words as *susceptible to committing murder.* (This ambiguity applies to Amiri Baraka's Clay, too; whereas Clay's monologue suggests he is susceptible to committing murder, the play's outcome proves that he is susceptible to being murdered, too.)

In the above passages, Hyacinthe utters trenchant truths about race, history, violence, and freedom through an idiom of madness. I want to highlight her insights about love, too. Regarding Liliane, Hyacinthe explains, "Zoom really loved her, I think. Victor-Jésus loved her. S. Bliss probably loved her too, but I've got to look through these watercolors, before I say. Oh hell, I loved Liliane, too: loved, cared, cherished, adored, craved, desired, blessed, yes, blessed. We all were blessed, to have the privilege to love her, Liliane, anybody's colored child, anybody's daughter, just like me. Stop. Stop. You are too close."[84] Hyacinthe attests to the bounty of love in Liliane's life, even within her most fraught relationships. Remarkably, Hyacinthe shifts from canonizing Liliane as a saintly icon of love to asserting Liliane's sublime ordinariness, her status as "anybody's colored child, anybody's daughter."

Hyacinthe claims affinity with Liliane, describing her friend as "just like me," but quickly retreats from that likeness, insisting "Stop. Stop. You are too close." Perhaps that likeness, that too-closeness, that existential adjacency is rooted in their shared madness. Hyacinthe proudly admits that Liliane "never thought I was crazy, least no more crazy than she was." If Liliane is also crazy, she might also be vulnerable to the degradation that Hyacinthe endures. Perhaps Hyacinthe's "Stop. Stop" is an attempt to ward Liliane away from that likeness—lest it lead Liliane to similar sorrow.

For all her narrative angst, Hyacinthe is a poignant speaker to deliver this tribute to her friend. Madness endows her words with startling candor, passionate crescendo, intensity of feeling, compulsive care, and unabashed vulnerability that are well-suited to expressing love. Moreover, Hyacinthe recites this homage in the idiom of her madness: an obsessive list-cum-tender litany for her friend.

In the introduction to her 1980 short play collection, *Three Pieces*, Ntozake Shange decries "the straightjacket that the english language slips over the minds of all americans."[85] To have Shange tell it, "american english" is a structure of domination that violently constricts "american" imagination, enshrines white supremacist logics, propagates antiblack grammars, thwarts insurgent expressions, and chokes demands for freedom.[86]

Shange's "straightjacket" metaphor conjures scenes of psychiatric confinement, where some captives are forced into such carceral garment. Impairing the use of its wearer's hands and arms, the straightjacket is officially intended to prevent detainees from physically harming themselves and others—which is to say, it is touted as a technology to thwart *mad violence*. In the process, the straightjacket exposes its captive to *Reasonable violence*, both physical and metaphysical, potentially perpetrated by hospital personnel, profiteers, bureaucrats, the psychiatric-industrial complex, and the broader psychonormative imagination. The straightjacket accomplishes this harm, not merely through physical fetters, but through symbolic violence: it is a uniform of abjection clung tight to the body, announcing its wearer's degraded status, frustrating its captive's agency and dignity.

Shange claims that all "americans" are debilitated by the "english" language, but she suggests that its straightjacket cleaves to black bodies with especially oppressive tightness and stickiness. Emphasizing the language's effect on black children, she writes, "i can't count the number of times i have viscerally wanted to attack deform n maim the language that i was taught to hate myself in / the language that perpetuates the notions that cause pain to every black child as he/she learns to speak of the world & the 'self.' "[87] Shange wants to "attack deform n maim the language," to do vengeful violence to the Symbolic Order wherein she was "taught to hate" herself, to metaphorically castrate its phallocentric weaponry. Lacan proposes that every subject entering the Symbolic Order undergoes a violent rupture from a primordial feeling of oneness with the world. For her part, Shange asserts that the black child confronts another, more sinister violence as she enunciates her black "i" and speaks her black "self." The "black child" speaking "english" confronts a history of antiblackness embedded in the language, in what Hortense Spillers calls "American Grammar." Recall Spillers's injunction that "dominant symbolic activity, the ruling episteme that releases the dynamics of naming and valuation, remains grounded in the originating metaphors of captivity and mutilation."[88] The pain Shange describes pulsates from the "captivity and mutilation" of that "dominant symbolic activity." If this is the case, then every black "i" uttered in "america" cites and recites material, symbolic, and psychic violence inflicted on black people.

Concerning the creation of *Three Pieces*, she confesses that "each of these pieces was excruciating to write / for i had to confront / again & again / those moments that had left me with no more than fury n homicidal desires."[89] Insofar as she harbors "fury n homicidal desires," Shange is like Liliane and her friends: "susceptible to murder." Also like Liliane, Shange performs masterful feats of sublimation amid "homicidal" angst and creates exquisite art in a discursive straightjacket. If "american english" is a carceral garment, Shange's writings teach us how to dance while caught in its binds, and maybe wiggle free. Her oeuvre abounds with black vernaculars, feminist articulations, complex wordplay, hood slangs, subversive syntax, motherwit, grammatical insurgency, incantatory phrases, curse words, orthographic insurrections, prophetic outbursts, violent exclamations, and mad idioms—all working to unbind the straightjacket and split its seams.

As an undergraduate student at Barnard College, Shange sublimated suicidal angst into social justice and artmaking. Theatre historian Phillip Effiong paints her as a paragon of sublimation: "She could hardly cope with the sense of alienation and bitterness that consumed her after her unsuccessful first marriage and the personal frustrations drove her into a suppressed rage that culminated in a series of suicide attempts. Failing to commit suicide, Shange channeled her anger into student protest, Civil Rights, and Black Liberation movements."[90] Shange graduated from Barnard College in 1970, four years before the debut of her monumental choreopoem, *for colored girls who've considered suicide / when the rainbow is enuf*. Remarkably, she harnessed the madness of a "colored girl" who attempted suicide into a sublime drama *for colored girls who have considered* it.

To close this chapter, I briefly return to the scene of Liliane's sweet sixteen slumber party. Bernadette Reeves—the newbie in Liliane's circle, a girl whose family just barely makes the cut for black elite status—beholds the neuroses of the girls and declares, "All you all are crazy as shit." Unfazed, Roxie replies, "There aren't many colored folks who aren't," proposing that the craziness of "colored folks" is a mundane matter of fact.[91] Hyacinthe chimes in with her own wisdom on the matter: "I don't make sense to other people, so they say I'm crazy. I get mad at them and then I might seem really crazy. But as far as I'm concerned, I don't know many Africans and descendants thereof who ain't halfway crazy. Plus, going crazy is so startling and scary to them once they realize their true state of mind, that they pretend sanity, much as they can. Now me, I've been crazed so long and so intensely, I'm really good at it, comfortable, you might say."[92]

Hyacinthe is a prison intellectual outlining a theory of black madness that overlaps with my own. When she professes that the label "crazy" is affixed to those who "don't make sense to" a powerful majority, she is describing a sort of *psychosocial madness*. When she mentions that "I get mad at them and then I might seem really crazy," she is sketching the conflation of *madness-as-anger* and *madness-as-insanity*. When she divulges that going crazy is "startling and scary," she is recounting her experience of *phenomenal madness*. Hyacinthe does not describe, but eventually lives, *medicalized madness*; her institutionalization is a testament to the medicalized degradation often afflicting persons deemed mentally ill.

Hyacinthe also insists that most black people are madpersons in disguise, merely "pretending" to be sane. To be black in the thick of antiblack worlds is a condition of such trauma, such chaos, such strangeness, such wonder, such alterity, such uncertainty, such antagonism, that it often feels mad. Thus, implies Hyacinthe, madness is an existential inheritance of most African-descended people. Those who pass as sane are those who feign sanity persuasively, whose masks fit snugly enough to conceal the craziness underneath.

When Hyacinthe announces that she is "good at" madness, she suggests that madness is not merely something that overtakes, encumbers, or otherwise acts upon a subject. Madness is something said subject can claim, wield, and *do*; something that one might learn to do *well*; something that might be adapted as methodology and praxis. Her own mad methods include donning a massive Afro in the face of family members who demand straight hair of their daughter; invoking "strange slavery talk" at slumber parties; expressing murderous angst at demure social luncheons; and articulating radical critiques of antiblackness and white supremacy in mad black rants.

From her hospital room years later, Hyacinthe wistfully ponders the lives of her friends, recalling their myriad dreams, adventures, romances, revelations, and transformations. Then she proclaims, "Lili can draw all this, all plain and clear for me and you. I know that. Lili can paint my craziness. She can paint it, build it, hammer and beat it outta nothin.'"[93] I want to describe Liliane's art, as Hyacinthe would, in a series of lists. Over the long arc of the novel, Liliane gives madness language and picture, color and form, texture and weight, blood and paint, brushstroke and hip-swerve, scent and irrepressible glow. She materializes madness, makes it a watercolor, or a curse word, or a love song, or a fancy dress, or an altar, or a knife, or a flower, so that it can be viewed, touched, recited, inhaled, held, handled, heard, pondered, admired, perhaps put to use, and perhaps put away.

Regarding the art Lili makes from madness, Hyacinthe explains:

> Lili sent me, actually sends me, drawings, photographs, papier-mâché images of who is in her life. She makes me feel like I was actually there, I could touch em, and smell em, and sometimes, I love em: Lili's friends, Lili's nemesis, niggahs what kicked Lili's ass, is what she let me experience with her.
>
> My social workers chastise me constantly cause I line my walls, the walls of my room, with Lili's drawings. "Why Miss Malveaux, you know you've never been any of these places; why you've never even been out of sight for more than eight hours." When my nurses talk like this, I don't say anything cause they don't know no better. Let me show you. That's what Lili says, "Let me show you."[94]

Liliane sends art objects that are like talismans holding traces of her sensations, emotions, companions. These objects vicariously transport Hyacinthe beyond those hospital walls and toward adventures with her friend. Naysaying nurses and unbelieving social workers cannot spoil this communion. With the help of Liliane's art, Hyacinthe imagines herself elsewhere and otherwise. Hopefully, these imaginative journeys are prelude to an exodus out of that hospital and toward something like liberation or at least a little peace of mind. As though preparing a path for her friend, Liliane offers to lead the way: "Let me show you."

From Ms. Liliane Lincoln, we turn to Ms. Lauryn Hill, who will show you and *tell you*, too.

CHAPTER FIVE

"THE PEOPLE INSIDE MY HEAD, TOO"

MS. LAURYN HILL SINGS TRUTH TO POWER
IN THE KEY OF MADNESS

HILL AND HORIZON

Heralded by a hip-hop beat, crooning love songs and rally cries, beaming black pride, and clamoring womanist wisdom, Ms. Lauryn Hill scaled the treacherous summit of global pop music stardom in the late 1990s.[1] Already famed as the lone woman member of the popular Afrodiasporic hip-hop trio called the Fugees, Hill released a solo debut album in 1998 that showcased her creative and commercial prowess apart from the men who were her bandmates. That solo album, *The Miseducation of Lauryn Hill*, is an ambitious amalgam of social commentary and infectious grooves spanning and fusing hip-hop, rhythm and blues, soul, rock, reggae, gospel, and beyond. *Miseducation* burst into the global music market and quickly became one of the most acclaimed and megaselling hip-hop albums in history.[2] Atop that treacherous height, Hill was hailed as musical genius and pop culture prophetess.[3]

Just three years later, to have many pundits tell it, Hill had fallen from the favor of the mainstream market and veered across the thin line said to separate genius from madness and prophecy from lunacy.[4] Remarkably, whether pundits ascribe to Hill the sublime intellect of a genius, the divine discernment of a prophetess, or the scandalous unruliness of a madwoman, they consistently set her apart from psychonormativity. (Remember that the genius, prophetess, and madwoman each access epistemic horizons unavailable to so-called normal-minded masses—though the genius and prophetess are imagined to inhabit spaces of elevation, while the madwoman is thought to dwell in a zone of debasement.) But Hill is no passive object in the debate about her alterity; she has repeatedly, emphatically portrayed herself as a psychosocial other. Hill has proclaimed "I've got the mind of a genius," suggested that her predicament reveals "how the world treats its prophets," announced "I'm crazy,"[5] and manifested each type in this trio of alterity. In Hill's own words, "I was never normal."[6]

Acknowledging the significance of Hill's black womanly command of genius and prophecy amid antiblack and sexist pop cultures and public spheres, I turn to the controversial case of "crazy."[7] To embrace madness is risky business for a black woman traversing those antiblack and sexist milieus, where black womanhood is double-crossed by myths of black subrational savagery and myths of female hysteria. The story of Hill is an instructive case study in what I call the *maddening of black genius*. This polysemous term denotes the derision of black radical creativity as "crazy"; the outrage of artists antagonized by such antiblackness; the mental distress that sometimes ensues; and, in Hill's case, the embrace of madness for song-making, self-making, and worldmaking.

In this chapter, I chart Hill's trajectory briefly before and mostly after she supposedly crossed the genius | madness border. I carefully watch and listen for phenomenal madness in her 2001 *MTV Unplugged No. 2.0* performance; I read a number of interviews and interludes where Hill frames her "crazy" conduct as psychosocial alterity; I chart how she invokes and literally instrumentalizes black rage on stage; and I examine textual and visual representations of Hill, mostly from mainstream media, that depict her as a woman askew. As mad methodologist, I track the "voices" that speak to Hill, I read for philosophy where pundits seek pathology, I find critical praxis where naysayers see only disruptive or "diva" misbehavior, and I glean incisive message where many merely perceive mess. Of course, I know that pathology might beget philosophy, misbehavior is sometimes praxis, and messes can contain message. Ultimately, this chapter charts how Hill speaks and sings truth to power in the key of madness, with a sound that sometimes booms and sometimes cracks. Her mad repertoire is rich with black feminist, womanist, antiracist, anti-racial-capitalist, and liberation resonance that I hope to amplify here.

Alongside Hill, this chapter features a guest appearance by another mad black musician: Kanye West. Deeply influenced by Hill and widely derided as crazy, West showcases another style of self-making in the key of madness.

Born in the spring of 1975 to black middle-class parents, Hill was raised in suburban South Orange, New Jersey. She is a member of America's post–Civil Rights generation, reared in a nation legally integrated but stubbornly socially segregated and white supremacist. Intimately familiar with middle-class suburbia, critically aware of the persistence of racial and class injustice, and raised in a family where blackness was celebrated, Hill's upbringing prepared her to navigate white mainstream cultures while honoring black vernacular and radical aesthetics.[8] Rather than recite a generic synopsis of Hill's career, I want to position her oeuvre within three pertinent genealogies of black American performance.

First, Hill participates in a long tradition of black protest music, in particular an iteration called *conscious hip-hop*. The conscious genre frequently features politically charged content, condemnation of social ills, protest provocations, and visions of social transformation, often delivered with didactic lyrics. Afrocentrism, black pride, antiracism, black feminism, and poor and working-class solidarity (not to mention respectability politics, reactionary black patriarchy, and conspiratorial homophobia) are among the worldviews that gather and clamor beneath the "conscious" banner. While the music is not the exclusive prerogative of avowedly "woke" artists, there are some performers whose consistent protest ethic set precedence for Hill's interventions: Gil Scott-Heron, Public Enemy, KRS-One, Arrested Development, and especially Queen Latifah are among them. In the late 1990s, conscious hip-hop contended with increasing commercialization of the broader genre and growing market demand for depictions of flashy materialism, spectacular hypersexuality, and black intraracial violence. *Miseducation* eschewed those market values and maintained a generally progressive message that centered black pride and self-determination, feminist and womanist ethics, and solidarity with poor people—along with messages about virtuous womanhood and proper manhood that appealed to respectability politics.[9]

Second, Hill stands in a lineage of twentieth- and twenty-first-century African American women musicians whose spectacular talent is shadowed and sometimes overshadowed by spectacular sorrow.[10] Like Hill during her *Unplugged* era, Billie Holiday, Nina Simone, Whitney Houston, and Mary J. Blige have all been black women musicians in public pain—black women enduring widely publicized and scrutinized personal traumas.[11] When such traumas are carefully, cautiously expressed in songs and interviews, they can alert popular audiences to some of the psycho-existential perils assailing black women in antiblack and misogynist milieus. Too often, however, portrayals of black-women-in-pain are careless, callous extensions of a perverse American tradition. As poet and critic Elizabeth Alexander explains it, "Black bodies in pain for public consumption have been an American national spectacle for centuries."[12] The rote replication and mass circulation of representations of black-women-in-pain upholds what Saidiya Hartman likewise calls "the spectacular character of black suffering," which coarsens audiences to the lived reality of such pain, aestheticizes that pain, opens it up for narcissistic projection, and reduces it to fetish for voyeuristic consumption.[13]

During and beyond her *Unplugged* incarnation, Hill fits within a third trajectory of black performance that is especially salient for my present purposes. She is among a cohort of African American popular musicians since the twentieth century who have mobilized "madness" as method and metaphor in radical performance praxis. Along with Hill, this group includes Mamie Smith, Charles Mingus, Sun Ra, Nina Simone, Kanye West, Kendrick Lamar, and Azealia Banks, among others. Like Hill, each persona on the preceding list is something of an iconoclast; each has ignited controversy; and each has manifested some version of psychosocial, medicalized, furious, and/or phenomenal madness. Nina Simone, vanguardist of the artistic arm of the Civil Rights Movement, is Hill's most poignant predecessor—another brown-skinned black woman and polymathic protest musician singing revolutionary sentiments in contralto tones. Early in her career, on a track called "Ready or Not" from the Fugees' 1996 *The Score* album, Hill explicitly likens herself to Simone. Repudiating the mobster-obsessed bravado of lesser emcees, Hill proclaims,

> While you imitating Al Capone
> I'll be Nina Simone
> and defecating on your microphone[14]

While others model themselves after mobsters, she chooses to channel and embody black revolutionary womanhood instead. Hill would later incorporate covers of Simone's "Sinnerman" and "Feeling Good" into her live performance repertoire; would record six of the sixteen tracks on the 2015 *Nina Revisited . . . A Tribute to Nina Simone* album; and would perform at Simone's 2018 induction into the Rock and Roll Hall of Fame.

From these panoramic views of US black popular performance since the twentieth century, I zoom back in on several key moments in Hill's individual trajectory. Her 1998 solo debut, *The Miseducation of Lauryn Hill*, was a massive commercial and critical success. It set the record for the highest first-week sales for a solo female debut in the history of the American *Billboard* chart, another for the most Grammy wins in a single year for any female artist, and yet another as the first hip-hop album in the Recording Academy's history to win album of the year.[15] *Rolling Stone*, *Spin*, and *Time* all ranked *Miseducation* the best album of 1998;[16] in 2003, VH1 named it the thirty-seventh greatest album ever;[17] and in 2008, *Entertainment Weekly* named *Miseducation* the second-best album of the preceding twenty-five years.[18] As of 2018, the album had sold approximately nineteen million units worldwide.[19]

Describing Hill's *Miseducation* incarnation, the *Village Voice* clamored that "she's almost forbiddingly perfect, but so thanks-to-god about it that it's impossible to begrudge her."[20] The *New York Times* proclaimed her to be a "visionary," who projected "a prophet's voice" and crafted a "miraculous" album.[21] *Essence* retrospectively anointed her "the hope of hip hop, pure and simple."[22] *The Source* crowned her "the flyest MC ever."[23] *Time* gushed, "Listen to her voice and hear a new world."[24] Furthermore, Hill was frequently praised for her brown-skinned, kinky-haired, dreadlocked beauty amid a pop culture that favors Eurocentric looks.

A brilliant lyricist, powerful vocalist, charismatic stage performer, and incisive commentator on race, sex, and spirituality, Hill became the "conscious" heroine of late 1990s hip-hop: genius, prophetess, and formidable race woman.[25] But within three years of *Miseducation*'s debut, Hill would allegedly snap. When she returned to the scorching limelight in 2001, the race woman had purportedly become a madwoman—though no less formidable.

THE VOICES

I had to work through *that voice* telling me, "People don't want to hear that. You ain't got no beat. Who do you think you are, playing that guitar?" I had to talk back to that voice and say, "You know what? Just because I have a guitar, it doesn't mean that changes me. I still rhyme, I still sing." The means that God gave me to express myself with right now.
—LAURYN HILL, MTV interview, 2001

[Speaks:] This is what *that voice* in your head says when you try to get peace of mind.... [Sings:] I gotta find peace of mind. —LAURYN HILL, "I Gotta Find Peace of Mind," 2001

You do have to do something with the insecurity, ghosts and demons that have been programmed in us for centuries. You have to master *the voices*.
—LAURYN HILL, *Essence* magazine, 2006

On July 21, 2001—nearly three years after her solo debut, and following a year-long hiatus from the national media scene—Hill recorded her second solo LP, the acoustic *Unplugged*, before a live audience at MTV's Times Square studios.[26] Released in 2002 as both audio album and video concert DVD, *Unplugged* unveiled a dramatically different Hill. She had shorn her trademark locks, abandoned her pristine vocal and visual presentation, removed that "forbiddingly perfect" armor, dismissed a massive entourage, repudiated her former persona, and picked up a new set of accoutrements: a guitar, a stool, a frequently hoarse voice, and by many accounts, including her own, a bit of "derangement."[27] Stories of devastating heartbreak, profound disillusionment with fame,[28] outrage at the incursions of capitalism, spiritual epiphany, and a nervous breakdown have circulated as explanations for Hill's dramatic reinvention. In performances and interviews illuminated throughout this chapter, Hill addresses or alludes to each of these hypotheses.

Unplugged contains thirteen songs (eleven original compositions and two covers), an expository "Intro," seven interludes, and an expository "Outro." Hill is the sole performer and the only instruments heard are her voice and her guitar. Presenting a more radical worldview than *Miseducation*, *Unplugged's* tracks and interludes address a range of social and structural issues including antiblackness, police brutality, colonialism, racial capitalism, political and clerical corruption, intimate partner abuse, organized rebellion, mental health, and madness.[29] The latter, my focus, is a recurring theme and modality on *Unplugged*, appearing most dramatically on four occasions that I will ponder in turn: the "Intro," then "Interlude 3," then a song called "I Gotta Find Peace of Mind," and finally, the "Outro."

Within two minutes of her arrival on stage, during a conversational "Intro" that precedes her first song, Hill inquires, "You guys are cool?" When an affirmative murmur comes from the crowd, she responds, "I'm talking to the people in my head, too." Hill and her studio audience—and maybe the people in her head—chuckle together. In a 2002 *Essence* magazine feature, poet and novelist Pearl Cleage recounts a similar exchange during a performance that year in Atlanta: "'You guys cool?' [Hill] asks the audience, and when we clap an enthusiastic yes, she laughs and points to her head. 'I'm talking to the people in my head too.'"[30] Hill's laughter highlights her playful double-entendre. On one level, the most literal and "rational" level, Hill refers to the sound technicians who speak to her via earpiece. But on a lower register, she conjures madness.

An adult who talks to the "people" inside her head might be diagnosed with schizophrenia—a medicalized madness that frequently entails the impression of sounds, often voices, in the affected mind. Hill's statement also evokes dissociative identity disorder, a psychotic condition that manifests as multiple personalities inhabiting a subject's psyche. To be clear, I am *not* suggesting that Hill is clinically schizophrenic or dissociative, nor am I proposing that she actually hears voices other than the technicians'. Instead, I am asserting that Hill, well aware that she has been diagnosed "crazy" by the tabloid press, is signifying (on) her alleged madness.

In other words, whether or not Hill *phenomenally* perceives multiple "people" inside her head, she summons *medicalized* madness to cast herself as *psychosocial* other. By dramatically invoking phenomena the audience cannot hear or see, she emphasizes that her intentions exceed what is available to their senses. She reminds spectators that they cannot facilely presume her performance to be exclusively for their consumption, that they are not privy to all the dynamics of her subjectivity and creativity, that she is in conversation and commiseration with other "people." While wired with a microphone, and thus primed for optimal audibility, Hill calls attention to what the studio audience cannot hear. While perched beneath a spotlight, and thus poised for maximal visibility, Hill conjures what the studio audience cannot see. If madness makes the madwoman inscrutable to normative understanding, Hill hints that she can exploit that inscrutability as a tool for opacity and radical concealment.

In her capacity as protest musician, Hill has claimed to speak to and for various counterpublics: "black youth," "poor people," "the have-nots," and "the voiceless" among them.[31] In this "Intro," Hill invokes the "people inside [her] head" as though they are a *symbolic counterpublic*: outside the dominant public sphere, inaudible to dominant hearing, invisible to dominant vision, but heard and seen by Hill who concerns herself with their articulations. That she repeatedly invokes "people inside her head" indicates more than spontaneous interjection; this is a thoughtful, concerted project of counterpublicity and mad performance.

People—and more precisely, *voices*—inside Hill's head do battle on *Unplugged*'s longest song, "I Gotta Find Peace of Mind." In general, I do not presume that song lyrics are direct references to the biographies of their creators; nor do I blithely conflate the *character* in a song with the *artist* who sings it. However, because Hill insists that *Unplugged* is a personal testimony about her actual life, I regard the song's protagonist as an iteration of Hill herself. Before she begins to sing, Hill announces, "See, this is what that voice in your head says when you try to get peace of mind." In the lyrics that follow, we encounter two voices who compete in a sort of war over her mind as she seeks "peace" within it.

At the start of the nine-minute track, Hill strums her guitar and softly, dreamily describes a lover who afflicts her:

> He says it's impossible, but I know it's possible
> He says there's no me without him
> Please help me forget about him
> He takes all my energy
> Trapped in my memory
> . . .
> I need to tell you all
> All the pain he's caused

"He" hinders her progress, eats away her energy, and infects her with insecurity. In these opening lines, as she describes "all the pain he's caused," Hill positions herself within that cohort of black women in pain.

"His" identity is ambiguous. Within the conventions of the heartbreak ballad, he may register as a hurtful, abusive man with whom she remains in malignant union. Within Hill's avowedly Judeo-Christian theology,[32] he resembles the devil who tempted Eve and taunted Job: stoking doubt, undermining faith, intending to cause ruin. Within the milieu of madness, "he" might be Hill's anguish condensed into a phantasmic, heckling voice.

Trauma theorist Cathy Caruth suggests that devastating trauma may tear open a psychic and existential wound in the subject. She describes a "sorrowful" "voice that cries out from the wound, a voice that witnesses a truth that [the traumatized subject] cannot fully know."[33] I call this entity a *talking wound*, in counterpoint to Freud's *talking cure*. A talking wound might speak in the "sorrowful voice" that Caruth describes, or with a sinister voice, like the one assailing Hill. In "I Gotta Find Peace of Mind," the talking wound—the one who "says it's impossible"—is a trauma clamoring in the consciousness of its victim, echoing like an evil refrain, intensifying hurt with each reiteration. This voice, this trauma that taunts, is part of a vicious chorus that Hill identifies as "insecurity, ghosts and demons that have been programmed in [black women] for centuries."[34] In some cases, those "ghosts and demons" can induce fundamental crises of perception, selfhood, and meaning that feel like phenomenal madness.

Fortunately, there is another figure in this songscape: a righteous, loving being who counteracts the one who "says it's impossible." This benevolent being redeems and uplifts Hill where the other degraded and oppressed her.[35] If that sinister figure incites fear and self-loathing, this affirming being brings "peace of mind." If that other figure is demonic, this figure is godly. Hill cries out:

> Oh you inspire me
> To be the higher me
> You make my desire pure
>
> . . .
>
> You are my peace of mind
> That old me is left behind

As Hill flees the one who "says it's impossible" and embraces the one who brings her "peace of mind," her volume rises and passion surges. In fact, the song is a prolonged musical and affective crescendo in which Hill moves tremulously toward peace of mind, and once at its threshold, pleads to that benevolent figure:

Please come free my mind!

Please come be my mind!

When Hill entreats the loving voice to "come be my mind," she seeks to surrender her discrete, autonomous self for the relief that merging with "him" will bring.

Many glibly dismissed Hill's *Unplugged* performance as a symptom of hysterical lovelorn womanhood, invoking sexist tropes of the overwrought and love-crazed hysteric come undone under the thumb of a domineering man.[36] It is possible to acknowledge the role that heartbreak might have played in Hill's distress without reducing Hill to a pitiful trope. Toward this end, it is worth noting that "I Gotta Find Peace of Mind" depicts a woman whose psychospiritual condition depends upon the deeds of two "hims." A figure identified as "he" is to blame for her deep sorrow; and ultimately, another "he" brings her "peace of mind." This scenario begs the question, *Shouldn't a woman-empowering praxis entail autonomous "peace of mind"—one that rises and sets in a woman's own sense of self?* Surely, self-starting and self-sustaining self-esteem are desirable conditions for empowered womanhood. However, it is crucial that Hill describes what appears to be joyful, beneficial, *willful* surrender. Within the complex emotional arc of the song, this surrender reads more like an act of hard-fought agency than a symptom of subjection. Once Hill submits to this benevolent being—a figure who might be the "wonderful God" she praises at the song's end—she achieves a sort of psychospiritual catharsis. By giving in, she lays down a burden, sheds a bit of what weighs her down, marshals her energy to "get free."

As Hill repeatedly utters, "Please come free my mind!" she begins to weep. Her voice strains and quivers as she proclaims, "Free your mind" and "It's possible," shifting focus from her individual plight to a vision of collective struggle and liberation. Chanting these phrases like mantras, Hill eventually seems to soothe herself; her voice and guitar lull to a lower register and quieter volume. But that calm erupts into one final paroxysm near the song's end. There as she thanks the "wonderful, merciful God" who brings her peace of mind, Hill weeps tears that dissolve language, leaving her struggling to sing. Her sobs seem to slosh away any trace of that "forbiddingly perfect" veneer, opening up to *radical revelation*: she comes undone before her audience, exposes spectacular vulnerability, and demands that we witness the sound of her grief and her gratitude.

The term *madness* cannot wholly caption this song. It is also a tale of heartbreak and healing, a portrait of a person overcoming staggering self-doubt, a parable of Armageddon writ small, and a spiritual testimony that culminates in a fit of spiritual ecstasy. The song is not merely mad—it is also traumatic, tragic, ecclesiastic, and ecstatic.

Still, Hill repeatedly foregrounds madness in the song and throughout *Unplugged*. I now shift to "Interlude 3," where Hill muses that "the view is that I'm, like, emotionally unstable which is reality—like you aren't." When she describes herself as "emotionally unstable," and then sarcastically interjects "like you aren't," Hill hails her audience into an affiliation of instability, a community of unruly minds. She seems to believe that emotional instability is so common a human condition that it can be presumed present in her listeners. Humming their assent, audience members seem to accept this interpellation and embrace the affiliation. After admitting her emotional instability, Hill deems herself a "mad scientist." She explains, "What I've realized I've become is one of those mad scientists who does the tests on themselves first, you see, to make sure that they work. . . . I'm not gonna give you something that I haven't tried and tested for myself." The proverbial "mad scientist" conducts dangerous experiments in obsessive pursuit of revelation and breakthrough. Although her experiments may be hazardous, Hill persists because she believes that the outcome—revelatory art—is worth the risk.

Several tracks on *Unplugged* depict God as a repressive being who demands restrictive religiosity.[37] To the contrary, "I Gotta Find Peace of Mind" portrays God as a spirit who vanquishes repression and abolishes inhibition. This vision of God is elaborated in the album's "Outro," where I now turn my attention. In her closing commentary on this final track of *Unplugged*, Hill opines that "we think that's God telling us 'feel guilty.' God is saying 'get free.' Confess, man. . . . It's just a bunch of repression. . . . Life is too valuable, man, for us to sit in these boxes all repressed, you know, afraid to admit what we're really going through." Hill's notion of "repression" differs from the standard psychoanalytic definition. Whereas Freud defines repression as the interment of traumatic thoughts, memories, and desires into the unconscious, Hill uses the term to describe a conscious and concerted process of self-stagnation.[38] Its resolution is not the excavation of memories from the unconscious, but rather the excavation of our true selves out of the "boxes" that imprison us. Hill seems to undergo a *breakdown* (coming undone before her audience), which is also a *breakthrough* (achieving revelation and catharsis), and a *breakout* (from those repressive "boxes") that helps her *break free* ("free your mind!" is a slogan she sings and seeks to embody).

In that "Outro," Hill further ponders such freedom and its relation to madness:

Yeah, I'm crazy and deranged, you know, and *I'm free.* . . . I might play these songs and twitch a little bit just so people know. . . . Y'all think that's a curse, I'm telling you, it's a blessing. . . . When I was a politician, boy, everybody, just all over me, you know, I didn't have a private moment at all. Not one private moment. Now that people think that I'm crazy and deranged, we have peace. Total peace. And so, listen: As far as I'm concerned, I'm crazy and deranged. As far as all y'all know, I'm crazy and deranged, you know, I'm emotionally unstable. . . . That's my story, I'm sticking to it.[39]

In 1998 and 1999, at the height of *Miseducation*'s popularity, Hill might have felt like "a politician." After all, her work entailed touring the country and world, presenting a polished persona at every turn, building a (fan) base, fielding demands that she represent her community, and enduring intense scrutiny while backed by a massive public relations machine (courtesy Columbia/Sony Records). These activities sound like the itinerary of a political candidate.

The new Hill has happily transformed from politician of respectability to madwoman. She claims that her "crazy and deranged" reputation helps her evade surveillance and preserve privacy. Perhaps her madness scares, bores, or confounds interlopers enough to keep them at bay—granting her the space to find "freedom" and "peace." I hasten to note that Hill's achievement of privacy-through-madness is eased by her privilege as a prominent musician. For the majority of black women—neither famous nor wealthy—to be viewed as "crazy and deranged" is to be especially vulnerable to *nullified privacy* and thwarted freedom in prisons and psychiatric wards.

Hill jests that she might "play these songs and twitch a little bit just so people know" that she's mad. A "twitch" is an abrupt and unruly bodily spasm typically associated with mental and/or neurological disability. Hill claims the twitch as a gesture within an embodied idiom of madness, a visual-corporeal cue in a mad performance repertoire, a kinesthetic sign that might be brandished to convey craziness and ward off interlopers. When Hill further proclaims, "That's my story and I'm sticking to it," she hints that there may be some other truth, some covert and withheld knowledge, beneath the "story" she tells. To be clear, neither Hill's talk of performing a twitch nor her winking insistence that she's sticking to her "story" necessarily imply that her madness is a ruse. It is possible to earnestly believe oneself crazy and strategically conceal it or expose it, present it or withhold it, downplay it or dramatize it within projects of self-making and self-defense.

Briefly, I want to ponder Hill's mad utterances on another "Outro," specifically the "Manifest/Outro," track that concludes the Fugees' 1996 album *The Score*. On this track, like "Peace of Mind," Hill describes madness induced by a hurtful man:

> You see, I loved hard once, but the love wasn't returned
> I found out the man I'd die for, he wasn't even concerned
> In time it turned, he tried to burn me like a perm
> Though my eyes saw the deception, my heart wouldn't let me learn
> . . .
> My heart must have died a thousand deaths
> Compared myself to Toni Braxton, thought I'd never catch my breath
> Nothing left, he stole the heart beating from my chest
> . . .
> Pain suppressed, will lead to cardiac arrest
> . . .
> I spent nights clutching my breasts overwhelmed by God's test
> I was God's best contemplating death with a Gillette
> But no man is ever worth the paradise manifest.[40]

These verses traverse the speaker's body as she details the visceral effects of unrequited love and emotional violence. The song's male antagonist deceives her, neglects her, betrays her, belittles her, and figuratively eviscerates her. The burnt scalp, the breathless lungs, the excised and still-beating heart, the clutched breasts, the unspecified stretch of skin threatened by razor blade: these are all corporeal points at which pain gathers and points from which pain emanates. But they are also existential coordinates where knowledge gathers, where wisdom originates. In fact, "Manifest/Outro" illuminates another sort of *talking wound*: one that clamors counsel. From these woundings, scorchings, and constrictions come revelation.

Hill's rapid, breathless, strident recitation redoubles the urgency of those lyrics. The verses crescendo and finally climax with the word *Gillette*, referring to the razor blade and potential instrument of the speaker's self-destruction. Thankfully, in the next instant, she coolly, knowingly announces the moral of the song: "But no man is ever worth the paradise manifest." She will not allow a neglectful or abusive man to be her undoing; nor should anyone else, if they heed her closing counsel. She speaks with the authority of a woman who has careened along the edge of destruction and survived to tell her cautionary tale.

Note that Hill's mention of a perm invokes black feminine embodiment in particular; the use of chemical agents to change hair texture is a familiar and frequent process for many black girls and women. Indeed, "Manifest/Outro," specifically evokes black womanhood driven to phenomenal and nearly suicidal madness. Hill testifies to the agony of degradation and the power of self-regard and self-affirmation. What results is an arresting depiction of black feminine pathos and expression of black feminist ethos.

LOSING IT

After her *Unplugged* performance, Hill was promptly deemed crazy by media pundits. She was "brainwashed" and "inexplicable," per *Fox News*.[41] She was "tore up. Tired. Lost" and "unwound," according to the *San Francisco Bay Guardian*.[42] She was "unhinged" in the *Los Angeles Times*.[43] She was "unglued" and "rambling," to have *Time* tell it.[44] She was "bizarre," "baffling," and "perversely fascinating," according to *Entertainment Weekly*.[45] She was "crazy" by *Vibe*'s standard.[46] Hill had embraced psychosocial alterity—and confessed mental distress and unruliness of mind—garnering widespread derision as "crazy."

Stoking speculation that Hill was mentally ill, her former Fugees bandmate and lover Wyclef Jean declared to *Rolling Stone*, "I felt sorry for her, because I think she needs psychiatric help. I felt like she's bipolar. You can't get angry with someone who's sick. So I even called her mom, and I stressed to her, 'Yo, you need to get her psychiatric help.' But I think they all fear her to death. She wasn't always like this—but if someone has the ego and you keep feeding the ego, it's going to turn monstrous."[47] Jean begins with the medicalized language of "psychiatric help," "bipolar," and concern for "someone who's sick," as though proposing a clinical intervention. Before long, he shifts from therapeutic idiom to the language of the grotesque, suggesting that Hill's ego, swollen with hubris, has bloated into a monstrosity that terrorizes even her loved ones. One wonders whether Jean's comments are inflected by the scorn of an ex-lover and ex-bandmate after personal and professional schism.

While a few commentators expressed concern with Hill's mental health and spiritual welfare (Pearl Cleage and Joan Morgan, both black feminists writing in *Essence*, belong on that brief list),[48] many seemed to relish the drama of such a steep and spectacular fall from favor. Beyond her emotional *Unplugged* performance, Hill's decision to walk away from massive earnings-potential likely colored her crazy in the view of devout capitalists. The commonsense of capitalism, where wealth is health and profit is paramount, is so deeply embedded in American Reason that any anticapitalist or antiprofit sentiments are liable to be deemed crazy.

Hill's early exaltation as prophetess and subsequent derision as mad-woman echo the tale of Cassandra, a tragic Trojan prophetess and madwoman of Classical Greek lore. In Aeschylus's *Agamemnon*, Cassandra is a revered diviner until she rebuffs the sexual advances of Apollo, the god of prophecy, and refuses to bear his offspring. To spite her, the vindictive god turns her gift into a curse, her adulation into abjection: she retains her prophetic ability, but no one believes her prophecies thereafter. Haunted by ghastly visions of her own murder and Trojan doom, vainly crying out for a sympathetic ear, Cassandra is ignored and reviled. Ultimately, her compatriots dismiss her at their own peril; her prophecies come true and Troy falls.[49]

In the Judeo-Christian paradigm, the prophet is often a holy insurrectionist, driven by divine inspiration to defy political and religious status quos. Philosopher and social theorist Cornel West contends that prophets are characterized by "vigilant disposition toward prevailing forms of individual and institutional evil," and "an unceasing suspicion of ossified and petrified forms of dogmatism."[50] By these measures, Hill's most brazen prophetic performance might have taken place at a 2003 Vatican Christmas concert. An invited guest of the pontiff, Hill interrupted her scheduled set to admonish church leaders for institutional cover-ups of child sexual abuse. She announced, "God has been a witness to the corruption of his leadership, of the exploitation and abuses which are the minimum that can be said for the clergy," and "I realize some of you may be offended by what I'm saying, but what do you say to the families who were betrayed by the people in whom they believed?"[51] Hill publicly rebuked a colossal global power—an institution that serves as moral arbiter for hundreds of millions of persons and has few rivals in influence or dominion across recorded history—while in person, on stage, at its headquarters, before its leadership. This is marvelously bold and risky business. It is an act of insurgent, *unruly will* that detractors derided as symptom of an *unruly mind*.

The US-based Catholic League condemned the performance as an "outburst" of madness. In a statement released weeks after her performance, League President Bill Donohue declared, "Hill's personal problems do not justify her rants against the Catholic Church. . . . Pathologically miserable, Hill has confessed to taking 'some lighter fluid and a match and burned everything I had built because the foundation was wrong.' It is no wonder that in one of her songs, she literally asks God to 'save me from myself.'"[52] He labels Hill "pathologically miserable" and dismisses her statements as "rants," coding her intervention as lunacy rather than prophecy. He reads Hill's insistence on burning down a faulty foundation as proof of an emotionally arsonous and self-destructive psyche.

Keeping in mind Donohue's denunciation of Hill, I want to reinvoke the figure of Cassandra. Hill's prophetic performance, the praise and adoration she garnered from powerful cultural arbiters, her spurning of power's advances, the punishment mobilized against her, and the dismissal of her insight as incoherent and crazy, all reflect the attempted *Cassandrafication* of Hill by powerful pundits and publics. However, Hill is no Cassandra. The disdain of dominion has not been her undoing. Instead, she participates in modes of sociality and fields of belonging outside the pop music mainstream. (Hill has described, for example, the fulfillment she achieves in her role as mother.[53] While many pundits insist that Hill's creativity has stalled in the twenty-first century, she has flourished procreatively. Nearly twenty-two years after *Miseducation*, Hill has released no studio albums—that is, she has borne no more desirable "offspring" for racial capitalism and its pop music–industrial complex—but she has given birth to six children.[54] She has chosen family over career and children over albums.) Also unlike Cassandra, Hill retains a critical mass of supporters, like her *Unplugged* studio audience, who defend, celebrate, and heed her proclamations.[55]

Far less receptive than that *Unplugged* audience were spectators at the Twenty-Fifth Annual Martin Luther King Jr. Concert Series in Brooklyn, New York, where Hill performed on August 6, 2007. The years between her 2001 *Unplugged* performance and this 2007 concert beheld her continued repudiations of celebrity culture, increased reclusion, tardy shows, vocal challenges, and rumors of outrageous "diva" behavior.[56] At this concert, Hill took the stage two hours late and confronted a cantankerous audience. In a *Village Voice* concert review titled "The Disorientation of Lauryn Hill," music journalist Rob Harvilla describes the scene:

> "Where Brooklyn at?" she asks. Brooklyn is at wit's end. "What took you so long?" demands one voice. "Sing something we know!" thunders another.
>
> Lauryn: "We gonna do some new things!"
> Crowd: "Uh-uh!"
> Lauryn [hurriedly]: "And we gonna do some old things!"
> Crowd: "Yeahhhhhh!"
> Lauryn then launches into an old thing that sounds new, as in unfamiliar, as in undesirable, as in uh-uh.[57]

In Harvilla's account, someone disrupts Hill to ask that she explain her tardiness. Another insists that she perform "something we know!" (probably music from her immensely popular *Miseducation* album). Still more resist her bid to perform "some new things!" The audience longs for *Miseducation*'s songs and most likely for *Miseducation*'s Hill. By demanding that she perform a familiar song, audience members pressure Hill to channel "that old" her: the "forbiddingly perfect" and deeply insecure media darling, the "politician" who lacked peace and privacy, the repressed woman who lived in a "box." Harvilla colorfully recounts that "for a half-hour, this show is absolutely terrifying, a volatile star versus a sweltering, irritated crowd. Apocalypse looms." He describes the clash between the audience's demand for the familiar and Hill's insistence on the radical; between the audience's stubborn nostalgia for the old "Lauryn" and the singer's emphatic insistence on the reinvented "Ms. Hill."

To have Harvilla tell it, Hill nominally indulges but substantively refuses the audience's preference for the familiar. She performs "something we know!" but it is altered so drastically that it feels strange. During this concert and nearly all others since her reemergence, Hill revamps *Miseducation* tracks, sometimes beyond recognition. She changes song keys, shuffles vocal arrangements, overhauls instrumental accompaniment, dramatically modulates volume, and radically accelerates the tempos of her nineties hits. In much of the concert footage circa that 2007 performance, Hill scats, raps, slurs, shouts, or pauses to catch breath during stanzas she had sung with melodic and rhythmic precision on their original tracks. It seems that Hill will only revisit her former persona if it is differently staged, differently intoned, differently arranged, differently accompanied, differently emoted, differently paced, and thus, hardly recognizable as that former persona at all.

This 2007 performance—and much of Hill's stage and public persona since 2001—instantiates what black feminist performance theorist Daphne Brooks calls an "Afro-alienation act." Proposing a theory of "black(ened)" diasporic performance in the late nineteenth and early twentieth centuries, wherein "the condition of alterity converts into cultural expressiveness and a specific strategy of cultural performances," Brooks asserts the following: "Just as [Bertolt] Brecht calls for actors to adapt 'socially critical' techniques in their performances so as to generate 'alienation effects' and to 'awaken' audiences to history, so too can we consider these historical figures [and performers] as critically de-familiarizing their own bodies by way of performance in order to yield alternative racial and gender epistemologies. By using performance tactics to signify of the social, cultural and ideological machinery that circumscribes African Americans, they intervene in the spectacular and systemic representational abjection of black peoples."[58]

Harvilla characterizes Hill's voice as a "malicious, inarticulate rasp." Hill's voice is "malicious" because it is an Afro-alienating sound that violently assaults the polished, slickly produced paradigm of late-nineties pop vocals. If her voice is "inarticulate," that is because it flouts the sensibilities of pop music (where catchy love odes and pristine heartbreak ballads reign supreme) and thus ceases to make hegemonic sense. Harvilla believes that Hill's struggling voice is a metonym for her life and mind. He declares that "Lauryn wails, sounding not a little crazy herself. [She performs] a song of passion and desperation now sung by someone with plenty of both, who realizes she's losing a crowd that probably assumes she's losing her mind—and maybe she is."[59] To have Harvilla tell it, Hill might be suffering an existential dispossession and nervous breakdown before his eyes and ears: losing her audience, losing her mind, losing her voice, and maybe gaining voices in her head instead.[60] For her part, Hill would likely claim that no matter what she is losing, she is gaining liberation: losing the whole world to gain back her soul.[61]

Harvilla further describes Hill's voice as "angry, vicious, unpleasant *by design*." While physiological vicissitudes have likely contributed to Hill's vocal changes, Harvilla rightly recognizes that "design" is also at work. Indeed, Hill deliberately and strategically brandishes her ailing voice. In an interview immediately after her 2001 *Unplugged* performance, Hill told MTV that "it used to kill me, but not anymore. It got to the point where I was like, 'Oh my God, it's reality.' My voice being raspy doesn't change the words. I'm sorry that I can't run up the scale and back, but this ain't about me. It's about people receiving encouragement to jump that battery and start living."[62] Unfortunately, for many reviewers this *is* about Hill. It seems that Harvilla, for instance, is distracted by Hill's hoarse vocals and thus less attentive to the messages conveyed with those vocals. Nevertheless, Hill marshals her hoarse voice and unpredictable stage performances in an effort to "'awaken' audiences to history": the fraught history of black female artistry in America, where black girls and women are targeted by those "insecurity, ghosts, and demons"; the sordid history of racial capitalism in pop music, where black performance is rabidly consumed, often to the detriment of performers; and the turbulent history of Hill's career.

Black feminist visual culture theorist Nicole Fleetwood advances a notion of the "visible seam" in black women's visual art. She theorizes the visible seam as "an aesthetic device and a discursive intervention that reveal the gaps and sutures of dominant visual narratives and the underpinning ideologies that maintain them."[63] Whereas Fleetwood's focus is on the visual, I want to synesthetically adapt her insights to the aural in order to caption Hill's performance. Analogous with the visible seam is what we might call the *resonant crack*: where the voice cracks, breaks, snaps, and is nevertheless transmitted to audiences in its riven condition. Hill refuses to force pristine vocals from her throat and ostensibly opts out of backing tracks available for live performance. Instead, Hill exposes and amplifies the cracks in her voice to draw attention to "gaps and sutures of dominant [musical] narratives and the underpinning ideologies that maintain them." Those ideologies include the (racial) capitalism and vicious profiteering that compel artists to conform to market trends even when it means self-abnegation.

Forty-three years before Hill's MLK performance, another black woman musician would marshal hoarse vocals in order to sound a shrill alarm to "'awaken' audiences to history." Jazz and blues vocalist Abbey Lincoln forged a cracking, Afro-alienating sound amid the tumult of the Civil Rights Movement. "Triptych: Prayer/Protest/Peace," Lincoln's 1964 collaboration with the Max Roach Quintet on the album *We Insist! Max Roach's Freedom Now Suite*, is an iconic protest song emerging from the movement. In the "Protest" section of the triptych, Lincoln's earsplitting shrieks and screeches are wordless exclamations of fury at racial injustice; she unleashes a piercing sound of black aural and existential angst that precedes and exceeds language. Because Lincoln's performance is commonly indexed within a Civil Rights–era protest tradition and emergent be-bop avant-garde, her wails are readily regarded as vocal innovation and political intervention.

Hill's vocally cracked resonance has not generally been read as innovation. Despite her repeated insistence that she wants and intends to showcase her hoarseness, Hill's raspy, jagged, cracking voice is still framed in pop punditry as *failure* and *loss of control.*

Practicing a mad methodology, I hear Hill's decision to perform with a faltering voice as an aesthetic-cum-political gesture, as experimentation and innovation in avant-garde black performance. Her cracked voice jolts audiences, resists *easy listening*, rejects the pop culture palatability she cultivated last millennium, and hopefully provokes conversation "about people receiving encouragement to jump that battery and start living."

INTRODUCING MS. HILL

Since circa 2005, Hill has demanded that she be addressed and billed as "Ms. Hill." Dismissed by some as a symptom of melodramatic egotism and delusional grandeur,[64] Hill's mandate accrues symbolic value amid the history of degrading names aimed at black people in America and elsewhere. Hill responds to a history stretching from chattel slavery through the Information Age, in which "boy," "gal," "Uncle," "Auntie," and even one's given first name are insidious counterparts to "nigger" in arsenals of antiblack speech. While some of these appellations may appear endearing, the fact is that within the broader matrix of title in the West (where reverence is signaled in formal prefix), white refusals to grant black people "Mr." and "Ms." prefixes have functioned to belittle them. By demanding the "Ms." honorific, Hill admonishes against a presumptuous first-name familiarity that rehearses (purposefully or inadvertently) rituals of antiblack appellation.

Near the start of "Mama's Baby, Papa's Maybe," Hortense Spillers recites a litany of epithets: "'Peaches' and 'Brown Sugar,' 'Sapphire' and 'Earth Mother,' 'Aunty,' 'Granny,' God's 'Holy Fool,' a 'Miss Ebony First,' or 'Black Woman at the Podium.'" She explains that the preceding "are markers so loaded with mythical prepossession that there is no easy way for the agents buried beneath them to come clean. . . . In order for me to speak a truer word concerning myself, I must strip down through layers of attenuated meanings, made an excess in time, over time, assigned by a particular historical order, and there await whatever marvels of my own inventiveness."[65] Spillers is describing an "American grammar" replete with discursive and symbolic violence that distorts and debases black womanhood. Though *Hill* is an Anglophone surname possibly forced upon her enslaved ancestors, Hill attempts to claim it, preceded by formal honorific, to signify respect within her own project of self-making and "inventiveness." She declares, "I'm Ms. Hill because I know I'm a wise woman. That is the respect I deserve."[66]

Another of Hill's directives: *Do not touch her.* In a 2006 *Essence* article, she recounts, "I was at a store one day when this woman started touching me and I said, 'Listen, ma'am, I don't like to be touched.' And she was offended. 'You don't like to be touched?!' Five years ago I would have said, 'Okay, touch me.' Now I'm like, 'I don't like to be touched, get off me!' I didn't always have the strength to do that. It's especially hard when you have the desire to be liked and make everyone happy."[67] Although there is no indication that this stranger means the musician physical harm, this touch is nevertheless a flagrant act of violation. This woman feels entitled to lay her hands on another person's body, and has the gall to become offended at the refusal, as though she's the victim in such an encounter, as though touching Hill is her right. Though the "Lauryn" of old would have abided this touch for the sake of niceness, "Ms. Hill" rebuffs it to protect her personal boundaries and corporeal security.

The musician's comments bring to mind innumerable contexts in which black people's bodies have been touched—pulled, prodded, poked, caressed, battered, penetrated—without permission. Auction blocks, slave quarters, alleyways, schoolyards, prison yards, doctor's offices, and yes, stores, have been constant sites of unwanted touch and violation perpetrated against black people. Hill insists on setting the terms for how people refer to her and how they approach her. She will not tolerate a stranger calling her "Lauryn," let alone, say, "bitch"; she will not abide an unwelcome tap on her shoulder, let alone, say, a strike or grab. Furthermore, she activates madness—in this case, anger—when she demands that antagonists "get off me!"

Six years after that *Essence* interview, Hill would further instrumentalize anger in a searing song called "Black Rage." Sung to the melody of Rodgers and Hammerstein's popular showtune "My Favorite Things," "Black Rage" is a masterful act of "signifyin(g)." The latter is defined by literary theorist Henry Louis Gates Jr. as the "repetition with revision" within a cultural production or practice—repetition that can function as "parody" and supply "severe critique."[68] Performing the song in October 2012 at a concert in Houston, Texas, Hill retained Rodgers's melody and lyrical meter, but otherwise drastically altered and signified on the tune.

Her rendition entails an accelerated tempo; a hard, driving drumbeat; a dissonant, staccato piano; a blaring electric guitar; and rapid-fire vocal delivery.[69] Most poignantly, Hill subverts the original song's cheery disposition with these woeful new lyrics:

> Black rage is founded on two-thirds a person
> Rapings and beatings and suffering that worsens
> Black human packages tied up in strings
> Black rage is founded on these kinds of things
>
> So when the dogs bite
> and when the beatings
> and when I'm feeling sad
> I simply remember all these kinds of things
> and then I don't fear so bad[70]

Where the phrase *raindrops* resides in the original song, Hill replaces it with "black rage"; "whiskers on kittens" is exchanged for "two-thirds a person"; the verse "bright copper kettles and warm woolen mittens" is supplanted by "rapings and beatings and suffering that worsens"; "brown paper packages tied up with strings" are traded for "black human packages tied up in strings." No longer a litany of childlike whimsies and delectable objects, the song is recast as a sinister inventory of violence, oppression, terror, and death. In additional lyrics, Hill scathingly indicts antiblack dominion, deftly invoking slavery, lynching, rape, racial capitalism, state-sanctioned police brutality, psychic violence, and myriad other atrocities. If the original song is a confection of idyllic fancies, Hill suggests that black slave labor and exploitation has cut the cane to provide such sweetness.

Remarkably, the recitation of these atrocities comforts Hill. She proclaims, "I simply remember these kinds of things and then I don't fear so bad." Knowing the harrowing history of "black rage" empowers her to critically process it and use it. Indeed, the song is not simply a description of black fury; it is an act of black fury, full of intensity and ferocity, instrumentalized for pedagogical and inspirational effect.[71] Ideally, Hill's lyrics encourage enraged black people to politicize their wrath in pursuit of social transformation. (And indeed, black people have long harnessed fury like fuel propelling them toward ballot boxes, picket lines, armed resistance, and riotous rebellion.) With "Black Rage," Hill takes up the mantle of Nina Simone, whose "Mississippi Goddam" was also a call to furious solidarity against antiblackness.

In her influential 1981 essay, "The Uses of Anger," black feminist poet and critic Audre Lorde writes, "Every woman has a well-stocked arsenal of anger against those oppressions, personal and institutional, which brought that anger into being. Focused with precision, it can become a powerful source of energy serving progress and change."[72] Heeding Lorde's counsel on the efficacy in anger, black feminist historian and critic Brittney Cooper rallies black women to cultivate "eloquent rage" as a "feminist superpower" in struggles against antiblackness and misogyny. Significantly, Cooper notes that such rage is not always "focused with precision," but might, in fact, be "messy as hell."[73] Cooper's black feminist praxis makes space for messiness and mistakes—and encourages extending generosity and grace—for those learning and growing to become feminist heroines. Hill models the "uses of anger," whether "focused" or "messy," as an instrument in protest music and a "powerful source of [sonic] energy serving progress and change."

Hill drew further attention to the violence of global white supremacy—and to the role of rage as a political affect animating social upheaval—when she lent her voice to the documentary film "Concerning Violence: Nine Scenes from the Anti-Imperialistic Self-Defense."[74] Directed by Swedish filmmaker Göran Hugo Olsson, the documentary entails archival footage of colonial carnage and devastation interwoven with selections from Frantz Fanon's *Wretched of the Earth*. Passages from Fanon's text are visually superimposed over the video footage while Hill reads them aloud, her voice aurally dubbed over the audio footage. She orates Fanon's account of the violence of colonialism and the violent revolution that will be its demise. Significantly, *Wretched of the Earth* does not so much incite anticolonial violence as it prophesizes the necessity and inevitability of such violence for revolutionary upheaval.

This material might have lent itself to impassioned and dramatic reading, but Hill delivers the lines with a stern, sober, stoic didacticism that serves the source text well. Because the images are often incendiary, horrific, and heart-breaking, one might take solace in the steadiness of Hill's voice. Perhaps her calm comes from the same fortitude she described on "Black Rage": "I simply remember all these kinds of things," including the relentlessness of antiblack-ness, the persistence of colonial violence, and the prospect of revolution, "and then I don't fear so bad."

THE BAG LADY'S REVENGE

To ponder the look of Hill's alleged madness, I examine a photograph of the musician performing at Heineken Music Hall in Amsterdam, Netherlands, on July 26, 2007. The image has circulated widely on tabloid websites, often captioned as "crazy" and presented as though it were transparent proof of Hill's madness. It has incited hundreds of online comments lamenting and ridiculing the vision of Hill therein.[75]

In the photograph, Hill dons an oversized black bowler hat atop a black and auburn Afro; large gold leaf earrings; thick tufts of false eyelashes; heavy foundation topped with bursts of purple blush on her cheeks; deep-purple lipstick with a darker purple lip liner; a large costume ring of orange, red, and gold on a hand that holds a microphone to her mouth; and a beige trench coat. The expression on Hill's face is arresting: her brow is wrinkled tightly, her nostrils are flared, her forehead is streaked with sweat and bulging veins, and her mouth is gaping as she sings or hollers or cries out.

Concerning Hill's appearance in like garb at a performance that same summer in Oakland, California, the *San Francisco Chronicle* reported that "Hill wore a green-and-yellow plaid jacket that appeared to be made of wool and an ankle-length black skirt, looking not unlike a bag lady one might encounter at a taco truck on International Boulevard."[76] Nearly five years later, *L.A. Weekly* claimed that "with her face plastered in red and blue make-up, and wearing an over-sized bag-lady style coat, she rambled and mumbled her way through the opening songs."[77] To these commentators, Hill resembles the crazy "bag lady" whose person is overloaded with accoutrements because there is no home with a closet to store them—who collects an excess of objects that clash, clutter, and seem to overdetermine her as visibly and visually wretched. A gendered abjection, bag ladyhood is womanhood ejected from the domestic sphere (which, according to patriarchal logics, is the appropriate space for femininity) and into the street. The presence of "lady" within the epithet ironically highlights such a woman's distance from conventional bourgeois ladyhood.

5.1 Ms. Lauryn Hill performing at Heineken Music Hall, Amsterdam, the Netherlands, on July 26, 2007. © 2007 Getty Images/Mark Venema.

As an alternative to bag ladyhood, Hill's appearance might be captioned as *bohemianism*: an aesthetic and political orientation that rejects bourgeois social norms, celebrates eccentricity, extols creativity, romanticizes starving artistry, and revels in nonconformist and unstructured living.[78] Hill has disclosed an ardor for fashion, and these outfits might reflect a sartorial bohemianism: combining her love of fashion-forward clothing with her eccentric, nonconformist, Afro-alienated propensities post-*Miseducation*.[79] Whereas those "bag lady" appellations suggest abjection and desolation, this bohemian reading emphasizes critical agency and creativity.

Regarding a similar outfit in 2007, *New York* magazine observed that she "wasn't exactly wearing a Halloween costume,"[80] coding her appearance as scary and even monstrous. The suggestion of monstrosity brings to mind the grotesque, which emphasizes "parts of the body that are open to the outside world. . . . *the open mouth*, the genital organs, the breasts, the phallus, the pot-belly, *the nose.*"[81] This freeze-frame of Hill is especially prone to grotesque readings because it captures her with mouth agape and nostrils flaring. When tabloid bloggers and media outlets published this image of Hill, they hailed her into the visual matrix of the grotesque.

Although antiblackness constantly codes black people's bodies as excessive, unwieldy, and grotesque within systems of symbolic violence, grotesquerie may paradoxically be wielded to combat such violence. Bakhtin declares that the grotesque, especially its mad aspect, possesses insurgent power: "The theme of madness is inherent to all grotesque forms, because madness makes men look at the world with different eyes, not dimmed by 'normal,' that is by commonplace ideas and judgments."[82] Indeed, through its dramatic distortion of the "normal," the grotesque can evince and encourage radical (re)visions of the world. Just as Hill's hoarse vocals and accelerated arrangements thwart *easy listening*, her visual presentation in this picture likewise thwarts *easy viewing*. For many who beheld this image in 2007—accustomed to Hill's trendier *Miseducation*-era appearance—the photograph likely incited a disconcerted double-take and lingering stare. Perhaps the photo even occasioned looking at Hill "with different eyes, not dimmed by 'normal,' that is by commonplace ideas and judgments" about how she could or should appear on stage. Ultimately, I regard this photograph as a portrait of Afro-alienation; it marshals mad grotesquerie to disrupt the hegemonic scene (and seen) of black female celebrity, popular performance, and racial capitalism circa 2007.

We need not rely on Bakhtin to explain Hill's "mad" conduct during this period; the emcee has proffered her own theory of madness and her own explanation for her "crazy" demeanor. At a Los Angeles concert with the briefly reunited Fugees in February 2006, she declared, "Ladies and gentlemen, I'm not crazy. I'm just a black woman who's super smart, who can't be bought and who can't be bribed. I'm not a machine. I give my people the truth. Today, if you're all of those things they think you're crazy. If that's the definition of crazy, then I'm crazy."[83] Hill indicts an antiblack, sexist, racially capitalist order that would commodify her, purchase her wholesale, and use her as a "machine" to mass-produce a hegemonic order at the expense of "the truth." Moreover, she recognizes that the epithet *crazy* is aimed at people who manifest an unruly will, who resist hegemonic co-optation, who are unintelligible to hegemonic common sense. She specifies that smart, defiant, honorable black womanhood is especially susceptible to such denigration.

Remarkably, Hill moves from a transgressive disavowal of craziness ("I'm not crazy") to a subversive claim of it ("then I'm crazy"). In her transgressive disavowal, she rejects the "crazy" label that has been assigned to her, but reinforces the premise that craziness is negative and should be shunned. In contrast, Hill's subversive embrace of madness undermines the fundamental logic of madness-as-derogatory and takes up madness as a banner of resistance. Madness might be desirable amid a corrupt world order that deems itself Reasonable.[84]

"IT ALL FALLS DOWN"

Ms. Lauryn Hill is not the only hip-hop iconoclast whose art practice and public persona mobilize mad black creativity. Kanye West has also scaled that treacherous summit of global stardom and ranks among the most critically acclaimed and commercially successful emcees in the history of hip-hop. His catalogue is a medley of kinetic protest anthems, impassioned ballads of love and heartbreak, and braggadocious odes to himself—sometimes all merged into a single track. West has a knack for swerving between boasts of extravagant power and confessions of staggering insecurity, engendering a sort of musical polarity that might analogize the psychiatric bipolarity he has publicly disclosed. I will return to West's self-professed bipolar "superpower" shortly, but first I want to locate him in relation to Hill.

We might think of West as Hill's sibling in a kinship of black musicians purportedly navigating "genius" and "madness" within the crucible of early twenty-first-century pop culture. West has expressed affinity and admiration for Hill, extolling her as "a beautiful, beautiful young lady that's inspired me, definitely,"[85] and admitting that he "listened to *The Miseducation of Lauryn Hill* at least a thousand times" while creating his own debut album *College Dropout* (2004).[86] Perhaps *Miseducation*, with its titular and thematic attention to (mis)education, influenced West's own scholastic titles and fixations on his first three albums: *College Dropout, Late Registration*, and *Graduation*.

In 2003, West sampled a snippet of Hill's *Unplugged* song, "Mystery of Iniquity," and prominently incorporated it into his mixtape track, "All Falls Down." In the song, West culls Hill's lyrics, "It all, all falls down / I'm telling you it all, it all falls down," a prophetic caution heralding the downfall of corporatist-colonialist-misogynist-racist regimes of deceit and delusion. He samples Hill's line as a constant refrain, more persistently present than a conventional chorus, as bits of Hill's admonition and accompanying guitar riff are interspersed amid West's verses. In the song, West describes black folks wading through the afterlife of slavery, the viciousness of antiblackness, the demands of respectability, the lure of materialism, and the haze of the American fever dream. He breathlessly proclaims:

> It seem, we living the American dream
> The people highest up got the lowest self esteem
>
> . . .
>
> Shine because they hate us, floss cause they degrade us
> We trying to buy back our forty acres
> And for that paper, look how low we'll stoop
> Even if you in a Benz, you still a nigga in a coupe [coop]
>
> . . .
>
> 'Cause they made us hate ourself and love they wealth

He describes black people who have access to monetary and cultural capital, who appear "successful" by prevailing neoliberal standards. And yet they are nonetheless—and in fact, all the more—spiritually unfulfilled, mentally distressed, morally bereft, self-loathing, and unfree.[87] West suggests that it is possible to physically occupy a luxury coupe car while existentially trapped in a chicken coop (a farm enclosure for hens, where chicken-loving black caricatures congregate in blackface minstrelsy). The façade may seem alluring, but it is unsound; eventually the structure "all falls down."

Whereas Hill was called crazy for her dramatic disruption of a papal status quo, West was deemed crazy for two dramatic disruptions of a presidential status quo. The first of West's interventions took place at a 2005 telethon raising money and awareness for New Orleans in the immediate aftermath of Hurricane Katrina. While on live television, he veered off the teleprompted script to declare, "George Bush doesn't care about black people." West was referring to systematic neglect and n ecropolitical devaluation of poor black people in New Orleans—all laid bare in the aftermath of Katrina, when thousands were left to die. (Of course, presidential indifference and malfeasance against black people long precedes and far exceeds the Bush administration. Historically, such malfeasance has been so common that one might presume it part of the presidential job description.) West also defied a deeply entrenched American psychonorm: the polite, conciliatory expression of national unity in the aftermath of national tragedy. Because of its function as unruly and disruptive speech, its violation of US postdisaster psychonorms, and its expression of righteous rage against black suffering and antiblack complicity, this public rebuke of George W. Bush was an act of mad black performance. It was as dramatic and compelling as any musical spectacle.

Over a decade later, West would attempt a very different intervention in presidential politics. At a November 2016 concert in San Jose, California, West confessed that he had not voted in the national election that month, but revealed that if he had, he would have cast his ballot for Donald Trump's presidency. Just four days later, West was hospitalized in Los Angeles for a "psychiatric emergency."[88] Speculation swirled that West's support of Trump was the symptom of a mental breakdown, proof that the musician had lost his mind.

Since then, West has repeatedly expressed admiration for Trump, whom he views as an "outsider" who managed to "infiltrate" the political establishment and affirm that "anything is possible."[89] In April 2018, in the lead-up to the November 2018 US midterm elections, West doubled down and tweeted that "the mob can't make me not love [Trump]. We are both dragon energy. He is my brother."[90] West's comments garnered accusations of treachery, stupidity, and insanity. Many continued to question West's soundness of mind, seeming to wonder: How could a man, once known for speaking truth to presidential power, endorse Trump's appalling presidency? What, but psychotic delusion, could spin a man to such a dramatic about-face? What, other than mental illness, could drive a black man to align with a presidency so clearly and categorically antithetical to black liberation? Such questions, however earnest and well-intentioned, reflect the psychonormative tendency to cast undesirable and inexplicable behavior as mental illness.

It seems to me that West's declarations that "Bush doesn't care about black people" in 2005 and that "the mob can't make me not love" Trump in 2018 were both intended as insurrectionary speech and political provocation to unsettle complacency. In critiquing Bush, West attempted to disrupt complacency about presidential antiblackness among (white) American public spheres. In endorsing Trump, West attempted to challenge an anti-Trump consensus among many of his peers in black communities and in hip-hop milieus. Of course, these two declarations lend themselves to drastically different political agendas. The first attempts to repudiate presidential antiblackness; the second effectively colludes with presidential antiblackness. The first speaks truth to power, calling out a necropolitical disregard for black life; the second bickers with disaffected masses about his right to "love" a pugnacious head of state.

West's foray into presidential drama was not his only spectacular controversy in 2018. In the month following his "dragon energy" declaration, West uttered these words in the offices of internet tabloid TMZ: "When you hear about slavery for four hundred years—for four hundred years? That sound like a choice. You were there for four hundred years and it's all of y'all? It's like we're mentally imprisoned."[91] To suggest that enslaved people categorically consented to their degradation is to reveal profound ignorance about the violent coercion and nullification of consent that characterized chattel slavery; or worse, it is to flaunt a victim-blaming antipathy toward the enslaved. However, I want to highlight the last sentence of the above statement: "It's like we're mentally imprisoned." West pivots from commentary on the history of chattel slavery to an assessment of present-day people who are in psychic bondage. It seems to me that West's intended emphasis, from the onset, is not antebellum abjection but twenty-first-century groupthink. The latter is West's longtime fixation; he has spent much of his career touting emancipation from societal status quos, escape from cultural conformity, and glory in a promised land of creative freedom. While challenging groupthink is a worthy mission, the problem is that West reduces chattel slavery to mere prologue and analogue in order to mount that challenge. In the process, he minimizes and mischaracterizes a world-historical atrocity.

The next day, West attempted to clarify his comments on slavery and emphasize his concern with twenty-first century, rather than antebellum, tethers. He tweeted, "The reason why I brought up the 400 years point is because we can't be mentally imprisoned for another 400 years. We need free thought now."[92] He added, "of course I know that slaves did not get shackled and put on a boat by free will" and "my point is for us to have stayed in that position even though the numbers were on our side means that we were mentally enslaved."[93] But if West is referring to the United States, he is wrong; historical data indicate that the numbers were not on the side of enslaved people. According to the 1860 census, only about 13 percent of the total US population was enslaved, and Mississippi and South Carolina were the only states with more enslaved than free persons. Fifty years earlier, as per the 1810 census, no state had a majority enslaved population.[94]

West's intentions are undermined by inaccuracy and obscured by reductive phrases—but there is a critical impetus, however inchoate, animating his remarks. West wants to emphasize the psychological degradation and violence to which enslaved people were subjected (in tandem with the physical). He means to point to the chaining and maiming of the mind that reinforced the chaining and maiming of the body, which caused some captives to internalize their subjection and become docile beings who favored their master's rule over freedom. However, such a position should not be labeled a "choice"; rather, it is a terrifying collapse of the will under the "soul-murderous" weight of chattel slavery.[95]

In that same recorded interview at TMZ's offices, West also asserted that "we're taught how to think, we're taught how to feel. We don't know how to think for ourselves, we don't know how to feel for ourselves . . . I felt a freedom in . . . just doing something that everybody tells you not to do." Perhaps his polemics originate in a desire to *feel freedom* even and especially through arbitrary acts of dissent and contrariness. It seems that West wants to go against the grain that surrounds him, no matter the direction of that grain. He seeks to stir the pot—whatever the ingredients, whoever's being fed. West is describing an *unruliness of will* mobilized against psychosocial norms, whatever those norms. Depending upon whose rules he is defying in a given instance, this mad contrariness may serve structures of dominion, movements for liberation, or both, or else.

In response to rumors of madness, West had this to say in a 2018 interview:

> They'll take something I'll say that's like absolutely inspired . . . but if they put something inspired in the wrong context it will come off as . . . I don't want to say "crazy" cause I also want to change the stigma of crazy and I want to change the stigma of mental health, period. I have not done no extra study on it, we at the beginning of it, we at the beginning of the conversation . . . but best believe I'ma take the stigma off the word *crazy*. But let's just say for now people will take something that's enlightened, put it in a different context and then call it crazy to try to diminish the impact and the value of what I'm actually saying.[96]

Frustrated by media outlets spinning his "inspired" statements as "crazy," West begins to defend himself against their characterizations. But he stops himself short, realizing that such defensiveness reinforces the notion that "crazy" is fundamentally negative. Like Hill, West recognizes that the term "crazy" is weaponized to punish people who transgress social norms. Like Hill, he initially disavows madness but then wonders whether madness should be claimed and embraced instead. Applying far more critical nuance to the matter of madness than he did to the subject of slavery, West plans to research mental illness with hopes of effectively destigmatizing it. Here he aspires to something like scholar-activism: an extensive process of "study" and "conversation" intended to disseminate knowledge that will transform public discourse and empower subjugated people.

In the same interview, West explains of his hospitalization, "There was elements about going to the hospital and having a breakdown or breakthrough that was fire. It was incredible, the feeling. . . . On the song 'Saint Pablo,' I said 'I'm praying an outerbody [*sic*] experience would happen so people could see my light.'" According to West, his breakdown did not dim his radiance; to the contrary, his breakdown was also a breakthrough that unleashed and intensified his light. While others pity West for allegedly going *out of his mind*, he rejoices in the supernatural sensation of going *out of his body* and exceeding the limits of his flesh. When West admits that he prayed for such an experience, he casts madness as divine intercession.

West likewise treats madness as a supernatural endowment in a track called "Yikes" on his 2018 *Ye* album:

> That's why I fuck with Ye
> See, that's my third person
> That's my bipolar shit, nigga, what?
> That's my superpower, nigga, ain't no disability
> I'm a superhero! I'm a superhero![97]

He flouts conventional perceptions of "disability" as affliction and dysfunction, instead touting his "bipolar shit" as a "superpower." The manic experience of bipolar disorder sometimes manifests as intense rushes of energy or feelings of invincibility—analogous to powers possessed by comic book superheroes. In casting manic depression as a superpower, West might be said to romanticize mental illness and obscure the hardship endured by many bipolar people.[98] However, West is describing his own experience in his own idiom of self-expression—not proposing a universal account of the condition. Furthermore, when we consider West's broader oeuvre, it is clear that he does not categorically romanticize madness. Rather, he regards and describes it with complex ambivalence: it is variously "beautiful" and "twisted"; euphoric and distressing; cause for grievance and for gratitude.[99]

A poignant expression of that ambivalence appears on the album cover for *Ye*. Pictured there are the words, "I hate being Bi-Polar its awesome [*sic*]," in handwritten, neon green letters, superimposed upon a photograph of a mountain range. West succinctly describes a conflicted experience that induces both *hate* and *awe* in him. Because it is both loathsome and awesome, his bipolar condition cannot be neatly plotted on one or another side of a clear-cut good | bad binary. It is both and neither and more. It is significant that West features these words on the cover of the album, unfurling a disability disclosure that will greet most listeners before they dive into the tracks. This disclosure invites audiences to foreground madness as a theme and analytic while listening to *Ye*.

In sum, West's madness is manifold. It is a phenomenal unruliness of mind, sometimes ecstatic and sometimes despondent. It is a medicalized diagnosis of bipolar disorder. It is anger at perceived groupthink. Moreover, West's madness is a psychosocial rebellion, an emphatic unruliness of will that he marshals, sometimes clumsily, to disrupt orthodoxy. Just as West regards his madness with ambivalence, I propose approaching him with a critical ambivalence that registers both the loathsome and awesome resonance in his articulations. Rather than fully dismiss or wholly embrace West, I dance between push and pull. Indeed, it is possible to appreciate his antiracist interventions while rebuking his antiblack provocations; to turn up the volume on his liberation anthems while muting his Trumpist overtures (or maybe chopping and screwing them beyond recognition); to rally against his dangerous ignorance even as we extend him radical compassion.

"START AGAIN"

Twenty-two years after the release of *Miseducation*, Hill continues to tour and headline various musical festivals, her concerts sometimes panned for vocal fluctuations, accelerated arrangements, and tardy starts. Indeed, Hill's now legendary lateness for shows is sometimes denounced as shameless divadom or a pathological inability to keep time; meanwhile, the nonarrival of a studio-recorded follow-up to *Miseducation* is decried, by some, as proof of arrested artistic development. Debates rage in the popular press, on social media, in concert halls, in beauty shops, and likely at Sony Music marketing meetings about Hill's legacy and future in the pop music industry.[100] All the while, she maintains a beloved community of fans who admire her black radical feminist audacity, relish the occasional singles she releases, recognize her enduring influence on popular music, patiently await her (studio album) return.

Hill's fans awaited her return with heightened suspense during three months in 2013. Convicted of federal tax evasion on at least $1.8 million in earnings, Hill spent ninety days in a minimum-security women's prison in Connecticut. But before her conviction, she issued a statement regarding the charges against her. In those remarks, posted on her website, Hill describes going "underground" for several years to protect herself and her family from an exploitative music industry and media machine. While off the grid, she explains, she performed infrequently, earned little income, and thus had to stockpile savings and withhold taxes to care financially for her family. She elaborates,

> I did not deliberately abandon my fans, nor did I deliberately abandon any responsibilities, but I did however put my safety, health and freedom and the freedom, safety and health of my family first over all other material concerns! I also embraced my right to resist a system intentionally opposing my right to whole and integral survival. . . . I conveyed all of this when questioned as to why I did not file taxes during this time period. Obviously,

the danger I faced was not accepted as reasonable grounds for deferring my tax payments, as authorities, who despite being told all of this, still chose to pursue action against me, as opposed to finding an alternative solution.[101]

She makes clear that her priorities do not align with IRS statutes and that her personal morality takes precedence over US legality. She also critiques the US justice system for its propensity to incarcerate, "as opposed to finding an alternative solution," in response to conflict or infraction. Although Hill's imprisonment was not tied to any psychiatric diagnosis, she shares an intimate knowledge of state-sanctioned captivity with the historical and fictional psychiatric detainees throughout this study. Furthermore, she occupies a continuum of black people held captive by Western governments in sites spanning seventeenth-century barracoons, nineteenth-century plantations, twentieth-century psychiatric hospitals, and twenty-first-century jails and prisons.

Back in 2002, Cleage had pondered Hill alongside a group of gifted black women performers who died young: "The life [Hill] had constructed was not the one she wanted to live. It had become more weight than she could carry without becoming a madwoman or a sadwoman or just one more name on a list that includes Billie Holiday and Florence Ballard and Dorothy Dandridge and all the sisters whose vibrant artistry couldn't save their lives."[102] Reciting a tragic litany—to which we might add the late Phyllis Hyman and Whitney Houston, among many others—Cleage identifies Hill as a "vibrant" black woman artist encumbered by market forces, public whims, creative frustrations, personal tragedy, and mental distress, all against the backdrop of structural antiblackness and misogyny. Thankfully, Hill is still living, performing, and creating, and thus does not belong on that funerary list.

Hill herself relates her predicament to a broader matrix of hardship endured by black women. In a 2006 interview with hip-hop feminist Joan Morgan, Hill professes:

It's really about the Black woman falling in love with her own image of beauty. I thought that a perfectly reciprocal relationship was an impossibility. That's that "Black woman is the mule of the world" thing. It says she can't get what she deserves, no matter how dope she is. And, you know, you have to go through the fear. You do have to do something with the insecurity, ghosts and demons that have been programmed in us for centuries. You have to master the voices, all the insecure and inadequate men who put garbage in a woman's mind, soul, spirit and psyche just so they can use her.[103]

Hill cites centuries of epistemic violence, psychological terror, sociopolitical degradation, and existential assault targeted at black women. She repudiates the "mule of the world" creed, which potentially naturalizes black female abjection and accepts a culture of foregone defeat. Instead, Hill instructs black women to "go through the fear," "to do something with the insecurity," and "master the voices" in order to realize self-love, reciprocal care, political autonomy, spiritual fulfillment, and liberation. It bears noting that Hill counsels black women to *master the voices*, rather than silence them. Her model of liberated black womanhood is capacious enough to incorporate those voices, though she might change their key, speed their tempo, raise their volume, and bid them sing "some new things."

In short, Ms. Lauryn Hill wields madness as a multivalent technology for insurgent performance and personhood. She invokes "the people inside her head" as a counterpublic set apart from normative public spheres; she brandishes craziness to fend off interlopers and pursue peace; she erupts into tears that erode and slosh away "forbiddingly perfect" façades; she raises her cracked voice in an effort to crack and shatter complacency; she overhauls hit records to disturb easy listening and demand critical listening instead; and she presents an Afro-alienated and Afro-alienating persona to challenge presumptions about how black womanhood can look, sound, and be in the world. Sometimes an assertion of freedom looks and sounds like an outburst of madness. Soon after her *Unplugged* concert, Hill described a new paradigm for performance, one founded in a mad will-to-freedom: "I don't have to check with nobody. I can stop. I can pause. I can mess up. I can start again. I can go to another song. I can do anything."[104]

Now I turn to Hill's generational peer, the comedian Dave Chappelle, who was called crazy for his own decision to start again.

CHAPTER SIX

THE JOKER'S WILD, BUT THAT NIGGA'S CRAZY
DAVE CHAPPELLE LAUGHS UNTIL IT HURTS

THE SNAP AND THE CLICK

"Loud and long" laughter typically signals comedic success: the louder and longer the laughter the better, like a chime for a comedian's job well done. Yet the reverse was true for Dave Chappelle on the set of his celebrated sketch comedy series, *Chappelle's Show*, in November 2004. While performing a blackface minstrel gag, Chappelle heard an outburst of loud and long laughter that sounded like a buzzer announcing defeat, or else a death knell tolling doom, or maybe a snap signifying something had broken. Here is the scene summarized in a May 2005 *Time* magazine feature: "At the taping [of the blackface sketch], one spectator, a white man [on the show's production staff], laughed particularly *loud and long*. His laughter struck Chappelle as wrong, and he wondered if the new season of his show had gone from sending up stereotypes to merely reinforcing them." According to Chappelle, "'It made me uncomfortable. As a matter of fact, that was the last thing I shot before I told myself I gotta take a fucking time out after this, because my head almost exploded.'"[1] An expert purveyor of racial satire—often distending racist stereotypes to grotesque proportions to burst them open and expose their absurd innards—Chappelle finally fed and poked the blackface monster. He got bit.

That monster was spawned in nineteenth-century New York City with white minstrels smearing dark pigment on their faces and performing obscene caricatures of black people as *coons*: lazy, lascivious, savage, apelike creatures forever chasing chickens and worshipping watermelons.[2] Perhaps, to Chappelle's ears, that "loud and long" outburst was inflected by histories of white pleasure in black abjection; perhaps he heard a ghostly echo of antiblack laughter, a centuries-old sinister sound skittering from the decks of slave ships to plantation porches to minstrel stages to that television studio.[3] Although the popularity of blackface declined amid the cultural impact of the US civil rights movement, the coon genre still rears its blackened head in twenty-first-century pop culture. Its lives and afterlives persist in myriad theatrical, cinematic, televisual, and musical amusements that spectacularize, fetishize, and humorize wretched blackness.

Chappelle's blackface foray, a sketch called "In-Flight Meal," begins with the comedian playing a demure version of himself ("Mr. Chappelle") seated in an airplane cabin.[4] A flight attendant approaches Mr. Chappelle and asks whether he would prefer fish or fried chicken for his in-flight meal. When the attendant utters the word *chicken*, a four-inch-tall blackface pixie, also played by Chappelle, magically appears atop a seat's headrest. Wearing a bellhop uniform, white gloves, coal-black makeup, and perceived only by Mr. Chappelle, the pixie performs a medley of minstrel shtick: shuffling, shucking, squealing, limbs flailing, howling profanities, waxing rhapsodic about chicken, and coaxing Mr. Chappelle to order and devour the fried bird with coonish glee. When the flight attendant informs Mr. Chappelle that the fish is all gone and chicken is his only choice, he is reluctant; he worries that eating the meal in public will affirm stereotypes of fried chicken–loving blackness. Meanwhile, the pixie persists like a proverbial demon on Mr. Chappelle's shoulder, goading him to act against his conscience.

I hasten to note that there is nothing fundamentally coonish or devilish about eating fried chicken while black.[5] Mr. Chappelle's discomfort seems rooted in a neurotic respectability: an anxious conformity to codes of proper behavior with hopes of earning a seat at the table of bourgeois liberal rights (where, apparently, *fried chicken will not be served*). Freedom-seeking black people would do well to prioritize liberation over respectability, to fight for a world where they can feast on whatever meals they please, at whichever table they prefer, maybe under open sky, without agonizing over appearances or fearing antiblack repercussions.[6] Eschewing these ethical and existential complexities, the sketch comes to a neat resolution; when another passenger offers to swap fish for the chicken, the pixie's plan is foiled and Mr. Chappelle's crisis is averted.

No such neat resolution came to quell Chappelle's malaise after the sketch wrapped. According to the comedian, "In-Flight Meal" was supposed to present a caricature of a racist caricature in order to expose its absurdity and diminish its insidious power. Alas, he suspected that his attempt to parody blackface minstrelsy merely replicated it. While interviewing Chappelle in 2006, talk show host Oprah Winfrey referred to the blackface incident as a "tipping point."[7] We might also describe this event as a *snap*: a sudden break, a violent upheaval, a mad and maddening eruption, a "head [that] nearly exploded." But this fateful moment was not merely a snap, it was also a *click*: an epiphany, a moment of clarity, a process of falling and fitting into place, the sound of the switch that turns on the light or loudspeaker revealing truth. According to Chappelle, the truth was that he was "doing sketches that were funny but socially irresponsible."[8] Just as the sound of a physical SNAP! and the sound of a physical CLICK! are sometimes equivalent to human hearing, it seems to me that Chappelle's snap was also a click. He was overtaken by violent frustration and poignant revelation; his head nearly exploded and his mind surely expanded, too.

In the wake of this snap/click, Chappelle attempted a pilgrimage to Mecca, Saudi Arabia, in search of spiritual renewal.[9] He made it as far as Turkey, but was denied a visa to enter the Saudi border, returned to work shortly after, and resumed filming for several months. However, in late April 2005, disillusioned with show business and troubled by treachery among his associates, Chappelle left again. This time, he absconded to South Africa for two fateful weeks—and this time, he never returned to the set to finish filming.[10]

Chappelle's departure shocked many amid the massive success of *Chappelle's Show*. Season 1 had become the top-selling television series DVD in history and season 2 had become the top-rated program on the Comedy Central cable network.[11] Spurred by Chappelle's profit potential, the network had offered him a $50 million contract to produce third and fourth seasons of the series. Instead, he fled the scorching spotlight of American stardom, rebuked the favor and praise of its powerbrokers, dissolved his collaboration with show cowriter Neal Brennan, and rebuffed that massive payout. James Lipton, host of *Inside the Actor's Studio*, voiced the questions vexing many devout capitalists: "How could one of the most promising comedians of recent history have left a successful television series? How could he have walked away from a $50 million contract? Who in his right mind could have done that?"[12] Within the cult of capitalism (where market values trump all other values, where the most cherished freedom is the free market, where profit is always the Reason/reason) Chappelle's refusal of $50 million seemed downright crazy.

Because Chappelle flouted those psychosocial norms of corporate capitalism, tabloids accused him of psychosocial madness. Moreover, rumors swirled that he was suffering severe mental illness, medicalized madness, which he emphatically denied.[13] Meanwhile, he disclosed furious madness, instigated by corporate constrictions and racial antagonisms. And insofar as he confessed intense distress and unruliness of mind—including a head that "almost exploded"—it would appear that he experienced phenomenal madness, too. Thus, all four iterations of madness are key to Chappelle's saga, whether at the level of tabloid gossip or on the register of lived experience.

Now that I have briefly narrated Chappelle's snap/click, I want to investigate a series of creaks, thumps, and booms that preceded and followed it. I mobilize mad methodology to chart scenes of madness in the comedian's lifeworld: his repeated warnings that he might snap and lose his mind; his mounting rage against antiblackness and racial capitalism; his comedic account of the madness of antiblackness; his theory and practice of black paranoia; his insistence that there is a conspiracy to paint him "insane"; and his drapetomaniacal journey to South Africa, charting and chasing a mad diaspora. I reveal how Chappelle frequently traffics in tropes, idioms, and performances of madness—playfully and poignantly consorting with it—even as he claims that he is not crazy.

TALKING CRAZY

Born in 1973 in Washington, DC, Chappelle is a member of America's post–civil rights generation as well as the "postsoul" cohort. Theorized by pop culture scholar Mark Anthony Neal, postsoul encompasses

> folks born between the 1963 March on Washington and the 1978 [Regents of the University of California v.] Bakke case, children of soul, if you will, who came to maturity in the age of Reaganomics, and experienced the change from urban industrialism to de-industrialism, from segregation to de-segregation, from essential notions of blackness to metanarratives on blackness, without any nostalgic allegiance to the past . . . but firmly in grasp of the existential concerns of this brave new world.[14]

Chappelle manifests many of these postsoul conditions: he often describes the effects of "Reaganomics" and "de-industrialism," like deepening poverty and surging crack-cocaine addiction in his hometown in the 1980s; he consistently mocks "essential notions of blackness" by presenting postmodern and parodic visions of black life; he refuses "nostalgic allegiance to the past" with his irreverent imaginings of civil rights iconography;[15] and he expresses "existential concerns" over the persistence of antiblackness in twenty-first-century America.

Chappelle is the son of a pair of black scholar-activists. His mother, Yvonne Seon, was appointed by Congolese Prime Minister Patrice Lumumba to serve as secretary of the high commission for the Inga Dam Project for the Democratic Republic of the Congo in the early 1960s. She subsequently worked in nonprofit advocacy benefiting sub-Saharan Africa, earned a doctorate in African and African American Humanities, and taught at several universities in and around DC.[16] His father, William David Chappelle III, was an antiracist human rights activist in Yellow Springs, Ohio, and taught music at Antioch College, a small liberal arts institution in the same town.[17] Chappelle's parents incorporated messages of black pride, knowledge of black history, and critiques of antiblackness into his rearing.[18]

When Chappelle was two years old his parents divorced, and so he split his youth between their homes. He spent his early years with his mother in a suburb outside DC, then lived his middle school years in rural Yellow Springs with his father. At fourteen, when he returned to his mom's care in DC, he beheld a town that looked to him "like a crack bomb had gone off."[19] Young Chappelle witnessed the catastrophic fallout from that "crack bomb"—communities blighted by addiction, drug economy turf wars, police surveillance and brutality, carceral extraction, and general human misery—amid the district's still-vibrant culture and still-robust black sociality. These years also saw the spread of *de-institutionalization*: a set of Reagan-era federal policies that defunded mental health services and shuttered psychiatric treatment facilities—effectively rerouting some severely mentally ill persons toward prison, homelessness, self-medication, or drug addiction. All this blight and beauty would influence Chappelle's comedic commentary in years to come.[20]

As a result of these adolescent migrations amid societal transformations, Chappelle was intimately familiar with the lifeworlds of overwhelmingly white, "hippy,"[21] rural Ohio; predominantly black, urban Washington, DC; and black middle-class suburbia outside DC. As film and media studies scholar Bambi Haggins explains, "The dual nature of his black experience—identity formation in predominantly black and predominantly white spaces—also informs his comic persona. Chappelle enjoys a sort of dual credibility."[22]

That "dual credibility" likely came in handy for Chappelle's role in *Half Baked* (1998), an interracial buddy comedy-*cum*-stoner flick that earned him a cult following. But Chappelle's breakthrough into mainstream celebrity came with his HBO stand-up special, *Killin' Them Softly*, filmed in 2000 in DC's Lincoln Theater.[23] The special is the site of two especially trenchant evocations of madness, the first occurring at the very start. As the opening credits roll and the comedian makes his way onto the stage, rapper DMX's 1999 hit single, "Party

Up," booms as musical accompaniment. In the song's chorus, the gravel-voiced emcee declares

> Y'all gon' make me lose my mind, up in here, up in here
> Y'all gon' make me go all out, up in here, up in here
> Y'all gon' make me act a fool, up in here, up in here
> Y'all gon' make me lose my cool, up in here, up in here[24]

Antagonized by "y'all," DMX chants a litany of warnings about an imminent snap. In musical persona, he threatens to lose his mind, to act a fool, to lose his cool, to go mad. Though it's called "Party Up," the song is not about good times and revelry. In fact, the lyrics are a series of artful threats and revenge fantasies aimed at the emcee's enemies. In a later passage of the song, not featured in Chappelle's opening, DMX details the pain he will cause "cowards" who provoke him:

> Nigga runnin' his mouth, I'm a blow his lung out
> Listen, yo' ass is about to be missin'
> You know who gon' find you? Some old man fishin'
> Grandma wishin' your soul's at rest
> But it's hard to digest with the size of the hole in your chest

The party promoted in the track's title is liable to turn into a massacre. The song takes part in a hip-hop tradition of larger-than-life bravado and menacing machismo, but DMX touts madness as the force fueling his bravado and deepening his menace. DMX is a prolific maker of mad black art in his own right. A survivor of dozens of stints in jail and prison, a former psychiatric detainee, and a person living with bipolar disorder, he makes music about blackness, masculinity, spiritual striving, existential agony, phenomenal madness, inter-species solidarity with his pit bull companions, and raucous rebellion against constrictive social norms. In the process, DMX takes up the formidable mantle of the "crazy nigger."[25]

As for Chappelle, if *Killin' Them Softly* heralds his ascent to stardom, it is significant that madness presides as he arrives. In the very same instant that he introduces himself to tastemakers consuming his HBO special, he playfully broadcasts the threat of losing his mind. Maybe Chappelle intends this as a lighthearted evocation of comedic "madness" and uninhibited abandon. Or maybe, on a lower frequency, he means to forecast his potential to cause trouble and "cut loose" if antagonized.[26] (And cut loose he did. Just five years later, maddened by clashes with racial capitalism and the pop culture industry, Chappelle would "go all out": out of his role on *Chappelle's Show*, out of the blinding media spotlight, out of the borders of the US nation-state, and, to have pundits tell it, out of his mind.)[27]

Killin' Them Softly's second evocation of madness comes when Chappelle shares a funny fable about "talking crazy." He explains, "I can't handle pressure. Sometimes pressure make me talk different," and continues:

> Sometimes I'll talk crazy just to make myself feel better. . . . Y'all do that? Just start talking like crazy. [Speaks in James Cagney–like "gangster" voice:] Ever heard this voice? That's how bad guys used to talk in the forties. . . . I talk like that, not all the time, but if somebody put the pressure on me, fuck it, I gotta cut loose. If the police pull me over, I'll talk crazy:
>
> "Son, do you know why we pulled you over?"
>
> [Cagney voice:] "'Cause I'm black, see, that's right . . ."
>
> "Stop talking like that!"
>
> [Cagney voice:] "Stop talking like what, copper? That's how I talk, see!"[28]

Chappelle sets this humorous anecdote at the ominous scene of a traffic stop where a black man talks crazy to a cop. This premise is so foreboding because unarmed black men are four times more likely than their white counterparts to be killed by police.[29] What's more, unarmed persons with untreated severe mental illness are sixteen times more likely to be subjected to deadly police force than are other unarmed civilians.[30] The math is staggering: to be black *and* appear crazy is to face a radically, exponentially greater risk of death relative to white, psychonormative majorities. When the officer commands him to stop talking crazy, Chappelle snaps back: "Stop talking like what, copper? That's how I talk, see!" In describing this flippant exchange, Chappelle's intentions are clearly comedic rather than documentary, and he is invested in humorous outlandishness rather than tragic verisimilitude. In real life, such a confrontation could quickly escalate to murderous state violence.

Even amid that mortal risk, Chappelle touts two critical uses for talking crazy. First is simply to "make [oneself] feel better" when under pressure, perhaps because it provides amusement and comedic outlet. Second is to "cut loose," to break free from constrictive social norms and codes of Reasonable propriety. But there is a third effect achieved by talking crazy in this anecdote: speaking truth to power, and more precisely, *wisecracking truth to power.* When asked if he knows why he's been pulled over, Chappelle alleges that cops targeted him because of his blackness. His retort is delivered comically but backed by deadly serious facticity; there is extensive sociological data indicating racial profiling of black people in traffic stops.[31] Chappelle deploys crazy talk, an idiom of madness, to critique racist policing with boisterous boldness that would discomfit most Reasonable people.

The themes of *living under pressure* and *cutting loose* appear elsewhere in Chappelle's oeuvre. Shifting from *Killin' Them Softly*, I turn to two sketches from *Chappelle's Show*, one portraying a black man living under pressure and the other depicting a black man cutting loose. These performances are starkly different in tone and aesthetic, but both contain incisive insights about the psychic life of black madness.

"The Niggar Family" appears on season 1 of *Chappelle's Show*.[32] A parody of 1950s family sitcoms like *Leave It to Beaver* and *Father Knows Best*, the sketch surrounds a clan of middle-class, suburban, cookie-cutter Caucasians surnamed "Niggar." The sketch's running gag is the comic irony each time they are called "Niggars," phonetically indistinguishable from "niggers." My primary concern is not any member of the Niggar clan. Instead I want to focus on a local "colored" milkman named "Clifton," played by Chappelle, who is friendly with the remarkably named family along his route. The most arresting moment in the sketch occurs at a fancy restaurant, where Clifton and his wife are out on a dinner date. As the two wait to be seated, Clifton hears the host call out "Niggar" and takes offense—that is, until he realizes that the word is directed at the adolescent son of the Niggar family, also on a date at the restaurant. With the misunderstanding cleared up, Clifton soon exclaims, "I bet you'll get the finest table a nigger's ever got in this restaurant!" Both couples laugh, and their laughter—*loud and long*—sounds strained, seems insincere.

Then Clifton catches his breath, turns directly to the camera, breaks the proverbial fourth wall, and plainly announces, "This racism is killing me inside." The words pierce through the loud and long laughter and are sobering amid an otherwise irreverent sketch. Before Clifton can elaborate his anguish and before any characters can respond, the camera cuts quickly to the next scene. Uttered by a black milkman servicing white suburbia in 1950s America, the declaration "This racism is killing me inside" could refer to countless antiblack injuries and indignities: Jim Crow degradation, antiblack labor exploitation, racialized poverty, white vigilante terrorism, mundane microaggressions, and on and on. Maybe Clifton tends to suffer such abuses quietly, but here he interrupts racism's regularly scheduled programming to disclose his hurt and confess a mental and existential crisis. One wonders whether the milkman's sentiments reflect Chappelle's own work-related trauma and whether this scene prophesizes Chappelle's eventual snap/click.

If "The Niggar Family" depicts madness that corrodes a person's insides, "Dave Gets Revenge" depicts madness that literally explodes outside.[33] One of the few sketches produced for the unfinished third season of *Chappelle's Show*, "Dave Gets Revenge" is a comedic payback fantasy and parody of psychopathy. Chappelle plays a villainous version of himself with a vendetta against those who wronged him before his fame. After disgracing an ex-girlfriend who dumped him and then humiliating a casting director who dismissed his talents, "Dave" makes his way to "Steve," the owner of a comedy club who once banned the comic from the venue. Before Steve realizes that he is a target for revenge, he apologizes for barring Dave from the club, expresses remorse, admits he always knew Dave would prosper, and melodramatically pleads for forgiveness. To heighten the effect, a maudlin violin scores the apology. Moreover, Steve speaks his penitence from a wheelchair, where he is confined because of an injury in a car accident. Within prevailing ableist logics, such a disability makes him a proper object of patronizing pity. The sketch both exploits and mocks such sentimentalism.

At first, Dave seems moved to mercy. He confesses his vengeful agenda as though he has experienced a change of heart. Then, suddenly, he hurls Steve and the wheelchair down a flight of steps, douses the comedy club with gasoline, and blows up the building with the man inside. Laughing fiendishly and strutting away from the wreckage, Dave snatches a baby from a blonde woman on the street and kicks the child into the air like a punted football. In this scene, Chappelle performs a psychopathic version of himself: manipulative, prone to wanton violence, lacking conscience, and immune to guilt. The comedian has spoken candidly about naysayers who dismissed his talents and sabotaged his early career. Perhaps the joke is a cathartic fantasy of revenge, an imaginative wish fulfillment.[34] In *Jokes and Their Relation to the Unconscious*, Freud writes that a hostile "tendentious" joke "will allow us to exploit something ridiculous in our enemy which we could not, on account of obstacles in the way, bring forward openly or consciously."[35] But "Dave Gets Revenge" does not usher its hostility into the recesses of its televisual unconscious or conceal its malice behind benign scenery. Instead, this skit literalizes, amplifies, spectacularizes, and openly flaunts its violent wish.

"The Niggar Family" and "Dave Gets Revenge" depict disparate responses to living under pressure. If there is a spectrum of reaction to such strain, Clifton could be said to occupy one end: the side of *passive endurance and slow corrosion* that kills him from the inside. Dave inhabits the opposite end: a proclivity for *violent vengeance and sudden explosion* that kills his antagonist. Juxtaposed, Clifton and Dave invite a meditation on long-suffering pacifism and mortal hostility as methods for confronting mad and maddening worlds. Maybe the viewer, inspired to ponder these polarities, will seek a happy medium: neither collapsing inward, nor erupting outward, but finding a liberated homeostasis somewhere in between.

"THE MAD REAL WORLD"

Chappelle has distinguished himself as an expert practitioner of the racial carnivalesque. Describing carnivalesque humor, Bakhtin emphasizes its "peculiar logic of the 'inside out' . . . of a continual shifting from top to bottom, from front to rear, of numerous parodies and travesties, humiliations, profanations, comic crownings and uncrownings."[36] Literary scholars Richard J. Gray II and Michael Putnam highlight the Bakhtinian inflections in Chappelle's work, suggesting that the comedian "relies strongly on the inversion of racial roles," where conventional tropes of blackness and whiteness are swapped for parodic effect.[37] I would add that Chappelle invites his audience to *read upside down*:[38] to capsize racial expectations, to regard the world from its underside, to swap black and white as though viewing a film negative of extant social arrangements— and hopefully, amid these inversions, to recognize the sheer obscenity of racist regimes. Gray and Putnam read racial inversions in "The Niggar Family" as well as in "Blind Supremacy" (the latter a trenchant sketch about a blind white supremacist who does not know that he is black).

There is another sketch in Chappelle's televisual universe that stages an explicitly "mad" racial inversion: "The Mad Real World."[39] Chappelle prefaces the sketch with remarks about *The Real World*, an iconic MTV "reality" television show that debuted in 1991. Each season of *The Real World* typically convenes seven young adults, strangers to one another, to cohabitate while being videotaped around the clock. Chappelle explains, "Every few years they always put a black guy on there and try and make him look crazy. . . . Like he'll freak out. . . . Of course he's gonna freak out, you put him around six of the craziest white people you can find, and then expect him to live a normal life." According to Chappelle, *The Real World* periodically casts a black man who is deliberately made to *look* crazy by white housemates who actually *are* crazy. He claims that the program stages and televises the traumatization and pathologization of black men. Notably, MTV (the station that aired *The Real World*) and Comedy Central (the station that aired *Chappelle's Show*) were both owned by mega-multinational media conglomerate Viacom. Thus, Chappelle's complaints about the purveyors of *The Real World* were allegations against his own employers. His willingness to wisecrack truth to power—not some abstract and distant power, but the corporation cutting his own paychecks—is incompatible with public relations protocols and corporate loyalty mandates governing neoliberal media. Such incompatibility would later drive him away from television altogether.

Continuing his introduction to the sketch, Chappelle proclaims, "They would not like it if we made a show where we put one white guy around six of the craziest black people we could find, would they? Well, guess what? I got a show just like that!" The faux show is called "The Mad Real World" and the "one white guy" is "Chad." Blond, naïve, happy-go-lucky, and fragile, he is essentially an effigy of privileged white manhood upon whom black women and men will exact comedic revenge. When Chad moves into the loft, he arrives to a scene where crowds of rowdy young black people are smoking weed, playing dice, drinking, and brawling—which is to say, they are performing and parodying stereotypes of unruly black youth.

From the time of Chad's arrival, he is treated as a quaint curiosity at best, but more often as a pale nuisance or walking punchline. What's more, he is repeatedly abused by his housemates. When his girlfriend "Katie" visits the loft, Chad's roommate "TyRee" (an "ex-convict" caricature) openly leers and masturbates while watching Chad and Katie kiss. Soon after, TyRee and his friend "Lysol" (fresh out of prison) kick Chad out of his own bed and entice Katie to sleep with Lysol as TyRee video records it. While horseplaying at a party in the loft, a housemate named "Tron," played by Chappelle, grips Chad in a sleeper hold until he passes out. Partiers swiftly steal Chad's wallet and shoes before TyRee and Lysol take his unconscious body upstairs, where, it is implied, they rape him. Later, when Chad's father visits, he is bullied and finally shanked for allegedly looking at another housemate, "Zondra," in a way that displeases her. Chad garners little sympathy from his housemates, who respond with amusement, contempt, or indifference.

When narrated on the page, these incidents read like an awful litany of violence and degradation. The humor comes from the sheer absurdity of the performances, where stereotypes of black criminality and white frailty are stretched to preposterous proportions, generating a satirical effect. What makes these events so outlandish is not only the extreme behavior of the black roommates; it is also that they act with brazen impunity and face no repercussions. In the current racial order, when crowds of black people cause white discomfort, let alone white injury, chances are that police will aggressively intervene.[40]

Chad eventually reaches his breaking point, his own snap event. When the housemates throw a party that keeps him awake all night with an early morning ahead, he storms into the common space, screams furiously at his cohabitants, and finally demands that they treat him with respect. As though shocked and affronted, they claim that his outburst makes them feel unsafe and promptly evict him from the home. Chappelle stages these outrageous indignities to lampoon what he views as a troubling real-life pattern: the antagonism and condemnation that black men endure on the actual MTV show and elsewhere.

The "mad" in the sketch's title is polysemous. It signifies the angry affect displayed by those black roommates from the start and Chad's outraged outburst that gets him kicked out at the end. "Mad" also denotes the chaotic atmosphere of the loft. Moreover, "mad" points to the sketch's carnivalesque capsizing of the white dominion and black precarity that are America's racial status quo. I want especially to note a fourth potential meaning of "mad" in the show's title. In hip-hop idiom, the word *mad* can signify abundance, intensity, and excess, essentially functioning as a synonym for *many*, *very*, or *extra*.[41] Thus, the title "The Mad Real World" suggests a heightened (and blackened) melodrama, beyond the already over-the-top antics featured on the actual show. It is noteworthy that hip-hop establishes a homonymic convergence between *mad*-as-crazy and *mad*-as-excessive. A similar convergence is at work when madness is regarded as cognitive or affective excess—that is, as the condition of an overwrought mind, cluttered with voices, crowded by personalities, fraught with emotion, bloated with angst, ready to spill outside itself.

Ultimately, Chappelle's faux reality show depicts a domain where vulnerable people are demeaned, vicious majorities rule, and suffering is met with indifference. In the process, Chappelle parodies not only an iconic television show called *The Real World*; he also satirizes the cruelty and injustice plaguing a real world that is sometimes called Earth.

"THUS, AFRICA"

Now we leave the "The Mad Real World," but linger in the trope of *madness as place*. Chappelle's snap/click activated a diasporic velocity in him: driving him to retreat from his New York City set and flee to Durban, South Africa; propelling him across national, hemispheric, and oceanic boundaries; and ushering him into diasporas of blackness and madness. Typically, *black diaspora* signifies the dispersal of black peoples from their ancestral homelands in Africa to various regions across the globe—a process spurred by transatlantic slavery as well as persecution, war, sanctuary-seeking, fugitivity, exile, carceral relocations, itinerant labor, and wanderlust, amid countless other sociopolitical and existential exigencies. Alongside black diaspora, I propose a novel notion of *mad diaspora* to refer to the scattering of mad persons from their homes by vicissitudes of foolish ships,[42] persecution, war, institutionalization, de-institutionalization, exile, fugitivity, dissociative fugues,[43] carceral relocations, abandonment, and snaps and clicks, among myriad other sociopolitical and existential conditions.

Like multitudes of black diasporans before him, Chappelle left home amid antiblack antagonisms (a blackface debacle). Like many mad voyagers before him, he left home amid mad vicissitudes (a head that "almost exploded"). To be clear, I am not equating Chappelle's escapade with, say, the passage of an African captive chained to a slave ship that sailed from Cape Coast to South Carolina in the eighteenth century. Nor am I conflating his voyage with, say, the trek of a mentally ill vagrant evicted from a psychiatric hospital in Chicago circa 1987 and hitchhiking to warmer climes in California. Nor am I suggesting parity between the transit of that black ship captive and that mad hitchhiker. Rather, I mean to highlight how being black in antiblack worlds and mad in antimad worlds often entails diaspora under duress—or at least diaspora under stress.

It is significant that Chappelle's diasporic velocity carried him to sub-Saharan Africa. In racial cartographies mapped by antiblackness since the Euro-Enlightenment, sub-Saharan Africa is frequently figured as a mad world unto itself. In chapter 1, I noted that Euro-Enlightenment philosophers like Kant, Hume, Jefferson, and Hegel imagined Africa as a pit of savagery and un-Reason that was utterly remote—as though across a vast metaphysical chasm—from the pantheon of Euromodern civilization and its Reason. It was Hegel who famously proclaimed that Africa "is no historical part of the world"[44] and that Africans inhabit a "completely wild and untamed state."[45] Hegel might characterize Chappelle's trip to Africa as a pilgrimage to the epicenter of unReason.

Such anti-African logics persist in the contemporary West, permeating news media, popular cinema, anthropological scholarship, and charitable campaigns that all treat Africa as an accretion of abject associations. In Western discourses, Africa frequently functions as metonym for war, violence, famine, drought, poverty, disease, despair, savagery, and madness. In the process, the geopolitical and sociocultural diversity of Africa—with its vast array of ethnic groups, cultures, cosmologies, histories, nations, political formations, and ways of life—is collapsed into an undifferentiated mass and mess.[46]

In the tabloid clamor about Chappelle's escapade, "Africa" and "crazy" were frequently invoked and yoked together. The gist was that Chappelle *went crazy* and *went to Africa*, as though the two were convergent journeys.[47] To the contrary, Chappelle described his trip as a "spiritual retreat" and claimed he traveled to South Africa to flee the madness of the US pop culture industry.[48] In particular, he absconded to the home of a close confidante in Durban where he could rest and clear his mind. He explained to *Time* magazine, "Let me tell you the things I can do here which I can't at home: think, eat, sleep, laugh. I'm an introspective dude. I enjoy my own thoughts sometimes. And I've been doing a lot of thinking here."[49] Chappelle describes South Africa as a refuge beyond the tentacles of the Hollywood monster. He designates South Africa as a space for thinking, contrary to Euro-Enlightenment conceptions of Africa as an unthinking continent and contrary to myths of Africa as a wild terrain teeming with bodies and sensuality but barren in mind and criticality.

Despite the anti-African bent of Western modernity, a range of black diasporans in the Americas and elsewhere—survivors of Middle Passage, nineteenth-century emigrationists, twentieth-century immigrants, Garveyites, Négritudists, Rastafarians, Pan-Africanists, Egyptophiles, DNA-aided ancestry seekers, would-be Wakandans, and comedians in search of respite—have regarded Africa as a site of belonging, sanctuary, and critical thinking.[50] Chappelle's account of South Africa belongs among these Afro-affirmative counternarratives. All the while, he is keenly aware of the prevailing master narratives that dominate Western notions of Africa. Interviewed by CNN in 2006, he offered this incisive observation: "I was only gone for two weeks . . . they act like I bought an apartment and everything. . . . I wonder if I went to London or something if it would have been as big of a deal."[51] For adherents to Hegel's anti-African conception of history and geography, one cannot have a *quick* stay in Africa, because visiting Africa means trudging through a bog of ontological slowness, belatedness, and backwardness. Hegel would have us believe that Africa is outside history, outside teleological time, left behind the hallowed march of Euromodernity. From such a vantage, the journey from the United States to South Africa does not merely span thousands of miles; it is a passage backward across centuries in time.

Despite his embrace of Africa as a space for critical thought and his critique of anti-African prejudices, Chappelle occasionally indulges those prejudices. His identity as an African American does not exempt him from absorbing anti-African logics and sentiments so ubiquitous in America and across the globe. When Winfrey asks him about reports that he traveled to South Africa for psychiatric treatment, Chappelle replies, "Who goes from America to Africa for medical attention?," garnering loud and long laughter from Winfrey and her audience. He continues, "It sounds like the most irresponsible journalism in the world. I cannot imagine being a journalist and hearing this from these people and just running with it."[52] The implication is that such a journey would be a reversal of the Reasonable route a sick person should travel for treatment: from Africa (coded as primitive) to the United States (coded as modern).

I recognize that, by many measures, the United States has a more advanced medical infrastructure than any sub-Saharan African nation.[53] To acknowledge this disparity is not anti-African in itself. What concerns me are the ideological propensities driving that loud and long laughter. (My worry is akin to Chappelle's own concern about the cause of that cackle on the set of his blackface sketch.) If the question, "Who goes from America to Africa for medical attention?" is a joke, its humor pivots upon a notion of Africa as a *literally laughable* alternative to America. More precisely, African infrastructure is the butt of the joke.

Chappelle's undifferentiated reference to "Africa" obscures the specificity of his destination. South Africa houses a well-appointed private health care sector (steeped in a complex and egregious history of settler-colonial racial capitalism) that will readily accommodate wealthy celebrity patients. And although Chappelle did not travel to South Africa for formal psychiatric treatment, he did travel there to improve his mental health. The United States may have a more sophisticated psychiatric infrastructure, but in Chappelle's case, South Africa yields a more desirable psychiatric outcome. In light of this specificity, Africa does not seem so laughable after all.

During Chappelle's 2008 interview with *Inside the Actor's Studio*, his references to Africa consistently incite audience laughter. I want to highlight three occasions of this Africa-induced hilarity. First, Chappelle recalls advice his father once shared about the price of fame: "He said . . . name your price in the beginning. If it ever gets more expensive than the price you name, get outta there." Chappelle pauses and then announces to the audience: "Thus, *Africa*." He leans back dramatically, but does not smile, as the audience erupts into cackles and applause. "Africa" is literally the punchline of the joke. Second, Chappelle invokes Africa to warn other creators that they, too, may find themselves fleeing from profit-obsessed Hollywood. With an ominous tone he insists that "everybody laughs at me, but just get your *Africa* tickets ready, baby, [loud audience laughter] because it's coming. It's coming. You have no idea." Third, when asked by James Lipton about a low period in his life, Chappelle describes his father's stroke in the late nineties and his own disappointment with the film *Half Baked*. Chappelle proclaims, "It was all these things and so much pressure. *Africa!*" The audience hoots and guffaws in response.[54]

In all three of these cases, Africa is a metonym for otherness, escape, and relief—but more precisely, *outlandish* otherness, *quixotic* escape, and *comic* relief. The ensuing laughter is inflected by the same sensibility as that mirth on the *Oprah Winfrey Show*: a presumption that Africa is a strange, maybe even *mad*, place to seek treatment and refuge. In sum, the chatter around Chappelle's trip to Africa bespeaks anti-African attitudes permeating Western popular discourse. Chappelle's invocations of "Africa" also reflect what we might describe as *Afro-ambivalent* feeling persisting among many black Americans: a tendency to harbor romantic reverence for an imagined African motherland while also internalizing anti-African ideologies that disdain the continent.[55]

Chappelle is not the first African American comedian to dramatically abscond to sub-Saharan Africa. In 1979, the iconic comic Richard Pryor traveled to Kenya in search of rest and solace. Like Chappelle, Pryor regarded his journey as a practice of self-care, an attempt to escape the angst and madness of his life in the United States. Pryor's trip came at the behest of his psychiatrist, who recommended it as therapeutic treatment amid Pryor's marital woes, drug addiction, and ailing mental health.[56] The voyage was a wondrous education for Pryor, who absorbed much knowledge about the people, politics, cultures, and ecology of Kenya. But his most profound revelation came as he sat in a Kenyan hotel lobby just before his return to the United States. Suddenly something *clicked*, and maybe it *snapped*, inside him:

> I was sitting in a hotel and a voice said to me . . . "Look around. What do you see?"
> I said "I see all colors of people doing everything."
> The voice said "Do you see any niggers?"
> I said "No."
> [The voice] said "You know why? Cause there aren't any."
> And it hit me like a shot, man, I started crying and shit . . . I've been here three weeks and I haven't even said it, I haven't even thought it . . . It made me say I've been wrong, I need to regroup my shit . . . I ain't never gonna call another black man "nigger."[57]

A disembodied voice speaks this epiphany directly into Pryor's consciousness. Usually, such uncanny utterances are attributed either to prophecy (where the voice is exalted as divine intercession) or mental illness (where the voice is diagnosed as aural hallucination). Whatever the source of Pryor's revelation, it convinces him that there is inexorable violence embedded in the word *nigger*, and it compels him to delete the term from his stand-up routines and his broader life vocabulary. If Africa is a dark continent, Pryor testifies that it contains a *radiant dark*, yielding enlightenment and epiphany.[58] Like Chappelle, Pryor rebuts myths of unthinking Africa and extols it as a site of critical thought.

Chappelle is frequently imagined as heir apparent to Pryor. In addition to their fateful journeys to Africa, the two share other remarkable affinities. Both used stand-up comedy to indict America's racial status quo and nevertheless gained large fan bases among white mainstream consumers (who seemed, sometimes, to blithely overlook the racially subversive aspects of their performances). Both were rumored to suffer from crack-cocaine addiction (though, importantly, Pryor has confirmed a history of abuse while Chappelle adamantly denies such claims). Both men prominently featured addict characters in their repertoires (Richard Pryor's wino was called "Mudbone" and Dave Chappelle's crack-cocaine fiend was named "Tyrone Biggums"). Both had brief and controversial stints as sketch comedy writer-performers on television. And most significant for my purposes, both men are mythologized as "crazy."[59]

I want to tarry with Pryor a while longer. Black feminist media scholar Audrey McCluskey notes that "being declared a 'crazy nigger' bestowed a reckless freedom upon [Pryor], and an abandon which he embraced. Historically, the designation of 'crazy nigger' generally identified someone who defied the dictates of convention. It could apply to a range of behaviors, including rebelling against injustice, being a social misfit, or acting 'buck wild' and just not giving a damn."[60] I have erstwhile described the "crazy nigger" as a highly politicized black vernacular archetype: a folk hero and vicarious insurrectionist for the radically inclined; or, to the contrary, a nuisance and bogeyman to racial conservatives. Citing the folklorist Zora Neale Hurston, the satirist Ishmael Reed offers a different but complementary take on this figure: "In . . . Hurston's book *Dust Tracks on a Road*, 'crazy' means 'witty.' That's what proletariat black people mean when they say 'crazy nigger.'"[61] This interpretation of the "crazy nigger" treats craziness as a mode of thought and a practice of sophisticated intelligence. Pryor epitomizes this figuration with his comic prowess. He might have been "reckless" and prone to "abandon"—terms suggesting unthinking impulsivity—but he was also marvelously deft and witty. The title of Pryor's 1974 breakthrough stand-up album, *That Nigger's Crazy*, declares and documents his early embrace of "crazy nigger" status, before his eventual disavowal of the latter word. Insofar as his decision to rebuke "nigger" was inspired by a disembodied voice, it seems that the "crazy" remained even after "nigger" resigned. In fact, "crazy" called for "nigger's" resignation.

While craziness might have been a source of fabulous creativity and epiphany for Pryor, it was sometimes the cause and symptom of distress. Some of his most uproarious stand-up material was forged from the wreckage of violent trauma: the severe beatings he received at the hands of his father and grandmother, the rape he suffered as a child, his struggles with drug addiction, his woe from heartbreak, a heart attack at age thirty-seven, suicidal ideation, and general vulnerability to antiblackness were all fodder for Pryor's tragicomic jokes.[62] McCluskey writes, "The demons that deviled him were like wicked muses that jolted his creative genius but gave him no peace. The edginess of his humor was matched by, or more accurately, perhaps, provoked by living life on the edge."[63]

Pryor's most spectacular traumatic-*cum*-comedic incident happened on June 9, 1980. On that day, "the edge" would take the shape of a mansion window and he would jump from it. Coming down from a freebasing binge, Pryor, in his own words, "was experiencing serious dementia. Stuck in a surreal landscape of constantly shifting emotions. No weight. Floating at the end of a tunnel. Miserably alone. Frightened. Voices growing louder, closing in. Wave after wave of depression."[64] Here, Pryor narrates an agonized and terrorized phenomenal madness. He describes a sensation of radical isolation and disorientation, as though dwelling inside a vacuum that renders him weightless, friendless, and unmoored without an anchor to hold. Amid his haze and dread, Pryor doused himself with rum, set himself on fire, leapt from the window of his southern California home, ran down a posh suburban street, and burned for minutes before police put out the flames.[65]

Though the incident was initially reported as an accident, Pryor refuted those reports. At a 1986 promotional junket for his semi-autobiographical film, *Jo Jo Dancer, Your Life Is Calling*, Pryor insisted, "I did try to kill myself. . . . I have only fragments of memory about exactly what happened that night, but I know I tried to kill myself. The pain . . . it had come to that." When further questioned about the incident, Pryor replied, "The point is I was crazy, and I couldn't take it anymore. Maybe you have to be crazy to understand it."[66] He describes a madness that is devastation (something he "couldn't take any more") and revelation (something that enables one to "understand"). This madness hurts, but it also thinks and knows.

"WHAT'S A BLACK MAN WITHOUT HIS PARANOIA INTACT?"

In a sketch called "Celebrity Trial Jury Selection," included on season 2 of *Chappelle's Show*, the comedian roasts racism, celebrity, and criminal justice in America. At the crux of the sketch is Chappelle's commentary on several celebrity court cases at the turn of the twenty-first century, including the O. J. Simpson trial of 1994 and 1995. That trial's outcome, a black man found "not guilty" of killing a white woman despite compelling evidence implicating him, was a dramatic reversal of the racial status quo of American jurisprudence.[67] Chappelle plays a dramatized version of himself, a jury candidate convinced that racist police and prosecutors are behind the indictment of Simpson—as well as the child sex abuse charges against celebrated musicians Michael Jackson and R. Kelly. These men stood accused of serious offenses that warrant sober contemplation, but this is not Chappelle's intention. Instead, his aim is to comically expose and excoriate antiblackness in the US criminal justice system.

Because of his deep distrust of US jurisprudence, "Mr. Chappelle" is suspicious of all evidence presented by prosecutors. During the R. Kelly jury selection scene, an exasperated white woman prosecutor chides him for his intractable insistence that Kelly is not guilty. Referring to purported video footage of Kelly urinating on a child, Mr. Chappelle declares, "Listen, lady, the burden of proof is on the state. On the state! You have got to prove, to me, beyond a reasonable doubt, whether or not this man is a pisser." When the prosecutor replies, "Aren't your doubts unreasonable?," Mr. Chappelle delivers a mini treatise on bias, corruption, and conspiracy in American law enforcement and jurisprudence: "No, it's not unreasonable. We talking about a justice system that had five hundred people whose cases were overturned by DNA evidence. I seen a tape where five cops beat up a nigga and they said that they had a reasonable doubt. I got my doubts, too! All right? How come they never found Biggie and Tupac's murderer, but they could arrest O. J. the next day? Nicole Simpson can't rap! I want justice! . . . This whole goddamned court is out of order!" Even as he mocks the gravity of abuse and murder charges, Mr. Chappelle decries the antiblack rigging of the US justice system, which has instigated innumerable wrongful convictions of African Americans.[68]

Chappelle prefaces the sketch with this announcement: "To me, it's all about reasonable doubt. What's a reasonable doubt to a white person, you know, might not be reasonable doubt to a black person." On the surface, it may seem that Chappelle is touting a racially essentialist logic, a belief that epistemology and ethics derive from race. Yet in a modern world structured by race and racialization, blackness often entails historical, experiential, and structural conditions informing one's *relation to Reason* (the Euro-Enlightenment–rooted hegemony) and one's *practice of reason* (the process of discernment within a particular logic system). Given that black people have been subjected to rampant police violence and terrorism, juridical malfeasance, false convictions, hyperincarceration, and categorical criminalization, their suspicion about American law and order is perfectly reasonable—even if it is not Reasonable. In fact, black people in the United States have developed a tradition I call *black countercriminology*, a set of critical theories and astute critiques of antiblack criminal "justice."[69] This countercriminological tradition marshals personal and collective memories of injustice, profound pessimism, intense suspicion, and robust wariness to engage the police state. I will return to such suspicious dispositions in my discussion of black paranoia later in this chapter. For now, I want to emphasize that this black reason is not an essentialist dogma emerging spontaneously from the epidermis of a *biologized blackness*. Rather, it is a critical intelligence emerging from an *existential blackness* as it confronts the atrocious violence of antiblackness.

Chappelle takes on corrupt cops and courts in a season 2 spoof called "Tron's Law and Order." Introducing the sketch, Chappelle suggests that American cops and courts systemically grant white people great advantage and cause black people grave harm. He proclaims that "there's like two legal systems, damned near," citing the wrist-slap punishments meted out to the white, wealthy, white-collar culprits behind the multibillion-dollar Enron and Tyco frauds. A parody of the procedural television drama *Law and Order*, "Tron's Law and Order" swaps the expected fates of a black crack dealer and a white Wall Street ponzi-schemer. Played by Chappelle, "Tron Carter" is an unabashed and unrepentant drug runner charged with trafficking crack cocaine. However, his trial resembles a social hour: he is coddled and pampered by police officers, flattered by prosecutors, favored by the courts, and gently handed a one-month sentence in the cushy "Club Fed." This is no slap on the wrist; it's more like a caress.

Whereas Tron Carter is caressed, "Charles Jeffries" is pummeled. A white man and white-collar corporate criminal, Charles is subjected to police terror tactics, violent arrest, interrogation-by-torture, public humiliation, planted evidence, presumed guilt, incompetent defense, hasty conviction by a black and brown jury, debasement as "a filthy, big-lipped beast" by the trial judge, and finally, a sentence of life in prison. Chappelle inverts the world of racist cops and courts, staging a role reversal where a black defendant is exalted while a white defendant is damned. This outrageous satire prompts us to read American jurisprudence upside down—and hopefully ponder the wide racial disparity and deep racist corruption at its foundation.[70]

From Chappelle's theory of racialized reason, I pivot to his theory of racialized madness, akin to what anthropologist John Jackson Jr. calls "racial paranoia." During his 2006 appearance on *The Oprah Winfrey Show*, Chappelle alleged that he was the target of a conspiracy to exploit, defame, and control him—all hatched by unnamed business associates after "ugly [contract] negotiations." In the interview, Chappelle explains, "I felt like in a lot of instances I was deliberately being put through stress because when you're a guy that generates money, people have a vested interest in controlling you." He further emphasizes that he was not "crazy," but that these associates were "trying to convince me I am insane. They were trying to get me to take psychotic medication. . . . I said I'm not taking this medicine, man, because I know how these people be trying to control you or maybe discredit you."[71] In describing this alleged conspiracy to Winfrey and others, Chappelle intended to convince people of his sanity. Ironically, though, his talk of mind-control and secret cabals stoked rumors that he was a paranoid delusional conspiracy theorist. When Winfrey remarks that "colleagues were quoted as saying that you had become increasingly paranoid. Would you say you were paranoid?," Chappelle replies, "Sure . . . What's a black man without his paranoia intact?"

To be paranoid is to comport oneself with radical caution and obsessive vigilance; it is to anticipate and pay painstaking attention to potential threats, even the most unlikely, far-fetched, and unReasonable. Responding to ongoing histories of surreptitious antiblackness in American law enforcement, courts, electoral politics, education, housing, media, and medicine, many black people have incorporated conspiracy theories, emphatic suspicion, and deep pessimism into their cognitive frameworks. They have operationalized what Jackson calls "racial paranoia: distrustful conjecture about purposeful race-based maliciousness and the 'benign neglect' of racial indifference."[72] On *Chappelle's Show*, in stand-up performances, and in interviews, Chappelle has espoused "paranoid" theories about the origin of AIDS, the dissemination of crack cocaine,[73] and the hyperincarceration of black people.

When Chappelle suggests that he would be unsound without his "paranoia intact," he touts paranoia as essential equipment for black subsistence amid antiblackness. Some fifty years earlier, in a 1957 letter, protest novelist Richard Wright professed a similar sentiment: "I know I am paranoid. But you know, any black man who is not paranoid is in serious shape. He should be in an asylum and kept under cover."[74] Wright proposes that paranoid blackness is healthy, while blithely credulous blackness is pathological. Likewise, in 1968, black psychiatrists Price Cobbs and William Grier elaborated this theory of black paranoia:

> Black men have stood so long in such peculiar jeopardy in America that a black norm has developed—a suspiciousness of one's environment which is necessary for survival. Black people, to a degree that approaches paranoia, must be ever alert to danger from their white fellow citizens. It is a cultural phenomenon peculiar to black Americans. And it is a posture so close to paranoid thinking that the mental disorder into which black people most frequently fall is paranoid psychosis.[75]

The above passage begins with reference to "black men," who are also the protagonists in Chappelle's and Wright's formulations. I hasten to interject that, despite the androcentric language used by Chappelle, Wright, Grier, and Cobbs, there is nothing essentially masculine or male about this paranoia. Black women, girls, and other femme people are assailed by collusions of antiblackness, misogyny, and femmephobia. They have at least as much cause to practice paranoia as "any black man."

As for their broader formulation, Cobbs and Grier propose that black people have harbored paranoia as a psychosocial adaptation for living in perpetual jeopardy. The doctors regard this paranoia as both pathological (a "disorder") and beneficial ("necessary for survival"), a poignant paradox that infuses the psychic life of blackness in America. It would seem that this is a case of black people going mad in order to not lose their minds or their lives.[76]

Cobbs and Grier emphasize the *longue durée* of this black paranoid disposition. I want to elaborate several hypothetical scenarios, across centuries, where critical paranoia might prove useful for black folks. Paranoia would come in handy for an enslaved black man in 1831 whose otherwise aloof "master" suddenly begins to inquire, with exacting interest, about hidden aspects of black social life and freedom dreams on the plantation. Paranoia would also come in handy for a domestic worker in the Jim Crow South whose white male employer has begun to compliment her, whenever they are alone, on how well her bust fills out her uniform; or for a poor black mother in the mid-twentieth-century urban North as she fields the prying questions of a snide social worker; or for a black patient who complains of radiating chest and shoulder pains, circa "postracial" 2010, and is hastily given Tylenol and sent home. Each of the preceding black social agents would do well to keep their "paranoia intact," to anticipate harms that might befall them if they proceed carelessly and credulously. For black people traversing antiblack terrains rigged with antiblack booby traps, paranoia has proven a valuable (if exhausting and imperfect) existential orientation and epistemological equipment.[77]

Note that this tradition of black paranoia precedes the late nineteenth-century and early twentieth-century "hermeneutics of suspicion" that philosopher Paul Ricoeur attributes to Marx, Nietzsche, and Freud.[78] It also precedes the "paranoid reading" practice that queer theorist Eve Sedgwick traces to late twentieth-century queer theory.[79] Ricoeur and Sedgwick are primarily concerned with suspicion and paranoia as interpretive methods and affective dispositions among critical theorists. In contrast, the paranoia that Chappelle describes is a *black common sense*, a black vernacular knowledge informing repertoires of everyday praxis among black masses. It is a broader structure of feeling and network of knowing than Ricoeur and Sedgwick's concepts (which tend to privilege textuality, high theory, and formal criticism).

One of the primary objects of Chappelle's paranoia is Neal Brennan, his former real-life interracial buddy and *Chappelle's Show* writing partner.[80] Their collaboration was fabulously successful and congenial for the first two seasons of the series. In 2004, Chappelle told Charlie Rose that "people think in terms of race. Because the show is so racially charged, they're amazed that a white person and a black person can be cohorts."[81] Chappelle submits his show as proof that interracial teamwork, and the varied perspectives it brings to bear, can produce trenchant commentary on race. I suspect that there was another practical benefit to their black-white creative collaboration: it might have mollified white liberal discomfort over some of the show's racially provocative content.[82] Brennan could serve as a racial alibi, affirming that Chappelle, for all his scathing lambasts of whiteness, was still a benign buddy to white audiences.

Whatever its advantages, their partnership came undone in late 2004 and early 2005. Chappelle refused to name Brennan or anyone else as a culprit in the conspiracy to control him, but he did acknowledge that the threat came from his "inner circle."[83] Because Brennan occupied that inner circle, because their partnership and friendship ended amid the *Chappelle's Show* debacle, and because of Brennan's own comments in the news media, we can surmise that Brennan was among those alleged antagonists. Interviewed by *Time*, Brennan revealed that the antagonistic feeling was mutual. He portrayed an irrational Chappelle who had become increasingly unruly on set in late 2004. Brennan explained, "I told him, 'You're not well,'" and further recounted:

> He would come with an idea, or I would come with an idea, pitch it to him, and he'd say that's funny. And from there we'd write it. He'd love it, say, "I can't wait to do it." We'd shoot it, and then at some point he'd start saying, "This sketch is racist, and I don't want this on the air." And I was like, "You like this sketch. What do you mean?" There was this confusing contradictory thing: he was calling his own writing racist.[84]

Considering that Brennan is an accomplished writer, he seems curiously out of touch with the vagaries and vicissitudes of artistic creation. Sometimes artmaking entails mercurial changes of mind; or feelings of frustration when artistic execution does not match creative vision; or periods of intense self-reflection and self-criticism. When Brennan insists, "You like this sketch," he elides such complexities and presumes to know Chappelle's desires better than Chappelle does.

Recounting Chappelle's worry about writing racist sketches, Brennan pivots from a posture of presumptuous certainty to an attitude of utter bewilderment. He finds it strange that Chappelle, a black man, fears his own writing could be antiblack. Perhaps Brennan believes that blackness precludes one from perpetrating antiblack racism. Alas, antiblackness is so insidious and ubiquitous in modernity that black people often internalize it, support it, practice it, and manifest it—knowingly or not—despite grave cost to themselves. If Brennan's ignorance and naïveté are the alternatives to Chappelle's paranoia, it is no wonder Chappelle wants to keep his "paranoia intact." Meanwhile, I wonder about Brennan, *How could someone who coauthored such trenchant racial satire be so blithely ignorant about the insidious workings of antiblackness?* In search of an answer, I arrive at a paranoid conclusion of my own: Perhaps Brennan's naïveté is feigned in order to paint himself innocent and sympathetic, while casting Chappelle as cryptic and crazy. If Chappelle is up against such cunning aggression, paranoia seems perfectly appropriate.

Beyond his own predicament, Chappelle deploys paranoia to ponder other celebrity scandals. In his interview with Lipton, Chappelle ruminates on rumors about the alleged craziness of two other entertainers, comedian Martin Lawrence and singer-songwriter Mariah Carey:

> What is happening in Hollywood that a guy that tough [Martin Lawrence] will be on the street waving a gun screaming "they are trying to kill me"? What's going on? Why is Dave Chappelle going to Africa? Why does Mariah Carey make a $100 million deal and take her clothes off on TRL? A weak person cannot get to sit here and talk to you. Ain't no weak people talking to you. The worst thing to call somebody is crazy. It's dismissive. I don't understand this person, so they're crazy. That's bullshit. These people are not crazy. They strong people. Maybe the environment is a little sick.[85]

The declaration "I don't understand this person, so they're crazy" is a pithy summary of psychosocial madness. When radical difference perplexes and vexes a psychonormative majority, such difference is frequently coded "crazy" by that majority. Much like I propose that psychosocial madness conveys more about the attitudes of supposedly sane communities than it reveals about "crazy" people, Chappelle claims that these allegations expose more about the "sick" state of Hollywood than about Lawrence and Carey. According to Chappelle, such acts of pseudodiagnosis are products of an exploitative and apathetic entertainment industry.

Chappelle also proposes that madness is incompatible with strength. To have him tell it, success in showbusiness demands strength, and "strong" people do not go "crazy." The implication is that going "crazy" indicates weakness and only afflicts people with frail constitutions. This widespread fallacy, a hallmark of psychonormative and antimad ideology, produces pernicious effects; it stigmatizes mentally ill people and potentially discourages them from seeking treatment for fear that they will appear weak. The truth is that "strong" people, powerful people, accomplished people, and brave people experience mental illness and suffer mental distress.[86] Furthermore, some are labeled "crazy" *precisely because they are strong*, because they possess an unruly will that disrupts the psychosocial status quo.

I want to zoom in upon Martin Lawrence's saga. A celebrated comedian and television auteur in his own right, Lawrence's breakout 1994 HBO stand-up special is called *You So Crazy*. That same expression would become his catch-phrase on his popular 1990s Fox sitcom, *Martin*. When directed at a comedian, the statement "You so crazy" may be high praise; qualities like uninhibitedness, unpredictability, eccentricity, and outburst are associated with "craziness" and regarded as assets in broad comedy. But beginning in 1995, Lawrence would be branded "crazy" with far more sinister inflection. *People* magazine reported that Martin was hospitalized in July 1995 after a "wild outburst" on a movie set.[87] In October 1996, Lawrence's then-wife, Patricia Lawrence, successfully filed a restraining order after he allegedly threatened to kill her. Her filing included this ominous claim: "Sometimes [Lawrence] is himself and sometimes he is not. I can never be sure."[88] The *Washington Post* reported that in January 1997, he became "increasingly manic and volatile" toward Tisha Campbell, his *Martin* costar, on the set of the hit series. She eventually sued Lawrence and the show, alleging that he harassed, threatened, and sexually assaulted her.[89] These accusations are grave. Such behaviors warrant careful attention and critical denunciation—not because they are *mad*, per se, but because they *do harm*. As I have argued, madness is not synonymous with malice. Madness can be a conduit for good, evil, and endless other effects. When madness does harm, that harm should be decisively addressed and thwarted. The same should be true when Reason does harm.

Chappelle's comments on *Actor's Studio* refer to a different incident involving Lawrence. In May 1998, according to news sources, Lawrence bounded into the busy intersection of Ventura Boulevard and Tyrone Avenue in the Sherman Oaks neighborhood of Los Angeles. A witness reported that he was acting like a "madman," darting from sidewalk to boulevard, flailing his arms, shouting obscenities at motorists, and also declaring "Don't give up!" "Fight the power!" and "Fight the establishment!" to passersby. Police later discovered that he was carrying a concealed and loaded pistol all the while (contrary to Chappelle's claim that Lawrence was "waving a gun").[90]

It is poignant that Lawrence's alleged breakdown inspired insurrectionary speech. "Fight the establishment!" and "Fight the power!" are slogans of radical protest. Defying that unspecified "power," Lawrence formed a one-man picket line, professed his seditious message in the public square, and rallied passersby to join him in the struggle. I wonder what particular power he was urging strangers to fight that day in Sherman Oaks. Maybe he had in mind the Los Angeles Police Department (LAPD), with its egregious history of antiblack violence, whose officers would soon arrive to detain him; or Hollywood executives trying to convert him into currency and commodity to be consumed in racial capitalism; or psychiatric medicine, authorized to subdue "manic and volatile" people; or antiblackness, always haunting and hunting black life; or maybe he was battling a heckling voice inside his head, audible only to him.

According to published reports, Lawrence was involved in a physical altercation with police on the scene, but emerged without injury.[91] It is worth pausing to reflect on the fact that a black, mad, aggressive, and armed man survived such a confrontation with the LAPD. Perhaps his celebrity protected him; after all, the incident happened only one year following the finale of his massively popular sitcom. Maybe he was spared by mercurial fate or sheer *mad* luck. Whatever human or divine agency protected Lawrence that day, police did not use deadly force. Instead, they arrested him, remanded him to Sherman Oaks Hospital (remarkably, not jail), and finally released him to the care of his personal physician. According to a statement from his publicist, doctors "found Mr. Lawrence to be suffering from a case of complete exhaustion and dehydration." This account omits any reference to madness or protest, reducing all the ruckus to a mere lack of sleep and want of water.[92]

Recall Chappelle's stand-up routine about "talking crazy" to police. Whereas Chappelle talked crazy from a theater stage, Lawrence brought crazy talk to the streets with stunning temerity. He raised his voice in the idiom of madness, enjoining startled strangers to "fight the power!"; he ranted and raved truth to power when its avatars arrived in a police cruiser; he physically tussled with power when it approached to arrest him; and he somehow survived intact. Lawrence's deeds are so risky, so utterly susceptible to deadly retribution, that they are incompatible with the self-preservationist convictions of most political paradigms. Perhaps a death-bound politics, a suicidal mission seeking to instrumentalize state violence to bring about one's own demise, would aspire to emulate this act of assailing police while mad, black, alone, and armed.

This incident at the intersection also bears a trenchant reminder: Sometimes curbside rants are really rally cries and statements of solidarity. Sometimes madpeople on boulevards are muttering revolutionary counsel that might encourage us—if only we would linger and listen for a while, before we rush to wherever it is we think we're going.

Now we come to the closing credits. At the end of each episode of *Chappelle's Show*, a frame appears with the logo for the comedian's production company, Pilot Boys Productions. That logo includes a photograph of Chappelle against an empty gray backdrop, cropped from the chest up, shirtless, wrists shackled, clutching a wad of cash in each hand, and casting a worried, incredulous gaze at the camera.[93] The shackles and bare chest bring to mind the scene of a slave auction, where black skin was exposed, inspected, and sometimes split open in spectacles of commoditized and brutalized flesh. Dubbed over this still frame, Chappelle's voice rings out: "I'M RICH, BEE-YOTCH!"

This picture portrays a person who has acquired money but lost his freedom, who is rich and enslaved, who embodies Kanye West's lyrical admonition, "For that paper, look how low we'll stoop / Even if you in a Benz, you still a nigga in a coop."[94] To be clear, I do not glibly equate Chappelle with a chattel slave. After all, he enjoyed creative control, exercised executive power, earned ample compensation, and eventually practiced his freedom to leave at will—all of which are conditions contrary to the status of "slave." Nevertheless, this picture points to a critical affinity that Chappelle shares with his enslaved ancestors: They are all entangled in, and existentially endangered by, racial capitalism. Furthermore, they are subjected to the superexploitation of racialized bodies, cultures, and labors toward the proliferation of white supremacist wealth and the maintenance of racial domination.

Chappelle's photograph is a visual allegory for racial capitalism in the twenty-first-century pop culture–industrial complex: black cultural producers earn money (those clutched bills) under constraint (the handcuffs), their bodies availed for consumption (the bare chest), as they sometimes endure profound angst and ambivalence (the troubled facial expression). Chappelle holds a dozen or so cash notes, but if we were to pan out, we might see barrels of money collected by mostly white stakeholders and owners. This is the bigger picture of racial capitalism and US pop culture: a few black cultural producers and administrators enjoy financial gains; however, deep structural wealth is held firmly in the unshackled grip of white stakeholders and owners.[95]

6.1 Detail from the logo for Dave Chappelle's Pilot Boys Productions.

Beyond shared subjection to racial exploitation, Chappelle bears another affinity with countless enslaved people, an affinity we might call *drapetomaniacal will*. Like his drapetomaniacal forerunners who harbored the "disease causing Negroes to run away,"[96] Chappelle followed a fugitive urge, resisted racial capitalism, slipped off the manacles, escaped the site of labor, took flight, and was deemed crazy for his efforts. In the process, he joined a *drapetomaniacal diaspora*: a dispersal of drapetomaniacal beings in search of freedom; a convergence of mad diaspora and black diaspora in a fugitive geography; an unruly, wayward propulsion that flees literal and metaphysical plantations; and a structure of sociality and solidarity stretching across these black-mad-fugitive formations. We can chart drapetomaniacal diaspora in Chappelle's restful meditation at the home of his confidant in South Africa; in Pryor's uncanny epiphany while sitting in the lobby of a Kenyan hotel; in Lawrence's insurgent speech at a crossroads in Southern California.

Drapetomaniacal sociality and solidarity were also at work when Ms. Lauryn Hill, our old friend, contacted Chappelle. She expressed her support and offered him compassionate advice, not least that he should "be truthful at all costs."[97] Who better than Hill to counsel Chappelle on the maddening of black genius? Who better to talk him through the travails of record-breaking post-soul black creativity as it chafes against the hegemonic hold of US pop culture? Like Hill, Chappelle endured a series of outrageous confrontations with racial capitalism. Like Hill, Chappelle was viewed as a scandalously strange psychosocial other. Like Hill, Chappelle was driven to unruliness of mind and deep distress. Like Hill, Chappelle was acclaimed as a mastermind for giving the world a masterpiece, and then defamed as a mad mind for refusing to give more.[98]

Dave Chappelle's drapetomaniacal drama illustrates how madness crosses space. Now, finally, I invite the reader to ponder how madness makes and takes time.

CHAPTER SEVEN

SONGS IN MADTIME

BLACK MUSIC, MADNESS, AND
METAPHYSICAL SYNCOPATION

SYNCOPATED SUBJECTS

Nina Simone is mad—and with good reason. Urged to "go slow,"[1] to keep calm amid the carnage of her people, to sing sedately with the bloody boot of antiblackness on her throat, she finally unleashed a "rush of fury" and outburst of song that came "quicker than [she] could write it down." In the aftermath of the Sixteenth Street Baptist Church bombing—a conspiracy to pulverize and terrorize black life—Simone detonated an explosion of her own—a musical conflagration meant to galvanize black life and resistance. The outcome is Simone's 1964 protest anthem, "Mississippi Goddam," the sound of freedom dreams deferred[2] blasting from the mouth of a black radical, black classical prophetess.[3]

It came as a rush of fury. . . . My explanation didn't make sense because the words tumbled out in a rush—I couldn't speak quickly enough to release the torrents inside my head. . . . I had it in my mind to kill someone, I didn't know who, but someone I could identify as being in the way of my people getting some justice for the first time in three hundred years. [My husband] didn't try to stop me, but just stood there for a while and said, "Nina, you don't know anything about killing. The only thing you've got is music." . . . I sat down at my piano. An hour later I came out of my apartment with the sheet music for "Mississippi Goddam" in my hand. It was my first civil rights song and it erupted from me quicker than I could write it down. —NINA SIMONE, *I Put a Spell on You: The Autobiography of Nina Simone*, 1992

I hear the roar of Simone's song, and the boom of the church bomb that preceded it, as opposing offensives in a war over the "racial time" of mid-twentieth century America.[4] Antiblack terrorism sought to suspend black people in a state of pseudocitizenship or else thrust them backward in time to formally enslaved rightlessness. Meanwhile, leaders of America's white liberal establishment, purported allies of racial progress, admonished civil rights leaders to *slowly* seek justice.[5] Into the din of terrorist explosions and liberalist admonitions, Nina Simone raised her resounding contralto and spit this searing malediction:

> This whole country is full of lies
> You're all gonna die and die like flies
> I don't trust you anymore
> You keep on saying "Go slow!"
> "Go slow!" But that's just the trouble
> [Band:] *Too slow!*
> Desegregation
> [Band:] *Too slow!*
> Mass participation
> [Band:] *Too slow!*
> Reunification
> [Band:] *Too slow!*
> Do things gradually
> [Band:] *Too slow!*
> But bring more tragedy
> [Band:] *Too slow!*

Simone recites a litany of structural transformations ("desegregation," "mass participation," and "reunification") perniciously postponed by a white supremacist status quo. Her band members exclaim "too slow!" like a battle cry to jump-start liberation, like a chant to drown out pleas for passive patience. In a live recording of the song at Carnegie Hall in 1964, Simone announces, "This is a showtune, but the show hasn't been written for it yet." Rather than idly await social transformation, Simone is planning for a show, and planning for a world, to come. She is Afrofuturist par excellence, restless to author and enter radical futures. (I imagine this as-yet-unwritten show in two parts: first, a stunning spectacle of revolutionary battles waged; second, a fantasia of liberation achieved and enjoyed. Somewhere, amid the grief and glory, there should be a requiem for Addie Mae Collins, Carol Denise McNair, Carole Robertson, and Cynthia Wesley, the four church girls whose deaths helped galvanize "Mississippi Goddam." Maybe some mad black artist reading these words will produce a show worthy of Simone's tune.)[6]

In video footage of Simone performing "Mississippi Goddam," fury seems to inflect her voice, furrow her brow, and propel her arms as she pounds the piano in thunderous fortissimo.[7] In addition to the rage that is so vividly and resonantly on display, three other modes of madness course through this performance. Simone invokes phenomenal madness when she sings of existential turmoil in the face of antiblackness. She manifests psychosocial madness as a brazen black woman shouting "Goddam!" into the snarling face of Jim Crow, defying white supremacist, antiblack psychonorms of mid-twentieth-century America. Furthermore, Simone lived with medicalized madness. In her autobiography, she details episodes of psychosis in the 1960s and describes symptoms later diagnosed as bipolar disorder and schizophrenia.[8] While it would be an error to reduce Simone's performance to *symptom*, we cannot preclude the possibility that mental illness impacted "Mississippi Goddam." It is possible, for example, that manic impulsivity and racing thoughts hastened her impatience, intensified her passion, emboldened her audacity, diminished her inhibition, and otherwise stoked her poignant delivery in the song. The copresence of mental illness does not disqualify Simone's artistry. Nor does it negate the immanent genius, revolutionary politics, and radical love that might interanimate her performance—along with madness, against madness, through madness, in madness, *as* madness.

Simone knew the power in mad performance and sought to instrumentalize it for radical ends. Describing her performance philosophy in the late 1960s, she divulged a desire to drive audiences crazy: "I want to shake people up so bad that when they leave a nightclub where I've performed, I just want them to be to pieces! . . . I want to go in that den of those elegant people with their old ideas, smugness, and just drive them insane!"[9] She longs to do righteous violence to smug audiences—to shatter their complacency and topple their sanity, making way for transformation. "Mississippi Goddam" does not merely describe violence, it does an aesthetic and epistemic violence that Simone wants to leverage toward revolution.

Regarding the relation between madness and musical form in "Mississippi Goddam," performance theorist Malik Gaines notes that Simone plays "over a bouncy 2/4 piano beat in a quick and witty pitter-patter" and that the "upbeat Vaudevillian quality belies the anger of the lyrical content and the earthy ferocity of [her] performance."[10] However, a quick cadence and jaunty delivery do not necessarily suggest levity. Bounciness might characterize a cheery skip through blooming pastures, but it might also mark a frenzied scramble through bloody trenches. I propose that Simone's "pitter patter" echoes the beat of a racing heart that is flustered and restless for change. I contend that Simone's "up-beat Vaudevillian" style does not belie but rather amplifies the mad, manic, impatient content of the lyrics. With her rapid-fire delivery, she

7.1 Nina Simone, blurred in a rush of fury, performs "Mississippi Goddam" in the Netherlands, 1965.

performs the refusal to "go slow" that she describes. Simone's autobiographical phrase, "a *rush* of *fury*," captures both the *quickening* and *maddening* momentum of the song.

In sum, it seems that madness, in various iterations, comprises much of the song's impetus, its method, its theme, its key, and perhaps its existential time signature. Regarding the latter, I propose that Simone performs "Mississippi Goddam" in *manic time*, within a broader matrix that I call *madtime*. Broadly, madtime signifies various modes of doing time and feeling time coinciding with spasms and rhythms of madness. Madtime is multidirectional and polymorphous, deranged and dreamy, unruly and askew, capacious and kaleidoscopic. It tears calendars, smashes clocks, ignores calls for timeliness, builds makeshift time machines, writes "poetry from the future,"[11] sings showtunes for the future, and dances to the lilt of the voices in your head. It might leap, twirl, moonwalk, or sit still when prompted to march in teleological lockstep. In the process, madtime defies the Eurocentric, heteronormative, capitalist, rationalist clock-time that reigns in the modern West. Let's call this dominant chronology *Western Standard Time.*

Western Standard Time periodizes the world, establishes normative timelines for both quotidian and epochal events, and institutes benchmarks for *the good life.* According to queer and trans theorist Jack Halberstam, such benchmarks include "the narrative coherence of adolescence—early adulthood—marriage—reproduction—child rearing—retirement—death."[12] In step with its veneer of "narrative coherence," Western Standard Time stages grand parades toward normative futures, toward narrow horizons of happily-ever-after tailored to white, heteronormative, middle-class, rationalist subjects. Exalted by Euromodernity, Western Standard Time accrues metaphysical prestige, as though it is a quintessential structure and deterministic force driving human history.[13]

Western Standard Time excludes Euromodernity's Others—black people, mad people, queer people, et al.—from its triumphal parade. These Others are often displaced to make way for the parade route, or sequestered to its sidelines, or trampled underfoot, or else conscripted, but only in token numbers, to march in its second line. Madtime disrupts the lockstep of the parade and obstructs its routes. Moreover, madtime constitutes a mode of *metaphysical syncopation*: a process that bends, cuts, tilts, turns, twists, inverts, shuffles, shifts, evades, eschews, rearranges, or otherwise disturbs the metaphysics of Western Standard Time, embarrassing its prestige.

Madtime consorts with other syncopated subjectivities, especially *queer time*, *crip time*, and *black time*, which I briefly sketch in turn. Regarding queer temporalities, literary theorist Elizabeth Freeman describes a "queer time" encompassing "ways of living aslant to dominant forms of object-choice, coupledom, family, marriage, sociability and self-presentation and thus out of synch with state-sponsored narratives of belonging and becoming."[14] Against hegemonic modes of historicity, modernity, and futurity, queer time takes up wayward projects like fantasy, speculation, camp, longing, loitering, cruising, melancholia, and backward feeling.[15] In the process, queer time conjures queer pasts, practices queer nows, and plots queer futures outside the oppressive schedules of heteronormativity.

Crip time is oriented to lived experiences of impairment and social constructions of disability, all while centering phenomenologies of the "crip." Articulated by feminist disability studies scholars like Alison Kafer and Ellen Samuels, crip temporality might be, for instance, recursive with chronic symptoms, paused by rest breaks, erratic with unpredictable bodies and minds, stretched over long periods of recovery, or routinized with medication administration.[16] Crip time variously rearranges normative life itineraries, so that, as Samuels explains, "Some of us contend with the impairments of old age while still young; some of us are treated like children no matter how old we get."[17] Kafer emphasizes crip time as an intervention against the hegemony of clock time: "Rather than bend disabled bodies and minds to meet the clock, crip time bends the clock to meet disabled bodies and minds."[18] Perhaps this bending can eventually break open the clock to admit the worldmaking capacities of the crip.

Concerning black temporalities, black nihilist philosopher Calvin Warren describes a "black time" born out of the "metaphysical violence" and "temporal domination" that Africans endured in transatlantic slavery.[19] Warren writes emphatically that *slavery is the vicious enterprise of situating a being outside the time of man and in the abyss of black time.*[20] I share Warren's concern with metaphysics and his conviction that blackness dwells outside the exclusionary "time of man," but I arrive at a different notion of black temporality. Against Warren's pessimistic formulation (and by "against" I might mean both *counter to* and *touching*), I offer another take on blackness and time. Frequently articulated in black vernacular traditions and practiced in black quotidian contexts, "colored people's time" resists the tyranny of clocks, takes its precious time, and saunters in late; or maybe it rushes in, breathless, shining with sweat, tardy but blessedly here just the same. Whether it is sauntering or scrambling, colored people's time seems to recalibrate clocks, rearrange minutes and years, bend time lines, and syncopate metaphysics so that said "colored" person is not late after all, but is right on time. As praxis, colored people's time is imbued with mighty agency, even if it is born in abysmal abjection. *The abyss may have no bottom, but blackness has no top, no limit.*

To chart madtime, I trace its presence in black expressive culture. I center a black repertoire, in part, because antiblackness casts black people as always already mad while framing Africa as ahistorical and outside teleological time.[21] Insofar as blackness bears dual ascriptions of madness and untimeliness in Western modernity, it is an exemplary site for thinking through madtime. But there are other, more important, reasons for centering blackness and black expressive culture in this chapter: Blackness often sponsors exquisite practices of musical and metaphysical syncopation, stages syncopated "disturbance or interruption of the regular flow,"[22] eludes official notation, disobeys the dominant beat, activates the offbeat, aestheticizes the offbeat, and abides in the offbeat. Indeed, myriad black musicians are experts at making music and forging lives in offbeats. No wonder they are apt instructors in the arts of musical and metaphysical syncopation.

The current chapter is indebted to a mad black musician and pioneer of early jazz, Charles "Buddy" Bolden, whose lives and afterlives fill the second chapter of this study. My interest in madtime is stoked, in part, by a bitter irony of Bolden's life and art: He helped innovate the rhythmic time of jazz (syncopation), but alas, he was eventually confined to an insane asylum and excluded from the epochal time of jazz (the Jazz Age). What's more, he supposedly suffered a mental breakdown, a snap, while marching in a New Orleans Labor Day parade in 1906. Such a procession is a poignant metaphor for Western Standard Time. After all, Labor Day parades originated as tributes to the proletariat labor that turned the gears, but could not set the time, of capital's clock.[23] Such processions stress *rank and file*, *pageantry*, *lockstep*, and *forward march*, which materialize, in turn, the tenets of *hierarchy*, *artifice*, *synchronicity*, and *teleology* that characterize Western Standard Time. It seems to me that when Bolden swerved off that parade route, he also swerved away from sanity, away from normative time, away from capital, away from Reason, away from History. He landed in a metaphysical offbeat, a mad place, a zone of exile, a rebel outpost indifferent to the rules of Western Standard Time.[24]

In the pages that follow, I sample the songs of Nina Simone, Charles Mingus, Lauryn Hill, Kendrick Lamar, and Frank Ocean—punctuated by the lyrical literatures of Amiri Baraka, Suzan-Lori Parks, and Toni Morrison—to produce a medley in madtime. It unfurls in four movements, each devoted to a mode of madtime: (1) the quick, restless time of *mania*; (2) the slow, sorrowful time of *depression*; (3) the infinite, exigent now of *schizophrenia*; and (4) the circling, spiraling sorrow of *melancholia*.[25] In each interlude, I describe the properties of a given form of madtime and analyze how it functions as an existential time signature in black music. In the spirit of syncopation, I deviate from traditional protocols of chronology, linearity, and historicism. Instead, I crisscross promiscuously between historical periods, chasing madtime wherever and whenever I hear it.

Throughout, I highlight what black liberation struggles might critically cull and ethically adapt from madtime. This emphasis reflects my belief that black freedom movements can gain much by foregrounding madness in their accounts of black life and agendas for black liberation. The fact is that some freedom-loving and freedom-fighting black people *get mad* and *go mad* amid onslaughts of antiblack violence, terror, degradation, and hurt. Too often, however, mad people are treated as casualties, and madness as mere liability, in revolutionary struggles. I insist that we honor the mad among our ranks, remembering that madness is "loaded with information and energy" that can inform and invigorate liberation movements.[26] I do not mean to romanticize mania, depression, schizophrenia, and melancholia. Nor do I recommend that revolutionary thinkers or liberation movements aspire to psychiatric disorder. I know that these conditions, at the level of lived symptoms and psychosocial stigmas, are painful for many. However, a condition can be a source of pain *and* a resource for revolution.

Epitomized in "Mississippi Goddam," manic time is a mad dash that outruns the speed limit of Western Standard Time. Zooming about with frantic force, this mode of madtime entails the racing thoughts, restlessness, hyperactivity, exhilaration, and impulsivity that mainstream psychiatry ascribes to mania.[27] As a provocation for protest, manic time resists hegemonic calls for passive patience and refuses to "go slow." It is a locus of energetic impatience and audacity that might be harnessed to expedite change.

To further clarify this manic mode of madtime, I revisit the music of jazz composer, bassist, memoirist, and self-avowed madman, Charles Mingus. Recall that in 1958—fifteen years into a career that yielded sublime jazz compositions and a reputation as the "Angry Man of Jazz"—Mingus found himself in New York City, struggling with severe fatigue, personal agony, and a possible flare-up of bipolar symptoms.[28] He admitted himself to Bellevue Psychiatric Hospital and claims he composed "All the Things You Could Be by Now If Sigmund Freud's Wife Was Your Mother" on his third day there. The song would appear on his 1960 album *Charles Mingus Presents Charles Mingus*.

In chapter 2, I examined the extraordinary conditions under which Mingus labored in Bellevue and the psychoanalytic evocations in the track's title. Now I want to emphasize the manic temporality of the track itself, manifesting in the musician's prefatory remarks and in the actual music. Before the instruments begin to play, Mingus offers words of introduction that are muffled, mumbled, and spoken so rapidly that they are difficult to discern: "And now, ladies and gentlemen, you have been such a wonderful audience. We have a special treat in store for you. This is a composition dedicated to all mothers. And it's titled 'All the Things You Could Be by Now If Sigmund Freud's Wife Was Your Mother,' which means if Sigmund Freud's wife was your mother, all the things you could be by now. Which means nothing."[29] If the slur and speed of his speech are not enough to evade understanding, Mingus concludes with another enigmatic gesture. He declares that the title means "nothing," nonchalantly negating the words he spoke just seconds before, and likely leaving many listeners puzzled. If madness evades Reasonable understanding, manic time accelerates that evasion to a speed that Reason might chase but cannot apprehend.

Before I explore the song's musical content, I want briefly to comment on its genealogy. "All the Things You Could Be by Now" is a radical and nearly unrecognizable reinterpretation of "All the Things You Are," a jazz standard composed by Jerome Kern and Oscar Hammerstein II. The lyrics of the original song read:

> You are the promised kiss of springtime
> That makes the lonely winter seem long
> You are the breathless hush of evening
> That trembles on the brink of a lovely song
> You are the angel glow that lights a star
> The dearest things I know are what you are
>
> Someday my happy arms will hold you
> And someday I'll know that moment divine
> When all the things you are, are mine[30]

Kern and Hammerstein's tune, as famously performed by Ella Fitzgerald, is about pleasurably deferred gratification and joyful anticipation. The song basks in that which is "promised" but not yet received, that which is "on the brink" but not yet arrived, that which is "someday" but not this day. The singer marvels at an adorable "you," who are perched on a distant but still vividly visible horizon. "You" are described as a celestial event: sunset, season, and starlight. It is noteworthy that all three of these natural phenomena help humankind measure the passage of time. But when Lady Ella sings the song, she is not parsing time, nor is she worried over its passage. Her canonical vocal rendition unfurls at a leisurely pace; she is so sure of "what you are" that she can confidently, happily wait. She seems to sing with blithe assurance that "you" will come.

Only retaining the broad musical structure of the original song, Mingus discards Kern's melody, excises Hammerstein's lyrics, accelerates it to manic time, and leads his ensemble in manic improvisation. The eight-and-a-half-minute cut features Ted Curson on trumpet, Eric Dolphy on alto sax, Dannie Richmond on drums, and Mingus on bass. In particular, the last two minutes of the track are dominated by rapid, strident, cacophonous outbursts of trumpet and saxophone. The two instruments wail various calls and responses like manic interlocutors in clamorous conversation. These brass and woodwind conversants sometimes bicker, sometimes speak in unison, sometimes murmur in agreement, and sometimes rant with excitement, often at dizzying speed, while drum and bass alternately heckle and cheer them on. Perhaps the song's clamorous quality mimics the squabble between Mingus's interior voices ("Mingus One, Two, and Three") described in his memoir.

The alterations within the song are heralded by the modifications in its title. From Hammerstein's indicative clause, "All the Things You *Are*," Mingus shifts to a subjunctive, "All the Things You *Could Be*," and then specifies a hypothetical status, "*If* Sigmund Freud's Wife Was Your Mother." Per this revised title, Mingus does not know who you are and cannot rest blithely assured like Fitzgerald could. Beyond his uncertainty about "you," Mingus faced other, more pressing, unknowns as he wrote the song. The man could not rest assured because he was trapped in a psychiatric hospital under the virulent "care" of an antiblack doctor. Maybe the song's manic speed reflects the restlessness of a psychiatric detainee craving release. Perhaps it reveals the impatience of a black person longing to escape the antiblackness looming near. Penned in a psychiatric institution, performed with great speed and fervor, and named to conjure histories of psychoanalysis, "All the Things" exemplifies music in manic time.

I want to linger at the site of confinement, even as I pivot to another performer, genre, and era in black music. Recall that Ms. Lauryn Hill was convicted in July 2013 of tax evasion and sentenced to three months in a minimum-security federal women's prison in Connecticut. On October 4, 2013, she was discharged from prison and, on that very same day, debuted a song called "Consumerism." It would seem that Hill, like Mingus, found artistic provocation in the site of confinement. Amid the compulsory stagnation and regimentation of carceral time, Hill created new music. The song was a surge of creativity held behind prison walls, a surge that Hill rushed to release (to the airwaves) upon her release (from prison).

Accompanied by a pounding drumbeat, a blaring electric guitar, and a sinuous flute that brings to mind "showdown" leitmotifs in film Westerns, Hill rhymes

> Television running through them like an organism
> Mechanism, despotism, poisoning the ecosystem
> Satanism running through them like a politician
> Hedonism, hypocrism, nihilism, narcissism
> Egotism running through them, need an exorcism
> . . .
> European fetishisms, terrorism running through them, on their
>   television
> Introversion, extra prison
> . . .
> Paranoia, skepticism, schizophrenic masochism
> Modernism has created modern prisons
> Neo-McCarthyisms, new colonialisms . . . [31]

Showdown music is fitting for the task at hand, as Hill sizes up a many-headed hydra of global structural evils. Insofar as consumerism tends to exalt consumer goods to the detriment of social good, it is one entry on a sinister list that also includes "despotism," "terrorism," and "new colonialisms." Hill repeatedly uses the term *running through them* to indicate that these evils are not merely surface; they course through the core of the corrupt world order Hill rebukes. "Like an organism," these "isms" resemble viral agents infesting a body politic, generating social ills.

(While illness metaphors may be poignant for dramatizing the insidiousness of structural evil, they potentially distort the experience of people living with illness. In this vein, I hasten to note that "schizophrenic masochism" appears in the song's sinister litany. Because schizophrenia is frequently imagined as an amalgamation of sickness and wickedness, it is a convenient trope to characterize the status quo as both ill and evil. Alas, such a trope stigmatizes schizophrenic people who, overwhelmingly, do not intend or perpetuate evil. We would do well to approach this verse with critical ambivalence, objecting to its problematic contents even as we endorse its progressive potential.)

The remarkable speed of Hill's postprison release of "Consumerism" was matched by the remarkable speed of her lyrical delivery on the track itself. The song is marvelously manic: Hill raps tongue-twisting words at an average of 6.5 syllables per second with virtuosic verbal dexterity. What's more, many of the words are esoteric, polysyllabic, and stacked back-to-back in dense wordblocks (i.e., "hedonism, hypocrism, nihilism, narcissism") without the respite of a breath between them. Hill's rapid-fire rhyming produces a sonic bombardment that is likely to disorient, frustrate, and overwhelm some listeners, much like those social evils disorient, frustrate, and overwhelm vulnerable populations. In other words, Hill's musical onslaught dramatizes and highlights the sociopolitical onslaught of those corrupt systems.

"Consumerism" is not Hill's first foray into manic music. Hill's live performances, especially since 2007, often feature manic remakes of *Miseducation*-era hits, including her catchy homily, "Doo-Wop (That Thing)," and her infectious fight song, "Lost Ones." Hill accelerates these popular tracks so dramatically that their lyrics are sometimes difficult to discern, and their beats are too rapid for casual dancing and easy grooving. Instead, Hill leads listeners on a high-speed chase: away from her "forbiddingly perfect"[32] former persona and toward the reinvented Ms. Hill who is radically honest and unabashedly flawed. Hill has expressed a desire to see her audiences "jump that battery and start living."[33] With these manic renditions, it seems that Hill hopes to jolt and jump-start those audiences to full throttle at warp speed. Hill's manic delivery, like her occasionally hoarse vocals and cacophonous arrangements (see chapter 5), resists *easy listening*. She solicits a nimble, attentive, difficult listening instead.

Noting this manic quality in a 2010 concert, the *Atlantic* reported that Hill "opened her set with a manic rendition of 'Lost Ones,' dancing and rhyming at spitfire speed. 'Ex-Factor' was not the same nuanced song of pain as it is on the album, but it had its own furious energy about it." In 2012, the *Washington Post* described a performance that "ended in a speedy punk-rock rave-up and a primal howl."[34] Remarkably, both reviews link observations about Hill's quickness and comments about her purported madness, as though her speed is symptom. In the *Atlantic*, her "manic" performance and "furious energy" are linked to "speed"; in the *Washington Post*, her "speedy" singing culminates in a "primal howl."

Ultimately, Hill's manic performances amplify the alterity, urgency, and difficulty that are key elements of her musical praxis post-*Miseducation*. Hill mobilizes manic time to call out a gamut of structural evils, dramatize the effect of those evils, thwart easy listening, radically revamp songs, disavow her former persona, jump-start audiences toward transformation, and showcase her tongue-twisting virtuosity all the while.

"I WILL STILL BE HERE": DEPRESSIVE TIME

Depressive time lags behind. It is a slow motion that mimics time sensations associated with depression. Among its properties are listlessness, inertia, delay, dragging, lingering, and what mainstream psychiatry labels "psychomotor retardation,"[35] the slowing of thoughts and physical movements. In popular music, speed frequently denotes mood. While fast tempos are associated with "upbeat" jubilation and levity, very slow music often evokes sorrow and solemnity.

What critical and ethical insights might we find, slowly and painstakingly, in depressive time? How might it be taken up within radical praxis? To address these queries, I look to the lifeworlds of enslaved black people in colonial and antebellum America. When slave traders ordered the enslaved to "step it up lively" on auction blocks, those captors were not only compelling their captives to feign joy (a process Saidiya Hartman calls "simulated jollity"), they were also demanding the performance of speed.[36] Compulsory speed was a perennial feature of chattel slavery. The lives of slaves were often circumscribed by demands for rapid "breeding"; quotas for breakneck agricultural output; the acceleration of enslaved childhood, so that tiny children were compelled to work and forced to wrestle with existential crises; the insistence that sick, injured, and postpartum slaves recuperate with impossible speed; and the hasty arrival of death for many.[37]

For a slave to tarry in depressive time, to drag her feet sorrowfully rather than "step it up lively," was to commit an act of defiance. Within their severely constricted repertoire of agency, slaves practiced *defiant slowness* (contrary to the *compliant slowness* rebuked in "Mississippi Goddam") through work slowdowns and malingering. When enslaved people used these tactics, they disrupted plantation economies, stalled the schedules of slavocracy, and decelerated racial capitalism.[38] In a telling linguistic convergence, *depression* is a negative keyword in both psychiatry and political economy, denoting a condition of crisis for the individual psyche or for national wealth. Even the American Psychiatric Association recognizes the connection between a depressed psyche and a depressed economy, emphasizing that depression diminishes one's will and capacity to work.[39] Indeed, depression slows the march toward capitalist productivity, flings a wrench into the neoliberal machine, and disrupts the corporate schedules of Western Standard Time.

Depressive time also centers and honors sorrow. Indeed, blackness and sorrow are constant companions in this "afterlife of slavery,"[40] where antiblack hurt and loss have induced staggering sadness in black folks. Then, to add insult to atrocity, agents of antiblackness and keepers of Western Standard Time tend to devalue that despair, insisting that black people *get over it* and *move on*. Depressive time stubbornly resists such prompting. Regarding the stubbornness of depression, feminist affect theorist Ann Cvetkovich proposes a practice of ethical depression, a willingness to "be patient with the moods and temporalities of depression, not moving too quickly to recuperate them or put them to good use. It might instead be important to let depression linger, to explore the feeling of remaining or resting in sadness without insisting that it be transformed or reconceived."[41] Depressive temporality, as I imagine it, opens up a nook and makes precious time for "resting in sadness." I am describing a depressive time that allows aggrieved subjects to *mobilize* their sorrow, ironically by *loitering* within it. Together, manic time and depressive time forge a counterhegemonic complement: manic time defies directives to *go slow* toward liberation, while depressive time refuses pressure to prematurely *get over* racial hurt.

In his 1961 poem, "Preface to a Twenty Volume Suicide Note," Amiri Baraka activates depressive time. The poem's title signals its depressive attachments on two registers: first, the name contains "suicide," which can be a grievous outcome of clinical depression; second, the title specifies an object, "a twenty volume suicide note," that evokes both sorrow and prolongment. Drafting such a long suicide note might feel excruciatingly slow and protracted for someone intent on cutting life short and hastening the arrival of death. "Preface" begins,

> Lately, I've become accustomed to the way
> The ground opens up and envelops me
> Each time I go out to walk the dog.
>
> . . .
>
> Things have come to that.
> And now, each night I count the stars.
> And each night I get the same number.
> And when they will not come to be counted,
> I count the holes they leave.

Both slowness and sorrow pervade these verses. The task of walking a dog and the pastime of stargazing are fraught with listless sadness. Within the poem, these mundane acts come to resemble funerary rituals. Baraka describes a malaise so consuming that it makes him lackadaisical about the Earth opening up beneath him and the cosmos rearranging itself above him. In the process, he documents the lifeworld of a black radicalizing poet at the dawn of a decade that would witness worldwide social upheaval.

Recorded live at the end of that same decade, Nina Simone's 1969 cover of Sandy Denny's "Who Knows Where the Time Goes?" also engenders a slow and sorrowful affect. In her spoken prelude to the song, Simone declares, "Time is a dictator, as we know it. Where does it go? What does it do? Most of all, is it alive? Is it a thing that we cannot touch and is it alive? And then one day you look in the mirror, you're old and you say where did the time go? We leave you with that one." After posing those sweeping existential queries, Simone listlessly sings:

> Across the morning sky
> All the birds are leaving
> How can they know
> That it's time to go?
>
> . . .
>
> Sad deserted shore
> Your fickle friends are leaving
> But I will still be here
> I have no thought of leaving

For I do not count the time

. . .

But I am not alone
As long as my love is near me
And I know it will be so
Until it's time to go[42]

Performing in the song's persona, Simone describes birds that instinctively know the season and migrate at the appointed time to the proper destination. To the contrary, people lose track of time, or refuse to count it, or else know it's time to go, but stay sullenly behind. The song lingers on that "sad deserted shore" with the speaker who has "no thought of leaving." Though her "love is near," the protagonist is still suspended in a slow-moving doldrum, still languid beneath the weight of a lingering loneliness. "Who Knows Where the Time Goes?" refuses to move on, models a depressive praxis, and draws the listener into its tarrying temporality and rueful feeling.

While the lyrics appear to portray personal loneliness and private grief, it is crucial to situate this performance within its broader geopolitical zeitgeist. Simone's live recording took place at the New York Philharmonic Hall in 1969, amid the fervor of the Vietnam War, the year of the Stonewall Rebellion, the year after the assassination of Martin Luther King Jr. (who Simone musically eulogized as "The King of Love"), and the year after what many mark as the end of the US civil rights movement.[43] In Simone's custody and in this historical context, lyrics about *romantic* love, lost *friends*, and passing *birds* doubly evoke *political* love, lost *leaders*, and passing *eras*. She endows a wistful love song with profound protest resonance.

That "King of Love" is the eponym for the annual Martin Luther King Jr. Concert Series, where Hill performed on August 6, 2007, in Brooklyn, New York. To the chagrin of audience members and media pundits, Hill arrived two hours late and unrepentant. In chapter 5, I pondered this performance in depth, but now I want to remark on the symbolic import of her lateness to an event named for King. Hill's *delinquency* is especially stark against the backdrop of King's legend, which is typically (and reductively) linked to notions of liberal *progress*. Hill's bodacious *defiance* is especially conspicuous when apposed with America's most revered icon of racial *reconciliation*.

This is one among many incidents of Hill's multihour tardiness to concerts post-*Unplugged*, as documented in countless disgruntled op-eds and social media posts that frame Hill's lateness as pathological.[44] In 2014, when an audience member at a UK concert asked Hill to explain her lateness, she replied, "Why am I late? . . . Because this is not robotic. This is a commodity of the soul and the emotions and every day is a different day. . . . Every day I'm dealing with different issues and I still pull myself up to come and give this performance. . . . Some days it takes more than others . . . because I'm not a machine, a robot." Assuring concertgoers that she is not beholden to their money, she continued, "There's never, like, a gun at your head at the ticket office or online to purchase a ticket. . . . everybody has choice in the situation. . . . I would never force anything on you. You can't force anything on me."[45] She intends to move at her own pace and perform in her own time, even when it comes at the cost of audience satisfaction and concert revenue. Hill will occasionally even point a peeved concertgoer to the exit and grant him a refund. She did so at a 2014 Chicago concert after an audience member reportedly flipped her his middle finger: "You can go and you can take all your money right back. . . . I do this because I love it, not because I owe you anything. . . . You can get on your blogs and you can tweet and you can say whatever you want to. I don't give a rat's ass. I do this because I love it."[46] Hill prioritizes her *love* for the music over *like* from the public and has (Afro-)alienated some fans in the process.[47]

Hill's nonrelease of a studio-recorded sequel to *Miseducation* has also garnered accusations of pathological slowness. Writing in GQ, music critic Amy Wallace explains that "[hip-hop producer] Questlove has a theory about what happens to black genius—what he calls 'a crazy psychological kind of stoppage that prevents them from following through. A sort of self-saboteur disorder.'"[48] To glib observers, "self-saboteur disorder" might seem apt to describe both Hill and Dave Chappelle. After all, each was widely anointed "genius," neither has yielded a "follow-through" in the vein of their earlier success, and each has been deemed "crazy."

The problem with Questlove's coinage—beyond its pseudopsychoanalyzing—is its emphatically commercialist and consumerist sensibility. The "stoppage" signified in his "self-saboteur disorder" is a drought in commercial productivity within an entertainment-industrial complex. If we assess Hill's follow-through in terms of a multiplatinum sophomore album or Chappelle's follow-through in terms of a hit fourth season on television, then, indeed, we are left with the impression of "stoppage." However, such assessments are calibrated to corporate clocks and earnings projections set by Columbia Records and Comedy Central, enshrining popularity and profitability above all else. Such narrow notions of productivity neglect vaster fields of creativity and fulfillment.

If we consider Hill's continued performance and productivity in various music festivals and small tours, it becomes clear that she does not suffer from "stoppage," but rather flows through routes outside the corporate mainstream. Moreover, if we decenter music altogether and foreground self-care, spiritual development, knowledge acquisition, familial proliferation, and other personal metrics of life accomplishment, Hill's trajectory is full of flow and progress.[49] I recognize that, say, clinical depression can stifle creativity and engender a "psychological kind of stoppage." However, commercial performance is not an appropriate measure for detecting or interpreting such psychological processes. Questlove's coinage (when applied to Hill and Chappelle) exemplifies a normative tendency to label behaviors "crazy" when they defy the status quo. If there is a sadness surrounding Hill's practice of depressive time, much of it comes from the patronizing pity of those who view her career as tragic.

Insofar as Hill instrumentalizes slowness, refuses to comply with corporate clocks, generates negative affect, endures accusations of madness, earns consumerist pity, and remains defiantly delinquent, she powerfully activates depressive time. In the process, she joins a long tradition of black refusals to perform timely labor, a legacy extending back to plantation slowdowns.

"IT IS ALWAYS NOW": SCHIZOPHRENIC TIME

My theory of schizophrenic time is provoked, in part, by Foucault's description of schizophrenia in *Madness: The Invention of an Idea*. He details a phenomenology of schizophrenia where "spatiotemporal coherence that is ordered in the here and now has collapsed, and all that remains is a chaos of successive heres and isolated moments," a "fragmented world," and "dispersed consciousness."[50] Foucault further avers that "the time without future or past in which [the schizophrenic] lives reflects his *inability to project himself into a future or recognize himself in a past*."[51]

Alongside and against Foucault's claim, I propose the following: Even if schizophrenic subjectivity cannot project into the past and future, it is utterly available to intrusions of the past and future into its now. Schizophrenic subjectivity, like all subjectivity, is vulnerable to irruptions of traumatic pasts and ominous futures into its precarious present. And if precarity is especially frequent in the lives of schizophrenic people, it is not merely because of an ontogenic, indwelling unruliness of mind. The cause is also sociogenic, the outcome of socially sanctioned persecutions animated by antimadness. In other words, the time-disruption that accompanies schizophrenia is not merely a process originating in the genetics, brain chemistry, or individual psyche of the schizophrenic subject. It is also the result of antimad violence—perpetrated on psychosocial, epistemic, clinical, carceral, and existential fronts—assaulting the life and time of the so-called schizophrenic.[52] When past trauma and future danger ambush your present, overrunning you at once from ahead and behind, you might be left feeling that "it is always now."[53] Now might seem to expand to eternity, and eternity might seem to contract into now.

Slavery weaponized something like schizophrenic time, aiming to isolate the enslaved in an abject now, estranged from both future and past (and yet utterly exposed to past trauma and future danger). Indeed, antiblack slavery sought to erase its captives from history, bridle their futurity, and consign them to an always already beleaguered present.[54] According to Hortense Spillers, antiblack slavery characterized the "slave" as "the essence of stillness," "fixed in time and space," manifesting an "undynamic human state."[55] Slavery's advocates claimed that such inertia was an ontogenic and ontological quality embedded in black slaves. The truth is that slavery imposed such fixity on enslaved people—with rope and chains to constrict physical movement and mental fetters to stifle imagination—thus fabricating tautological "proof" of its own specious claims. Even beyond formal abolition, agents of antiblackness still allege that there is no black history, there is no black future, just *a bleak black now*. All the while, structural antiblackness works to produce that bleak black now, to enforce and sustain black abjection.

Yet there are lessons to glean in and from schizophrenic time. Insofar as it collapses everything into an exigent now, schizophrenic time *frustrates the fantasy of teleology and resists the lure of nostalgia*. And because schizophrenic time entails a "chaos of successive" nows, each now yielding novel perils and opportunities, it might prompt extraordinary vigilance, adaptability, and improvisation. For those of us entrenched in radical flux and uncertainty—who have no choice but to live *in the moment*—schizophrenic time can teach and caution us about the chaos of now. On a different register, philosophers Gilles Deleuze and Félix Guattari discern radical potential in schizophrenia. They regard it as a repository of generative desire that thwarts the oppressive incursions of capitalism and psychoanalysis. According to Deleuze and Guattari, capitalism and psychoanalysis are structures of domination that stagnate human desire and prune people into repressed, docile, and utterly governable subjects. The authors depict the schizophrenic as a psychoexistential outlaw who resides "somewhere else, beyond or behind or below problems" that concern the normative (neurotic) ego.[56] Perhaps the schizophrenic can venture "beyond or behind or below" Western Standard Time, too.

Playwright Suzan-Lori Parks dramatizes schizophrenic time in her 1990 play, *The Death of the Last Black Man in the Whole Entire World*. The script does not conform to a conventional plotline or lend itself to linear recounting. Rather, it is a dreamy, uncanny meditation on the black dead as objects of memory, mourning, history, erasure, and resurrection. In a series of recursive speeches and dialogues, a surreal cast of characters—many named to evoke crude caricatures of blackness—ponder the deaths of the last black man in the world. Parks has likened the play's rhizomatic repetition and revision to free jazz.[57] This musicality makes the drama especially auspicious for inclusion among these songs in madtime.

In *The Death of the Last Black Man*, the primary protagonists are a husband and wife who lack proper names but are identified with captions: "Black Man with Watermelon" and "Black Woman with Fried Drumstick." Thus named, the two are tethered to totems of stereotyped, minstrelized, abjected blackness. The play opens as Black Man returns home from the dead to Black Woman and the two rendezvous on their porch. This is not Black Man's first return from the dead, for he has died many gory, spectacular deaths. He has "burst into flames," ostensibly by spontaneous combustion;[58] been "juiced" in an electric chair;[59] been asphyxiated and "swingin" at the end of a lynching rope;[60] gone "splat" at the bottom of a twenty-three-story fall;[61] and suffocated while buried alive. His deaths are strewn across centuries, as Black Woman explains: "Yesterday today next summer tomorrow just uh moment uhgoh in 1317 dieded thuh last black man in thuh whole entire world."[62] That he is the *final* black man implies that his death comes at the end of an extinction event or (gendered) genocide, but the script provides no such context. The play simply unfurls a world where black manhood is on the verge of vanishing, a fate only narrowly avoided because this last man keeps doggedly returning. It is unclear how black women are faring amid this extinction event—whether they remain in great numbers, or are dwindling, or whether Black Woman, like Black Man, is a sole survivor.

Theirs is a gendered division of labor: Black Man's work is *death* and *weary return*, while Black Woman's work is *grief* and *weary waiting*. Each repeats their appointed task over and over again, interceded by encounters on that porch. Black Man explains, "We sittin on this porch right now aint we. Uh huhn. Aaah. Yes. Sittin right here right now on it in it ainthuh first time either iduhnt it. Yep. Nope. . . . There is uh Now and there is uh Then. Ssall there is. (I bein in uh Now: uh Now bein in uh Then: I bein, in Now in Then, in I will be. I was be too but thats uh Then thats past. . . . Thuh me-has-been sits in thuh be-me: we sit on this porch. Same porch. Same me.") Black Man's speech performs the scrambling of spacetime that it purports to describe.[63] The passage zigzags across grammatical tense and dissolves syntactic norms, much as Black Man zigzags across timespace and dissolves the metaphysical borders between death and life. On that porch, the present ("Now"), the past ("Then"), and the future ("will be") all crowd together, like eternity crammed onto a porch swing, like the fabric of spacetime folded into a picnic blanket.

Also present in the play are supporting characters such as "Queen-Then-Pharaoh Hatshepsut," "Before Columbus," and "Old Man River,"[64] who intrude upon the proceedings like hallucinations made flesh, like voices in one's head given platforms and bullhorns, like dissociative doppelgangers of Black Woman and Black Man, like "stereotype pixies" run amuck.[65] I high-light these three figures because their names signify epochs of human history: "Queen-Then-Pharaoh Hatshepsut" evokes ancient Egypt during Hatshepsut's reign (circa 1500 BC); "Before Columbus" conjures the Americas before Euro-pean Conquest (before 1492 AD); and "Old Man River" brings to mind the US South around the "nadir" of African American history (circa 1900 AD). Although these eras span millennia, they all converge and condense into the imminence of a deathly *now* where Black Man is dying. It is as though time itself collapses beneath the corpse of black death—and suddenly the ancient past, the coming summer, a minute ago, post-Reconstruction, 1317, and to-morrow all come caving into the present. The play dramatizes and blackens Foucault's assertion that "spatiotemporal coherence that is ordered in the here and now has collapsed, and all that remains is a chaos of successive heres and isolated moments."

Black Man frequently expresses a frustrated desire to move his hands, a gesture that might symbolize the power to handle, to act upon, to exercise agency.[66] The play ends when Black Woman declares, "The black man he move. He move. He hans," and the entire cast replies, "Hold it. Hold it. Hold it. Hold it. Hold it. Hold it. Hold it."[67] Performance theorist Soyica Colbert argues that *The Death of the Last Black Man*, especially "the suspension of the play in the final words," "challenges the audience to abide with the trauma of racial violence and continue to work through it."[68] I want to suggest that such suspension and traumatized abiding are quintessential qualities of schizophrenic time. Colbert further asserts that the play "uses theater's visibility to situate all time in the now."[69] This is precisely the situation and function of schizophrenic time.

To communicate the relentlessness of black death, the play cannot abide by linear, realist techniques of conventional Western theater. Parks resorts, in-stead, to a mad dramaturgy: conjuring a frenzy of voices and memories—and jamming them into a tenuous now—to dramatize the frenzy of a world whose last Black Man is dying. Insofar as the play concerns death and prolonged processes of mourning, it also contains melancholic inflections. However, the play lingers in an endless here-and-now of black death, rather than longing for a gone-and-lost of the black dead; thus its primary habitus is schizophrenic time.

Hip-hop artist Kendrick Lamar also mobilizes schizophrenic time to probe black death. Lamar came to mainstream fame in 2012 and 2013, the same period when the killing of Trayvon Martin and subsequent acquittal of George Zimmerman haunted American public spheres and invigorated the Movement (and many movements) for Black Lives. Lamar has since emerged as a booming voice and prophetic exhorter in the #BlackLivesMatter soundscape. In confessional songs and interviews, he manifests a persona fraught with effervescent joy, "depression," radical hope, "suicidal thoughts," staggering doubt, and worldmaking love. He also exposes the structures of antiblackness, materialism, and toxic patriarchy that imperil him, while illuminating the systems of community, art, and love that sustain him.[70]

In "The Blacker the Berry," a track on his 2015 *To Pimp a Butterfly* album, Lamar activates schizophrenic time. The song depicts a black protagonist corrupted by antiblack trauma and antagonism. At the start of the song, he mumbles, slurs, and growls barely decipherable words—utterances in the idiom of madness—over high, ominous strings and blaring bass. Even when those opening words are deciphered and transcribed, they resist facile understanding:

> Everything black, I don't want black
> I want everything black, I ain't need black
> Some white, some black, I ain't mean black
> I want everything black
> Want all things black, I don't need black[71]

In character, Lamar recites a series of self-contradictions that suggest profound indecision and unruliness of mind—like the clamor of a man debating with a voice inside his head. Blackness is alternately claimed and denied in an intrapsychic tug-of-war. He darts among a series of nows, each disjointed from the one before: a *now* in which black is everything, a *now* in which black disappears, a *now* in which black is wanted, a *now* in which black is unwanted, a *now* in which black is needed, a *now* in which black is dismissed, a *now* in which black is accidental, a *now* in which black is on purpose. Lamar performs a schizophrenic temporality that fractures continuity, resists coherency, refuses resolution, inhabits "a chaos of successive" nows, and yields a series of paradoxes.

In a subsequent verse, Lamar declares "I'm black as the moon." Insofar as the moon typically appears pale to earthly observers, this declaration upends empirical commonsense. But there is another mad resonance in this black moon.

Folklore and philosophy extending back to ancient Greece claim that full moons induce madness—a belief enshrined in the word *lunatic*, from the Latin root *luna*, meaning *moon*. Thus, Lamar likens himself to a maddening celestial body and colors it black. When he later claims that "I'm black as the heart of a fucking Aryan," an allusion to white supremacist Nazis, he once again conjures a paradoxical blackness, a blackness whose description inverts expectation. Not only does this lyric liken a black speaker to a white supremacist, it also ascribes blackness, via a black heart, to a person invested in white purity. The lyric suggests an uncanny likeness and gnarled entanglement between the speaker's blackness and the antiblackness that assails him.

That entanglement is laid bare later in the song. Lamar's speaker announces that he is homicidal, but places the blame on an antiblack instigator who "hates" him, whose "plan is to terminate [his] culture," who "made [him] a killer." Lamar's speaker proceeds to diagnose the madness of antiblackness, judging it to be paranoid, antisocial, and self-loathing. Addressing agents of antiblackness, he proclaims, "You're evil" and "You hate me just as much as you hate yourself." Twenty-two years earlier, in a 1993 interview with Charlie Rose, Toni Morrison had mused about the psychopathology of white supremacy. With a taunting lilt, she interrogated an imagined white racist: "I take your [whiteness] away, and there you are all strung out and all you got is your little self. And what is that? What are you without racism? Are you any good? Are you still strong? Still smart? You still like yourself?"[72] As though answering Morrison's question, Lamar suggests that such racists do not merely *dislike* themselves, they *hate* themselves.

Beyond its "chaos of successive" nows and its evocations of psychosis, the track explicitly invokes schizophrenia. In the song's persona, Lamar confesses:

> Six in the mornin', fire in the street
> Burn, baby burn, that's all I wanna see
> And sometimes I get off watchin' you die in vain
> It's such a shame
> They may call me crazy
> They may say I suffer from schizophrenia or somethin'
> But homie, you made me[73]

Here the emcee performs a sinister sort of madness, a pyromaniacal persona who takes pleasure in witnessing burning streets and finds sadistic joy in "watchin' you die in vain." After confessing this malice, he mentions schizophrenia, invoking rampant associations between the condition and evil. Whereas

Hill mentions "schizophrenic masochism" on "Consumerism," Lamar conjures a schizophrenic sadism on "The Blacker the Berry." I hasten to note that the vast majority of schizophrenic people are not malevolent sadists or villainous evildoers; in fact, for example, "schizophrenic individuals who live in community settings and don't abuse drugs are more likely to be victims than perpetrators of violent crimes."[74]

After admitting that people "may say I suffer from schizophrenia," Lamar's speaker interjects "but homie, you made me." Like his insistence that "you made me a killer," the speaker blames his malice on an antiblack Other. Once again, Lamar portrays a cruel bond between a black man and an antiblack antagonist—an antagonist who is intent upon terminating, and yet responsible for making, that black man. To be clear, the speaker's claim that "you made me" is not conciliatory, not deferent, not a plea for affinity. To the contrary, "you made me" is an acerbic accusation, a laying of blame, a warning that just desserts will be served, an announcement that the harm you made might come back to burn you, to watch you "die in vain."

In "The Blacker the Berry," the madness of an antiblack world and the madness of a sadistic black persona entangle in a noxious knot. However, I want to disentangle the knot and emphasize that these are drastically different strains of madness. The (outlaw) madness channeled by Lamar should not be conflated with the (hegemonic) madness of antiblackness. Antiblackness is often agonized, distressed, and unruly—which is to say, it endures phenomenal madness—but it is not psychosocial alterity or insurgency. Antiblackness is commensurate with, not divergent from, America's psychosocial norms. In short, *antiblack blues ain't like Lamar's blues.*[75]

All the while, I recognize that Lamar's representation of a malevolent person under the sign of "schizophrenia" lends itself to the stigmatization of people living with the condition. We would do well to approach these verses with critical ambivalence, to sit with the simultaneity of their radical resonance and capitulation to stereotype. Critical ambivalence trains us to critique the potentially antimad content in "The Blacker the Berry," even as we note that the song's potentially schizophrenic protagonist is complex and conscientious, not some crude and flat caricature. Moreover, it is worth noting that antiblackness, not schizophrenia, is the song's archvillain—and a possibly schizophrenic persona is entrusted with the task of condemning that villain. To delegate such a crucial role to a madman is a remarkable gesture amid an antimad world. Ultimately, then, Lamar conjures schizophrenia to convey the insidiousness of antiblackness, to rebuke it, and to warn of the violence it spawns.

In the final phrase of the novel *Sula*, Morrison describes the wail of a woman longing for her deceased friend: "It had no bottom and it had no top, just circles and circles of sorrow."[76] These words trace the shape of melancholic time. Defined by Freud as "pathological mourning," melancholia occurs when a subject loses some precious "object," whether person, aspiration, ideal, or otherwise.[77] The subject feels profound grief but also festering resentment for the object because it has abandoned her. To combat the trauma of the loss, she attempts to keep the object with her by incorporating it, along with that resentment, into her own ego.

I propose that melancholia is existential time travel and the melancholic subject is time traveler. The process begins when that cherished object is torn away from the subject. What results is a *psychic wound that is also a tear in time* opening toward the memory of the lost object. Here is the itinerary of the melancholic time traveler: she enters that tear in time and travels backward into an idealized past where the lost object existed; she retrieves a fantasy of that lost object and carries it, bound up with reproach, back into her deficient present; she unloads the sorrowful cargo into her own ego; and then she repeats the melancholic journey again and again, from aggrieved present to idealized past to aggrieved present to idealized past, along circles and circles of sorrow.

What insights might this melancholic time traveler teach critical theory and liberation praxis? How might melancholia incite, inform, and inspire our protest? Psychoanalytic thinkers David Eng and Shinhee Han offer a compelling reply to these queries. Theorizing the insurgent uses of melancholia, they highlight a "militant refusal on the part of the ego to let go," which is "at the heart of melancholia's productive political potentials."[78] Likewise, black feminist theorist Sara Clarke Kaplan, following Anne Cheng's distinction between personal grief and politicized grievance, suggests that we approach "melancholia not as a private, backward-looking phenomenon of paralyzing psychic conflict, but as an embodied individual and collective psychic practice with the political potential to transform grief into the articulation of grievances that traverse continents and cross time."[79] Following Eng, Han, Cheng, and Kaplan, I envision a melancholic subject who refuses to let go of her lost object, who clutches and brandishes it, who clamorously proclaims her loss while picketing in circles of sorrow. I hear a melancholic picketer whose mournful wails (of grief) are always already also petitions for redress (from grievance).

To further elaborate the insurgent potential in melancholic time, I return to the lifeworlds of enslaved people, a melancholic turn and return that I keep performing in this chapter. Some slaveholders adopted a belief in black insentience, and thus treated their captives as brutes: insensitive to pain, estranged from tenderness, and incapable of deep feeling. Other slaveholders were keenly aware of the reality of black pain, cultivating an expert knowledge of that pain, and systematically inducing it to dominate and terrorize their captives.[80] Both believers in black insentience and instrumentalists of black pain subjected enslaved black people to astounding abuse: from body-destroying work demands, to gruesome acts of physical and sexual violence, to psychological torture, to the severing of kinship ties that sociologist Orlando Patterson calls "natal alienation."[81] That latter harm, the theft of kin, meant that enslaved people amassed a colossal store of melancholic objects. As a consequence, melancholia was a sprawling and towering structure of feeling in the lifeworlds of slaves.

Literary theorist Éva Tettenborn describes melancholic slaves forced to feign happiness. She writes that "beyond being an assault on the slave's sadness, the master's order to sing or dance . . . or to prepare for a party instead of a funeral . . . is an expression of a severe white anxiety regarding the slave's potential for melancholia [which] would threaten the system because it presupposes and claims the existence of the black subject and thus contests the limitations imposed on slaves."[82] Melancholia entails the incorporation of the lost "object" into the "self," but according to the logics of chattel slavery, neither that lost object, nor even the self, belonged to the black slave. According to Tettenborn, a slave's melancholic act of "claiming possession of someone to whom he or she has become attached" undermined the slaveholder's legal prerogative to wholly possess the enslaved.[83] This melancholic structure of feeling has outlasted formal chattel slavery and still stands ominously today. It is the accumulation and calcification of what Hartman describes as the "interminable grief engendered by slavery and its aftermath."[84] This melancholia is not only a microlevel phenomenal time characterizing the everyday experience of individuals. It is also a macrolevel, world-historical epoch initiated by the global catastrophe of Atlantic slavery.

On a different register, themes of freedom and unfreedom concern Ms. Lauryn Hill on "I Gotta Find Peace of Mind," the longest musical track on *MTV Unplugged 2.0*. The song, introduced in chapter 5, is a nine-minute testimony of a woman rebuking an emotional abuser, vanquishing self-doubt, realizing faith, and striving toward something like serenity. I return to the song to amplify a particular musical gesture within it that activates melancholic time. Recalling her former subjection to an abusive partner, the song's speaker tearfully repeats, "That old me is left behind."[85] The phrase *That old me* is a double entendre. On the one hand, it signifies a bygone version of the woman within the song. On the other hand, the term denotes Hill's "forbiddingly perfect" and widely lauded *Miseducation* persona beyond the song—a persona she would later renounce, a persona effectively dead and gone, a persona that seems to induce melancholic longing and reproach in the musician. Toward the end of the song, Hill entreats her audience to "free your mind" and "get free now." While weeping, she sings the word *free* fifteen times, generating a melancolic refrain, a vocal circle of sorrow that sounds like a freedom chant. It is as though the singer harnesses the kinetic energy in her spinning sorrow and finally lurches loose to freewheel toward freedom.

Unplugged 2.0 was lambasted for melodic redundancy within songs and lengthy interludes between songs. *Newsweek* lamented Hill's "rambling monologues," one of which, according to *Entertainment Weekly*, "meanders on for an interminable 12 minutes."[86] The *Village Voice* called *Unplugged* "a full-length double-CD of wordy strophic strolls that often last six, seven, eight minutes, accompanied solely by a solo guitar Hill can barely strum (the first finger-picked figure occurs on track 10, where it repeats dozens upon dozens of times, arghh)."[87] The words *rambling*, *meanders*, *interminable*, and *repeats* all evoke the circuitous time of melancholia. These reviewers are describing and decrying a performance in melancholic time: a sonic sadness that clamors for a lost object, troubles normative temporality, travels in sorrowful circles, and repeats itself over and over again.

I finally pivot to one last practitioner of melancholic time. Singer-songwriter Frank Ocean crafts exquisite anthems for starry-eyed lovers and sorrow songs for the brokenhearted. His 2016 visual album, *Endless*, is a potent potion of hip-hop, rhythm and blues, electronica, and ambient music surrounding three central themes: love, loss, and labor. More precisely, most of the songs on *Endless* concern the affective labor of losing love, which is to say, melancholia. Ocean's lyrical attention to such labor finds visual analog in the long-form video released with the album. That video is black-and-white footage of multiple Frank Oceans (he is visually cloned into two and sometimes three figures) who mill about in an industrial workshop space. The Oceans are collaborating to build a wooden spiral staircase that extends just a few yards into the air before ending abruptly—and thus, not properly ending at all. If one regards a staircase teleologically—as an entity whose inherent purpose and *end* is to traverse multiple landings—then Ocean's staircase does not fulfill its telos.

Without end, it achieves an *endlessness* suited to the album's title. Perhaps the staircase is a sculptural representation of melancholia, of spiraling sorrow left undone.

In particular, a track called "Wither" activates melancholic affect and time:

> Over where the trees burn down
> Place where the fields went down in flames
> You could put a hole in the ground
> Throw seeds and dance for rain
>
> . . .
>
> Hope a garden grows where we dance this afternoon
> Hope our children walk by spring when flowers bloom
>
> . . .
>
> Pray they'll get to see me, me wither
> See me wither[88]

"Wither" is a song about romance and death. The first three lines depict burning trees, scorched fields, and a "hole in the ground" that, in the aftermath of fiery destruction, might be mistaken for a grave. However, the fourth line reveals that the hole is a seedbed, the tomb is actually an earthen womb. Then the lyrics shift to livelier acts of planting seeds and dancing with a lover under open sky. Their dance will bring rain to wet the soil and water their love. Ocean hopes that the rain-soaked ground beneath their feet will someday spring a garden for their children to enjoy.

Alas, this garden of love grows in a wider field of loss. Ocean prays his children will get to see him wither, but he does not know for sure; he cannot guarantee that he'll be around long enough to wither before his children's eyes. In confessing this uncertainty, Ocean anticipates his own disappearance and envisions himself as a lost object departed from his children. And even if his children do get to see him wither, they are beholding his decline and the approach of his demise. While Ocean sings about withering, singer-songwriter Jazmine Sullivan croons mournful tones and melancholic riffs in the background. The only instrumental accompaniment is a guitar that slowly, listlessly alternates the same two chords over and over. That guitar strums circles of sorrow.

Let's tarry with Ocean's prayer. When he sings "Pray they get to see me, me wither," I have hitherto read those last two syllables as the word *wither*, meaning to wilt or deteriorate. However, I want to consider another possible interpretation of those syllables: "with her." Ingeniously, Ocean exploits the phonetic similarity between "wither" and "with her" so that the sound signifying his decay might also signify his lover. In just two crooned syllables on one short breath, Ocean dramatizes the convergence of love ("with her") and loss ("wither") that is the fluttering heart of melancholia.

Remarkably, these ambiguous syllables contain the song's only potential reference to the gender of the lover. It is possible that the word is only "wither" and that the beloved is not "her" at all—an intriguing prospect in light of Ocean's 2012 public disclosure of same-gender desire.[89] Days after posting that revelation on a blog, Ocean released his *Channel Orange* album, featuring several expressions of amorous desire for a "him." One such occasion occurs on a sorrow song called "Bad Religion." This song's beloved is gendered as "him," but alas, he does not reciprocate the love. Ocean sings:

> This unrequited love
> to me it's nothing but a one-man cult
> and cyanide in my styrofoam cup
> I can never make him love me
> never make him
> love me
> love me
> love me
> love me
> love me
> love me
> love me
> love me
> love me
> love me[90]

What begins as a concession that "I can never make him / love me" soon sounds like a demand for "him" to "love me." The phrase *love me* is uttered ten times, each iteration drifting further away from "I can never make him," so that "love me" eventually seems to hover alone like an autonomous declaration. Just *love me*. This shift from concession ("I can never make him love me") to injunction ("love me") is also a shift from surrendering the lost object to doggedly claiming it. In other words, this stanza charts a metamorphosis from mourning to melancholia.

On one register, "Bad Religion" is an artifact of the queer tragic, a testament to the sorrow that often assails queer affection in anti-queer worlds. When Ocean divulges that he's holding a cyanide-laced drink, he invokes tropes of the lonely, suicidal, tragic queer person. I hasten to emphasize that if queerness is tragic, it is because structural homophobia and queer-antagonism bully, punish, kill, and mute queer personhood and love. What's more, a tragic analytic cannot wholly hold this "Bad Religion." The song is not merely elegy. It is also a dogged fight song, an incantation, a prayer, and a clamor for black queer love audible above the white noise of antiblackness and homophobia.

Returning, finally, to "Wither." As the track nears its close, Ocean melismatically wails the word *be* eight times. The word is dubbed over the final verses so that one hears "be, be, be, be, be, be, be, be" floating through the songscape, untethered to the syntax of those verses. The repeated syllable sounds like a mantra affirming *be*ing despite the withering that awaits. From Ocean's mouth, a melancholic melisma is a method to sound out convergences of death and romance, tomb and womb, wither and with her, misery and fantasy, loss and love: pairings that frequently haunt black and queer life. It is poignant that this melancholic "Wither" appears on an album called *Endless*. Melancholia, after all, is mourning that does not want to rest or subside. It would rather wander in "circles and circles of sorrow," with "no bottom," "no top," no end. It would rather be, well, *endless*.

I leave the reader-listener to linger in the echo of this mad music and in the resonance of these parting questions: How else might music in madtime enrich our protest playlists? What more might our liberation struggles achieve by staging actions in madtime—and at what cost? While pursuing justice and joy, how might we activate madtime in the rhythm of our footsteps, our keystrokes, our chants, our dances, our breaths? How might madtime set the deadline for our demands, the turn-up time for our block party, the appointed moment for our rest, the zero hour for our revolution? To echo the words of singer-philosopher Erykah Badu, what could I achieve by going "out my mind, just in time"?[91] What about you?

I have assembled an ensemble of mad black musicians performing in madtime: a manic time that rushes forth to demand change; a depressive time that slowly honors and tends to its sorrow; a schizophrenic time that is "always now," refusing easy nostalgia and blithe teleology; and a melancholic time that travels backward to retrieve its lost objects, no matter how heavy the load. Having culled lessons from each mode of madtime, I want to acknowledge the risks that haunt these temporalities. Manic time might rush recklessly into danger; depressive time might become so deeply wedged in woe that it does not ever get free; schizophrenic time might be crushed between history's hurt[92] and future's threat; melancholic time might collapse under the weight of the lost and dead that it carries. And yet, these admissions do not negate the potential in madtime. Remember that madness is manifold, potentially a wellspring of inspiration as well as a pit of frustration—and some pits hold seeds. Remember, also, always, that the abyss may have no bottom . . . but blackness has no top, no limit.

Are you still holding tight?

THE NUTTY PROFESSOR (A CONFESSION)

1.

Confined to a cell in Cook County Jail, Bigger Thomas awaits his doom. The protagonist of Richard Wright's 1940 novel, *Native Son*, Bigger is held behind iron bars—but deeper still, he dwells behind an existential wall he has erected around himself, "a barrier of protection between him and the world he feared," a petrified hardness to keep out "racial hurt."[1] Nineteen years into a life rife with such hurt, and amid the bleak backdrop of Depression-era Chicago, Bigger accidentally kills a wealthy white heiress named Mary Dalton. While on the run, in a fit of spite and desperation, he rapes and deliberately murders Bessie Mears, a woe-weary black woman who is sometimes his girlfriend. Bigger is soon exposed, declared public enemy, deluged with public hatred, violently apprehended, convicted of Mary's (but not Bessie's) rape and murder, and quickly condemned to death.[2]

Bigger's jailhouse malaise is interrupted by the arrival of the "balmy" figure described in the epigraph: a mad black scholar writing a book. Hurled into the cell, the balmy man breaches Bigger's existential wall, so that "his hate and shame vanished in the face of his dread of this insane man turning suddenly upon him."[3] Considering all the brutality Bigger has endured, all the harm he has inflicted, all the peril he faces from guards and inmates inside that jail, all the animus from mobs outside, it is remarkable that he is so unnerved by a

> "He's balmy!" a white man said. "Make 'em take 'im outta your cell. He'll kill you. He went off his nut from studying too much at the university. He was writing a book on how colored people live and he says somebody stole all the facts he'd found. He says he's got to the bottom of why colored folks are treated bad and he's going to tell the president and have things changed, see? He's *nuts*!"
> —RICHARD WRIGHT, *Native Son*, 1940

solitary black man seeking social transformation. Maybe Bigger agrees with that white inmate shouting warnings nearby. According to that white inmate, the urge to battle antiblackness and the will to seek racial justice bespeak a nutty mind: "He says he's got to the bottom of why colored folks are treated bad and he's going to tell the president and have things changed, see? He's *nuts!*"

Meanwhile, the balmy man screams truth to power and literally rattles the cage. Bigger beholds that "the man's eyes were blood-red; the corners of his lips were white with foam. Sweat glistened on his brown face. He clutched the bars with such frenzy that when he yelled his entire body vibrated. He seemed so agonized."[4] The balmy man's madness entails an unruliness of bodily surges and eruptions: blood rushing into his eyes, foam bubbling from his mouth, sweat seeping from his face, shouts flying out his throat, convulsions coursing through his body, agony emanating from his flesh. However, his madness is as thoughtful as it is visceral, as politicized as it is agonized. When the mad scholar finally speaks for himself, he claims to have uncovered a vast antiblack conspiracy:

> "You're afraid of me!" the man shouted. "That's why you put me in here! But I'll tell the President anyhow! I'll tell 'im you make us live in such crowded conditions on the South Side that one out of every ten of us is insane! I'll tell 'im that you dump all the stale foods into the Black Belt and sell them for more than you can get anywhere else! I'll tell 'im you tax us, but you won't build hospitals! I'll tell 'im the schools are so crowded that they breed perverts! I'll tell 'im you hire us last and fire us first! I'll tell the President and the League of Nations."[5]

While others may dismiss these words as rant and rave, I read them as a condensed research report, the fruit of interdisciplinary investigation into structural antiblackness in Chicago. He describes a municipal conspiracy spanning housing, medical care, education, foodways, taxation, and employment, all systematically degrading black life. Based on his own declarations and those remarks from the white inmate, it would seem that the balmy man's crimes are as follows: amassing damning evidence against city government, alerting others to his findings, expressing his fury aloud in public, planning to petition the president and League of Nations, and mobilizing to battle the evil he's exposed. These acts are treasonous transgressions against antiblackness and white supremacy.

If that white inmate knows so much about the balmy scholar, let's suppose he knows the notorious allegations against Bigger—including the untrue charges that Bigger raped a white woman. Insofar as fantasies of black rapists enthralled white supremacist imagination in early and mid-twentieth-century

America (and beyond), one might expect the inmate to treat Bigger with special enmity. Yet in this scene, the white inmate shows no sign of malice toward Bigger. Instead, he seems to regard Bigger as a sensible and sympathetic figure whose safety is in jeopardy, who ought to be warned. Why this sympathy for an alleged rapist and apathy toward a scholar-activist?

I venture this answer: To the sensibilities of antiblackness, Bigger's actual and alleged crimes are less menacing than the balmy man's revelations. White supremacists and antiblack racists may loathe Bigger, but their loathing is likely mixed with a smug sense of rectitude. After all, Bigger would seem to affirm their fantasies of black male brutality and therefore justify their regimes of segregation, pathologization, criminalization, and annihilation. The mad black scholar, on the other hand, belies their fantasies of black depravity and inferiority. He announces that black people are not constitutionally depraved or inferior, but rather are subjected to the depraved machinations and inferior conditions wrought by antiblackness.[6] Furthermore, as antilynching heroine Ida B. Wells had insisted decades earlier, there is no factual basis for white supremacist fear of black bogeymen ravishing white damsels in droves. However, there is ample cause for white supremacy to dread black radical planning and struggle.[7] The balmy black man is so terrifying because he conducts such planning and struggle.

Alas, he has no time to detail his findings or elaborate his agenda, because "soon a group of men dressed in white came running in with a stretcher. They unlocked the cell and grabbed the yelling man, laced him in a straitjacket, flung him into a stretcher and carted him away."[8] During his brief appearance in *Native Son*, this balmy black scholar manifests all four modes of madness theorized in this study. His madness is rage against the systematic degradation of black people; it is the psychosocial alterity of black insurrection against antiblack Reason; and it is an agonized unruliness of body that bespeaks an unruliness of mind. Furthermore, if the balmy man is not already diagnosed, those white-clad orderlies will carry him into a psycho-carceral industrial complex. There, he will likely be branded with some medicalized madness, perhaps paranoid schizophrenia, and forcibly confined. In total, the madman's presence persists for about two pages. Nevermore does he appear in the book, nor is he ever mentioned again.

For all his textual transience, the balmy man leaves a monumental impression in my imagination. Mad, black, reviled, exiled, deviant, defiant, critical, ethical, writhing under the threat of annihilation, and quickly receding from view, he deserves all the care and rigor that mad methodology brings to bear. I shudder and flounder as I wonder: What vertigo might a black captive undergo—might a mad prisoner undergo—his data stolen, his work dismissed, his arms strapped into a straitjacket, his body hurled onto a stretcher, then laid supine, then wheeled away into a paratextual elsewhere, into *"nowhere* at all"?[9]

As a practice of radical compassion and what Saidiya Hartman calls "critical fabulation,"[10] I want to dream a subjunctive scenario where this mad black scholar regains his freedom. I imagine him finding his stolen data, then finishing his manuscript, then publishing it to great fanfare and controversy, then delivering it to the president and the League of Nations, then appealing to human rights and social justice movements with greater moral authority, then organizing mad and black masses, and eventually achieving something like revolution or relief. I picture his book on a shelf of volumes about black Chicago in the mid-twentieth century, nestled between St. Clair Drake and Horace Cayton's 1945 ethnography *Black Metropolis* and Gwendolyn Brooks's 1945 poetry collection *A Street in Bronzeville*. In this subjunctive world, *the book is bound and the man is free.*

I want freedom for him and for the mad and black prisoners held, in real life, in Cook County Jail today. In 2015, an estimated one-third of the jail's one hundred thousand inmates were living with some form of mental illness. This means that Cook County Jail was effectively the largest psychiatric facility in the United States. For a jail to lead the nation in housing mentally ill persons is a devastating testament to the failure of our public health infrastructure to grapple with mental illness. Also in 2015, 67 percent of the jail's inmates were black, though only 25 percent of Cook County's residents are black, a devastating testament to the racialization of America's carceral state.[11]

As a mad methodologist, it is my business to abide with the balmy man and his real-life counterparts; to highlight the insight in his "nutty" outburst; to amplify his rebuke of state-sanctioned antiblackness and antimadness; and to extend radical compassion to him and to others who endure such struggle. Beneath and beyond my radical compassion, I also feel something like *ordinary affinity* toward him. If radical compassion is driven by political imagination and resolve, ordinary affinity is far more rudimentary—it is simple solidarity born of likeness and shared experience. I feel this kinship because I am a mad black scholar, too. In fact, I am a mad methodologist in at least two senses: first, I am a scholar who theorizes and mobilizes mad methodology; second, I am a madman devising methods for ethical madness. I know, firsthand, the ordeal of being a mad black scholar while writing a mad black book while braving an antiblack-antimad world.[12]

Incidentally, *balmy* means both *insane* and *soothing*.

2.

My own madness is a conspiracy of cruel ironies that won't let me rest: a need for cleanliness that erupts into mess; an urge for order that spawns disorder; a tendency toward doubt that will undoubtedly surface; a tyrannical self-rule that is utterly unruly; intrusive thoughts that are as much indigenous as they are invaders to my mind; ghastly obsessions that are as repulsive as they are transfixing; an ineffable feeling that demands constant explanation; a past-glutted regret that wants to devour my future; a drive toward perfection that fucks things up. And then there are the ritual practices: the rinses, revisions, rehearsals, recountings, countings, meditations, medications, inspections, prayers, atonements, and confessions militated against that anguish but only ever provide provisional relief. Eventually, the sheer dirtiness, the strangeness, the bloodiness, the meanness, the nastiness of this world comes rushing or creeping in.

If there is a spectrum of stigma about mental illness in American popular imagination, obsessive compulsive disorder (OCD) is typically treated as a lesser mental illness, a milder madness. It does not incite the terror that swarms around schizophrenia and dissociative identity disorder (often confused and conflated in popular representations). Nor does it inspire the pathos that solemnly gathers around major depressive disorder. Instead, OCD is cast as mere idiosyncrasy: an irksome tendency to nitpick and split hairs, or, more favorably, an admirable perfectionism. This spectrum of stigma is vividly displayed in popular cinema. Schizophrenia and dissociative identity disorder are frequent fixations of horror films, where supposedly schizophrenic or dissociative "psychos" spawn mayhem and murder. Depression is sometimes depicted in melodramatic and sentimental cinema, often the consequence of heterosexual heartbreak and healed by romantic redemption or cheerful friends. Meanwhile, obsessive compulsive disorder is frequent fodder for comedy, where symptoms become foibles and compulsive rituals resemble comic routines.[13] OCD incurs less social stigma than do schizophrenia and depression—but this knowledge yields little relief when I am scrubbing my skin down to the soul.

How to Go Mad is the symptom and fruit of its author's madness. Put otherwise, this book both suffers and benefits from my own balminess. That suffering lies in the staggering worry, excruciating revision, and the overpowering urge to turn the work over and over and over and over and under and over and under in my mind until my mind is raw and the work feels worn and frayed. That suffering comes from the hurtful conviction that this book will fail. When I read these words in print, I will see—with a marvelous singularity of vision that could be mistaken for divination or hallucination—errors and omissions that will drive me to unruliness of mind. I do not believe that I will ever finish this book, no matter that you are reading it now. I will never feel that it has achieved closure or completion. It is endless. No copyedit, no print run, no smell of fresh pages under elegant cover, no esteemed award, no slot on a bookshelf, no pages spread wide on an eager lap will ever convince me that this book is done. There's this aching feeling that some essential example or insight is missing; that a misplaced quotation mark or lost footnote will unhinge the integrity of the work; that some flamboyant typo will show up, uninvited, to an utterly important sentence and enthrall your attention (while the embarrassed sentence bows and disappears).

But what of the benefit? For one, this afterword owes its existence and substance to my compulsion to confess. (Truth be told, this entire book is a coded confession.) More broadly, madness suffuses the ethical, critical, and radical impetus for *How to Go Mad*. What I mean is that this book is devoutly ethical, trained by a superpowered superego that commands, and relishes, acts of goodness. This book is painstakingly critical, sharing my propensity to question everything, to take nothing for granted, to seek the secrets buried underneath any placid surface, to find fault everywhere, to work to make it better. This book is intensely radical, inheriting my inclination to think and dream at the limits, beyond the limits, and further still, but never *still*, because my mind keeps darting, keeps pacing. OCD intensifies another elemental force coursing through this book, its most vital feature of all, its care. At the palpitating heart of *How to Go Mad* is care: both careful and caring, both worrisome and loving.

I considered creating a manuscript in the format of my madness. Such a book would sometimes forgo grammar and sometimes adhere fanatically to it. It would veer between immaculate eloquence and impenetrable ramblings. It would occasionally dispense with the left-to-right, top-to-bottom, front-to-back trajectory typical among English-language books, moving in zigzags, spirals, and wormholes instead. It might include blank pages, murals worth of marginalia, volumes of parenthetical digressions, miles of strikethroughs, meticulous lists to rival telephone books, drafts of paragraphs juxtaposed with their revisions, and bars of mad "black redaction,"[14] deprioritizing decipherability in order to achieve phenomenal fidelity. Or maybe my madness demands precisely what you are reading now: painstaking study, obsessive care, radical imagination, and fever dreaming all gathered together, held tight, and condensed into one hundred thousand throbbing words.

I sometimes wonder whether I accidentally actualize Frantz Fanon's prayer at the end of *Black Skin, White Masks*: "Oh, my body! Make me always a man who questions."[15] If I am a man, I am a man who always questions, who is driven to ask with a visceral urgency as irresistible and insatiable as an itch in a fold of my brain. *Oh, my body!* Every belief, every word, every phrase, every observation, every proposition, every citation, every punctuation mark is subjected to ruthless doubt and vicious interrogation. The conventions of grammar oblige me to end most of these sentences with periods, but there are ghostly, invisible lines curling and hovering over most of these tiny dots. What I mean is that most of the periods in this book are interrogation marks in disguise. Most of these declarations are really restless questions underneath.

This restlessness thwarts tranquility—but thankfully, it also refuses complacency. This restlessness is an eternal doubting—and fortunately, also, a tireless probing. My refusal of respite resembles what dancer-choreographer and movement theorist Martha Graham describes as the artist's "queer divine dissatisfaction, a blessed unrest that keeps us marching."[16] (*Divine* and *blessed!* After all my effort to avoid romanticizing madness, here I seem to sanctify it. Remember, though, that madness is capacious enough to hold the sensation of blessing and curse at once.) Now it is time to slow my march, though I will not stop. This is a procession without end, without rest, without closure. It is always in process, always awake, always open.

3.

Fanon, that peerless mad methodologist, that black-skinned man who yearned always to question, once asked this: "What indeed could be more grotesque than an educated man, a man with a diploma, having in consequence understood a good many things, among others that 'it was unfortunate to be a Negro,' proclaiming that his skin was beautiful and that the 'big black hole' was a source of truth[?]" Answering himself, Fanon ironically insisted that this Negro "must be mad, for it was unthinkable that he could be right."[17]

I entered this study from "nowhere at all" and here I arrive at a "big black hole." Many such arrivals and black holes punctuate *How to Go Mad*. Sometimes the big black hole is the hold of a slave ship careening through a "fruitless place,"[18] and sometimes it is the cabin of a spaceship cruising to otherworldly paradise. Sometimes the big black hole is a "deep black mouth"[19] that shrieks and smiles and bites and laughs—when it is not blowing a jazz riff or singing a melancholic melisma. Sometimes it is a humble "hole in the ground,"[20] fit to hold and nourish seeds, or else a colossal breach in the cosmos, fit to hold the whole galaxy steady. It might be a pit collapsing into nothingness and then a wellspring brimming to infinity.[21] This big black hole collects and emits strangeness, wonder, violence, terror, splendor, care, love, and truth, mixed with madness, which I have tried to impart to you. For believing this truth, Fanon foretells that I *must be mad*. If you've made it this far, and if you've found some truth down here, with me, then maybe you're mad, too.

Now let go.

NOTES

Chapter One: Mad Is a Place

Epigraphs: Michel Foucault, *Madness and Civilization: A History of Insanity in the Age of Reason*, trans. Richard Howard (New York: Vintage, 1988), 11; emphasis mine; Hortense Spillers, "Mama's Baby, Papa's Maybe: An American Grammar Book," *Diacritics* 17, no. 2 (summer 1987): 72.

1 The phrase *freedom dreams* comes from Robin D. G. Kelley's theorization of black radical thought in *Freedom Dreams: The Black Radical Imagination* (Boston: Beacon Press, 2002). My reference to "blood in my eyes" recalls the title of George Jackson's prison memoir, *Blood in My Eye* (New York: Random House, 1992).

2 Christina Sharpe theorizes the "wake" of the slave ship—and its various historical and existential effects—in her book, *In the Wake: On Blackness and Being* (Durham, NC: Duke University Press, 2016).

3 Frantz Fanon, *Black Skin, White Masks*, trans. Charles Lam Markmann (London: Pluto Press, 1986), 2.

4 Regarding the Afropessimistic perspective, see Frank B. Wilderson III, *Red, White, and Black: Cinema and the Structure of U.S. Antagonisms* (Durham, NC: Duke University Press, 2010).

5 Spillers, "Mama's Baby, Papa's Maybe," 72; emphasis in original.

6 See Winifred B. Maher and Brendan Maher, "The Ship of Fools: Stultifera Navis or Ignis Fatuus?," *American Psychologist* 37, no. 7 (1982): 756–61.

7 Concerning these controversies over the number dead and the harm done in the Middle Passage, see Maria Diedrich and Henry Louis Gates Jr., eds., *Black Imagination and the Middle Passage* (New York: Oxford University Press, 1999); Herbert S. Klein, Stanley L. Engerman, Robin Haines, and Ralph Shlomowitz, "Transoceanic Mortality: The Slave Trade in Comparative Perspective," *William and Mary Quarterly* 58, no. 1 (2001): 93–117; Patrick Manning and William S. Griffiths, "Divining the Unprovable: Simulating the Demography of African Slavery," *Journal of Interdisciplinary History* 19, no. 2 (1988): 177–201.

8 Hortense Spillers, Saidiya Hartman, Farah Jasmine Griffin, Shelly Eversley, and Jennifer L. Morgan, "'Whatcha Gonna Do?': Revisiting 'Mama's Baby, Papa's Maybe: An American Grammar Book,'" *Women's Studies Quarterly* 35, nos. 1–2 (2007): 308.

9 Spillers, "Mama's Baby, Papa's Maybe," 72.

10 *Collins English Dictionary*, http://collinsdictionary.com/. My attention to the spatial registers of the word *derange* parallels Foucault's emphasis upon the etymology of the word *delirium*. He writes: "The simplest and most general definition we can give of classical madness is indeed *delirium*: 'This word is derived from lira, a furrow; so that deliro actually means to move out of the furrow, away from the proper path of reason.'" Foucault, *Madness and Civilization*, 99–100; citing *Dictionnaire universel de medicine*, vol. III, translated, 1746–48.

11 Marcus Rediker generates an extensive cultural and social history of the slave ship in *The Slave Ship: A Human History* (New York: Penguin, 2007).

12 According to Foucault's account, ships of fools peaked in prevalence during the fourteenth and fifteenth centuries (*Madness and Civilization*, 8). Meanwhile, slave ships began to proliferate after the 1452 issuance of the papal bull *Dum Diversas*, which sanctioned Catholic nations in perpetual enslavement of "pagan" peoples, and granted moral license to Portugal to take its place at the vanguard of the Atlantic slave trade. If Foucault's account of the ship of fools is historically accurate, the two sorts of vessels overlapped in time. A packed slave ship and a ship of fools would scarcely encounter each other in space, though, since laden slave ships primarily traversed the Atlantic Ocean, while ships of fools, if they physically existed, commuted primarily along Europe's internal rivers and canals.

13 Wordference.com, *reason* from *Random House Unabridged Dictionary* 2020.

14 See V. B. Schneider, "What Is It to Be Rational?" *Philosophy Now: A Magazine of Ideas* 1, no. 1 (summer 1991), https://philosophynow.org/issues/1/What_Is_It_To_Be_Rational; Achille Mbembe, *Necropolitics* (Durham, NC: Duke University Press, 2019); and James Bohman and William Rehg, eds., *Deliberative Democracy: Essays on Reason and Politics* (Cambridge, MA: MIT Press, 1997).

15 Regarding the exclusions of nonwhite people from Enlightenment ideals, see Emmanuel Chukwudi Eze, ed., *Race and the Enlightenment: A Reader* (Malden, MA: Blackwell, 1997). Eze compiles key passages on race authored by David Hume, Thomas Jefferson, and Immanuel Kant, and other philosophers. Essays excerpted include David Hume, "Of the Populousness of Ancient Nations" and "Of National Characters"; Immanuel Kant, "Geography" and "On National Characters"; and Thomas Jefferson, "Notes on the State of Virginia."

Concerning the exclusion of women from Enlightenment ideals, see Susanne Lettow, "Feminism and the Enlightenment," in *Companion to Feminist Philosophy*, ed. Ann Gary, Serene Khader, Alison Stone (London: Routledge, 2017), 94–107. See also Carina Pape, "'Race,' 'Sex,' and 'Gender': Intersections, Naturalistic Fallacies, and the Age of Reason," in *Thinking about the Enlightenment: Modernity and its Ramifications,* ed. Martin L. Davies (London: Routledge, 2016).

Regarding the exclusion of poor people from Enlightenment ideals, see Fred Powell, "Civil Society History IV: Enlightenment," in *International Encyclopedia of Civil Society*, ed. Helmut Anheier and Stefan Toepler (New York: Springer, 2010).

16 Mbembe, *Necropolitics*, 67.

17 See Eze, *Race and the Enlightenment*.

18 I use the masculine possessive pronoun *his* because the patriarchal protocols of early modern Europe dictated that the paradigmatic early modern person was male. Regarding the function of such othering and ontological foiling in colonial and antebellum America, Toni Morrison proclaims that "black slavery enriched [America's] creative possibilities. For in that construction of blackness *and* enslavement could be found not only the not-free but also, with the dramatic polarity created by skin color, the projection of the not-me. The result was a playground for the imagination." *Playing in the Dark: Whiteness and the Literary Imagination* (New York: Vintage, 1993), 38. These formulations exist within a broader system of binaries—man|woman, light|dark, mind|body, and good|evil, among them—that structure Western modernity and arrange its epistemic orders.

19 In his own articulation of the centrality of black slavery to the invention of Western modernity, Paul Gilroy designates the slave ship as the "central organizing symbol." He announces that "getting on board [the slave ship] promises a means to reconceptualise the orthodox relationship between modernity and what passes for its prehistory. . . . [M]odernity might itself be thought to begin in the constitutive relationship with outsiders that both found and temper a self-conscious sense of western civilization." Paul Gilroy, *The Black Atlantic: Modernity and Double Consciousness* (London: Verso, 1993), 17.

20 In "The Case of Blackness," *Criticism* 50, no. 22 (2008), Fred Moten describes a (black) "radicalism" that is "the performance of a general critique of the proper" (177).

21 Rinaldo Walcott, *Black Like Who? Writing Black Canada* (Toronto: Insomniac Press, 1997), xiv.

22 In *Wayward Lives, Beautiful Experiments: Intimate Histories of Social Upheaval* (New York: W. W. Norton, 2019), Saidiya Hartman honors and centers black girls and women who "have been credited with nothing: they remain surplus women of no significance, girls deemed unfit for history and destined to be minor figures" (xv).

23 My notion of black radical creativity is influenced by Angela Y. Davis, *Blues Legacies and Black Feminism: Gertrude "Ma" Rainey, Bessie Smith, and Billie Holiday* (New York: Pantheon, 1998); Cedric Robinson, *Black Marxism: The Making of the Black Radical Tradition*, 2nd ed. (Chapel Hill: University of North Carolina Press, 2000); Robin D. G. Kelly, *Freedom Dreams: The Black Radical Imagination* (Boston: Beacon, 2002); and Fred Moten, *In the Break: The Aesthetics of the Black Radical Tradition* (Minneapolis: University of Minnesota Press, 2003).

24 Though the term *insanity* has been disavowed by the Anglophone medical establishment since the 1920s, its clinical connotation endures in its current legalistic and colloquial usage. See Janet A. Tighe, "'What's in a Name?': A Brief Foray into the History of Insanity in England and the United States," *Journal of the American Academy of Psychiatry and the Law* 33, no. 2 (2005): 252–58.

25 See "Schizophrenia Spectrum and Other Psychotic Disorders," *Diagnostic and Statistical Manual of Mental Disorders*, 5th ed. (Arlington, VA: American

Psychiatric Association, 2013), https://doi-org.proxy-um.researchport.umd.edu /10.1176/appi.books.9780890425596.dsm02.

26 Regarding the myriad frames through which schizophrenic symptoms have been interpreted, see John M. Ingham, *Psychological Anthropology Reconsidered* (Cambridge: Cambridge University Press, 1996); John Weir Perry, *Trials of the Visionary Mind: Spiritual Emergency and the Renewal Process* (Albany: SUNY Press, 1998); Dick Russell, "How a West African Shaman Helped My Schizophrenic Son in a Way Western Medicine Couldn't," *Washington Post*, March 24, 2015; Tanya Marie Luhrmann and Jocelyn Marrow, eds., *Our Most Troubling Madness: Case Studies in Schizophrenia across Cultures* (Oakland: University of California Press, 2016); and Ann Cooke, ed., *Understanding Psychosis and Schizophrenia*, rev. ed. (Leicester, UK: British Psychological Society, 2017).

27 Concerning the pathologization of blackness, see, for example, Sander Gilman, *Difference and Pathology: Stereotypes of Sexuality, Race, and Madness* (Ithaca, NY: Cornell University Press, 1985) (especially chapter 5); and Jonathan Metzl, *The Protest Psychosis: How Schizophrenia Became a Black Disease* (Boston: Beacon, 2009). Concerning the pathologization of (rebellious) femininity, see Maria Ramas, "Freud's Dora, Dora's Hysteria: The Negation of a Woman's Rebellion," *Feminist Studies* 6, no. 3 (1980). Regarding the pathologization of transness, see Cecilia Dhejne, Roy van Vlerken, Gunter Heylens, and Jon Arcelus, "Mental Health and Gender Dysphoria: A Review of the Literature," *International Review of Psychiatry* 28, no. 1 (2016): 44–57. Concerning the pathologization of homosexuality, see Ronald Bayer, *Homosexuality and American Psychiatry: The Politics of Diagnosis* (Princeton, NJ: Princeton University Press, 1987). Concerning the pathologization of poverty, see Helena Hansen, Philippe Bourgois, and Ernest Drucker, "Pathologizing Poverty: New Forms of Diagnosis, Disability, and Structural Stigma under Welfare Reform," *Social Science and Medicine* 103 (2014): 76–83.

28 For an especially eloquent discussion of how hegemonic judgments impact science and medicine in the United States, see Steven Epstein, *Impure Science: AIDS, Activism, and the Politics of Knowledge* (Berkeley: University of California Press, 1996). My declaration that "no science is pure" is inspired, in part, by Epstein's study and its title.

29 The words are lyrics from Solange, "Mad," *A Seat at the Table* (New York: Saint/ Columbia, 2016).

30 Kelly Baker Josephs arrives at a similar conclusion. She observes, "While mad can define a person, situation, or event, it more often describes the person attempting to define said person, situation, or event. That is, the term says as much, if not more, about the subject employing it as about the object it attempts to label" in *Disturbers of the Peace: Representations of Madness in Anglophone Caribbean Literature* (Charlottesville: University of Virginia Press, 2013), 8.

31 Regarding "critical ambivalence," I have written elsewhere that "Sometimes it is useful, even crucial, to tarry in the openness of ambiguity; in the strategic vantage point available in the interstice (the better to look both ways and beyond); in

the capacious bothness of ambivalence; in the sheer potential in irresolution . . . Lingering in ambivalence, we can access multiple, even dissonant, vantages at once, before pivoting, if we finally choose to pivot, toward decisive motion. To be clear, I am not describing an impotent ambivalence that relinquishes or thwarts politics. Rather, I am proposing an instrumental ambivalence that harnesses the energetic motion and friction and tension of ambivalent feeling. Such energy might propel progressive and radical movement." La Marr Jurelle Bruce, "Shore, Unsure: Loitering as a Way of Life," *GLQ* 5, no. 2 (2019): 357.

32 Audre Lorde, "The Uses of Anger: Women Responding to Racism," in *Sister Outsider: Essays and Speeches* (Berkeley, CA: Crossing Press, 1984), 127.

33 In *Scenes of Subjection: Terror, Slavery, and Self-Making in Nineteenth-Century America*, Saidiya Hartman unpacks the epistemic violence wrought by hegemonic *empathy*. She writes: "Properly speaking, empathy is a projection of oneself into another in order to better understand the other or 'the projection of one's own personality into an object, with the attribution to the object of one's own emotions.'" Hartman further writes that "by exploiting the vulnerability of the captive body as a vessel for the uses, thoughts, and feelings of others, the humanity extended to the slave inadvertently confirms the expectations and desires definitive of the relations of chattel slavery . . . empathy is double-edged, for in making the other's suffering one's own, this suffering is occluded by the other's obliteration." Saidiya Hartman, *Scenes of Subjection: Terror, Slavery, and Self-Making in Nineteenth-Century America* (New York: Oxford University Press, 1997), 18–19.

   Empathy entails a projection of oneself *into* another's shoes, a feeling into their predicament, and an imaginative occupation, as it were, of their perspective. The *em-* in *empathy* is a prefix signifying "to put (something) into or on" (as per "en-, prefix1," *OED Online*, Oxford University Press, https://www-oed-com/view/Entry/61499). I prefer *compassion*, containing the prefix *com-*, signifying that which is "together, together with, in combination or union" (as per "com-, prefix," *OED Online*, Oxford University Press, https://www-oed-com/view/Entry/36719?rskey=hS5I9y&result=2).

34 For further information on positivism as a philosophical tradition and orientation, see Seth B. Abrutyn, "Positivism," in *Oxford Bibliographies in Sociology* (Oxford: Oxford University Press, 2013).

35 Regarding these respective parapositivist formulations, see Hebrews 11:1–31 in the King James Bible; Édouard Glissant, *Poetics of Relation*, trans. Betsy Wang (Ann Arbor: University of Michigan Press, 1997); Avery F. Gordon, *Ghostly Matters: Haunting and the Sociological Imagination* (Minneapolis: University of Minnesota Press, 2008); Saidiya Hartman, "Venus in Two Acts," *Small Axe* 12, no. 2 (2008): 1–14; Jack Halberstam, *Female Masculinity* (Durham, NC: Duke University Press, 1998), 13; Patricia J. Williams, "Gathering the Ghosts," *A-Line* (August 30, 2018), https://alinejournal.com/vol-1-no-3-4/gathering-the-ghosts.

36 I am grateful to the audience at the 2018 Harold Stirling Lecture at Vanderbilt University for encouraging me to center this *unknowability*. Special thanks to Robert Engelman for his important comments on this matter.

37 Édouard Glissant, *The Collected Poems of Édouard Glissant* (Minneapolis: University of Minnesota Press, 2005), xxxii–xxxiii. Bracketed definitions in original.

38 Kelley, *Freedom Dreams*.

39 Moten, *In the Break*, 39.

40 Daphne Brooks, *Bodies in Dissent: Spectacular Performances of Race and Freedom, 1850–1910* (Durham, NC: Duke University Press, 2006).

41 D. Scott Miller, "Afrosurrealist Manifesto: Black Is the New Black—A 21st Century Manifesto," *D. Scott Miller: AfroSurreal Generation*, May 20, 2009, http://dscotmiller.blogspot.com/2009/05/afrosurreal.html.

42 Sarah Cervenak, *Wandering: Philosophical Performances of Racial and Sexual Freedom* (Durham, NC: Duke University Press, 2014).

43 L. H. Stallings, *Funk the Erotic: Transaesthetics and Black Sexual Cultures* (Champaign: University of Illinois Press, 2015).

44 GerShun Avilez, *Radical Aesthetics and Modern Black Nationalism* (Champaign: University of Illinois Press, 2016).

45 Emma Bell provides a pithy genealogy of the embrace of madness by Western artists and theorists. See Emma Bell, "Imagine Madness: Madness, Revolution, Ressentiment and Critical Theory," *Madness: Probing the Boundaries*, Interdisciplinary.Net 1st Global Conference, Mansfield College, Oxford, September 2008, unpublished.

46 Plato, "Phaedrus," in *Symposium and Phaedrus* (Mineola, NY: Dover, 2012), 79.

47 William Shakespeare, *The Tragedy of Hamlet, Prince of Denmark* (Washington, DC: Folger Shakespeare Library, n.d.), II.II.204–5, www.folgerdigitaltexts.org.

48 Edgar Allen Poe, "Eleonara," *Edgar Allan Poe: Complete Tales and Poems* (Edison, NJ: Castle Books, 2002), 591.

49 Friedrich Nietzsche, *Daybreak: Thoughts on the Prejudices of Morality*, trans. R. J. Hollingdale (Cambridge: Cambridge University Press, 1997), 13–14.

50 Foucault, *Madness and Civilization*, especially chapters 1–3.

51 Gilles Deleuze and Félix Guattari, *Anti-Oedipus: Capitalism and Schizophrenia* (Minneapolis: University of Minnesota Press, 1983). That this list of Western canon-dwellers from antiquity through postmodernity consists entirely of white men reflects the gendered and racialized exclusions that permeate Western canonicity.

52 Within disability studies, I am especially inspired by the critical race interventions of Christopher Bell; the queer "crip" provocations of Robert McRuer; the feminist-materialist correctives of Nirmala Erevelles; Alison Kafer's careful critique of the social construction of "health," and the harm it potentially perpetrates on people deemed unhealthy or pathological; and the recent black feminist intersectional innovations of Sami Schalk and Therí Pickens. Significantly, each of the aforementioned scholars recognizes and theorizes how disability is co-constitutive with other categories of difference.

See Christopher Bell, "Introducing White Disability Studies: A Modest Proposal," in *The Disability Studies Reader* (2nd ed.), ed. Lennard J. Davis (New York: Routledge, 2006); Robert McRuer, "Compulsory Able-Bodiedness and Queer/Disabled Existence," in *Disability Studies: Enabling the Humanities*, ed. Sharon L.

Snyder, Brenda Jo Brueggemann, and Rosemarie Garland-Thomson (New York: Modern Language Association, 2002); Nirmala Erevelles and Andrea Minear, "Unspeakable Offenses: Untangling Race and Disability in Discourses of Intersectionality," *Journal of Literary and Cultural Disability Studies* 4, no. 2 (2010): 127–45; Margaret Price, "The Bodymind Problem and the Possibilities of Pain," *Hypatia* 30, no. 1 (2014): 268–84; Alison Kafer, "Health Rebels: A Crip Manifesto for Social Justice," https://www.youtube.com/watch?v=YqcOUD1pBKw (2017); Sami Schalk, *Bodyminds Reimagined: (Dis)ability, Race, and Gender in Black Women's Speculative Fiction* (Durham, NC: Duke University Press, 2018); and Therí Alyce Pickens, *Black Madness :: Mad Blackness* (Durham, NC: Duke University Press, 2019).

53 Regarding the medical and social models of disability, see Justin Anthony Haegele and Samuel Hodge, "Disability Discourse: Overview and Critiques of the Medical and Social Models," *Quest* 68, no. 2 (2016): 193–206; Tom Shakespeare, "The Social Model of Disability," in *The Disability Studies Reader* (2nd ed.), ed. Lennard J. Davis (New York: Routledge, 2006), 214–21; Rosemarie Garland-Thomson, "Feminist Disability Studies," *Signs* 30, no. 2 (2005): 1557 87; and Arlene S. Kanter, *The Development of Disability Rights under International Law: From Charity to Human Rights* (New York: Routledge, 2015).

54 Brenda A. LeFrançois, Robert Menzies, and Geoffrey Reaume, "Introducing Mad Studies," in *Mad Matters: A Critical Reader in Canadian Mad Studies* (Toronto: Canadian Scholars' Press, 2013), 10.

55 LeFrançois, Menzies, and Reaume, "Introducing Mad Studies," 13.

56 LeFrançois, Menzies, and Reaume, "Introducing Mad Studies," 13.

57 Tanja Aho, Liat Ben-Moshe, and Leon J. Hilton, "Mad Futures: Affect/Theory/Violence," *American Quarterly* 69, no. 2 (2017): 291–302.

58 According to the landmark MacArthur Violence Risk Assessment Study, mental illness alone does not correspond to a statistically significant increased likelihood of committing violent crimes. However, the mentally ill are significantly more likely to be victims of violent crimes. See John Monahan, Henry J. Steadman, Eric Silver, Paul S. Appelbaum, Pamela Clark Robbins, Edward P. Mulvey, Loren H. Roth, et al., *Rethinking Risk Assessment: The MacArthur Study of Mental Disorder and Violence* (Oxford: Oxford University Press, 2001). See also MacArthur Research Network on Mental Health and the Law, "The MacArthur Violence Risk Assessment Study: September 2005 Update of the Executive Summary," MacArthur Research Network, http://www.macarthur.virginia.edu/risk.html.

59 Elizabeth Donaldson, "The Corpus of the Madwoman: Toward a Feminist Disability Studies Theory of Embodiment and Mental Illness," *NWSA Journal* 14, no. 3 (autumn 2002): 102.

60 Robert J. Barrett, "The 'Schizophrenic' and the Liminal Persona in Modern Society," *Culture, Medicine and Psychiatry* 22, no. 4 (December 1998): 488.

61 The section head echoes the title and theme of Soyica Colbert's *Black Movements: Performance and Cultural Politics* (New Brunswick, NJ: Rutgers University Press,

2017), with its emphasis upon the convergence of physical movement and social movement.

62 Sociologist Orlando Patterson suggests that the status of the slave is one of "social death," which entails three primary characteristics: violent subjection, natal alienation, and general dishonor. See Orlando Patterson, *Slavery and Social Death: A Comparative Study* (Cambridge, MA: Harvard University Press, 1982), 1–16.

63 For an extended account of suicide as a mode of agency among slaves, see Terri L. Snyder, *The Power to Die: Slavery and Suicide in British North America* (Chicago: University of Chicago Press, 2015).

64 Concerning the campaign of confinement that swept Europe in the seventeenth and eighteenth centuries—and in particular the treatment of purportedly violent madmen—Foucault writes that "those chained to the cell walls were no longer men whose minds had wandered, but beasts preyed upon by a natural frenzy. . . . This model of animality prevailed in the asylums and gave them their cagelike aspect, their look of the menagerie" (Foucault, *Madness and Civilization*, 72). Alas, Foucault does not connect the "animality" imputed to the insane and the animality concomitantly ascribed to Africans; he does not note any resemblance between "cagelike" asylum technology and cagelike slave ship and plantation technology. Foucault fails to critically engage the matter of blackness—especially noteworthy considering the importance of blackness as foil to whiteness in the drama of Western modernity and the worldwide colonial and racial upheavals concurrent with the composition of *History of Madness*. For a discussion of asylums in the mid-twentieth century (based on extensive ethnographic research), see Erving Goffman, *Asylums: Essays on the Social Situation of Mental Patients and Other Inmates* (New York: Anchor Books, 1961).

65 Benjamin Reiss, *Theaters of Madness: Insane Asylums and Nineteenth-Century American Culture* (Chicago: University of Chicago Press, 2008), 15. Regarding the "association of blackness and madness," Gilman explains that is "product of distortive fantasies of both the black and the mad. . . . Both are focuses for the projection of Western culture's anxieties" in *Difference and Pathology*, 148.

66 For a rich exegesis of diaspora as process, see Brent Hayes Edwards, *The Practice of Diaspora: Literature, Translation, and the Rise of Black Internationalism* (Cambridge, MA: Harvard University Press, 2003).

67 Samuel Cartwright, "Diseases and Peculiarities of the Negro Race," *DeBow's Review: Southern and Western States* 11 (1851): 331.

68 Frank Wilderson suggests that black people in modernity are subjected to relentless and categorical social death, which positions them structurally as slaves. Wilderson writes "Blackness and slaveness cannot be dis-imbricated, cannot be pulled apart." See Frank B. Wilderson III, "Blacks and the Master/ Slave Relation," in *Afro-pessimism: An Introduction* (Minneapolis: Racked and Dispatched, 2017), 15–30, https://rackedanddispatched.noblogs.org/files/2017 /01/Afro-Pessimism2.pdf.

69 Cartwright, "Diseases and Peculiarities of the Negro Race," 332.

70 Cartwright, "Diseases and Peculiarities of the Negro Race," 333. John C. Calhoun, prominent proslavery senator, similarly asserted that freedom had a detrimental impact on the mental health of blacks. As Douglas C. Baynton explains, "John C. Calhoun, senator from South Carolina and one of the most influential spokesmen for the slave states, thought it a powerful argument in defense of slavery that the 'number of deaf and dumb, blind, idiots, and insane, of the negroes in the States that have changed the ancient relation between the races' was seven times higher than in the slave states." See Douglas C. Baynton, "Disability and the Justification of Inequality in American History," in *The Disability Studies Reader*, ed. Lennard J. Davis (New York: Routledge, 2017), 20.

71 Regarding such pathologization of black freedom, Barbara Browning writes that "the terrifying contagion which the United States really feared in 1793 [amid the Haitian Revolution] was the contagion of black political empowerment." See Barbara Browning, *Infectious Rhythm: Metaphors of Contagion and the Spread of African Culture* (New York: Routledge, 1998), 82. US slaveholders feared that black slaves might be inspired by Louverture to seek *black* revolution and *black* liberty—not to be confused with the decidedly *white* revolution and *white* liberty accomplished by the slave-holding, settler-colonial state in 1776.

72 Robert W. Wood, *Memorial of Edward Jarvis, M.D.* (Boston: American Statistical Association, 1885), 11.

73 Toni Morrison quoted in Paul Gilroy, "Living Memory: A Meeting with Toni Morrison," in *Small Acts* (Essex, UK: Serpent's Tail, 1993), 178. Morrison's insight about "deliberately going mad, as one of the characters says, 'in order not to lose your mind,'" helped inspire the title of the present book.

74 Toni Morrison, *Beloved* (New York: Knopf, 1987), 192.

75 The name *schoolteacher* is written in lowercase in the novel. I have preserved that syntax in my own usage.

76 Margaret Garner's fate was different. She, her husband, and her surviving offspring were *confiscated*, as it were, and plunged back into Southern slavery. Avery Gordon offers a poignant meditation on the life of Margaret Garner in *Ghostly Matters* (Minneapolis: University of Minnesota Press, 1997), 137–92.

77 Nat Turner and Thomas Gray, *The Confessions of Nat Turner, the Leader of the Late Insurrection in Southampton* (Baltimore: T. R. Gray, 1831); electronic edition (Chapel Hill: University of North Carolina, 1999), 254, https://docsouth.unc.edu/neh/turner/turner.html.

78 Turner and Gray, *The Confessions of Nat Turner*, 246.

79 Turner and Gray, *The Confessions of Nat Turner*, 261–62.

80 Nietzsche, *Daybreak*, 14; emphasis in original.

81 For further insights on the figure of the "crazy nigger," see Nathan McCall, *Makes Me Wanna Holla: A Young Black Man in America* (New York: Vintage, 1994), 55–56; and Adam Gussow, "'Shoot Myself a Cop': Mamie Smith's 'Crazy Blues' as Social Text," *Callaloo* 25, no. 1 (2002): 8–44.

82 See Rayford Logan, *The Negro in American Life and Thought: The Nadir, 1877–1901* (New York: Dial Press, 1954).

83 W. E. B. Du Bois, *The Souls of Black Folk* (Oxford: Oxford University Press, 2007), 8.

84 This passage is excerpted from a letter originally published in American Surrealist magazine *View*, in 1941. See the full text of the letter in Suzanne Césaire, "The Domain of the Marvelous," in *Surrealist Women: An International Anthology*, ed. Penelope Rosemont (Austin: University of Texas Press, 1998).

85 Along with Aimé Césaire, Léopold Senghor and Léon Damas are credited with cofounding the Négritude Movement. As described on the back cover of the Wesleyan Poetry Series edition of *Notebook of a Return to the Native Land*, "Césaire considered his style a 'beneficial madness' that could 'break into the forbidden' and reach the powerful and overlooked aspects of black culture." See Aimé Césaire, *Notebook of a Return to the Native Land*, trans. Clayton Eshleman (Middletown, CT: Wesleyan University Press, 2001), back cover.

86 Aimé Césaire, *Notebook of a Return to the Native Land*, 18.

87 Fanon, *Black Skin, White Masks*, 14.

88 Fanon, *Black Skin, White Masks*, 2.

89 Hortense Spillers, "'All the Things You Could Be by Now, If Sigmund Freud's Wife Was Your Mother': Psychoanalysis and Race," *boundary 2*, 23, no. 3 (autumn 1996): 88.

90 Spillers, "Mama's Baby," 72.

91 Alongside the works of Fanon and Spillers, the following studies mobilize psychoanalysis to analyze the lives of various peoples of color: Claudia Tate, *Psychoanalysis and Black Novels: Desire and the Protocols of Race* (Oxford: Oxford University Press, 1998); Anne Anlin Cheng, *The Melancholy of Race: Psychoanalysis, Assimilation, and Hidden Grief* (Oxford: Oxford University Press, 2001); David Eng and Shinhee Han, *Racial Melancholia, Racial Dissociation: On the Social and Psychic Lives of Asian Americans* (Durham, NC: Duke University Press, 2018); Margo Crawford, *Dilution Anxiety and the Black Phallus* (Columbus: Ohio State University Press, 2008); Badia Sahar Ahad, *Freud Upside Down: African American Literature and Psychoanalytic Culture* (Champaign: University of Illinois Press, 2010); and Michelle Stephens, *Skin Acts: Race, Psychoanalysis, and the Black Male Performer* (Durham, NC: Duke University Press, 2014).

92 William Grier and Price Cobbs, *Black Rage* (New York: Basic Books, 1992).

93 Regarding Malcolm X's legendary status as "the angriest black man in America," see TaNoah Morgan, "Malcolm X Gets Stamp of Approval; Leader Honored on King's Birthday by Government He Faulted," *Baltimore Sun*, January 16, 1999, and Frank James, "The Malcolm X Factor," *Chicago Tribune*, November 8, 1991.

94 Martin Luther King, "September 27, 1966: MLK—A Riot Is the Language of the Unheard," interview with Mike Wallace, *60 Minutes*, 1966, YouTube video, https://www.youtube.com/watch?v=_KoBWXjJv5s.

95 Both Szasz and Laing rebuked coercive forms of psychiatric treatment, pursuing radical therapeutic alternatives. Szasz suggested "autonomous psychotherapy," wherein the therapist would not medicalize or pathologize the patient, but rather

would unobtrusively converse with the patient and serve as "catalyst" for the patient's own self-discovery. See Thomas Szasz, *The Ethics of Psychoanalysis: The Theory and Method of Autonomous Psychotherapy* (New York: Basic Books, 1965). Meanwhile, Laing experimented with patient-therapist cohabitation in an immersive therapeutic community. See Cheryl McGeachan, "'The World Is Full of Big Bad Wolves': Investigating the Experimental Therapeutic Spaces of R. D. Laing and Aaron Esterson," *History of Psychiatry* 25, no. 3 (2014): 283–98.

96 See Alvin F. Poussaint, "Is Extreme Racism a Mental Illness?," *Western Journal of Medicine* 176, no. 1 (2002): 4; and Joy DeGruy, *Post Traumatic Slave Syndrome: America's Legacy of Enduring Injury and Healing* (Milwaukee, WI: Uptone Press, 2005).

97 Robert C. Schwartz and David M. Blankenship, "Racial Disparities in Psychotic Disorder Diagnosis: A Review of Empirical Literature," *World Journal of Psychiatry* 4, no. 4 (2014): 135.

98 Metzl, *The Protest Psychosis*, ix. Concerning the psychopathologization of Africanity and blackness, see, for example, Cartwright, "Diseases and Peculiarities of the Negro Race"; Grier and Cobbs, *Black Rage*; Metzl, *The Protest Psychosis*.

99 Metzl, *The Protest Psychosis*, ix.

100 Regarding these stereotypes of Sapphires and Jezebels, see Patricia Hill Collins, *Black Feminist Thought: Knowledge, Consciousness, and the Politics of Empowerment* (Boston: Unwin Hyman, 1990).

101 See Fanon, *Black Skin, White Masks*; Grier and Cobbs, *Black Rage*; Alvin F. Poussaint, "Is Extreme Racism a Mental Illness?" *Western Journal of Medicine* 176, vol. 1, no. 4 (2002); and Metzl, *The Protest Psychosis*.

102 Fanon, *Black Skin, White Masks*, 14.

103 Toni Morrison and Charlie Rose, "Novelist Toni Morrison Looks Back on Her Youth and Family and Presents Her Newest Book, 'Jazz,'" *The Charlie Rose Show*, PBS, May 7, 1993, https://charlierose.com/episodes/18778.

104 Poussaint, "Is Extreme Racism a Mental Illness?," 4.

105 Regarding Trump's alleged madness, see, for example, Bandy X. Lee, ed., *The Dangerous Case of Donald Trump: 27 Psychiatrists and Mental Health Experts Assess a President* (New York: St. Martin's Press, 2017); and Keith Olbermann, *Trump Is F*cking Crazy* (New York: Penguin Random House, 2017).

106 I'Nasah Crockett, "'Raving Amazons': Antiblackness and Misogynoir in Social Media," *Model View Culture*, June 30, 2014, https://modelviewculture.com/pieces/raving-amazons-antiblackness-and-misogynoir-in-social-media.

107 Realizing the derogatory power in allegations of madness and pathologizing rhetoric, Trump argues that his opposition suffers from "Trump Derangement Syndrome"—as though suspicion of presidential malfeasance must be delusion, as though acts of protest are bouts of hysteria, as though speaking truth to his power is rant and rave. See Anne Flaherty, "Trump's Diagnosis for Critics: 'Trump Derangement Syndrome,'" *Associated Press News*, July 18, 2018, https://apnews.com/48225d1360864dcb861b12e5cda12a32.

108 I am grateful to Wendell Holbrook for his invocation of a mad jazz ensemble in his response to my own keynote, "Looking for Lauryn: Madness, Genius, and the Black Prophetess," at the "Ruminations on Blackness" conference at Rutgers University, New Brunswick, NJ, in 2011.

109 Amiri Baraka, *Dutchman and the Slave* (New York: Harper Perennial, 1971), 35.

110 It bears mentioning that there are extraordinary depictions and practices of madness in black expressive culture that I do not address at length in this book. I could write another dozen chapters on Huey Newton's call for radical personal and collective upheaval under the sign of "revolutionary suicide"; on Beauford Delaney's exquisite portraits produced as he lived with schizophrenia and was eventually destitute in a French insane asylum in 1979; on Kara Walker's paper silhouettes of perverse plantation scenes that resemble Rorschach inkblots and reveal the racial madness that is America's inheritance; or the final flourish of George C. Wolfe's *The Colored Museum* (1986), when the character Topsy chants "THERE'S MADNESS IN ME, AND THAT MADNESS SETS ME FREE," before beckoning the full cast of characters and announcing, "My power is in my . . ." to which they respond, "*Madness!*"; or Victor LaValle's *The Ecstatic* (2002), whose darkly comedic narrator is "a girthy goon suffering bouts of dementia"; or Gloria Naylor's *1996* (2007), a semifictionalized memoir espousing conspiracy theories about government-led mind control and read, by many, as an account of paranoid madness. I encourage the reader to seek out these mad artists and materials.

111 See Elizabeth Alexander, *The Black Interior* (Minneapolis: Graywolf Press, 2004), 79.

112 Monnica Williams, qtd. in Kenya Downs, "When Black Death Goes Viral, It Can Trigger PTSD-like Trauma," PBS *News Hour*, PBS.org, July 22, 2016, www.pbs.org /newshour/nation/black-pain-gone-viral-racism-graphic-videos-can-create-ptsd -like-trauma. See also Jacob Bor, Atheendar S. Venkataramani, David R. Williams, and Alexander C. Tsai, "Police Killings and Their Spillover Effects on the Mental Health of Black Americans: A Population-based, Quasi-Experimental Study," *Lancet* 392 (10), no. 144 (July 2018). Regarding racial trauma, see Kristin N. Williams-Washington and Chmaika P. Mills, "African American Historical Trauma: Creating an Inclusive Measure," *Journal of Multicultural Counseling and Development* 46, no. 4 (2018): 246–63. See also E. Ann Kaplan, *Trauma Culture: The Politics of Terror and Loss in Media and Literature* (New Brunswick, NJ: Rutgers University Press, 2005), especially chapter 4, "Vicarious Trauma and 'Empty' Empathy: Media Images of Rwanda and the Iraq War."

113 Doris A. Fuller et al. report that mentally ill people are sixteen times more likely to be killed in encounters with law enforcement. See Doris A. Fuller, H. Richard Lamb, Michael Biasotti, and John Snook, "Overlooked in the Undercounted: The Role of Mental Illness in Fatal Law Enforcement Encounters" (Arlington, VA: Treatment Advocacy Center, 2015), TACReports.org/overlooked-undercounted.

114 Surveying civilian mortality in encounters with police officers 2010–14, James W. Buehler determined that black males 10+ years old were 2.8 times as likely as their

white counterparts to die in lethal encounters with police. See Buehler, "Racial/Ethnic Disparities in the Use of Lethal Force by US Police, 2010–2014," *American Journal of Public Health* 107, no. 2 (February 2017). According to the Mapping Police Violence Project, in 2019, black people were three times as likely as their white counterparts to be killed by police; https://mappingpoliceviolence.org/.

115 Concerning Eleanor Bumpurs, see Michael Wilson, "When Mental Illness Meets Police Firepower; Shift in Training for Officers Reflects Lessons of Encounters Gone Awry," *The New York Times*, December 28, 2003; Nirmala Erevelles and Andrea Minear, "Unspeakable Offenses: Untangling Race and Disability in Discourses of Intersectionality," *Journal of Literary and Cultural Disability Studies* 4, no. 2 (2010): 127–45. Regarding Anthony Hill, see Richard Fausset, "Police Killing of Unarmed Georgia Man Leaves Another Town in Disbelief," *New York Times*, March 11, 2015; Christian Boone, "Who Was Anthony Hill? Figure in DeKalb Police Shooting Case Suffered from Mental Illness," *Atlanta Journal-Constitution*, January 22, 2016. With respect to Danny Ray Thomas, see Shaun King, "Danny Ray Thomas Was a Broken Man Who Needed Help. Instead He Was Gunned Down by a Cop in Broad Daylight," *The Intercept*, March 30, 2018; Alex Horton, "A Deputy in Houston Shot and Killed an Unarmed Black Man—Days after Stephon Clark's Death," *Washington Post*, March 24, 2018. Concerning Isaiah Lewis, see Tasneem Nashrulla, "An Unarmed Teen Was Running Around Naked in an Oklahoma Neighborhood. Then Police Shot and Killed Him," *Buzzfeednews.com*, May 2, 2019. Regarding Deborah Danner, see Kenrya Rankin, "NYPD Officer Kills Deborah Danner, Mentally Ill Black Woman," *Colorlines.com*, October 19, 2016, and Joseph Goldstein and James C. McKinley Jr., "Police Sergeant Acquitted in Killing of Mentally Ill Woman" *New York Times*, February 15, 2018.

116 Harry Elam, *The Past as Present in the Drama of August Wilson* (Ann Arbor: University of Michigan Press, 2004), 60.

117 I share this commitment with Pickens, whose *Black Madness :: Mad Blackness* is devoted to placing these fields in critical conversation.

118 Lauryn Hill and Joan Morgan, "They Call Me Ms. Hill," *Essence*, December 2009, https://www.essence.com/news/they-call-me-ms-hill/.

119 This "first man" designation appears in the title of Donald Marquis's biography of Bolden, *In Search of Buddy Bolden: First Man of Jazz* (Baton Rouge: Louisiana State University Press, 2005).

Chapter Two: "He Blew His Brains Out through the Trumpet"

Epigraph: Natasha Trethewey, "Calling His Children Home," *Callaloo* 19, no. 2 (1996): 351.

1 Cultural studies scholar Krin Gabbard credits Bolden with inventing jazz among other pathbreaking accomplishments in trumpet-playing and black masculine performance. Gabbard writes, "Buddy Bolden did more than invent jazz. He took hold of the royal, ceremonial, and military aspects of the trumpet and remade

them for black culture. He invented a new breed of black masculinity, essentially teaching subsequent generations of black men how to strut their stuff as men while delighting the same whites who might otherwise have brutally punished their expressions of black masculinity." Krin Gabbard, *'Hotter than That: The Trumpet, Jazz, and American Culture* (New York: Faber and Faber, 2008), 30.

The 2019 narrative film *Bolden* was promoted as the story of the "inventor" of jazz. See Daniel Pritzker, dir., *Bolden* (New York: Abramorama, 2019), film. For an example of that "inventor" rhetoric in the film's promotion, see "Bolden: The Story behind the Movie: How the 'Inventor of Jazz' Was Brought to Life Onscreen," *JazzTimes,* April 26, 2019, https://jazztimes.com/features/profiles /bolden-the-story-behind-the-movie/.

Famed trumpeter Wynton Marsalis has repeatedly described Bolden as "inventor" of jazz, including in promotion of *Bolden* (which he executive produced). See Gary Graff, "Wynton Marsalis on Bringing the Story of Jazz Originator Buddy Bolden to the Big Screen," *Billboard.com*, April 23, 2019, https://www.billboard.com/articles/news/8508244/wynton-marsalis-buddy -bolden-movie.

2 Notably, none of these newspaper stories concerned Bolden's musical achieve-ments. All were about a violent incident when Bolden (perhaps in the midst of a paranoid schizophrenic episode) attacked a family member with a pitcher. The three articles (none with named writers) include "Mauled His Mother-in-Law," *The Daily Picayune*, March 27, 1906; "Strikes Mother with Water Pitcher," *The New Orleans Item*, March 28, 1906; and "Alcoholic Indulgence Converts Negro Patient into a Dangerous Man," *The Daily States*, March 28, 1906. For further information, see Donald Marquis, *In Search of Buddy Bolden: First Man of Jazz* (Baton Rouge: Louisiana State University Press, 1978), 113–26. See also James Karst, "A Newly Discovered Account of Jazz Legend Buddy Bolden's Mental Decline," *Nola.com*, January 6, 2019.

3 For an investigation of the mystery surrounding Bolden's remains, see J. David Maxson, "Burying the King Again: Buddy Bolden's Jazz Funeral and Defleshed Memory," *Rhetoric Society Quarterly* 48, no. 5 (2018): 516–36.

4 See interviews with Bud Scott and Kid Ory in *Hear Me Talkin' to Ya: The Story of Jazz as Told by the Men Who Made It*, ed. Nat Shapiro and Nat Hentoff (Mine-ola, NY: Dover, 1966), 37, 38. See also Marquis, *In Search of Buddy Bolden*, 62–63; Gabbard, *Hotter Than That*, 15.

5 Performance theorist and theater historian Joseph Roach formulates the "circum-Atlantic" framework—emphasizing multidirectional transatlantic circuits of cultural exchange—in his influential text *Cities of the Dead: Circum-Atlantic Per-formance* (New York: Columbia University Press, 1996).

6 Regarding Bolden's performances at Lincoln Park, see Marquis, *In Search of Buddy Bolden*, 59–63. For a broader history of the park, which was located in the Gert Town section of New Orleans from 1902 to 1930, see Kevin McQueeny, "Playing with Jim Crow: African American Private Parks in Early Twentieth Century New Orleans" (MA thesis, University of New Orleans, 2005).

7 For further information on the storied history of Storyville, and its twenty-year stretch (1897–1917) as a bustling red-light district in New Orleans, see Emily Epstein Landau, *Spectacular Wickedness: Sex, Race, and Memory in Storyville, New Orleans* (Baton Rouge: Louisiana State University Press, 2013). See also Alecia P. Long, *The Great Southern Babylon: Sex, Race, and Respectability in New Orleans, 1865–1920* (Baton Rouge: Louisiana State University Press, 2005).

8 Nathaniel Mackey, *Bedouin Hornbook* (Los Angeles: Sun and Moon Press, 1997), 42.

9 Fred Moten, *In the Break: The Aesthetics of the Black Radical Tradition* (Minneapolis: University of Minnesota Press, 2003), 99.

10 Mikhail Bakhtin, *Rabelais and His World* (Bloomington: Indiana University Press, 1984), 26, 39; emphasis mine.

11 Roach, *Cities of the Dead*, 2.

12 My use of *fabulation* is indebted to Saidiya Hartman's formulation of "critical fabulation," in "Venus in Two Acts," *Small Axe* 12, no. 2 (2008): 1–14. See also Tavia Nyong'o's concept of "Afro-fabulation" in *Afro-Fabulations: The Queer Drama of Black Life* (New York: NYU Press, 2018).

13 I cull this phrase from Duke Ellington's song, "Hey Buddy Bolden," which includes the lyric, "He woke up the working people and kept the easy living." See Nina Simone, "Hey Buddy Bolden," *Nina Simone Sings Ellington!* (Colpix, 1962).

14 There are two intriguing cinematic depictions of Bolden that exigencies of time and space do not permit me to incorporate into this discussion. The first is John Akomfrah, dir., *Precarity* (London: Smoking Dog Films, 2018), a three-channel experimental art film screened at the Nasher Museum of Art at Duke University. The second is Daniel Pritzker, dir., *Bolden* (2019), a narrative film.

15 At its peak in 1905, the Buddy Bolden Band included Willie Cornish on trombone, Jimmy Johnson on string bass, Frank Lewis on clarinet, Brock Mumford on guitar, Cornelius Tillman on drums, and Willie Warner on clarinet (Marquis, *In Search of Buddy Bolden*, 76). Around 1906, soon before Bolden's institutionalization, Frank Dusen would replace Cornish on trombone. Countless other musicians played with the band as auxiliary players when core members were unavailable. Lorenzo Staultz, an auxiliary member who played guitar and contributed vocals, was one of Bolden's preferred crooners for the lyrics of "Funky Butt Blues." See Vic Hobson, "Buddy Bolden's Blues," *The Jazz Archivist: A Newsletter of the William Ransom Hogan Jazz Archive* 21 (2008): 8.

16 Concerning Bolden's alleged womanizing, Sidney Bechet described this apocryphal tableau of Bolden with a few of his female devotees: "One woman, she'd have his trumpet, and another, she'd carry his watch, and another, she'd have his handkerchief, and maybe there'd be another one who wouldn't have nothing to carry, but she'd be there all the same hoping to carry something home," in Sidney Bechet, *Treat It Gentle: An Autobiography* (New York: Hill and Wang, 1960), 84. Concerning Bolden's affinity for liquor, Jelly Roll Morton famously declared that "he drank all the whiskey he could find" (Morton, Library of Congress 1658A).

Concerning Bolden's alleged "sporting life," see Gabbard, *Hotter Than That*, 16–18.

17 Marquis, *In Search of Buddy Bolden*, 92–98.

18 For an extensive account of Bolden's youth and young adulthood, see Marquis, *In Search of Buddy Bolden*, 1–48. Trumpeter Mutt Carey proclaimed that "when you came right down to it, the man who started the big noise in jazz was Buddy Bolden. Yes, he was a powerful trumpet player and a good one too. I guess he deserves credit for starting it all," in Shapiro and Hentoff, *Hear Me Talkin' to Ya*, 35. Bunk Johnson designated Bolden's Band as "the first band to play jazz" (Shapiro and Hentoff, *Hear Me Talkin' to Ya*, 36).

19 Salim Washington, "All the Things You Could Be by Now: Charles Mingus Presents Charles Mingus and the Limits of Avant-Garde Jazz," in *Uptown Conversation: The New Jazz Studies*, ed. Robert O'Meally, Brent Hayes Edwards, and Farah Jasmine Griffin (New York: Columbia University Press, 2004), 28.

20 Fred Moten and Adam Fitzgerald, "An Interview with Fred Moten, Part I," *Literary Hub* 5 (August 2015), *Lithub.com*; emphases mine.

21 The definitive Morton biography is Alan Lomax, *Mister Jelly Roll: The Fortunes of Jelly Roll Morton* (Berkeley: University of California Press, 2001).

22 Morton, Library of Congress 1658A.

23 Morton, Library of Congress 1658B.

24 See Danny Barker, *Buddy Bolden and the Last Days of Storyville* (London: Cassell Press, 1998), 6–9; Marquis, *In Search of Buddy Bolden*, 56–63; John McCusker, *Creole Trombone: Kid Ory and the Early Years of Jazz* (Jackson: University Press of Mississippi, 2012), 53–66.

25 In an interview compiled by Shapiro and Hentoff, New Orleans jazz guitarist and composer and author Danny Barker would proclaim that "they talk about Buddy Bolden—how, on some night [*sic*], you could hear his horn ten miles away. Well, it could have happened because the city of New Orleans has a different kind of acoustics from other cities. There is water all around the city. There is also water all under the city, which is one of the reasons why they would bury people overground—in tombs, mounds, et cetera—because if you dug over three feet deep, you would come up with water" (Shapiro and Hentoff, *Hear Me Talkin' to Ya*, 38). Still, it would have been a remarkable feat for such an aquatic acoustic effect to carry sound over twelve miles—especially with noise-obstructing edifices and 300,000 residents in the city.

26 Alan Lomax, *Mister Jelly Roll: The Fortunes of Jelly Roll Morton, New Orleans Creole and "Inventor of Jazz"* (Berkeley: University of California Press, 2001), xvi–xvii.

27 See Tom Bethell, "The Legend of Buddy Bolden," *National Review* 31, no. 3 (January 19, 1979); Joseph Bonney, "Jazz Great Buddy Bolden Could Be Heard a Mile Away," *New Orleans Times-Picayune*, May 1, 1978 (Hogan Jazz Archive, Tulane University, New Orleans); Marquis, *In Search of Buddy Bolden*, 7, 43–44, 57, 95, 102; Shapiro and Hentoff, *Hear Me Talkin' to Ya*, 38.

28 Marquis, *In Search of Buddy Bolden*, 70.

29 We might also read Bolden as practitioner of a sort of queer domesticity. For all his rumored heterosexual exploits, Bolden was also a queerish figure: he frequented illicit sexworlds in community with sex workers; he queered fatherhood, inaugurating a nonreproductive parentage and nonheteronormative kinship with his "children"; and he made his home on funky dance floors and in parks—spaces that would serve as social and erotic hubs for queer folks decades later. Thanks to Soyica Colbert for pushing me to ponder the queerness of Bolden.

30 Alan Lomax, "Alan Lomax Collection," Library of Congress, Washington, DC, May–December 1938, 1658B.

31 Bolden's asylum admission paperwork suggested that his mental illness was alcohol induced. See Marquis, *In Search of Buddy Bolden*, 121.

32 Marquis, *In Search of Buddy Bolden*, 124.

33 Marquis, *In Search of Buddy Bolden*, 123–24.

34 Marquis, *In Search of Buddy Bolden*, 116, 118.

35 Marquis, *In Search of Buddy Bolden*, 112.

36 British psychiatry professor and jazz devotee Sean A. Spence suggests that "Given that Bolden was credited with the introduction of improvisation into jazz performance . . . it is of note that his resort to improvisation was attributed at the time to a falling-off technical proficiency. This leads to the possible conclusion that 'jazz' (as improvisation) music arose from the attempts of a cognitively impaired performer to execute novel performances" (Sean Spence, "Dementia Praecox and the Birth of Jazz" [abstract of paper presented at the Royal College of Psychiatrists Summer Meeting], Hogan Jazz Archives, Tulane University, New Orleans). While I share Spence's interest in the connections between Bolden's purported madness and his music, I reject Spence's suggestion that "it may be that [Bolden] had to improvise because he could not play the tunes in a useful way" and Spence's "possible conclusion" that jazz improvisation emerges by sheer accident as a result of impairment ("Jazz Is Not an Illness," *New Orleans Times-Picayune*, July 14, 2001, Hogan Jazz Archives, Tulane University, New Orleans). To the contrary, improvisatory jazz demands an *extraordinary aptitude* for "novel performances"— not to mention a remarkable dexterity with time, rhythm, tone, and modulation. A musician unable to "execute novel performances" would be better suited for the scripted predictability of, say, classical music. More broadly, even if psychosis were the origin of Bolden's improvisational acumen, no individual pathology— nor individual genius, for that matter—should be singularly credited with "the generation of a new art form" called jazz. In truth, masses of people collaborated to make jazz and are disregarded in Spence's account of a solitary progenitor, technical failure, and accidental creation.

37 Marquis, *In Search of Buddy Bolden*, 126.

38 Marquis, *In Search of Buddy Bolden*, 128.

39 Marquis, *In Search of Buddy Bolden*, 129.

40 Gabbard, *Hotter Than That*, 24.

41 Marquis, *In Search of Buddy Bolden*, 131.

42 Maxson, "Burying the King Again."

43 Trombone player Willie Cornish claimed he wrote "Funky Butt Blues." See Hobson, 8.

44 Barker, *Buddy Bolden and the Last Days of Storyville*, 31.

45 Christina Sharpe identifies "anti-blackness as total climate" in *In the Wake: On Blackness and Being* (Durham, NC: Duke University Press, 2016), 105. Elaborating the significance of "weather" as an organzing principle in her text, Sharpe explains, "In my text, the weather is the totality of our environments; the weather is the total climate; and that climate is anti-black" (104).

46 Simone, "Hey Buddy Bolden."

47 Concerning Simone's diagnosis with schizophrenia, see Nadine Cohodas, *Princess Noire: The Tumultuous Reign of Nina Simone* (Chapel Hill: University of North Carolina Press, 2012), 337. Regarding her diagnosis with bipolar disorder, see Liz Garbus, dir., *What Happened Miss Simone?* (Netflix, 2015).

48 Wilson, *Seven Guitars*, 71.

49 Wilson, *Seven Guitars*, 26.

50 Wilson, *Seven Guitars*, 71.

51 Wilson, *Seven Guitars*, 71.

52 As Harry Elam notes, among Wilson's mad characters, "Madness largely results from symbolic confrontations with white power structures. These encounters cause ruptures and schisms for the characters that parallel primal scenes of loss, rupture, and schism within the experiences of Africans in America." Harry Elam, *The Past as Present in the Drama of August Wilson* (Ann Arbor: University of Michigan Press, 2004), 64.

 Hedley's status as unrecognized "King" evokes the prince-as-pauper narrative archetype: the story of a royal figure flung temporarily into abjection, often via mistaken identity, and later restored to his rightful lofty station. The quintessential prince-as-pauper is Jesus Christ: a poor boy born in a manger in Bethlehem, later employed as a carpenter in Jerusalem, eventually accused of madness, thereafter subjected to state-sanctioned persecution, torture, and murder, before he was finally vindicated and restored to the heavenly throne that was his from the start. Bolden instantiates the prince-as-pauper paradigm on a different register. Bolden was "King," had throngs of followers who heeded him when he called them home, was decisive in the advent of one of the most canonical art forms of the twentieth century, but would die a pauper in a rural Louisiana asylum. Hedley locates himself within this paradigm, too. He is an unacknowledged "King" subjected to ridicule and persecution. If Bolden was restored to princely glory, it wasn't in his historical life, but in his mythical afterlife (or maybe in a spiritual afterlife in the next world). Hedley himself recognizes this affinity, explaining, "I always want to be a big man. Like Jesus Christ was a big man. He was the Son of the Father. I too. I am the son of my father" (Wilson, *Seven Guitars*, 71–72).

53 Wilson, *Seven Guitars*, 68.

54 Wilson, *Seven Guitars*, 113.

55 See Armstrong, "Black and Blue," *Satch Plays Fats: The Music of Fats Waller* (New York: Columbia, 1955). See also Ralph Ellison, *Invisible Man* (New York: Random House, 1995), 14.

56 Lawrence Jackson, *Ralph Ellison: Emergence of Genius* (New York: Wiley, 2002), 426.

57 At the close of *Invisible Man*, after narrating his futile attempts to assimilate to the world aboveground, he ends with this provocation to the reader: "Who knows but that, on the lower frequencies, I speak for you?" (581).

58 I refer to Michael Ondaatje's fictionalized character by the name "Buddy," as distinguished from the historical Bolden who is my broader object of inquiry in this chapter.

59 Michael Ondaatje, *Coming through Slaughter* (New York: Vintage International, 1996), 13.

60 Ondaatje, *Coming through Slaughter*, 24. The mention of "customers in the chair" alludes to Bolden's supposed career as a barber—another legend refuted in Marquis's biography.

61 Ondaatje, *Coming through Slaughter*, 15–16.

62 Ondaatje, *Coming through Slaughter*, 37–38.

63 Ondaatje, *Coming through Slaughter*, 130.

64 Ondaatje, *Coming through Slaughter*, 131.

65 Ondaatje, *Coming through Slaughter*, 130.

66 Concerning *jouissance*, see Leo Bersani, "Is the Rectum a Grave?" and "A Conversation with Leo Bersani," in *Is the Rectum a Grave? And Other Essays* (Chicago: University of Chicago Press, 2010); and Amber Musser, *Sensual Excess: Queer Femininity and Brown Jouissance* (New York: NYU Press, 2018).

67 Ondaatje, *Coming through Slaughter*, 133.

68 Ondaatje, *Coming through Slaughter*, 156.

69 Ondaatje, *Coming through Slaughter*, 156.

70 Other examples of Mingus describing his life in his own words include Thomas Reichman, dir., *Mingus: Charles Mingus* (Inlet Films, 1968); and John Goodman and Sy Johnson, *Mingus Speaks* (Berkeley: University of California Press, 2013). For further writings by Sun Ra, see Adam Everette Abraham, ed., *Sun Ra: Collected Works, Vol. 1—Immeasurable Equation* (Chandler, AZ: Phaelos Books and Mediawerks, 2005); and James Wolf and Hartmut Geerken, eds., *Sun Ra: The Immeasurable Equation—The Collected Prose and Poetry* (Wartaweil, Germany: Waitawhile Press, 2006).

71 Szwed, *Space Is the Place: The Lives and Times of Sun Ra* (New York: Da Capo Press, 1998), 5.

72 Szwed, *Space Is the Place*, 5.

73 Szwed, *Space Is the Place*, 6.

74 Szwed, *Space Is the Place*, 5.

75 Szwed, *Space Is the Place*, 5.

76 The surrealist designation suits Sun Ra in several respects. At the level of ideology, he posits Egypt and Saturn as spaces where the laws of earthly metaphysics and

human governance are replaced by strange, fantastical, and utopian possibility—akin to what surrealists would deem the "Marvelous." At the level of technique, Sun Ra demanded that his Arkestra members forgo transcription, rhythm, melody, and conventional aesthetic concerns in order to play primal, spontaneous, intuitive sounds according to their whims in a given moment. His praise of unhinged improvisation closely resembles the surrealist practice of automatism. See André Breton, "Manifesto of Surrealism" (1924), in *Manifestoes of Surrealism*, trans. Richard Seaver and Helen R. Lane (Ann Arbor: University of Michigan Press, 1969).

77 Szwed, *Space Is the Place*, 46.

78 Szwed, *Space Is the Place*, 44.

79 Szwed, *Space Is the Place*, 45.

80 Szwed, *Space Is the Place*, 6.

81 Regarding the de-pathologization of homosexuality in mainstream psychiatry, see Neel Burton, "When Homosexuality Stopped Being a Mental Disorder: Not until 1987 Did Homosexuality Completely Fall out of the DSM," *Psychology Today*, September 18, 2015, https://www.psychologytoday.com/us/blog/hide -and-seek/201509/when-homosexuality-stopped-being-mental-disorder. See also Jack Drescher, "Out of DSM: Depathologizing Homosexuality," *Behavioral Sciences* 5, no. 4 (2015): 565–75, https://www.ncbi.nlm.nih.gov/pmc/articles /PMC4695779/.

82 See Szwed, *Space Is the Place*, 193–200.

83 For an extensive discography of Sun Ra's work, see Szwed, *Space Is the Place*, 425–48.

84 See Szwed, *Space Is the Place*, 93–103, 193–98.

85 See Daniel Pritzker, dir., *Bolden* (New York: Abramorama, 2019); and John Coney, dir., *Space Is the Place* (San Francisco: Harte, 2015).

86 Coney, *Space Is the Place*.

87 Charles Mingus's significance to American music is aptly summarized by Salim Washington in his essay, "All the Things You Could Be by Now: *Charles Mingus Presents Charles Mingus* and the Limits of Avant-Garde Jazz": "Mingus is truly one of [America's] representative composers because of the unusual breadth of his musical influences, the depth with which he assimilated them, and the degree to which he synthesized them into a personal voice, avoiding both simple mimicry and postmodern pastiche" (in *Uptown Conversations*, ed. George Lewis, Brent Edwards, Farah Jasmine Griffin [New York: Columbia University Press, 2003], 35).

88 Charles Mingus, *Beneath the Underdog: His World as Composed by Mingus* (New York: Vintage, 1991).

89 Mingus, *Beneath the Underdog*, 3.

90 Mingus, *Beneath the Underdog*, 4.

91 Georg Wilhelm Friedrich Hegel, *The Philosophy of History* (New York: Dover, 1956), 99.

92 Mingus, *Beneath the Underdog*, 297.

93 See "Dissociative Disorders," *Diagnostic and Statistical Manual of Mental Disorders: DSM 5* (Arlington, VA: American Psychiatric Association, 2013), https://doi-org.proxy-um.researchport.umd.edu/10.1176/appi.books.9780890425596.dsm08.

94 Mingus, *Beneath the Underdog*, 14–15.

95 For an extended account of the historical interrelations between Nazism and Jim Crow, see Glenda Gilmore, *Defying Dixie: The Radical Roots of Civil Rights: 1919–1950* (New York: W. W. Norton, 2009), especially chapter 4, "The Nazis and Dixie."

96 Mingus, *Beneath the Underdog*, 333.

97 In Toni Morrison's 1987 novel *Beloved*, schoolteacher is a slaveholder who tortures, debases, and ravages enslaved people under the guise of scientific inquiry.

98 Charles Mingus, *Charles Mingus Presents Charles Mingus* (New York: Candid Records, 1960).

99 Though this phrase literally applies to the scenario of uncertain paternity conjured in Mingus's title, it doubles as the title of Hortense J. Spillers's preeminent essay, "Mama's Baby, Papa's Maybe: An American Grammar Book." Therein, she investigates racial and sexual abjection that permeate American history, genealogy, and beyond. See Spillers, "Mama's Baby, Papa's Maybe: An American Grammar Book," *Diacritics* 17, no. 2, *Culture and Countermemory: The "American" Connection* (summer 1987): 65–81.

100 The album's title begs the question *Who is Freud to you?* This is an incisive provocation for black studies scholars adapting psychoanalysis to read black life and mine black madness. Hortense Spillers addressed this concern in "All the Things You Could Be by Now If Sigmund Freud's Wife Was Your Mother: Race and Psychoanalysis," named after Mingus's track.

101 I am thinking of Spillers's formulation of "flesh" in "Mama's Baby, Papa's Maybe." She writes, "I would make a distinction in this case between 'body' and 'flesh' and impose that distinction as the central one between captive and liberated subject-positions. In that sense, before the 'body' there is 'flesh,' that zero degree of social conceptualization that does not escape concealment under the brush of discourse, or the reflexes of iconography" (67).

I envision a miscegenated psychoanalysis that may be codified as part of the official "body"/corpus of psychoanalytic practice, but contains fundamental elements (fleshly material, so to speak) that precede and exceed Freud.

102 In *Lose Your Mother: A Journey along the Atlantic Slave Route* (New York: Farrar, Straus and Giroux, 2007), Saidiya Hartman describes the afterlife of slavery as follows: "If slavery persists as an issue in the political life of black America, it is not because of an antiquarian obsession with bygone days or the burden of a too-long memory, but because black lives are still imperiled and devalued by a racial calculus and a political arithmetic that were entrenched centuries ago. This is the afterlife of slavery—skewed life chances, limited access to health and education, premature death, incarceration, and impoverishment" (6).

103 Regarding the lives of these jazz icons, see, respectively: Dave Gelly, *Being Prez: The Life and Music of Lester Young* (New York: Oxford University Press, 2007);

Guthrie Ramsey, *The Amazing Bud Powell: Black Genius, Jazz History, and the Challenge of Bebop* (Berkeley: University of California Press, 2013); Robin D. G. Kelley, *Thelonious Monk: The Life and Times of an American Original* (New York: Free Press, 2009); and Stanley Crouch, *Kansas City Lightning: The Rise and Times of Charlie Parker* (New York: HarperCollins, 2013).

104 That this list is a *fraternity* populated entirely by men is evidence of the often-gendered division of labor in jazz music, especially in the first half of the twentieth century. For various reasons—including a belief that the wandering life of jazz touring was unfeminine or that masculine bodies were best suited for certain instruments—women were granted fewer opportunities in jazz music. Many women have thrived as popular jazz singers—but usually as the sole woman within a given ensemble.

Feminist musicologist and cultural historian Sherrie Tucker has generated excellent scholarship on women jazz instrumentalists. See Sherrie Tucker, *Swing Shift: "All-Girl" Bands of the 1940s* (Durham, NC: Duke University Press, 2000); Sherrie Tucker, "Big Ears: Listening for Gender in Jazz Studies," *Current Musicology* 71–73 (spring 2001/2002): 375–408; and Nichole Rustin and Sherrie Tucker, eds., *Big Ears: Listening for Gender in Jazz Studies* (Durham, NC: Duke University Press, 2008). For a powerful broader account of jazz and female subjectivity, see Farah Jasmine Griffin, *If You Can't Be Free, Be a Mystery: In Search of Billie Holiday* (New York: One World/Ballantine, 2002).

105 I have found no statistics on the rate of African Americans imprisoned while living with serious mental illness in the early and mid-twentieth century. Alas, because so many people went undiagnosed and because imprisoned black people in Jim Crow America were subjected to profound neglect, apathy, and carelessness, it might not be possible to know. While deinstitutionalization in the 1960s–1980s might have rerouted seriously mentally ill people from hospitals to prison in general, mentally ill black people were *already* dispro-portionately in jails and prisons on account of hyperincarceration. Regarding the twenty-first century: According to a 2010 report by Torrey et al., there were three times as many seriously mentally ill persons in jails or prisons as in hospitals in 2004–5. The report also finds that 40 percent of seriously mentally ill people will spend time in jail or prison during their lifetimes. This study does not index race, but considering the hyperincarceration of black people in the United States, the data are surely even more bleak among black people in the United States who are seriously mentally ill. See E. Fuller Torrey, Aaron Ken-nard, Don Eslinger, Richard Lamb, and James Pavle, "More Mentally Ill Persons Are in Jails and Prisons Than Hospitals: A Survey of the States" (Arlington, VA: Treatment Advocacy Center, 2010).

106 Michel Foucault, *Madness: The Invention of an Idea* (previously published as *Mental Illness and Psychology*) (New York: Harper Perennial, 2011), 85–86.

107 See Daphne A. Brooks, "A New Voice of the Blues," in *A New Literary History of America*, ed. Greil Marcus and Werner Sollors (Cambridge, MA: Harvard University Press, 2012).

Interlude: "No Wiggles in the Dark of Her Soul"

Epigraph: Amiri Baraka, *Dutchman and the Slave* (New York: Harper Perennial, 1971), 35.

1   In the same year that *Dutchman* debuted, and within the same politicized cultural milieu of the Black Arts Movement, Adrienne Kennedy premiered her tragic surrealist drama, *Funnyhouse of the Negro*. Kennedy's protagonist is a "pallid Negro" woman ravaged by racial trauma and gone mad.

2   For an especially vivid account of such negrophobic fantasies of black male sexual savagery, see Frantz Fanon, *Black Skin, White Masks*, trans. Charles Lam Markmann (New York: Grove Press, [1952] 1994), especially "Chapter Six: The Negro and Psychopathology." *Dutchman*'s provocative depiction of a deadly encounter between a black man and white woman brings to mind Richard Wright's 1940 novel *Native Son*—published nearly twenty-five years earlier. See Richard Wright, *Native Son* (New York: HarperCollins, 1993).

3   For an extended discussion of the gender dynamics in *Dutchman*, including how the play stages Clay's emasculation and Lula's endowment with phallic power, see Matthew Rebhorn, "Flaying Dutchman: Masochism, Minstrelsy, and the Gender Politics of Amiri Baraka's 'Dutchman,'" *Callaloo* 26, no. 3 (2003): 796–812.

4   W. E. B. Du Bois, *The Souls of Black Folk* (New York: Signet Classic, 1995), 45.

5   Frantz Fanon, *The Wretched of the Earth*, trans. Constance Farrington (New York: Grove Press, 1963), 94. Fanon did not endorse arbitrary or unending violence, but rather saw it as an instrument toward political upheaval and anticolonial liberation.

6   Freud variously formulates sublimation in such essays as "Civilization and Its Discontents," "The Ego and the Id," and especially "Leonardo da Vinci and a Memory of His Childhood." For a comprehensive overview of psychoanalytic sublimation, see Hans Loewald, *Sublimation: Inquires into Theoretical Psychoanalysis* (New Haven, CT: Yale University Press, 1988). For a useful review of ambiguities and contestations around Freud's concept of sublimation, see Ken Gemes, "Freud and Nietzsche on Sublimation," *The Journal of Nietzsche Studies*, no. 38 (autumn 2009): 38–59.

7   Fanon, *Black Skin, White Masks*, trans. Charles Lam Markmann (New York: Grove Press, [1952] 1994), 150.

8   Regarding the complex lives, worldviews, and political practices of such "respectable" women, see Evelyn Brooks Higginbotham, *Righteous Discontent: The Women's Movement in the Black Baptist Church, 1880–1920* (Cambridge, MA: Harvard University Press, 1993).

9   For further insight on brazen rejections of respectability and sublimation among African Americans, see Cathy J. Cohen, "Deviance as Resistance: A New Research Agenda for the Study of Black Politics," *Du Bois Review: Social Science Research on Race* 1, no. 1 (2004): 27–45.

10 Amiri Baraka, "The Revolutionary Theatre," in *Home: Social Essays* (New York, Akashic Books, 2009), 237.

11 Amiri Baraka, "Black Art," in *The LeRoi Jones/Amiri Baraka Reader*, ed. William J. Harris (New York: Basic Books, 1999), 219.

12 Baraka, "The Revolutionary Theatre," 240; emphasis mine.

13 Frank Lords, dir., *Nina Simone—The Legend* (London: British Broadcasting Corporation, 1992).

14 Joel Gold, dir., *Nina: A Historical Perspective* (New York: Cinemagic, 1970).

15 Hortense J. Spillers, "Mama's Baby, Papa's Maybe: An American Grammar Book," *Diacritics* 17, no. 2 (summer 1987), 68.

16 As a black woman born in the American South in 1894, just a generation after emancipation, Smith likely encountered antagonisms and perils that Clay—a middle-class, mid-twentieth-century man—has never known. Antiblackness, misogyny, patriarchy, and sexual vulnerability and violence—in various concatenations on interpersonal and structural registers—stalked black womanhood at every turn. Concerning the life and art of Bessie Smith, see Chris Albertson, *Bessie*, rev. and expanded ed. (New Haven, CT: Yale University Press, 2003).

17 Paul Oliver, "Smith (née Robinson), Mamie," *The New Grove Dictionary of Jazz* (New York: Oxford University Press, 2003).

18 For an extensive exegesis of the song, see Adam Gussow, "'Shoot Myself a Cop': Mamie Smith's 'Crazy Blues' as Social Text," *Callaloo* 25, no. 1 (2002): 8–44.

19 *Dutchman* was originally produced in 1964 and is set in roughly the same period. Clay is twenty years old in the play, which would date his birth to around 1944.

Chapter Three: The Blood-Stained Bed

Epigraph: Gayl Jones, *Eva's Man* (1976), in *The Healing, Corregidora, Eva's Man* (New York: Griot Editions, 1999).

1 Jones, *Eva's Man*, 484.

2 Frederick Douglass, *Narrative of the Life of Frederick Douglass, An American Slave: Written By Himself* (1845) (New Haven, CT: Yale University Press, 2001), 16.

3 See Darlene Clark Hine, "Rape and the Inner Lives of Black Women in the Middle West," *Signs* 14, no. 4 (1989): 912–20; Hazel V. Carby, "Policing the Black Woman's Body in an Urban Context," *Critical Inquiry* 18, no. 4 (1992): 738–55; Saidiya Hartman, "Venus in Two Acts," *Small Axe* 12, no. 2 (2008): 1–14; Danielle L. McGuire, *At the Dark End of the Street: Black Women, Rape, and Resistance—A New History of the Civil Rights Movement from Rosa Parks to the Rise of Black Power* (New York: Knopf, 2010).

4 See, for example, Biman Basu, "Public and Private Discourses and the Black Female Subject: Gayl Jones' *Eva's Man*," *Callaloo* 19, no. 1 (winter 1996): 193–208. See also Carol Margaret Davison, "'Love 'em and Lynch 'em': The Castration Motif in Gayl Jones's *Eva's Man*," *African American Review* 29, no. 3 (autumn 1995): 393–410.

5 When Caminero-Santangelo proposes that "the madwoman can't speak," she forecloses the expressive potential of the madwoman. I want to insist that madwomen do speak, though not necessarily in heroic rally cries or political slogans

or readily discernible accounts of political subjectivity. Sometimes madwomen speak in shrieks, manic "rants," bursts of weeping, or mumbled asides—utterances that may not register in dominant public spheres, but have performative and communicative value among the mad black protagonists convened in this study. And even if a madwoman remains silent, she may manifest a resonant silence that is communicative and agential. Indeed, the processes of silently observing, refusing to answer, and moving about stealthily unheard are all examples of agency smuggled beneath the cover of silence. See Marta Caminero-Santangelo, *The Madwoman Can't Speak: Or Why Insanity Is Not Subversive* (Ithaca, NY: Cornell University Press, 1998).

6 Jones, *Eva's Man*, 477.

7 For further information on repetition compulsion, see Sigmund Freud, "Beyond the Pleasure Principle," in *The Freud Reader*, ed. Peter Gay (New York: W. W. Norton, 1989), 594–625. See also Hans Loewald, "Some Considerations on Repetition and Repetition Compulsion," *International Journal of Psychoanalysis* 52 (1971): 59–66. Regarding post-traumatic stress disorder (PTSD), see American Psychiatric Association, "Post-Traumatic Stress Disorder" in *Diagnostic and Statistical Manual of Mental Disorders: DSM 5* (Arlington, VA: American Psychiatric Association, 2013). https://doi.org/10.1176/appi.books.9780890425596.dsm05.

8 Freud, "Beyond the Pleasure Principle," 611.

9 Freud, "The Ego and the Id," 645.

10 Freud, "Beyond the Pleasure Principle," 613.

11 Freud, "Beyond the Pleasure Principle," 621.

12 Jones, *Eva's Man*, 521.

13 As Jones explains it, "In Eva's mind, time and people become fluid. Time has little chronological sequence, and the characters seem to coalesce into one personality," in Claudia Tate, "Interview with Gayl Jones," *Black American Literature Forum* 13, no. 4 (winter 1979): 146.

14 Jones, *Eva's Man*, 509.

15 Jones, *Eva's Man*, 635.

16 Candice Jenkins, *Private Lives, Proper Relations: Regulating Black Intimacy* (Minneapolis: University of Minnesota Press, 2007), 158.

17 In her discussion of Gayl Jones's first novel, *Corregidora* (1975), Christina Sharpe explores "transgenerational trauma" (54) and "transgenerational racial hatred [and] sexual violence" (56) as experienced by black women. See Christina Sharpe, *Monstrous Intimacies: Making Post-Slavery Subjects* (Durham, NC: Duke University Press, 2010).

18 Jones, *Eva's Man*, 639.

19 Tate, "Interview," 143.

20 Tate, "Interview," 143.

21 Charles Rowell, "An Interview with Gayl Jones," *Callaloo* 16 (1982): 33.

22 Here I am building upon insights from literary critics Donia Allen Elizabeth and Cheryl Wall on the blues tradition in Jones's work. Donia Allen Elizabeth astutely asserts that Jones "adapts formal devices, among them repetition, call

and response and the blues break to reveal crucial aspects of her character's lives and struggles, as well as important themes in her work in general." Donia Allen Elizabeth, "The Role of the Blues in Gayl Jones's 'Corregidora,'" *Callaloo* 25, no.1 (2002): 257. See also Cheryl A. Wall, "Trouble in Mind: Blues and History in *Corregidora*," in *Worrying the Line: Black Women Writers, Lineage, and Literary Tradition* (Chapel Hill: University of North Carolina Press, 2005).

23 Jones, *Eva's Man*, 477.

24 Angela Y. Davis, *Blues Legacies and Black Feminism: Gertrude "Ma" Rainey, Bessie Smith, and Billie Holiday* (New York: Pantheon, 1998), 21.

25 The figure of the blueswoman is not singularly characterized by sorrow, death, and vengeance. She is also characterized by sly wit and humor, alluring charisma, unabashed sexuality, and social intelligence.

26 Jones, *Eva's Man*, 511.

27 Jones, *Eva's Man*, 603.

28 Ursa Corregidora is the protagonist of Jones's debut novel *Corregidora*, published in 1975, one year before *Eva's Man*. The two novels may be read as a diptych addressing such themes as black female abjection, male predation and domination, encroachments of past trauma upon vexed presents, and "blues ritual."

Ursa is a blues singer whose songs sublimate peculiar anguish and rage. For as long as she can remember, she has been haunted by secondhand and third-hand memories of her long-dead ancestor, a man called Corregidora. He was an incestuous "Portuguese slave breeder and whore-monger" (292–93) who set up shop in nineteenth-century Brazil. Remembering and reciting his wickedness is a definitive ritual that binds the Corregidora women. They devise a familial oral tradition—indeed, a storytelling art—devoted to preserving the memory of slavery's horrors and of Corregidora's peculiar malevolence. Of her great-grandmother, Ursa remembers: "It was as if the words were helping her, as if the words repeated again and again could be a substitute for memory, were somehow more than memory. As if it were only the words that kept her anger" (295). Ursa describes an exemplary sublimation: Her great-grandmother channels "anger"—a mode of madness—into storytelling. She sublimates that terrible memory, and the madness it engenders, into a narrative. The narrative constitutes a blues ritual.

Regarding *Corregidora*, see Sharpe, *Monstrous Intimacies*; Madhu Dubey, "Gayl Jones and the Matrilineal Metaphor of Tradition," *Signs: Journal of Women in Culture and Society* 20, no. 21 (1995): 245–67; and Jennifer Cognard-Black, "'I Said Nothing': The Rhetoric of Silence and Gayl Jones's 'Corregidora,'" *NWSA Journal* 13, no. 1 (2001): 40–60.

29 Regarding disaster-fixation and morbid curiosity (what is often called the "train wreck" phenomenon), see Amrisha Vaish, Tobias Grossmann, and Amanda Woodward, "Not All Emotions Are Created Equal: The Negativity Bias in Social-Emotional Development," *Psychology Bulletin* 134, no. 3 (2008): 383–403. See also Eric G. Wilson, *Everyone Loves a Good Train Wreck: Why We Can't Look Away* (New York: Farrar, Straus and Giroux, 2013).

30 Jones, *Eva's Man*, 575.

31 Jones, *Eva's Man*, 489.

32 Jones, *Eva's Man*, 489.

33 Jones, *Eva's Man*, 579–80.

34 In their 1968 manifesto *Black Rage*, Grier and Cobbs relay an uncannily similar real-life story: "In the 1950s a young white southern lawyer, newly returned from a New England law school, was assigned a case by his law firm involving a Negro woman and her property. He soon realized that his task was to have the woman committed to an institution as insane and to arrange for the acquisition of her property by a client of the law firm. He resigned from the firm and took on the woman's defense. He learned of similar cases and, by defending them, earned the enmity of his colleagues. Threats were made on his life and he fled the state for his own safety." William Grier and Price Cobbs, *Black Rage* (New York: Basic Books, 1992), 107.

35 Jones, *Eva's Man*, 595.

36 Jones, qtd. in Clabough, "Toward an All-Inclusive Structure: The Early Fiction of Gayl Jones," *Callaloo* 29, no. 2 (spring 2006): 636.

37 Jones, *Eva's Man*, 521.

38 Jones, *Eva's Man*, 548.

39 Jones, *Eva's Man*, 549.

40 Jones, *Eva's Man*, 570.

41 I am inspired by Foucault's discussion of the "polymorphous incitements to discourse" about sexuality that proliferate in the modern West. These incitements urge people to announce their sexualities to clergy (in religious confession) and psychoanalysts (in talk therapy), among other arbiters of normative discourse. See Michel Foucault, *The History of Sexuality: An Introduction: Volume I*, trans. Robert Hurley (New York: Vintage Books, 1990), 34.

42 See Michael Dawson, *Black Visions: The Roots of Contemporary African-American Political Ideologies* (Chicago: University of Chicago Press, 2003), 1–44.

43 Foucault, *The History of Sexuality*, 34. For insight on how the injunction to speak in the juridical context can be an exposure to racial victimization and humiliation, see, for example, Danielle McGuire, "'It Was Like All of Us Had Been Raped': Sexual Violence, Community Mobilization, and the African American Freedom Struggle," *Journal of American History* 91, no. 3 (December 2004): 906–31.

44 Foucault, *History of Sexuality*, 27.

45 Aliyyah Abdur-Rahman, *Against the Closet: Black Political Longing and the Erotics of Race* (Durham, NC: Duke University Press, 2012), 30–32.

46 Dori Laub, "Bearing Witness or the Vicissitudes of Listening," in *Testimony: Crises of Witnessing in Literature, Psychoanalysis, and History* (New York: Routledge, 1991), 60, 65.

47 Audre Lorde, "The Transformation of Silence into Language and Action," in *Sister Outsider* (Berkeley, CA: Crossing Press, 1984), 41.

48 See James C. Scott, *Domination and the Arts of Resistance: Hidden Transcripts* (New Haven, CT: Yale University Press, 1990).

49 Kevin Quashie has generated critical work on black quiet and is very careful to distinguish *quiet* from *silence*. He writes: "Quiet is often used interchangeably with silence or stillness, but the notion of quiet in the pages that follow is neither motionless nor without sound. Quiet, instead, is a metaphor for the full range of one's inner life—one's desires, ambitions, hungers, vulnerabilities, fears" (6). Furthermore, he observes, "Indeed, the expressiveness of silence is often aware of an audience, a watcher or listener whose presence is the reason for the withholding—it is an expressiveness which is intent and even defiant. This is a key difference between the two terms because in its inwardness, the aesthetic of quiet is watcherless" (22). My emphasis is on the withholding silence that Quashie indicates is outside his focus. Kevin Quashie, *The Sovereignty of Quiet: Beyond Resistance in Black Culture* (New Brunswick, NJ: Rutgers University Press, 2012).

50 Jones, *Eva's Man*, 627.

51 Jones, *Eva's Man*, 590.

52 Jones, *Eva's Man*, 553.

53 Casey Clabough, *Gayl Jones: The Language of Voice and Freedom in Her Writings* (Jefferson, NC: McFarland, 2008), 29.

54 Jones, *Eva's Man*, 622; emphasis in original.

55 Jones, *Eva's Man*, 567.

56 Jones, *Eva's Man*, 600.

57 Mikhail Bakhtin, *Rabelais and His World* (Bloomington: Indiana University Press, 1984), 26.

58 Jones, *Eva's Man*, 529.

59 Jones, *Eva's Man*, 490.

60 Regarding Spillers formulation of "the flesh," see Hortense Spillers, "Mama's Baby, Papa's Maybe: An American Grammar Book," *Diacritics* 17, no. 2 (summer 1987): 67. See also Alexander Weheliye, *Habeas Viscus: Racializing Assemblages, Biopolitics, and Black Feminist Theories of the Human* (Durham, NC: Duke University Press, 2014), 33–45.

61 Carol Margaret Davison, "'Love 'em and Lynch 'em': The Castration Motif in Gayl Jones's *Eva's Man*," *African American Review* 29, no. 3 (autumn 1995): 398–99.

62 Audre Lorde, "*Eva's Man*," in *I Am Your Sister: Collected and Unpublished Writings of Audre Lorde*, ed. Rudolph Byrd, Johnnetta Betsch Cole, and Beverly Guy-Sheftall (New York: Oxford University Press, 2009), 153.

63 For a data-driven discussion of the precarity of black girls and women amid misogynist and antiblack contexts, see Asha DuMonthier, Chandra Childers, and Jessica Milli, *The Status of Black Women in the United States* (Washington, DC: Institute for Women's Policy Research, 2017).

64 This phrase is culled from the lyric, "Southern trees bear strange fruit / Blood on the leaves and blood at the roots" that opens Billie Holiday's "Strange Fruit," Commodore Records, 1938. Lyrics written by Abel Meeropol.

65 Sharpe, *Monstrous Intimacies*, 3.

66 Sharpe, *Monstrous Intimacies*, 9.

67 According to Ovid's account of the myth, Medusa "was once very beautiful, and sought by many, / And was admired most for her beautiful hair. . . . / They say that Neptune, lord of the sea, / Violated her in the temple of Minerva. / The goddess hid her chaste eyes behind her aegis, / But so that the crime might not go unpunished, / She changed the Gorgon's hair to loathsome snakes, / Which the goddess now, to terrify her enemies, / With numbing fear, wears on her breast-plate." See Ovid, *Metamorphoses*, trans. Stanley Lombardo (Indianapolis: Hackett Publishing, 2010), 117.

68 Regarding rape and victim-blaming, see Madeleine van der Bruggen and Amy Grubb, "A Review of the Literature Relating to Rape Victim Blaming: An Analysis of the Impact of Observer and Victim Characteristics on Attribution of Blame in Rape Cases," *Aggression and Violent Behavior* 19, no. 5 (September–October 2014): 523–31; William H. George and Lorraine J. Martínez, "Victim Blaming in Rape: Effects of Victim and Perpetrator Race, Type of Rape, and Participant Racism," *Psychology of Women Quarterly* 26, no. 2 (June 2002): 110–19; Rebecca M. Hayes, Katherine Lorenz, and Kristin A. Bell, "Victim Blaming Others: Rape Myth Acceptance and the Just World Belief," *Feminist Criminology* 8, no. 3 (2013): 202–20.

69 Jones, *Eva's Man*, 482, 507.

70 Jones, *Eva's Man*, 549.

71 Jones, *Eva's Man*, 507.

72 Jones, *Eva's Man*, 640–41.

73 Jones, *Eva's Man*, 643.

74 In her landmark essay, "Visual Pleasure and Narrative Cinema," British feminist film theorist Laura Mulvey famously theorizes male gaze: the male-centered, scopophilic, "controlling" perspective (a perspective nearly ubiquitous in contemporary cinema) that acts to objectify, sexualize, and consume females on screen and elsewhere. See Laura Mulvey, "Visual Pleasure and Narrative Cinema," in *Feminism and Film Theory*, ed. Constance Penley (New York: Routledge, Chapman, and Hall, 1988), 57–68.

75 See Sigmund Freud, "Medusa's Head," in *Sexuality and the Psychology of Love* (New York: Touchstone, 1997), 202.

76 For further information on the Medusa myth, including feminine and/or feminist imaginings of Medusa from Hélène Cixous, Rita Dove, Sarah Kofman, and Sylvia Plath, see Marjorie Garber and Nancy J. Vickers, eds., *The Medusa Reader* (New York: Routledge, 2003).

77 Jones, *Eva's Man*, 51.

78 Jones, *Eva's Man*, 480. See also Jenkins, *Private Lives, Proper Relations*, 166–73.

79 Jones, *Eva's Man*, 502.

80 Jones, *Eva's Man*, 502.

81 Jones, *Eva's Man*, 592.

82 Jones, *Eva's Man*, 645–46; emphasis in original.

83 Jones, *Eva's Man*, 635.

84 In the introduction to *Wandering: Philosophical Performances of Racial and Sexual Freedom*, Sarah Cervenak offers a rich reading of the significance of bus riding and the broader thematic of wandering in Jones's *Corregidora*. See Sarah Cervenak, *Wandering: Philosophical Performances of Racial and Sexual Freedom* (Durham, NC: Duke University Press, 2014), 1–23.

85 Jones, *Eva's Man*, 649.

86 Basu, "Public and Private Discourses and the Black Female Subject," 197.

87 The phrase *bitter crops* is inspired by the lyrics, "Here is a fruit for the crows to pluck / . . . For the sun to rot, for the tree to drop / Here is a strange and bitter crop" that conclude Billie Holiday's "Strange Fruit," Commodore Records, 1938. Lyrics written by Abel Meeropol.

88 Gayl Jones, "Asylum," in *White Rat: Stories* (New York: Harlem Moon Press, 2005), 68.

89 Jones, "Asylum," 67.

90 Jones, "Asylum," 67.

91 Jones, "Asylum," 69.

92 Jones, "Asylum," 70.

93 Examples of such racist medicine range from J. Marion Sims's experiments on female slaves, to the extraction of cells from Henrietta Lacks without her consent, to the Tuskegee syphilis experiments, to nonconsensual sterilization of black and brown women in the American South and in Puerto Rico, to the pathologization of black and brown schoolchildren in "special education."

94 The Tuskegee syphilis experiments ran from 1932 to 1972. Jones composed the stories that would become *White Rat* between 1970 and 1977.

95 Jones, "Asylum," 70.

96 Jones, "Asylum," 70.

97 Walter Benjamin advises historians to "brush history against the grain" in "Theses on the Philosophy of History" in his essay collections, *Illuminations* (New York: Harcourt, Brace Jovanovich, 1968), 257. Jacques Derrida elaborates "deconstruction" as a mode of textual analysis in *Of Grammatology*, trans. Gayatri Spivak (Baltimore: Johns Hopkins University Press, 1976). bell hooks explores a tradition of insurgent "oppositional gaze" deployed by black women in "The Oppositional Gaze: Black Female Spectators," published in her essay collection, *Black Looks: Race and Representation* (New York: Routledge, 1992), 115–32.

98 Tate, "Interview," 142.

99 Tate, "Interview," 146.

100 For further discussion of the sociological burden thrust upon black art, see Dexter Fisher and Robert Stepto, "Introduction," in *Afro-American Literature: The Reconstruction of Instruction* (New York: Modern Language Association of America, 1979).

101 For further details, see Sally Eckhoff, "The Terrible Mystery of Gayl Jones," *Salon.com* (February 26, 1998). See also Peter Manso, "Chronicle of a Tragedy Foretold," *New York Times Magazine* (July 19, 1998).

102 Manso, "Chronicle of a Tragedy Foretold."

103 Spillers, "Mama's Baby, Papa's Maybe," 261.

104 See Achille Mbembe, "Necropolitics," trans. Libby Meintjes, *Public Culture* 15, no. 1 (winter 2003): 11–40. According to Mbembe, necropolitics entails "figures of sovereignty whose central project is not the struggle for autonomy but *the generalized instrumentalization of human existence and the material destruction of human bodies and populations*" (Mbembe, "Necropolitics," 14; emphasis in original). Mbembe precisely contradicts the liberal thesis that modern, democratic, first-world governmentality is animated by the confederation of rational humans pursuing mutual liberty and autonomy. Mbembe regards necroplitics as the *standard*—not the exception—of modern statehood. Necropower threatens ethnic minorities, women, sexual minorities, the poor, subaltern people, and other besieged people variously configured throughout the world. Mbembe argues that "vast populations are subjected to conditions of life conferring upon them the status of *living dead*" (40).

105 See Mbembe, "Necropolitics," 40; emphases in original.

Chapter Four: A Portrait of the Artist as a Mad Black Woman

1 Virginia Woolf, *A Room of One's Own*, ed. Mark Hussey (Orlando, FL: Harcourt, [1929] 2005). This chapter's title riffs on James Joyce's *Portrait of the Artist as a Young Man* (1916) (London: Penguin, 1992).

2 Alice Walker, "In Search of Our Mother's Gardens," in *In Search of Our Mother's Gardens: Womanist Prose* (San Diego: Harcourt and Brace, 1983).

3 Ntozake Shange, *Liliane: Resurrection of the Daughter* (New York: St. Martin's, 1994), 190.

4 Shange, *Liliane*, 251. This conscious sublimation is a technology of black respectability politics and racial uplift. Indeed, sublimation has functioned as a perennial element of black American bourgeois socialization, particularly during periods of heightened racial antagonism and contestation in the American public sphere, like the 1950s and 1960s. Assailed by racist fantasies of black violence and licentiousness—and committed to rebuking those fantasies—many respectable blacks have perfected sublimation as a science and an art. Concerning the intricate protocols of respectability politics, see Evelyn Brooks Higginbotham, *Righteous Discontent: The Women's Movement in the Black Baptist Church, 1880–1920* (Cambridge, MA: Harvard University Press, 1993); Candice Jenkins, *Private Lives, Proper Relations: Regulating Black Intimacy* (Minneapolis: University of Minnesota Press, 2007); and see Cathy J. Cohen, "Deviance as Resistance: A New Research Agenda for the Study of Black Politics," *Du Bois Review: Social Science Research on Race* 1, no. 1 (2004).

5 I use "goods" as a double-entendre in this sentence to signify both a public good (that which is viewed as ethical, moral, benevolent, and beneficial to a general public and society) and a consumer good (a commodity intended for capitalist consumption and thus, from capital's perspective, viewed as ethical, moral, benevolent, and beneficial to the public).

6   For other poignant examples of Shange's black women artist protagonists, see her play *Spell #7*, in *Three Pieces* (New York: St. Martin's, 1992), and her novel *Sassafras, Cypress, and Indigo* (New York: Picador, 1996).

7   Black women fiction writers who achieved formidable critical and commercial success during this period include Shange, Toni Morrison, Alice Walker, Gayl Jones, Toni Cade Bambara, Octavia Butler, Gloria Naylor, and Terry McMillan, among others. Concerning literary criticism of the era, consider, for example, Barbara Smith's "Toward a Black Feminist Criticism" (1978); Deborah McDowell's "New Directions for Black Feminist Criticism" (1980); Hazel Carby's "'Woman's Era': Rethinking Black Feminist Theory" (1987); Barbara Christian's "The Race for Theory" (1987); Mae Henderson's "Speaking in Tongues: Dialogics, Dialectics, and the Black Woman Writer's Literary Tradition" (1989); and Valerie Smith's "Black Feminist Theory and the Representation of the 'Other'" (1989). All the preceding are anthologized in Michael Awkward, ed., *African American Literary Theory: A Reader* (New York: NYU Press, 2000). Farah Jasmine Griffin details these developments in "That the Mothers May Soar and the Daughters May Know Their Names: A Retrospective of Black Feminist Literary Criticism," *Signs* 32, no. 2 (winter 2007): 483–507.

8   Concerning the "feminist sex wars," see, for example, Carol Vance, ed., *Pleasure and Danger: Exploring Female Sexuality* (Boston: Routledge and Kegan Paul, 1984); and Catharine MacKinnon, *Feminism Unmodified: Discourse on Life and Law* (Cambridge, MA: Harvard University Press, 1987).

9   Brenda Lyons and Ntozake Shange, "Interview with Ntozake Shange," *The Massachusetts Review* 28, no. 4 (1987): 693.

10 Concerning black feminist vexation over *Eva's Man* at the time of its publication, see "All about Eva: Eva's Man," *New York Times Book Review* (May 16, 1976), 36–37; and Audre Lorde, "Eva's Man," in *I Am Your Sister: Collected and Unpublished Writings of Audre Lorde*, ed. Rudolph Byrd, Johnnetta Betsch Cole, and Beverly Guy-Sheftall (New York: Oxford University Press, 2009).

11 Shange, *Liliane*, 16. In describing wayward womanhood, I am riffing on Saidiya Hartman's extensive illumination of such womanhood in her *Wayward Lives, Beautiful Experiments: Intimate Histories of Social Upheaval* (New York: W. W. Norton, 2019).

12 Carol Margaret Davison describes the dental castration as "the most direct, shocking, and brutal attack on phallocentrism in African American literature." "'Love 'em and Lynch 'em': The Castration Motif in Gayl Jones's *Eva's Man*," *African American Review* 29, no. 3 (autumn 1995): 14.

13 Shange, qtd. in Jeffrey B. Rubin, *The Good Life: Psychoanalytic Reflections on Love, Ethics, Creativity, and Spirituality* (Albany: State University of New York Press, 2004), 14.

14 For another useful discussion of the theatricality of psychoanalysis, see Edward Baron Turk, "Comedy and Psychoanalysis: The Verbal Component," *Philosophy and Rhetoric* 12, no. 2 (spring 1979): 95–113.

15 Shange, *Liliane*, 3.

16 For readers first opening *Liliane*, there will likely be confusion about the meaning of the long dashes, the purpose of the line breaks, and the identities of the speakers. When I began the book, I read far enough to clarify who was who, and then I counted dashes backward to the very beginning of the section in order to chart their dialogue precisely.

17 Shange, *Liliane*, 179.

18 Shange, *Liliane*, 179.

19 Shange, *Liliane*, 4.

20 Shange, *Liliane*, 7.

21 Shange, *Liliane*, 6.

22 Thanks to Elizabeth Alexander for prompting me to think through the symbolism in this name.

23 Shange, *Liliane*, 44.

24 Shange, *Liliane*, 187.

25 Alice Walker, *In Search of Our Mother's Gardens: Womanist Prose* (New York: Harcourt, 2004), 241.

26 Shange, *Liliane*, 190.

27 Shange, *Liliane*, 193.

28 E. Franklin Frazier, *Black Bourgeoisie* (New York: Free Press, 1997), 232.

29 Shange, *Liliane*, 251.

30 In the novel *Sula*, Morrison describes similar outrage—among the black men of The Bottom—at the notion of a black woman willingly sleeping with a white man: "It was the men who gave her the final label, who fingerprinted her for all time. They were the ones who said she was guilty of the unforgivable thing—the thing for which there was no understanding, no excuse, no compassion. The route from which there was no way back, the dirt that could not ever be washed away. They said that Sula slept with white men. . . . There was nothing lower she could do, nothing filthier. . . . They insisted that all unions between white men and black women be rape; for a black woman to be willing was literally unthinkable." In Toni Morrison, *Sula* (New York: Knopf, 1973), 112–13.

31 Shange, *Liliane*, 180.

32 Shange, *Liliane*, 125–26.

33 Gayl Jones, *Eva's Man* (1976), in *The Healing, Corregidora, Eva's Man* (New York: Griot Editions, 1999), 509.

34 Shange, *Liliane*, 249–50.

35 Shange, *Liliane*, 16.

36 Brent Hayes Edwards, *The Practice of Diaspora: Literature, Translation, and the Rise of Black Internationalism* (Cambridge, MA: Harvard University Press, 2003), 220.

37 Edwards, *The Practice of Diaspora*, 220. For an extensive account of the vagabond international, see Edwards, chapter four, "Vagabond Internationalism: Claude McKay's *Banjo*," 187–240.

38 McKay, qtd. in Edwards, *The Practice of Diaspora*, 206.

39 McKay, qtd. in Edwards, *The Practice of Diaspora*, 206.

40 Shange, *Liliane*, 21.

41 Jones, *Eva's Man*, 518.

42 Shange, *Liliane*, 27.

43 See Margaret Mitchell, *Gone with the Wind* (New York: Macmillan, 1936), and the film adaptation, Victor Fleming, dir. *Gone with the Wind* (Beverly Hills, CA: Metro-Goldwyn-Mayer, 1939).

44 Shange, *Liliane*, 15–16.

45 Shange, *Liliane*, 19.

46 I am referring to the New Testament Book of John, chapter 1, verse 14: "And the Word was made flesh, and dwelt among us, (and we beheld his glory, the glory as of the only begotten of the Father) full of grace and truth" (King James Bible).

47 Shange, *Liliane*, 80.

48 Shange, *Liliane*, 81.

49 Shange, *Liliane*, 81.

50 Shange, *Liliane*, 80. Emphasis mine.

51 Shange, *Liliane*, 66.

52 Dino Franco Felluga, *Critical Theory: The Key Concepts* (New York: Routledge, 2015), 182.

53 Shange, *Liliane*, 68.

54 Shange, *Liliane*, 67.

55 Shange, *Liliane*, 74.

56 Lorde, "The Uses of Anger," in *Sister Outsider* (Berkeley, CA: Crossing Press, 1984), 127.

57 Shange, *Liliane*, 133.

58 Shange, *Liliane*, 134.

59 Shange, *Liliane*, 140.

60 Shange, *Liliane*, 139.

61 It is worth noting that the question *Who do you think you are?* might also be mobilized insurgently, to check and challenge someone's abuse of power.

62 Shange, *Liliane*, 141.

63 Shange, *Liliane*, 141.

64 Shange, *Liliane*, 143.

65 Shange, *Liliane*, 124.

66 Shange, *Liliane*, 124.

67 Shange, *Liliane*, 108–9.

68 Shange, *Liliane*, 108.

69 Shange, *Liliane*, 112–13.

70 Shange, *Liliane*, 112.

71 It is worth noting that Sawyer Malveaux also dons insurgent hair. According to Liliane, he "had a process. No I don't mean anything respectable-looking like Duke Ellington or Ray Robinson, but some wildass colored-looking 'do' that challenged Brook Benton and Lil Richard. The boy had nerve" (109). For all his "nerve" and all his violation of protocols for respectable presentation, Sawyer's

parents do not punish him. Once again, it appears that Sawyer's malehood protects him from the sort of reprisal meted out against his sister.

72 Shange, *Liliane*, 259.
73 Shange, *Liliane*, 258.
74 Shange, *Liliane*, 259.
75 Shange, *Liliane*, 258.
76 Shange, *Liliane*, 261.
77 Shange, *Liliane*, 240, 242.
78 Althusser distinguishes between the "repressive state apparatus" and "ideological state apparatus" in "Ideology and Ideological State Apparatuses (Notes Towards an Investigation)" (1970) in *Cultural Theory: An Anthology*, ed. Imre Szeman, Timothy Kaposy (Oxford: Wiley-Blackwell, 2010).
79 Shange, *Liliane*, 259.
80 Wolfgang Karrer, "Gayl Jones: Asylum," in *The African American Short Story 1970 to 1990: A Collection of Critical Essays*, ed. Wolfgang Karrer and Barbara Puschmann-Nalenz (Trier, Germany: Wissenschaftlicher Verlag Trier, 1993), 96.
81 Shange, *Liliane*, 261.
82 Shange, *Liliane*, 261–62.
83 Shange, *Liliane*, 263.
84 Shange, *Liliane*, 265.
85 Ntozake Shange, *Three Pieces* (New York: St. Martin's, 1992), xii.
86 Shange, *Three Pieces*, ix–xvi.
87 Shange, *Three Pieces*, xii.
88 Hortense Spillers, "Mama's Baby, Papa's Maybe: An American Grammar Book," *Diacritics* 17, no. 2 (summer 1987): 261.
89 Shange, *Three Pieces*, xiii.
90 Phillip U. Effiong, *In Search of a Model for African-American Drama: A Study of Selected Plays by Lorraine Hansberry, Amiri Baraka, and Ntozake Shange* (Lanham, MD: University Press of America, 2000), 132.
91 Shange, *Liliane*, 241–42.
92 Shange, *Liliane*, 257.
93 Shange, *Liliane*, 265.
94 Shange, *Liliane*, 262–63.

Chapter Five: "The People inside My Head, Too"

1 For critical discussions of feminist, womanist, and broadly woman-empowering praxis in hip-hop, see Joan Morgan, "Fly-Girls, Bitches, and Hoes: Notes of a Hip-Hop Feminist," *Social Text* 45 (winter 1995); Imani Perry, *Prophets of the Hood: Politics and Poetics in Hip Hop* (Durham, NC: Duke University Press, 2004); Janell Hobson and R. Dianne Bartlow, "Introduction: Representin': Women, Hip-Hop, and Popular Music," *Meridians* 8, no. 1 (2008); Cheryl L. Keyes, "Empowering Self, Making Choices, Creating Spaces: Black Female Identity via Rap Music Performance," *The Journal of American Folklore* 113, no. 449 (summer 2000).

2 *Miseducation* set the record for the highest first-week sales for a solo female debut in the history of the American *Billboard* chart. See Edna Gundersen, "Lauryn Hill's Debut Smashes Record," *USA Today*, September 3, 1998.

3 Regarding Hill as "genius," the *Amsterdam News* celebrated Hill's "creative genius" (Okoampa-Ahoofe); popular R&B musician John Legend would later declare, "She's truly a genius"; *Rolling Stone* would retrospectively refer to Hill's status as "self contained musical genius" (Touré); and *The Atlantic* would later emphasize that "Hill's genius came not from her proximity to her Fugees bandmates, Wyclef Jean and Pras Michél, but from within" (Giorgis). See Kwame Okoampa-Ahoofe Jr., "The Creative Genius of Lauryn Hill," *New York Amsterdam News*, February 17, 2000, 18; John Legend qtd. in "A Dream Comes True for John Legend," Sony Urban Music/Columbia Records, August 23, 2005, https://www.sony.com/content/sony/en/en_us/SCA/company-news/press-releases/sony-music-entertainment/2005/a-dream-comes-true-for-john-legend.html; Touré, "The Mystery of Lauryn Hill," *Rolling Stone*, October 30, 2003, http://www.rollingstone.com/news/story/5940100/the_mystery_of_lauryn_hill; Hannah Giorgis, "The Complicated Female Genius of Lauryn Hill," *The Atlantic*, August 27, 2018, https://www.theatlantic.com/entertainment/archive/2018/08/the-complicated-female-genius-of-lauryn-hill/568612/.

Concerning Hill as "prophet," the *New York Times* designated Hill a "visionary" issuing a "prophet's voice," and characterized *Miseducation* as "miraculous" (Powers); the *Village Voice* would declare, "months before [the 9/11 attacks]—on the Fourth of July, no less, at an African Arts Festival in Brooklyn—Lauryn was the lone hiphop voice making prophetic pronouncements: *I don't respect your system. I won't protect your system. The system is a joke. You'd be smart to save your soul, and escape this mind control. These traditions are a lie*" (Lewis); and *Trace* magazine would publish a feature on Hill: "The Prophet: Lauryn Hill" (Grunitzky). See Ann Powers, "Crossing Back Over from Profane to Sacred," *New York Times*, August 23, 1998, https://search.proquest.com/docview/431022705?accountid=14696; Miles Marshall Lewis, "Reality Soundbites: Lauryn Hill's *MTV Unplugged 2.0*," *The Village Voice*, July 3–9, 2002, https://www.villagevoice.com/2002/07/02/reality-soundbites/, emphasis in original; Claude Grunitzky, "The Prophet: Lauryn Hill," *Trace Magazine*, July 2005.

4 Concerning Hill's supposed transformation to madwoman, see, for example, Sylvia Chan, "On the Verge: *Unplugged* Captures Lauryn Hill Unwound," *San Francisco Bay Guardian*, June 12, 2002; Roger Friedman, "Lauryn Hill: Brainwashed?," *FoxNews.com*, June 11, 2002; Josh Tyrangiel, "Unplugged and Unglued," *Time*, May 13, 2002.

5 Lauryn Hill, "Outro," *MTV Unplugged No. 2.0* (New York: Columbia/Sony, 2002).

6 John Legend and Lauryn Hill, "So High (Cloud 9 Remix)," Getting Out Our Dreams/Sony Urban Music/Columbia, 2005; Hill, "Outro," *Unplugged*.

7 Farah Jasmine Griffin astutely asserts that "since the earliest days of our nation, black women were thought to be incapable of possessing genius; their achieve-

ments were considered the very opposite of intellectual accomplishment. All persons of African descent were thought to be unfit for advanced intellectual endeavor. Black women in particular were body, feeling, emotion and sexuality." In Farah Jasmine Griffin, *If You Can't Be Free, Be a Mystery: In Search of Billie Holiday* (New York: One World/Ballantine, 2002), 14.

Also aware of the racist-sexist logics informing conferral of the *genius* title in American popular culture, Hill herself suggests, "They'll never throw the genius title to a sister. They'll just call her a 'diva' and think it's a compliment," in "Lauryn Hill Speaks Out on How Motherhood Made Her Sexy and Why She's Not a Diva," *Jet*, February 8, 1999, 39.

8 The following passage is from Hill's description of her teenage sociocultural geography: "'You'll see that my house is right on the borderline of the suburbs and the ghetto,' Hill says, pointing to the projects of Newark that loom just beyond her family's backyard fence. 'I always had this duality. I went to school with a lot of white kids—it was really like a suburban environment—but I lived with black kids. . . . I grew up with two kinds of people in my life." See Alec Foege, "Fugees: Leaders of the New Cool," *Rolling Stone*, September 5, 1996, https://www.rollingstone.com/music/music-news/the-fugees-leaders-of-the-new-cool-244125/.

9 See, for example, Lauryn Hill, "Doo Wop (That Thing)," *The Miseducation of Lauryn Hill* (Ruffhouse/Columbia, 1998).

10 My thoughts on Hill's performance of pain are influenced by Daphne Brooks's lecture "Bring the Pain," which was delivered at Columbia University's Institute for Research in African American Studies in December 2009.

11 Regarding Billie Holiday (perhaps the quintessential icon of black womanhood in pain in popular music), scholar Monica Casper cautions that "reading the singer's legacy primarily through a lens of trauma transforms her into a kind of spectacle, not unlike the racialized showcase of lynching itself. Billie Holiday was a woman, not a song. . . . And she was/is not merely the embodiment of historical trauma." See Monica Casper, "Race, Trauma, and 'Strange Fruit,'" *The Feminist Wire*, April 7, 2012, https://thefeministwire.com/2012/04/on-race-trauma-and-strange-fruit/.

12 Elizabeth Alexander, "'Can You Be BLACK and Look at This?': Reading the Rodney King Video(s)," *Public Culture* (fall 1994): 79.

13 Saidiya Hartman, *Scenes of Subjection: Terror, Slavery, and Self-Making in Nineteenth-Century America* (New York: Oxford University Press, 1997), 3. See also Alexander, "Can You Be BLACK and Look at This?"; Deborah Walker King, *African Americans and the Culture of Pain* (Charlottesville: University of Virginia Press, 2008), 5–7.

14 Fugees, "Ready or Not," *The Score* (New York: Columbia Records/Sony, 1996).

15 See Gundersen, "Lauryn Hill's Debut Smashes Record."

16 "*Rolling Stone* 1998 Critics," http://www.rocklistmusic.co.uk/rolling.htm#98; "*Spin* Albums of the Year 1998," http://www.rocklistmusic.co.uk/spinend.htm; "Music: The Best of 1998 Music," *Time*, December 21, 1998, http://www.time.com/time/magazine/article/0,9171,989884,00.html.

17 Dan Collins, "VH1 Offers Best Album List," *CBSNews.com*, January 4, 2001, https://www.cbsnews.com/news/vh1-offers-best-album-list.

18 "The New Classics: Music," *Entertainment Weekly*, June 18, 2007, https://ew.com /article/2007/06/18/new-classics-music.

19 Alex Gale, "On My Own: The Best Solo Breakouts," *Bet.com*, October 2012, https://www.bet.com/music/photos/2012/10/on-my-own-the-best-solo -breakouts.html.

20 Sia Michel, "Dream-Girl Disenfranchised," *Village Voice*, September 1, 1998, https://www.villagevoice.com/1998/09/01/educating-lauryn/.

21 Ann Powers, "Crossing Back Over from Profane to Sacred," *New York Times*, August 23, 1998, http://www.nytimes.com/1998/08/23/arts/pop-jazz-crossing -back-over-from-profane-to-sacred.html?src=pm.

22 Joan Morgan, "They Call Me Ms. Hill," *Essence*, January 2006, http://www .essence.com/essence/themix/entertainment/0,16109,1149478,00.html.

23 "Lauryn Hill Is the Flyest MC Ever," *The Source*, September 1998.

24 "Music: The Best of 1998 Music," *Time*, December 21, 1998, http://www.time.com /time/magazine/article/0,9171,989884,00.html.

25 Hill's remarkable success was facilitated by several historical forces. She achieved her solo success at the commercial height of hip-hop; her musical and sartorial samples of the 1960s and 1970s tapped into an abiding cultural nostalgia and reverence for classic soul; she enjoyed the legacies of civil rights and second-wave feminism in forging spaces for black and female creativities; she tapped into a long legacy of brilliant black women performers who hadn't been granted the "genius" title; she benefited from Clinton-era multiculturalism that putatively celebrated cultural and creative difference; and she was, after all, extraordinarily multitalented.

26 Section epigraphs: Lauryn Hill and Sway Calloway, "Lauryn Hill: Redemption Song," *MTVNews.com*, 2001; Lauryn Hill, "I Gotta Find Peace of Mind," *Unplugged*; Pearl Cleage, "Looking for Lauryn," *Essence* (July 2002), 90.

27 Hill, "Outro."

28 In a *Rolling Stone* exposé of the legal drama around the album's credits and royalties, music journalist Touré writes that "the album was released crediting Hill with having produced, written, and arranged all the music except one track, and Hill was established as a self-contained musical genius." Four *Miseducation* musicians filed suit against Hill and alleged that they had not received proper credit or renumeration for the album. The case was resolved out of court for an undisclosed financial settlement, and Hill has been reticent and guarded in addressing it ever since. See Touré, "The Mystery of Lauryn Hill."

29 Hill explores police brutality and organized rebellion in "I Find It Hard to Say (Rebel)"; corruption among political and religious leaders is addressed in "The Mystery of Iniquity"; slavery and colonialism are invoked in "The Conquering Lion"; and misogyny and intimate partner abuse are explored in "Adam Lives in Theory," and "I Gotta Find Peace of Mind."

30 Hill, qtd. in Cleage, "Looking for Lauryn."

31 For Hill's description of her commitment to "black people" and particularly "black youth," see "Lauryn Hill–Howard Stern Interview 1996," YouTube video, October 23, 2007, https://www.youtube.com/watch?v=HDaG9Zz7J0Y. Concerning Hill's investment in "poor people," "the have-nots," and "the voiceless," see her interview in Peter Spirer, dir., *Rhyme and Reason* (Los Angeles: Miramax, 1997).

32 See, for example, "Oh, Jerusalem" and "Adam Lives in Theory."

33 Cathy Caruth, *Unclaimed Experience: Trauma, Narrative, and History* (Baltimore: Johns Hopkins University Press, 1996), 2–3.

34 Hill, qtd. in Morgan. For an extensive discussion of some of these "ghosts and demons," see Patricia Hill Collins, *Black Feminist Thought: Knowledge, Consciousness, and the Politics of Empowerment* (New York: Routledge, 2000), especially the chapters "Work, Family, and Black Women's Oppression," "Mammies, Matriarchs, and Other Controlling Images," and "Black Women's Love Relationships."

35 If this redemptive lover corresponds to a specific incarnated being, he might have been Rohan Marley, Hill's former "spiritual" husband (Mcgee and Tresniowski), son of musical insurgent Bob Marley, and father of the five eldest of Hill's now six children. Rohan Marley attends the *Unplugged* performance taping, and for a few seconds toward the song's climax the camera lingers over him as he solemnly watches Hill sing and weep. Tiffany McGee and Alex Tresniowski, "What Ever Happened to . . . Lauryn Hill?," *People*, August 18, 2008, http://www.people.com/people/archive/article/0,,20221692,00.html.

36 In his 2013 autobiography *Purpose: An Immigrant Story*, Wyclef Jean writes that "Lauryn would go from extreme passion to extreme anger with little warning." Further, he writes "since [their romantic relationship] didn't work out—and it tore her up emotionally—a lot of people blamed me for Lauryn's emotional instability and artistic inconsistency afterward," and "I've been told by many angry people who are also her fans that if I hadn't messed with her, she would not have gone so insane" (68). Wyclef Jean and Anthony Bozza, *Purpose: An Immigrant Story* (New York: HarperCollins, 2012).

37 See Lauryn Hill, "Adam Lives in Theory," "The Mystery of Iniquity," and "Oh Jerusalem," *Unplugged*.

38 See Freud, "Repression," in *The Freud Reader*, ed. Peter Gay (New York: W. W. Norton, 1989), 568–71.

39 Hill, "Outro."

40 Fugees, "Manifest/Outro," *The Score* (New York: Columbia Records/Sony, 1996).

41 Roger Friedman, "Lauryn Hill: Brainwashed?," *FoxNews.com*, June 11, 2002, http://www.foxnews.com/story/0,2933,54993,00.html.

42 Sylvia Chan, "On the Verge: *Unplugged* Captures Lauryn Hill Unwound," *San Francisco Bay Guardian*, June 12, 2002, http://www.sfbg.com/36/37/art_music_lauryn.html.

43 Robert Hilburn, "Hill Continues Her Lofty Course," *Los Angeles Times*, July 15, 2002, http://articles.latimes.com/2002/jul/15/entertainment/et-hilburn15.

44 Josh Tyrangiel, "Unplugged and Unglued," May 13, 2002, http://www.time.com /time/magazine/article/0,9171,1002421,00.html.

45 David Browne, "Review: Lauryn Hill's 'Unplugged' Draining," *Entertainment Weekly*, May 8, 2002, https://www.cnn.com/2002/SHOWBIZ/Music/05/08/ew .rec.mus.hill/.

46 Keith Murphy, "7 Ways Lauryn Hill Can Make Us Forget a Decade of Crazy," Vibe.com, July 10, 2010, https://www.vibe.com/2010/07/7-ways-lauryn-hill-can -make-us-forget-decade-crazy.

47 Wyclef Jean, qtd. in Brian Hiatt, "Wyclef Jean Q&A: How the Ex-Fugee Got His Groove Back," *Rolling Stone*, November 29, 2007, http://www.rollingstone.com /music/news/wyclef-jean-q-a-how-the-ex-fugee-got-his-groove-back-20071129. After the Fugees' tremendous success, some pundits wondered whether Hill's talent was subordinate to—or even ventriloquized by—Jean (See Touré 2003). Some of these misgivings were surely symptomatic of racist-sexist logics that were unable to accept the existence of (black) female genius. If Jean believes that Hill's success relied upon his genius, he might be the figure who "says it's impossible without him," in "I Gotta Find Peace of Mind" (that is, "impossible" for Hill to have a viable career without him on her production credits list). *Miseducation* proved this proposition false—but incited its own controversy over credit and intellectual property.

48 See Cleage, "Looking for Lauryn"; and Morgan, "They Call Me Ms. Hill."

49 See Aeschylus, *The Oresteia*, trans. Robert Fagles (New York: Penguin, 1984). For a feminist reading of Cassandra, see Schapira, *The Cassandra Complex: Living with Disbelief*.

50 Cornel West, "The Making of an American Radical Democrat of African Descent," *The Cornel West Reader* (New York: Basic Civitas Books, 2000), 14. Perhaps the two most prominent Judeo-Christian prophets, Moses and Jesus Christ, are exemplars of this paradigm. Moses challenged Egyptian dominion, and Christ challenged the authority of the Pharisees and Romans.

51 "Lauryn Hill Speaks Out against Abusive Priests in the Church," *Jet,* January 12, 2004, 50.

52 Bill Donohue, "Lauryn Hill Flips Her Lid," *Catholic League*, January 22, 2004, https://www.catholicleague.org/lauryn-hill-flips-her-lid/.

53 In 2013 Hill explained, "Right now my focus is just being a good mother. If I could do that properly, I'd be really, really happy. If I could be half the parent that my parents were to me, then I'd be very happy. Like any woman on the planet who decides to have children, that's an extremely important role. You have these empty vessels that you have to fill with all the information, and all the knowledge and all the proper tools for them to end up being happy, healthy, compassionate, caring people. That's really crucial to me. So I love music, and I always put my 100% into making music, but now I have to put 200% into being a mother." Quoted in Simon Witter, "Lauryn Hill: 'I'm Not Afraid to Be the Person I Am,'" *The Guardian*, August 21, 2013, https://www.theguardian.com/music/2013/aug/21/rocks-back-pages-lauryn-hill.

54 Hill's eldest child, Zion, was born before the release of *Miseducation*.

55 Joan Morgan examines and exemplifies this sustained support in *She Begat This: 20 Years of the Miseducation of Lauryn Hill* (New York: Atria, 2018).

56 For an account of Hill's putatively difficult behaviors, see Zoe Chace, "The Many Voices of Lauryn Hill," *NPR: Music*, June 28, 2010, https://www.npr.org/2010/06/28/128149135/the-many-voices-of-lauryn-hill.

57 Rob Harvilla, "The Disorientation of Lauryn Hill," *The Village Voice*, August 7, 2007, https://www.villagevoice.com/2007/08/07/the-disorientation-of-lauryn-hill/.

58 Daphne Brooks, *Bodies in Dissent: Spectacular Performances of Race and Freedom, 1850–1910* (Durham, NC: Duke University Press, 2006), 4–5.

59 Harvilla, "The Disorientation of Lauryn Hill."

60 Thanks to Sylvia Chong for highlighting the irony of losing her physical voice while confronting voices in her head.

61 My observation that "she seems to believe that she is losing the whole world to gain back her soul" is a riff on Matthew 16:26 as rendered in the King James Bible, which reads: "For what shall it profit a man, if he shall gain the whole world, and lose his own soul?"

62 Hill and Calloway, "Lauryn Hill: Redemption Song."

63 Nicole Fleetwood, *Troubling Vision: Performance, Visuality, and Blackness* (Chicago: University of Chicago Press, 2011), 113.

64 McGee and Tresniowski, "What Ever Happened to . . . Lauryn Hill?"

65 Hortense Spillers, "Mama's Baby, Papa's Maybe: An American Grammar Book," *Diacritics* 17, no. 2 (summer 1987), 65.

66 Hill, qtd. in Morgan, "They Call Me Ms. Hill."

67 Hill, qtd. in Morgan, "They Call Me Ms. Hill."

68   Henry Louis Gates Jr., *The Signifyin' Monkey: A Theory of African-American Literary Criticism* (New York: Oxford University Press, 1988), xxiv, xxvii. This aptly applies to Hill's provocative retooling of the show tune "My Favorite Things." The most iconic version of "My Favorite Things" is performed principally by Julie Andrews on the soundtrack to the 1965 film version of *The Sound of Music*. The music is composed by Rodgers and the lyrics are written by Hammerstein.

69 Footage from this performance can be viewed at Mcoast, "Lauryn Hill in Houston Texas oct 31 2012 Live New Sing Black Rage/and Explain [*sic*]," YouTube video, November 1, 2012, https://www.youtube.com/watch?v=oo_fpRttaV4.

70 Hill, "Black Rage," *Life Is Good/Black Rage Tour*, October 31, 2012.

71 Discussing the *Life Is Good/Black Rage Tour*, Hill proclaimed: "As artists we have opportunity to help the public evolve, raise consciousness and awareness, teach, heal, enlighten and inspire in ways the democratic process may not be able to touch. So we keep it moving" (Hill, qtd. in Kennedy). See Gerrick D. Kennedy, "Nas, Ms. Lauryn Hill Announce Joint Fall Tour," *Los Angeles Times*, September 19, 2012, https://www.latimes.com/entertainment/music/la-xpm-2012-sep-19-la-et-ms-nas-ms-lauryn-hill-announce-joint-tour-20120919-story.html.

72 Audre Lorde, "The Uses of Anger," in *Sister Outsider* (Berkeley, CA: Crossing Press, 1984), 280.

73 Brittney Cooper, *Eloquent Rage: A Black Feminist Discovers Her Superpower* (New York: St. Martin's, 2018), 5–6.

74 Regarding Hill's role in the film, director Göran Hugo Olsson explains: "We had mutual friends, and through them, I knew she was into Fanon. She was in prison at the time for tax problems. I wrote to her, and she responded immediately saying, 'I'm reading Fanon in my cell every evening.' She was released on a Friday. Monday morning she went into the studio." See Göran Hugo Olsson and Rachel Segal Hamilton, "'Concerning Violence' Is a New Meditation on Africa's Struggle for Freedom," *Vice.com*, November 24, 2014, https://www.vice.com/en_us/article/jmb47p/concerning-violence-rachel-segal -hamilton-320.

75 For especially virulent examples of the circulation of these images, see, for example, Perez Hilton, "Lauryn Hill Is a Song Thief! And a Bitch!," July 31, 2007, https://perezhilton.com/lauryn-hill-is-a-song-thief; and Perez Hilton, "Lauryn Hill Has Completely Lost Her Mind!," July 26, 2007, https://perezhilton.com /lauryn-hill-has-completely-lost-her-mind.

76 Lee Hildebrand, "Late Start, New Approach Disappoint Lauryn Hill Fans at Oakland Concert," *San Francisco Chronicle*, June 29, 2007, https://www.sfgate .com/music/article/Late-start-new-approach-disappoint-Lauryn-Hill-2584129 .php.

77 Phillip Mlynar, "Lauryn Hill's Top 5 Career-Torpedoing Tendencies," *L.A. Weekly*, February 14, 2012, https://www.laweekly.com/lauryn-hills-top-5-career -torpedoing-tendencies/.

78 Thanks to Elizabeth Alexander for encouraging me to think through Hill's poten-tial bohemianism.

79 See Grunitzky, "The Prophet: Lauryn Hill"; Morgan, "They Call Me Ms. Hill."

80 Jada Yuan, "Lauryn Hill: Not Crazy after All These Years?," *New York Magazine*, October 26, 2006, http://nymag.com/daily/intel/2006/10/lauryn_hill_not _crazy_after_al.html.

81 Mikhail Bakhtin, *Rabelais and His World* (Bloomington: Indiana University Press, 1984), 26. Emphasis mine.

82 Bakhtin, *Rabelais and His World*, 39.

83 Hill, qtd. in Ernest Hardy, "Fugee-L.A.," in *L.A. Weekly*, February 10, 2006, http://www.laweekly.com/index.php?option=com_lawcontent&task=view&id =12609&Itemid=125.

84 In "Notes on Deconstructing 'the Popular,' " cultural theorist Stuart Hall writes that "opposing arguments are easy to mount. [In contrast,] changing the terms of an argument is exceedingly difficult, since the dominant definition of the problem acquires, by repetition, and by the weight of the credibility of those who propose or subscribe it, the warrant of 'common sense.' Arguments which hold to this defi-nition of the problem are read as straying from 'the point.' So part of the struggle is over the way the problem is formulated: the terms of the debate, and the logic it entails" (5). Stuart Hall, "Notes on Deconstructing 'the Popular,' " in *Cultural Theory and Popular Culture: A Reader (Fourth Edition)*, ed. John Story (Essex,

UK: Pearson Education, 2009). What I have described as Hill's transgressive disavowal corresponds to what Hall labels an "opposing argument." Her subversive
embrace evinces the process of "changing the terms of the argument." She shifts
from the former to the latter in the course of just a few sentences.

85 West utters these words on the mixtape version of "All Falls Down" on *Freshman Adjustment* (Chicago: Chi Town Gettin' Down, 2004).

86 Austin Scaggs, "Kanye West: No Kicks from Champagne," *Rolling Stone*, December 30, 2004, https://www.rollingstone.com/music/news/kanye-west-no-kicks -from-champagne-20041230.

87 Cornel West similarly describes "a significant black middle class, highly anxiety-ridden, insecure, willing to be co-opted and incorporated into the powers that be, concerned with racism to the degree that it poses constraints on upward social mobility." See Cornel West, "The Political Intellectual," *The Cornel West Reader* (New York: Basic Civitas Books, 2000), 284.

88 Joe Coscarelli, "Kanye West Is Hospitalized for 'Psychiatric Emergency' Hours after Canceling Tour," *New York Times*, November 21, 2016, https://www.nytimes .com/2016/11/21/arts/music/kanye-west-hospitalized-exhaustion.html.

89 In an interview with radio personality Charlamagne tha God, West declared, "The fact that [Trump] won, it's like it proves something. It proves that anything is possible in America . . . that Donald Trump is the president of America. . . . When I see an outsider infiltrate, I connect with that." See Kanye West, "Kanye West/Charlamagne Interview," YouTube video, May 1, 2018, https://youtu.be /zxwfDlhJIpw.

90 Kanye West, @kanyewest, "You don't have to agree with trump but the mob can't make me not love him. We are both dragon energy. He is my brother. I love everyone. I don't agree with everything anyone does. That's what makes us individuals. And we have the right to independent thought." Twitter, April 25, 2018, 12:30 p.m., https://twitter.com/kanyewest/status/989179757651574784 ?s=20.

91 "Kanye West Stirs Up TMZ Newsroom Over Trump, Slavery, Free Thought," May 1, 2018, https://www.tmz.com/2018/05/01/kanye-west-tmz-live-slavery -trump.

92 Kanye West, @kanyewest, "The reason why I brought up the 400 years point is because we can't be mentally imprisoned for another 400 years. We need free thought now. Even the statement was an example of free thought[.] It was just an idea." Twitter, May 1, 2018, 7:56 p.m.

93 Kanye West, @kanyewest, "To make myself clear. of course I know that slaves did not get shackled and put on a boat by free will." Twitter, May 1, 2018, 7:30 p.m.; Kanye West, @kanyewest, "My point is for us to have stayed in that position even though the numbers were on our side means that we were mentally enslaved." Twitter, May 1, 2018, 7:30 p.m., https://twitter.com/kanyewest/status /991459400018624512.

94 Jenny Bourne, "Slavery in the United States," *EH.Net Encyclopedia*, March 26, 2008, http://eh.net/encyclopedia/slavery-in-the-united-states.

95 See Nell Irvin Painter, "Soul-Murder and Slavery: Toward a Fully Loaded Cost Accounting," in *Southern History across the Color Line* (Chapel Hill: University of North Carolina Press, 2002).

96 Kanye West, "Kanye West/Charlemagne Interview," May 1, 2018, YouTube video, https://www.youtube.com/watch?v=zxwfDlhJIpw.

97 Kanye West, "Yikes," *Ye* (New York: GOOD Music/Def Jam, 2018).

98 For a persuasive critique of the trope of the "supercrip"—a disabled person who has supposedly surmounted the "tragedy" of their disability and can thus be a source of melodramatic inspiration and an object of patronizing praise from nondisabled people—see Sami Schalk, "Reevaluating the Supercrip," *Journal of Literary and Cultural Disability Studies* 10, no. 1 (2016): 71–86.

99 In using the terms *beautiful* and *twisted*, I am alluding to the title of West's fifth studio album, *My Beautiful Dark Twisted Fantasy* (New York: Roc-A-Fella/Def Jam, 2010). Madness is a frequent fixation of West's albums: deep depression and melancholia are the foremost moods and themes on *808s and Heartbreak* (2008); *My Beautiful Dark and Twisted Fantasy* (2010) stages megalomania and narcissistic excess; and *Yeezus* (2013) seems intent on generating a sonic and lyrical chaos.

100 Regarding the range of laudatory and derogatory assessments of Hill's career, see Morgan, *She Begat This*; Chace; McGee and Tresniowski; Murphy; Mylnar; Yuan.

101 "Ms Lauryn Hill," June 8, 2012, https://mslaurynhill.com/.

102 See Cleage, "Looking for Lauryn."

103 Hill, qtd. in Morgan, "They Call Me Ms. Hill."

104 Hill and Calloway, "Lauryn Hill: Redemption Song."

Chapter Six: The Joker's Wild, but That Nigga's Crazy

The phrase *that nigga's crazy* is a modification of the title of Richard Pryor's 1974 stand-up album, *That Nigger's Crazy*. I have deliberately softened the "er" to "a," changing "nigger" to "nigga." The latter pronunciation corresponds to its casual and/or affectionate use in the black vernacular milieu that I inhabit.

1 Christopher John Farley, "Dave Speaks," *Time*, May 14, 2005, http://content.time.com/time/magazine/article/0,9171,1061512,00.html. Emphasis mine.

2 For more extensive exploration of blackface minstrelsy, see Eric Lott, *Love and Theft: Blackface Minstrelsy and the American Working Class* (New York: Oxford University Press, 1993); W. T. Lhamon, *Raising Cain: Blackface Performance from Jim Crow to Hip Hop* (Cambridge, MA: Harvard University Press, 2000); and Louis Chude-Sokei, *The Last "Darky": Bert Williams, Black-on-Black Minstrelsy, and the African Diaspora* (Durham, NC: Duke University Press, 2006).

3 For compelling histories and readings of black abjection as American amusement, see Lott, *Love and Theft*; and Saidiya Hartman, *Scenes of Subjection: Terror, Slavery, and Self-Making in Nineteenth-Century America* (New York: Oxford University Press, 1997), especially the chapter "Innocent Amusements."

4 The sketch was originally titled "The Nigger Pixie," with footage depicting a blackface pixie haunting Rodney King and Tiger Woods. However, the material that made it to television was heavily truncated and absent the King and Woods scenes. See Devin Gordon, "Fears of a Clown," *Newsweek*, May 15, 2005, https://www.newsweek.com/fears-clown-118667. The sketch was part of a broader series of sketches entitled "Stereotype Pixies"—a "Hispanic," "Asian," and "white" pixie also make appearances—but none are loaded with such onerous culture baggage as the black(face) pixie. See *Chappelle's Show—The Lost Episodes*, "In-Flight Meal," Episode 2, aired July 16, 2006, writ. Dave Chappelle and Neal Brennan, Comedy Central (2006), DVD.

5 Black feminist food studies scholar Psyche Williams-Forson is completing a book-length study about the politics of food shaming in black life, tentatively called "Eating While Black: Food Shaming and Food Policing in Black Communities." See Psyche Williams-Forson, "The Future of Food Studies—Intersectionality," *Notes on the Field* (Graduate Association for Food Studies) 6, no. 1 (June 16, 2019), https://gradfoodstudies.org/2019/06/16/the-future-of-food-studies-intersectionality/.

6 For further rumination on the material and symbolic significance of fried chicken and black life, see Psyche Williams-Forson, *Building Houses Out of Chicken Legs: Black Women, Food, and Power* (Chapel Hill: University of North Carolina Press, 2006).

7 Dave Chappelle and Oprah Winfrey, "Why Comedian Dave Chappelle Walked away from $50 Million | The Oprah Winfrey Show | OWN," aired February 2, 2006, YouTube.com, https://www.youtube.com/watch?v=tlScX2stRuo.

8 Chappelle and Winfrey, "Why Comedian Dave Chappelle Walked away from $50 Million."

9 See Farley, "Dave Speaks"; Chappelle and Winfrey, "Why Comedian Dave Chappelle Walked away from $50 Million."

10 See Josh Wolk, "Chappelle's No Show," *Entertainment Weekly*, May 11, 2005, https://ew.com/article/2005/05/11/chappelles-no-show/.

11 See Gary Susman, "New 'Chappelle' DVD Is Fastest-Selling TV Disc Ever," *Entertainment Weekly*, June 1, 2005, https://ew.com/article/2005/06/01/new-chappelle-dvd-fastest-selling-tv-disc-ever/.

12 Dave Chappelle and James Lipton, "Dave Chappelle," *Inside the Actor's Studio*, aired February 12, 2008, Bravo TV.

13 Oprah Winfrey interviewed Chappelle about widespread rumors that he was mentally ill and/or addicted to crack-cocaine. Chappelle denied both allegations. See Chappelle and Winfrey, "Why Comedian Dave Chappelle Walked away from $50 Million."

14 Mark Anthony Neal, *Soul Babies: Black Popular Culture and the Post-soul Aesthetic* (New York: Routledge, 2002), 3.

15 A notable example of this irreverence is a season 2 sketch called "Profiles in Courage: Toilet Pioneer." When a black man named "Cyrus Holloway" gets a bad case of "mud butt" (diarrhea) and rushes to a white bathroom, he initiates the de-

segregation of toilets in Alabama. The sketch includes lots of scatological humor (including gleeful talk of "mud butt" and "doody"), a bag of feces, plenty of flatulent noises, and America's first civil rights "shit-in." See "Profiles in Courage: Toilet Pioneer," *Chappelle's Show—Season Two*, Episode 13, aired April 14, 2004, written by Dave Chappelle and Neal Brennan, *Comedy Central* (2005), DVD.

16 Chappelle and Lipton, "Dave Chappelle." For further information on Chappelle's mother, see "Yvonne Seon," *The History Makers: The Nation's Largest African-American Video Oral History Collection*, https://www.thehistorymakers.org/biography/yvonne-seon-39.

17 Chappelle and Lipton, "Dave Chappelle."

18 For example, Tyrone Simpson examines the "black nationalist" inflections in Chappelle's comedy. See Tyrone Simpson, "When Keeping It Real Goes Wrong: Pryor, Chappelle, and the Comedic Politics of Post-Soul," in *Richard Pryor: The Life and Legacy of a "Crazy" Black Man*, ed. Audrey Thomas McCluskey (Bloomington: Indiana University Press, 2008), 106–38.

19 Chappelle and Lipton, "Dave Chappelle."

20 In a season 1 sketch called "World's Greatest Wars," Tyrone Biggums meets a gang leader named "Corn Row Wallace" in 1982, when the two become cellmates in prison. Tyrone raves about a new type of cocaine—crack cocaine—and how lucrative it will be once it hits the street en masse. Corn Row instructs his minions to start selling it, and thus sparks the rise of crack cocaine in Chicago. See "World's Greatest Wars," *Chappelle's Show—Season One*, Episode 10, aired March 26, 2003, written by Dave Chappelle and Neal Brennan, Comedy Central (2004), DVD.

21 Chappelle and Lipton, "Dave Chappelle."

22 Bambi Haggins, *Laughing Mad: The Black Comic Persona in Post-Soul America* (New Brunswick, NJ: Rutgers University Press, 2007), 179.

23 Stan Latham, dir., *Dave Chappelle: Killin' Them Softly*, aired July 26, 2000, HBO.

24 DMX, "Party Up (Up in Here)," . . . *And Then There Was X* (New York: Def Jam Records, 1999).

25 DMX, also known as Earl Simmons, came to fame in the late 1990s and achieved extraordinary success. From 1998 through 2003, he released five number-one albums—and became the first and only artist in the history of the chart to have his first five albums debut atop the *Billboard* 200. See "DMX Proves 'Grand Champ' on Album Chart," *Billboard.com*, September 24, 2003, https://www.billboard.com/articles/news/68953/dmx-proves-grand-champ-on-album-chart.

Since then, he has been a frequent subject of tabloid attention for alleged drug abuse, erratic behavior, and repeated imprisonments on charges including drug possession, animal cruelty, attempted carjacking, and impersonation of a law enforcement officer. For an overview of DMX's travails and triumphs, see Mark Anthony Green, "Dark Man X: The Resurrection," *GQ*, September 23, 2019, https://www.gq.com/story/dmx-the-resurrection. In late 2010 at a sentencing for probation violation, an Arizona judge suggested he had an "undiagnosed mental condition" and ordered him to spend seven months in a mental health unit of Arizona State Prison. See Niki D'Andrea, "DMX Moved to Mental-Health Unit at Arizona State Prison Complex," *Phoenix New Times* blog, December 27, 2010, https://www.phoenixnewtimes.com/news/dmx-moved-to-mental-health-unit -at-arizona-state-prison-complex-6645350. DMX discloses his bipolar disorder in this interview soon after his release from that Arizona Prison, in "DMX Speaks on His Bipolar Disorder, Drug Addiction—ABC15," YouTube.com, August 11, 2011, https://www.youtube.com/watch?v=tlScX2stRuohttps://www.youtube .com/watch?time_continue=8&v=VZ6QkCS8gNQ&feature=emb_title.

26 Latham, dir., *Dave Chappelle: Killin' Them Softly*.

27 Regarding reports that Chappelle was dealing with a "really quite serious" mental health crisis, see Associated Press, "Report: Dave Chappelle in a Mental Health Facility," May 11, 2005, https://www.today.com/popculture/report-chappelle -mental-health-facility-wbna7821711. Concerning Chappelle's responses to said accusations, see Chappelle and Winfrey, "Why Comedian Dave Chappelle Walked away from $50 Million"; Chappelle and Lipton, "Dave Chappelle."

28 Latham, dir., *Dave Chappelle: Killin' Them Softly*.

29 Regarding the rate of unarmed black men killed by police, see Joe Fox, Adrian Blanco, Jennifer Jenkins, Julie Tate, and Wesley Lowery, "What We've Learned about Police Shootings 5 Years after Ferguson," *The Washington Post*, August 9, 2019, https://www.washingtonpost.com/nation/2019/08/09/what-weve-learned -about-police-shootings-years-after-ferguson/?arc404=true.

30 For data indicating that mentally ill people are sixteen times more likely to be killed in encounters with law enforcement, see Doris A. Fuller, H. Richard Lamb, Michael Biasotti, and John Snook, "Overlooked in the Undercounted: The Role of Mental Illness in Fatal Law Enforcement Encounters," Treatment Advocacy Center, 2015, TACReports.org/overlooked-undercounted. For an account of the peculiar perils facing those who are both black and seriously mentally ill, see Shaun King, "If You Are Black and in a Mental Health Crisis, 911 Can Be a Death Sentence," September 29, 2019, https://theintercept.com/2019/09/29/police -shootings-mental-health/.

31 The Stanford Open Policing Project—dedicated to "gathering, analyzing, and releasing records from millions of traffic stops by law enforcement agencies across the country" in order to "help researchers, journalists, and policymakers inves- tigate and improve interactions between police and the public"—reports that black people nationwide are 20 percent more likely to be stopped than their white counterparts. See "Findings," Stanford Open Policing Project, 2020, https:// openpolicing.stanford.edu/.

This discrepancy is far more dramatic in particular jurisdictions. For example, black motorists in Missouri and California are respectively 95 percent and 250 percent more likely to be pulled over than their white counterparts. See Associated Press, "Report: California Cops More Likely to Stop Black Drivers," January 2, 2020, https://www.usnews.com/news/best-states/california/articles /2020-01-02/report-california-cops-more-likely-to-stop-black-drivers; and

Associated Press, "Missouri Police Still Disproportionately Stop Black Drivers," May 29, 2020, https://www.usnews.com/news/best-states/missouri/articles/2020 -05-29/missouri-police-still-disproportionately-stop-black-drivers.

32 "The Niggar Family," *Chappelle's Show—Season Two*, Episode 2, aired January 28, 2004, written by Dave Chappelle and Neal Brennan, Comedy Central (2005), DVD.

33 "Dave Gets Revenge," *Chappelle's Show—The Lost Episodes,* Episode 1, aired July 9, 2006, written by Dave Chappelle and Neal Brennan, Comedy Central (2006), DVD.

34 Chappelle and Lipton, "Dave Chappelle."

35 Sigmund Freud, *Jokes and Their Relation to the Unconscious*, trans. James Strachey (New York: W. W. Norton, 1990), 122–23.

36 Mikhail Bakhtin, *Rabelais and His World* (Bloomington: Indiana University Press, 1984), 11.

37 Richard Gray II and Michael Putnam, "Exploring Niggerdom: Racial Inversion in Language Taboos in Chappelle's Show," in *The Comedy of Dave Chappelle*, ed. Kevin Wisniewski (Jefferson, NC: McFarland, 2009), 16.

38 This notion of reading upside down is inspired by the unnamed woman psychiatric detainee of Gayl Jones's 1977 short story, "Asylum." As a psychiatrist observes her and takes notes about her, she looks back—observing him and reading his notes, though they are upside down from her perspective. I adapt reading upside down as model for mad counterreading. See chapter 3.

39 "The Mad Real World," *Chappelle's Show—Season One*, Episode 6, aired February 26, 2003, written by Dave Chappelle and Neal Brennan, Comedy Central (2004), DVD.

40 See Vesla Mae Weaver, "Why White People Keep Calling the Cops on Black Americans," May 29, 2018, *Vox*, https://www.vox.com/first-person/2018/5/17 /17362100/starbucks-racial-profiling-yale-airbnb-911.

41 Regarding associations with madness and excess vis-à-vis this hip-hop idiom, see also Therí Alyce Pickens, *Black Madness :: Mad Blackness* (Durham, NC: Duke University Press, 2019), 51.

42 As noted in chapter 1, Foucault regards the ship of fools as a physical, material entity when describing it in *Madness and Civilization*. However, historians of medieval and early modern Europe have questioned whether ships of fools ever physically existed. Many believe that the ship of fools was only a literary and visual conceit. See Winifred B. Maher and Brendan Maher, "The Ship of Fools: Stultifera Navis or Ignis Fatuus?," *American Psychologist* 37, no. 7 (1982): 756–61.

43 "Fugue" was a psychiatric diagnosis that proliferated briefly in late nineteenth-century Europe. It purportedly entailed "mad travel": a compulsive wandering, often across great distances, accompanied by amnesia and dissociation. See Ian Hacking, *Mad Travelers: Reflections on the Reality of Transient Mental Illnesses* (Cambridge, MA: Harvard University Press, 2002).

44 Georg Wilhelm Friedrich Hegel, *The Philosophy of History* (New York: Dover, 1956), 99.

45 Hegel, *The Philosophy of History*, 93.

46 Concerning American opinions and notions of the continent of Africa, see Michael McCarthy, *Dark Continent: Africa as Seen by Americans* (Westport, CT: Greenwood, 1983); V. Y. Mudimbe, *The Idea of Africa* (Bloomington: Indiana University Press, 1994); Curtis Keim and Carolyn Somerville, *Mistaking Africa: Curiosities and Inventions of the American Mind*, 4th ed. (New York: Routledge, 2018).

47 For three instances of tabloids flippantly pairing and merging Africa and madness, see Sara Stewart, "What Are You Laughing At? Back from Africa, Back on Film, Dave Chappelle Won't Back Down," February 16, 2006, https://nypost.com/2006/02/19/what-are-you-laughing-at-back-from-africa-back-on-film-dave-chappelle-wont-back-down/; cganemccalla, "Top 5 Black Comic Meltdowns: Dave Chappelle Goes to Africa," *NewsOne.com*, November 17, 2008, https://newsone.com/40592/top-5-black-comic-meltdowns/; and Amos Barshad, "On The Skit That 'Killed' Chappelle's Show," *The Fader*, July 29, 2016, https://www.thefader.com/2016/07/29/skit-that-killed-chappelles-show.

For critical discussions of this association of "Africa" and madness in tabloid reporting around Chappelle, see John L. Jackson Jr., *Racial Paranoia: The Unintended Consequences of Political Correctness* (New York: Basic Books, 2008), vii–xiv; and Dannagal Goldthwaite Young, *Irony and Outrage: The Polarized Landscape of Rage, Fear, and Laughter in the United States* (New York: Oxford University Press, 2019), 128.

48 Farley, "Dave Speaks."

49 Christopher Farley, "On the Beach with Dave Chappelle," *Time*, May 15, 2005, http://content.time.com/time/arts/article/0,8599,1061415,00.html.

50 The facts of continental Africa are complicated: neocolonialisms, internecine warfare, genocide, and the proliferation of HIV/AIDS exist alongside African ingenuity, rich and complex cultural practices, progressive and liberatory struggles, and intense promise and optimism. Concerning the complicated sociopolitical dimensions of contemporary Africa, see Mahmood Mahdani, *Citizen and Subject: Contemporary Africa and the Legacy of Late Colonialism* (Princeton, NJ: Princeton University Press, 1996). For incisive discussions of African American fantasies of and longing for "Africa," see Saidiya Hartman, *Lose Your Mother: A Journey along the Atlantic Slave Route* (New York: Farrar, Straus and Giroux, 2007). See also Salamishah Tillet, "In the Shadow of the Castle: (Trans)Nationalism, African American Tourism, and Gorée Island," *Research in African Literatures* 40, no. 4 (2009): 122–41.

51 Dave Chappelle and Anderson Cooper, "Chappelle's Story," *Anderson Cooper 360*, aired July 10, 2006, CNN. Transcript at http://transcripts.cnn.com/transcripts/0607/10/acd.02.html.

52 Chappelle and Winfrey, "Why Comedian Dave Chappelle Walked away from $50 Million."

53 Five years before Chappelle's fateful trip to South Africa, the World Health Organization published an extensive study (including a ranking) of overall health infrastructure for 191 nations. The United States ranked number 37, above

all sub-Saharan African nations. See Ajay Tandon, Christopher Murray, Jeremy Lauer, and David Evans, "Measuring Overall Health System Performance for 191 Countries" (Geneva: World Health Organization, 2000), https://www.who.int /healthinfo/paper30.pdf.

54 Chappelle and Lipton, "Dave Chappelle."

55 Regarding complex and sometimes ambivalent attitudes that some African Americans hold about the African continent, see Bernard Makhosezwe Magubane, *The Ties That Bind: African-American Consciousness of Africa*, 2nd ed. (Trenton, NJ: African World Press, 1987); and Nemata Blyden, *African Americans and Africa: A New History* (New Haven, CT: Yale University Press, 2019).

56 Regarding that psychiatrist's role in encouraging Pryor to venture to Kenya, see Derrick Z. Jackson, "Opinion: The N-Word and Richard Pryor," *New York Times*, December 15, 2005, https://www.nytimes.com/2005/12/15/opinion/the -nwordand-richard-pryor.html.

57 Joe Layton, dir., *Richard Pryor: Live on the Sunset Strip* (Los Angeles: Columbia Pictures, 1982).

58 Concerning Pryor's journey to Kenya, see Richard Pryor, *Pryor Convictions* (New York: Knopf, 1995).

59 For incisive discussions of the affinities between Pryor and Chappelle, see Glenda Carpio, *Laughing Fit to Kill: Black Humor in the Fictions of Slavery* (New York: Oxford University Press, 2008); and Simpson, "When Keeping It Real Goes Wrong," 106–38.

60 Audrey McCluskey, "Richard Pryor: Comic Genius, Tortured Soul," in *Richard Pryor: The Life and Legacy of a "Crazy" Black Man*, ed. Audrey Thomas McCluskey (Bloomington: Indiana University Press, 2008), 1.

61 Ishmael Reed, *Conversations with Ishmael Reed*, ed. Bruce Dick and Amritjit Singh (Jackson: University Press of Mississippi, 1995), 22.

62 In his autobiography, Pryor candidly discusses struggles with abandonment, abuse, addiction, and mental health—and illuminates how those traumas inform and infuse his comedy. See Richard Pryor and Todd Gold, *Pryor Convictions* (New York: Knopf, 1995). Many of the essays in *Richard Pryor: The Life and Legacy of a "Crazy" Black Man*, also explore Pryor's incorporation of personal pain and precarity into his performances. Regarding the use of tragedy in Pryor's stand-up, see, for example, Jeff Margolis, dir., *Richard Pryor: Live in Concert*, MPI Home Video, 1979.

63 McCluskey, "Richard Pryor: Comic Genius, Tortured Soul," 12.

64 Pryor and Gold, *Pryor Convictions*, 187–88.

65 Pryor and Gold, *Pryor Convictions*, 189–90.

66 Pryor, qtd. in Gene Siskel, "Richard Pryor Comes Clean in Harrowing Recap of Life," *Chicago Tribune*, May 4, 1986, https://www.chicagotribune.com/news/ct -xpm-1986-05-04-8602010470-story.html.

67 Among the most infamous historical examples of antiblack jurisprudence in the United States are the "Scottsboro Boys" case in Alabama in 1931 and the "Central Park Five" case in New York in 1989–90. In both incidents, groups of black boys

and young men were wrongly convicted of gang raping white women or a white woman. Regarding the Scottsboro case, see Dan T. Carter, *Scottsboro: A Tragedy of the American South* (Baton Rouge: Louisiana State University Press, 2007). Concerning the Central Park Five case, see Sarah Burns, *The Central Park Five: The Untold Story behind One of New York City's Most Infamous Crimes* (New York: Knopf, 2011).

68 See Sophia Kerby, "The Top 10 Most Startling Facts about People of Color and Criminal Justice in the United States: A Look at the Racial Disparities Inherent in Our Nation's Criminal-Justice System," Center for American Progress, March 13, 2012, https://www.americanprogress.org/issues/race/news/2012/03/13/11351/the-top-10-most-startling-facts-about-people-of-color-and-criminal-justice-in-the-united-states/. I hasten to emphasize the role of wealth and fame in influencing juridical outcomes. Simpson and Jackson's "not guilty" verdicts likely reflect their access to ultra-expensive, high-powered legal teams who service celebrities in the entertainment industry.

69 For a thorough examination of racial injustice in American law enforcement and juridical systems, see, for example Michelle Alexander, *The New Jim Crow: Mass Incarceration in the Age of Colorblindness* (New York: The New Press, 2012).

70 Concerning racial disparities in conviction and sentencing, see "Racial Disparities in Sentencing," American Civil Liberties Union, 2014, https://www.aclu.org/sites/default/files/assets/141027_iachr_racial_disparities_aclu_submission_0.pdf.

71 Chappelle and Winfrey, "Why Comedian Dave Chappelle Walked away from $50 Million."

72 Jackson, *Racial Paranoia*, 1.

73 On Chappelle's conspiracy theories about the origin of crack cocaine and AIDS, see "Pretty White Girl Sings Dave's Thoughts," *Chappelle's Show—Season One*, Episode 2, aired January 29, 2003, written by Dave Chappelle and Neal Brennan, Comedy Central (2004), DVD. Concerning the prison-industrial complex, see "Celebrity Trial Jury Selection," *Chappelle's Show—Season Two*, Episode 9, aired March 17, 2004, written by Dave Chappelle and Neal Brennan, Comedy Central (2005), DVD.

74 Hazel Rowley, *Richard Wright: The Life and Times* (New York: Henry Holt, 2001), 490–91.

75 William Grier and Price Cobbs, *Black Rage* (New York: Basic Books, 1992), 206.

76 I am riffing on Toni Morrison's trenchant insight on black women and madness: "Black women had to deal with post-modern problems in the nineteenth century and earlier. . . . Certain kinds of dissolution, the loss of and the need to reconstruct certain kinds of stability. Certain kinds of madness, deliberately going mad in order, as one of the characters [from the novel *Beloved*] says, 'in order not to lose your mind.' These strategies for survival made the truly modern person. They're a response to predatory Western phenomena." Toni Morrison, qtd. in Paul Gilroy, "Living Memory: A Meeting with Toni Morrison," in *Small Acts* (Essex, UK: Serpent's Tail, 1993), 178.

77 Concerning the incorporation of conspiracy theories into black American political consciousness, see Anita M. Waters, "Conspiracy Theories as Ethnosociologies: Explanation and Intention in African American Political Culture," *Journal of Black Studies* 28 (September 1997): 112–25; Jackson, *Racial Paranoia*; and R. L'Heureux Lewis, "Racial Conspiracy and Research," in *The Search for the Legacy of the USPHS Syphilis Study at Tuskegee*, ed. Ralph V. Katz and Rueben Warren (Lanham, MD: Lexington Books, 2011).

78 Paul Ricoeur, *Freud and Philosophy: An Essay on Interpretation* (New Haven, CT: Yale University Press, 1970), 30–36.

79 Eve Kosofsky Sedgwick, "Paranoid Reading and Reparative Reading, or, You're So Paranoid, You Probably Think This Essay Is about You," in *Touching Feeling: Affect, Pedagogy, Performativity* (Durham, NC: Duke University Press, 2003), 123–51.

80 Bambi Haggins discusses Chappelle's frequent forays into the buddy genre and his skill in "transforming [buddy characters] into overdetermined and self-conscious parodies of those character types" (Haggins, *Laughing Mad*, 184). She narrates Chappelle's rise to cinematic fame in buddy films including *Robin Hood: Men in Tights*, *Half Baked*, and *You've Got Mail*; in a short-lived late 1990s television show actually called *Buddies*; and in his comedic anecdotes in *Killin' Them Softly*.

81 Chappelle, qtd. in Haggins, *Laughing Mad*, 207.

82 Chappelle suggests that pundits emphasize this interracial collaboration in order to dispel anxieties that he is playing the "race card" and "being divisive." See Dave Chappelle and Charlie Rose, "Dave Chappelle Discusses Culture and 'Chappelle's Show,'" *The Charlie Rose Show*, PBS, April 28, 2004, https://charlierose.com/videos/5454. For a discussion of radical politics in Chappelle's oeuvre, see Chiwen Bao, "Haunted: Dave Chappelle's Radical Racial Politics in the Context of Co-Opted Blackness," in *The Comedy of Dave Chappelle*, ed. Kevin Wisniewski (Jefferson, NC: McFarland, 2009), 167–83.

83 Farley, "Dave Speaks."

84 Farley, "Dave Speaks."

85 Chappelle and Lipton, "Dave Chappelle."

86 Among such "strong" black artists who have admitted to mental illness and breakdowns are writer Ntozake Shange, musician Nina Simone, and Chappelle's own role model, comedian Richard Pryor.

87 Steven Lang, "Disorderly Conduct," *People*, May 12, 1997, https://people.com/archive/disorderly-conduct-vol-47-no-18/.

88 Sharon Waxman, "The Tragedy of the Comic," *Washington Post*, June 24, 1997, https://www.washingtonpost.com/wp-srv/style/longterm/movies/review97/fmartinlawrence.htm.

89 Waxman, "The Tragedy of the Comic."

90 Margaret Ramirez, "Comedian Martin Lawrence Runs into Street, Yells at Cars," *Los Angeles Times*, May 8, 1996, https://www.latimes.com/archives/la-xpm-1996-05-08-me-1744-story.html.

91 Ramirez, "Comedian Martin Lawrence Runs into Street, Yells at Cars."

92 Ramirez, "Comedian Martin Lawrence Runs into Street, Yells at Cars."

93 Significantly, the cover of Richard Pryor's eponymous stand-up album contained an image of Pryor sitting in front of a cave in a loincloth with a bow and arrow and a shell necklace. McCluskey suggests that "[h]is nakedness . . . denotes the truthfulness of his confessional style, as well as the danger and vulnerability that threaten to overtake his primitive defenses" ("Richard Pryor: Comic Genius, Tortured Soul," 3), but he is also signifying on colonial and racist representations of indigenous African and indigenous American peoples.

94 Kanye West, "All Falls Down," *Freshman Adjustment* (Chicago: Chi Town Gettin' Down, 2004).

95 As of 2016, the average net wealth of white families in the U.S. was ten times that of black families. See Kriston McIntosh, Emily Moss, Ryan Nunn, and Jay Shambaugh, "Examining the Black-White Wealth Gap" (Washington, DC: The Brookings Institution, February 27, 2020), https://www.brookings.edu/blog/up -front/2020/02/27/examining-the-black-white-wealth-gap/.

96 Samuel Cartwright, "Diseases and Peculiarities of the Negro Race," *DeBow's Review: Southern and Western States* 11 (1851): 331.

97 Farley, "Dave Speaks."

98 See, for example, Gordon, "Fears of a Clown"; Josh Wolk, "Chappelle's No Show" *Entertainment Weekly*, May 11, 2005, https://ew.com/article/2005 /05/11/chappelles-no-show/; and Associated Press, "Report: Chappelle in Mental Health Facility," *NBCNews.com*, May 12, 2005, https://www.today.com /popculture/report-chappelle-mental-health-facility-wbna7821711.

Chapter Seven: Songs in Madtime

Epigraph: Simone, *I Put a Spell on You: The Autobiography of Nina Simone* (New York: Pantheon), 89–90.

1 Simone sings, "This whole country is full of lies / You're all gonna die and die like flies / I don't trust you any more / You keep on saying "Go slow!" / . . . But that's just the trouble" in "Mississippi Goddam," *Nina Simone in Concert* (New York: Phillips, 1964).

2 I am invoking both Robin D. G. Kelly's formulation of "freedom dreams" in *Freedom Dreams: The Black Radical Imagination* and Langston Hughes's vision of "a dream deferred" in the poem "Harlem," from his 1951 poetry collection *Montage of a Dream Deferred* (New York: Holt, 1951).

3 In a 1997 interview with *Details* magazine, Simone expressed her discomfort with being labeled a "jazz" musician and instead embraced the category of "black classical music." She explained, "To most white people, jazz means black and jazz means dirt and that's not what I play. I play black classical music. That's why I don't like the term 'jazz,' and Duke Ellington didn't either—it's a term that's simply used to identify black people." Nina Simone and Brantley Bardin, "Simone Says," *Details*, January 1997, http://brantleybardin.com/_articles/hits_nina _simone.html.

4 Several scholars have theorized race and temporality under the signifier *ra-cial time*. I am especially influenced by political theorist Michael Hanchard's formulation: "Racial time is defined as the inequalities of temporality that result from power relations between racially dominant and subordinate groups. When coupled with the distinct temporal modalities that relations of dominance and subordination produce, racial time has operated as a structural effect upon the politics of racial difference. Its effects can be seen in the daily interactions—grand and quotidian in multiracial societies." Michael Hanchard, "Afro-Modernity: Temporality, Politics, and the African Diaspora," *Public Culture* 11, no. 1 (1999): 253. For other theorizations of "racial time," see Howard Winant, *Racial Conditions: Politics, Theory, Comparisons* (Minneapolis: University of Minnesota Press, 1994), 115–17; Anthony Reed, *Freedom Time: The Poetics and Politics of Black Experimental Writing* (Baltimore: Johns Hopkins University Press, 2014), 207–14; and Charles Mills, "The Chronopolitics of Racial Time," *Time and Society* 29, no. 2 (2020): 297–317.

5 Martin Luther King Jr.—icon of the civil rights movement whose revolutionary richness is often abstracted into a milquetoast dream, or flattened into a token of triumphal assimilation in popular memory—wrote these words concerning racial time: "I have yet to engage in a direct action campaign that was 'well timed' in the view of those who have not suffered unduly from the disease of segregation. For years now I have heard the word 'Wait!' It rings in the ear of every Negro with piercing familiarity. This 'Wait' has almost always meant 'Never.'" Martin Luther King Jr., "Letter from Birmingham Jail," in Martin Luther King Jr., *Why We Can't Wait* (New York: Signet Classics, 2000), 64–84.

6 For further insight on "Mississippi Goddam," see Daphne Brooks, "Nina Simone's Triple Play," *Callaloo* 34, no. 1 (2011): 176–97; Danielle C. Heard, "'Don't Let Me Be Misunderstood': Nina Simone's Theater of Invisibility," *Callaloo* 35, no. 4 (2012): 1056–84; and Malik Gaines, "The Quadruple-Consciousness of Nina Simone," *Women and Performance: A Journal of Feminist Theory* 23, no. 2 (2013): 248–67.

7 Hip Hop Library, "Nina Simone—Mississippi Goddam (Live in Netherlands)," YouTube video 5, no. 27 (December 19, 2015), https://www.youtube.com/watch?v=ghhaREDM3X8.

8 Concerning Simone's diagnosis with schizophrenia, see Nadine Cohodas, *Princess Noire: The Tumultuous Reign of Nina Simone* (Chapel Hill: University of North Carolina Press, 2012), 337. Regarding Simone's diagnosis with bipolar disorder, see Liz Garbus, dir., *What Happened, Miss Simone?* (Netflix, 2015).

9 Peter Rodis, dir. *Nina Simone: A Historical Perspective*, 1970.

10 Gaines, "The Quadruple-Consciousness of Nina Simone," 253.

11 In *The Eighteenth Brumaire of Louis Bonaparte*, political economist and philosopher Karl Marx professes that "the social revolution of the nineteenth century can only create its poetry from the future, not from the past." See Karl Marx, *Surveys from Exile: Political Writing Vol. 2*, ed. David Fernbach (London: Penguin, 1973), 149.

12 Carolyn Dinshaw, Lee Edelman, Roderick A. Ferguson, Carla Freccero, Elizabeth Freeman, Jack Halberstam, Annamarie Jagose, Christopher Nealon, and Nguyen

Tan Hoang, "Theorizing Queer Temporalities: A Roundtable Discussion," *GLQ* 13, no. 2 (2007): 182.

13 For powerful critiques of the racialization of metaphysics, see Calvin Warren, "Black Time: Slavery, Metaphysics, and the Logic of Wellness," in *The Psychic Hold of Slavery: Legacies in American Expressive Culture*, ed. Soyica Diggs Colbert, Robert J. Patterson, Aida Levy-Hussen (New Brunswick, NJ: Rutgers University Press, 2016), 55–68; and Michael Lackey, "Redeeming the Post-Metaphysical Promise of J. Saunders Redding's 'America,'" *CR: The New Centennial Review* 12, no. 3 (2012): 217–43.

14 Elizabeth Freeman, *Time Binds: Queer Temporalities, Queer Histories* (Durham, NC: Duke University Press, 2010), xv.

15 Regarding "cruising," see José Esteban Muñoz, *Cruising Utopia: The Then and There of Queer Futurity* (New York: NYU Press, 2009). Regarding "backward feeling" see Heather Love, *Feeling Backward: Loss and the Politics of Queer History* (Cambridge, MA: Harvard University Press, 2007). For further consideration of loitering, see Bruce, "Shore, Unsure."

16 Regarding "crip time," see Alison Kafer, *Feminist Queer Crip* (Bloomington: Indiana University Press, 2013), 25–46; and Ellen Samuels, "Six Ways of Looking at Crip Time," *Disability Studies Quarterly* 37, no. 3 (2017), https://dsq-sds.org/article/view/5824/4684.

17 Samuels, "Six Ways of Looking at Crip Time."

18 Kafer, *Feminist Queer Crip,* 27.

19 Warren, "Black Time," 58–61.

20 Warren, "Black Time," 62; emphasis in original.

21 Regarding that erasure from history, I am thinking, for example, of Hegel's contention that Africa "is no historical part of the world" and that its people live in a "completely wild and untamed state." Such sentiments were mobilized to justify slavery and colonialism as *civilizing* forces. See Georg Wilhelm Friedrich Hegel, *The Philosophy of History* (New York: Dover, 1956), 93, 99.

22 Miles Hoffman, *The NPR Classical Music Companion: An Essential Guide for Enlightened Listening* (New York: Houghton Mifflin, 1997), 239.

23 Karl Marx describes this as "labor time" within his theory of historical materialism in *A Contribution to the Critique of Political Economy* (Chicago: Charles Kerr, 1904), 23–29. I am aware of the revolutionary potential Marx ascribes to the proletariat—a potential that categorically opposes the hegemony of capitalism. However, the state-sanctioned occasion of Labor Day honors proletariat labor inasmuch as it sustains and benefits the broader project of capital. Bolden swerved away from that paradigm.

24 Bolden is a poignant case study of the adversity that often assails black radical creativity in antiblack worlds. Thankfully, he is also an exemplar of the improvisational and syncopative genius that often animates such creativity. While Fred Moten has riffed on the improvisational character of black expressive cultures (see Moten, *In the Break: The Aesthetics of the Black Radical Tradition* [Minneapolis: University of Minnesota Press, 2003]), I accent the principle of syncopation here.

I hasten to note that black creativity is not only improvisational and syncopative but also studied and meditative.

25 There are chapters and books to be written about the asynchronic times of "dissociative identity disorder," the ritualized time of the "obsessive compulsive disorder," and beyond.

26 Nicole Fleetwood proposes a related notion of "penal time," which she describes as "time as punishment" (23) and "punishment measured as time in captivity or under state supervision, such as parole" (8) in *Marking Time: Art in the Age of Mass Incarceration* (Cambridge, MA: Harvard University Press, 2020).

27 "Bipolar I Disorder," *Diagnostic and Statistical Manual of Mental Disorders: DSM 5* (Arlington, VA: American Psychiatric Association, 2013), https://dsm -psychiatryonline-org.proxy-um.researchport.umd.edu/doi/full/10.1176/appi .books.9780890425596.dsm03.

28 Concerning Charles Mingus's brief stint in Bellevue, see Mingus, *Beneath the Underdog: His World as Composed by Mingus* (New York: Vintage, 1991), 327–48.

29 Charles Mingus, "All the Things You Could Be by Now If Sigmund Freud's Wife Was Your Mother," *Charles Mingus Presents Charles Mingus* (New York: Candid Records, 1960).

30 Ella Fitzgerald, "All the Things You Are," in *Ella Fitzgerald Sings the Jerome Kern Song Book* (New York: Verve, 1963). Remarkably, Frank Sinatra, Barbra Streisand, Carmen McRae, Michael Jackson, Norm Lewis, Audra McDonald, and many others have recorded vocal covers of the song. John Coltrane, Charlie Parker, and Miles Davis, among many others, have recorded jazz instrumental renditions.

31 Lauryn Hill, "Consumerism" (New York: Sony/Columbia, 2013).

32 Sia Michel, "Dream-Girl Disenfranchised," *Village Voice*, September 1, 1998, https://www.villagevoice.com/1998/09/01/educating-lauryn/.

33 Lauryn Hill and Sway Calloway, "Lauryn Hill: Redemption Song," *MTVNews.com*, (2001).

34 Aylin Zafar, "In Defense of Lauryn Hill," *The Atlantic*, September 1, 2010, https:// www.theatlantic.com/entertainment/archive/2010/09/in-defense-of-lauryn-hill /62343/; and Charles Richards, "Lauryn Hill Moves Her R&B toward Progres- sive Rock," *Washington Post*, March 1, 2012, https://www.washingtonpost.com /lifestyle/style/lauryn-hill-moves-her-randb-toward-progressive-rock/2012/03/01 /gIQAYkzMlR_story.html; emphases mine.

35 American Psychiatric Association, *DSM-5*, "Bipolar I Disorder."

36 Regarding these wretched performances of "stepping it up lively" and "simulated jollity," see Saidiya Hartman, *Scenes of Subjection: Terror, Slavery, and Self-Making in Nineteenth-Century America* (New York: Oxford University Press, 1997), 23, 36–38.

37 For a compelling account of how slaveholders worked to control all aspects of slaves' time and weaponized temporality within their arsenal of domination, see Walter Johnson, "Possible Pasts: Some Speculations on Time, Temporality, and the History of Atlantic," *Amerikastudien/American Studies* 45, no. 4 (2000): 485–99.

38 Concerning the use of work slowdowns within campaigns of subterranean resistance, see Walter Johnson, "Possible Pasts." Regarding the potential resistant
power of stillness, see Harvey Young, *Embodying Black Experience: Stillness,
Critical Memory, and the Black Body* (Ann Arbor: University of Michigan Press,
2010). Young illuminates historical cases in which the "performance of stillness
opens up new possibilities for critical reading strategies, and, indeed, positionings
for cultural historians and scholars" (44).

39 American Psychiatric Association, DSM-5, "Bipolar I Disorder."

40 Regarding the afterlife of slavery, see Saidiya Hartman, *Lose Your Mother: A Journey along the Atlantic Slave Trade Route* (New York: Farrar, Straus and Giroux,
2007), 6.

41 Ann Cvetkovich, *Depression: A Public Feeling* (Durham, NC: Duke University
Press, 2012), 14.

42 Nina Simone, "Who Knows Where the Time Goes?" *Black Gold* (New York:
RCA Records, 1970).

43 In the aftermath of King's death, Simone wrote and recorded a musical elegy and
eulogy for him called "Why? (The King of Love Is Dead)," *'Nuff Said!* (New
York: RCA Records, 1968)

44 See, for example, Elijah J. Watson, "'Don't Waste Your Money on Her': Lauryn
Hill Angers Toronto Fans for Late Performance," *OkayPlayer*, July 2018,
https://www.okayplayer.com/music/lauryn-hill-angers-toronto-fans-for-late
-performance.html; Kiersten Willis, "Lauryn Hill Fans Trash Singer after She
Showed up Late Again to Concert," *Atlanta Black Star*, July 20, 2018, https://
atlantablackstar.com/2018/07/20/lauryn-hill-fans-trash-singer-after-she-showed
-up-late-again-to-concert/; Jewel Wicker, "Concert Review: Lauryn Hill Shows
up More than 2 Hours Late to Atlanta Show," *Atlanta Journal-Constitution*,
May 7, 2016, https://www.ajc.com/blog/music/concert-review-lauryn-hill-shows
-more-than-hours-late-atlanta-show/kkFJSBQjLkeWlKGiyXOU7O/. For an
especially dramatic account of Hill's lateness, see Rob Harvilla, "The Disorientation of Lauryn Hill," *Village Voice*, August 7, 2007, https://www.villagevoice.com
/2007/08/07/the-disorientation-of-lauryn-hill/.

45 Blacktainment, "Lauryn Hill Defensively Tells Fan Why She Was Late for UK
Concert," YouTube video, October 3, 2014, https://www.youtube.com/watch?v
=QAnelMUofS4.

46 "Lauryn Hill—Shows Up LATE for Concert Then Lectures Fan on Respect!,"
TMZ, July 23, 2014, https://www.tmz.com/2014/07/23/lauryn-hill-concert-video
-rant-disrespectful-fan-house-of-blues/.

47 I am gesturing toward Daphne Brooks's formulation of "Afro-alienation act."
See Brooks, *Bodies in Dissent: Spectacular Performances of Race and Freedom,
1850–1910* (Durham, NC: Duke University Press, 2006), 4–5.

48 Amy Wallace, "Amen! (D'Angelo's Back)," *GQ*, June 2012.

49 Hill has born and raised six children since 1998 (the year *Miseducation* debuted). Of
course, this familial and maternal accomplishment does not serve the interests of
music executives and (some) fans who would rather she beget albums than children.

50 Michel Foucault, *Madness: The Invention of an Idea* (previously published as *Mental Illness and Psychology*) (New York: Harper Perennial, 2011), 29. Other clinicians have articulated similar observations. Writing in *Schizophrenia Bulletin* in 2016, a team of psychiatrists explained, "With the fracturing of the time flow [in schizophrenia], we observe an itemization of now-moments in consciousness so that each now-moment in a person's stream of consciousness will be experienced as detached from the previous one and from the following." See Giovanni Stanghellini, Massimo Ballerini, Simona Presenza, Milena Mancini, Andrea Raballo, Stefano Blasi, and John Cutting, "Psychopathology of Lived Time: Abnormal Time Experience in Persons with Schizophrenia," *Schizophrenia Bulletin* 42, no. 1 (2016): 45–55.

51 Foucault, *Madness: The Invention of an Idea*, 29, 47; emphasis mine.

52 Multiple studies indicate, as Wehring and Carpenter explain, that "persons with schizophrenia are more likely to be the victims of violence than to perpetrate violence." See Heidi J. Wehring and William T. Carpenter, "Violence and Schizophrenia," *Schizophrenia Bulletin* 37, no. 5 (2011): 877. See also Linda A. Teplin, Gary M. McClelland, Karen M. Abram, and Dana A. Weiner, "Crime Victimization in Adults with Severe Mental Illness: Comparison with the National Crime Victimization Survey," *Archives of General Psychiatry* 62, no. 8 (2005): 911–21; John S. Brekke, Cathy Prindle, Sung Woo Bae, and Jeffrey D. Long, "Risks for Individuals with Schizophrenia Who Are Living in the Community," *Psychiatric Services* 52, no. 10 (2001): 1358–66; and Wehring and Carpenter, "Violence and Schizophrenia," 877–78.

53 Toni Morrison, *Beloved* (New York: Knopf, 1987), 210. Saidiya Hartman similarly asserts, "The distinction between the past and the present founders on the interminable grief engendered by slavery and its aftermath," in "The Time of Slavery," *South Atlantic Quarterly* 101, no. 4 (2002): 758.

54 Regarding that erasure from history, I am thinking, again, of Hegel's *The Philosophy of History*. There, he refers to Africa as "the land of childhood, which lying beyond the day of self-conscious history, is enveloped in the dark mantle of Night" and claims that the continent "is no historical part of the world; it has no movement or development to exhibit" (93).

55 Hortense Spillers, "Mama's Baby, Papa's Maybe: An American Grammar Book," *Diacritics* 17, no. 2 (summer 1987), 78.

56 Gilles Deleuze and Félix Guattari, *Anti-Oedipus: Capitalism and Schizophrenia* (Minneapolis: University of Minnesota Press, 1983), 23.

57 When asked about musical influences on her work, Parks explains, "I listened to Ornette Coleman practically all the time when I was writing [*The Death of the Last Black Man in the Whole Entire World*]. The play moves like that." Suzan-Lori Parks and Han Ong, "Suzan-Lori Parks by Han Ong," *BOMB Magazine*, April 1, 1994. Coleman is known for innovating free jazz, a jazz subgenre emerging in the 1960s that attempted to abolish any fixed rules of tempo, harmony, and chord changes, encouraging the performer to practice radical, freewheeling improvisation.

58 Suzan-Lori Parks, *The Death of the Last Black Man in the Whole Entire World*, *Theater* 21, no. 3 (1990): 83.

59 Parks, *The Death of the Last Black Man in the Whole Entire World*, 85.

60 Parks, *The Death of the Last Black Man in the Whole Entire World*, 89.

61 Parks, *The Death of the Last Black Man in the Whole Entire World*, 82.

62 Parks, *The Death of the Last Black Man in the Whole Entire World*, 82.

63 Parks, *The Death of the Last Black Man in the Whole Entire World*, 92.

64 Adrienne Kennedy's 1964 play, *Funnyhouse of a Negro*, also unfurls an elaborate dramatization of schizophrenic time. The "pallid Negro"—the biracial woman protagonist of *Funnyhouse*—cohabits that house with her multiple personalities and psychotic hallucinations made manifest in a drama that bizarrely skews subjectivity, space, and time. That protagonist experiences herself as first-century Jesus Christ, nineteenth-century British royalty, and twentieth-century Congolese freedom-fighting martyr colliding in a mishmash of trauma within the ever-arriving and ever-vanishing present of theatrical performance. Portraying its protagonist's terrifying lifeworld, *Funnyhouse* yields devastating critiques of racial and sexual abjection in civil rights–era America. See Adrienne Kennedy, *Funnyhouse of a Negro: A Play in One Act* (New York: Samuel French, 1969).

65 "Stereotype pixie" is a reference to Dave Chappelle's 2005 blackface minstrel parody performed on *Chappelle's Show* (described in chapter 4).

66 Regarding the significance of Black Man moving his hands in the play, see Soyica Diggs Colbert, "'When I Die, I Won't Stay Dead': The Future of the Human in Suzan-Lori Parks's *The Death of the Last Black Man in the Whole Entire World*," *Boundary 2*, 39, no. 3 (2012): 191–93.

67 Parks, *The Death of the Last Black Man in the Whole Entire World*, 94.

68 Colbert, "'When I Die, I Won't Stay Dead,'" 196.

69 Colbert, "'When I Die, I Won't Stay Dead,'" 196.

70 In a 2015 interview with Rob Markman, Lamar disclosed that he lives with depression. It is not clear whether he has been clinically diagnosed with depression or is using the term colloquially to describe intense sadness. In the same interview Lamar describes suicidal thoughts that have haunted him. See "Kendrick Lamar Talks about 'u,' His Depression and Suicidal Thoughts (Pt. 2) | MTV News," YouTube video, April 1, 2015, https://youtu.be/Hu4Pz9PjolI.

71 Kendrick Lamar, "The Blacker the Berry," *To Pimp a Butterfly* (Carson, CA: Top Dawg/Interscope Records, 2015).

72 Toni Morrison and Charlie Rose, "Novelist Toni Morrison Looks Back on Her Youth and Family and Presents Her Newest Book, 'Jazz,'" *The Charlie Rose Show*, PBS, May 7, 1993, https://charlierose.com/episodes/18778.

73 Lamar, "The Blacker the Berry."

74 This quotation comes from Gilien Silsby, "People with Schizophrenia Are Often Targets for Criminals," *USC News*, October 22, 2001, https://news.usc.edu/4303/People-With-Schizophrenia-Are-Often-Targets-for-Criminals/. Silsby is citing and summarizing the findings in John S. Brekke, Cathy Prindle, Sung Woo Bae, and Jeffrey D. Long, "Risks for Individuals with Schizophrenia Who Are Living

in the Community," *Psychiatric Services* 52, no. 10 (2001): 1358–66. According to Eric Elbogen and Sally Johnson, writing in *Archives of General Psychiatry*, "Bivariate analyses showed that the incidence of violence was higher for people with severe mental illness, but only significantly so for those with co-occurring substance abuse and/or dependence. Multivariate analyses revealed that severe mental illness alone did not predict future violence." See Eric B. Elbogen and Sally C. Johnson, "The Intricate Link between Violence and Mental Disorder: Results from the National Epidemiologic Survey on Alcohol and Related Conditions," *Archives of General Psychiatry* 66, no. 2 (2009): 152–61.

75 I am riffing on the title of Bebe Moore Campbell's 1992 novel, *Your Blues Ain't Like Mine* (New York: Random House, 1992), which is inspired by the murder of Emmitt Till and the courage of his mother, Mamie Till-Bradley.

76 Toni Morrison, *Sula*, 174.

77 Sigmund Freud, "Mourning and Melancholia," in *The Freud Reader*, ed. Peter Gay (New York: W. W. Norton, 1989), 587.

78 David Eng and Shinhee Han, "A Dialogue on Racial Melancholia" in *Loss: The Politics of Mourning*, ed. David Eng and David Kazanjian (Berkeley: University of California Press, 2002), 365. Eng and Han also propose a melancholic ethic: "[The] preservation of the threatened object might be seen . . . as a type of ethical hold on the part of the melancholic ego. The mourner, in contrast, has no such ethics. The mourner is perfectly content with killing off the lost object, declaring it to be dead yet again within the domain of the psyche" (365).

79 Sara Clarke Kaplan, "Souls at the Crossroads, Africans on the Water: The Politics of Diasporic Melancholia," *Callaloo* 30, no. 2 (2007): 513. Concerning "racial melancholia" and the distinction between "grief" and "grievance," see Anne Anlin Cheng, *The Melancholy of Race: Psychoanalysis, Assimilation, and Hidden Grief* (New York: Oxford University Press, 2001).

80 Concerning both the belief in black insentience and the instrumentalization of black pain by slaveholders and others, see Deborah Walker King, *African Americans and the Culture of Pain* (Charlottesville: University of Virginia Press, 2008).

81 Orlando Patterson, *Slavery and Social Death: A Comparative Study* (Cambridge, MA: Harvard University Press, 1982), 5–10.

82 Éva Tettenborn, "Melancholia as Resistance in Contemporary African American Literature," *MELUS* 31, no. 3 (2006): 109.

83 Tettenborn, "Melancholia as Resistance," 109.

84 Saidiya Hartman, "The Time of Slavery," 758.

85 Lauryn Hill, "I Gotta Find Peace of Mind," *MTV Unplugged 2.0* (Columbia/Sony, 2002).

86 Jeff Giles, "Songs in the Key of Strife: Lauryn Hill Comes Unplugged," *Newsweek*, May 13, 2002, http://www.newsweek.com/id/64512; David Browne, "Review: Lauryn Hill's 'Unplugged' Draining," *Entertainment Weekly*, May 8, 2002, https://www.cnn.com/2002/SHOWBIZ/Music/05/08/ew.rec.mus.hill/.

87 Robert Christgau, "Not Hop, Stomp," *Village Voice*, April 22, 2003, https://www.villagevoice.com/2003/04/22/not-hop-stomp/.

88 Frank Ocean, "Wither," *Endless* (New York: Def Jam, 2016).

89 In a letter posted to his public Tumblr account, Ocean recounted his nineteen-year-old self falling in love with a young man in an enchanted summer when "time would glide." Eventually, though, the love became "malignant." See Frank Ocean, "thank you's," https://frankocean.tumblr.com/post/26473798723.

90 Frank Ocean, "Bad Religion," *Channel Orange* (New York: Def Jam, 2012).

91 Erykah Badu, "Out My Mind, Just in Time," *New Amerykah Part Two (Return of the Ankh)* (New York: Universal Motown Records, 2010).

92 Saidiya Hartman describes "the history that hurts—the still unfolding narrative of captivity, dispossession, and domination that engenders the black subject in the Americas" in *Scenes of Subjection*, 51.

Afterword: The Nutty Professor (A Confession)

Epigraph: Richard Wright, *Native Son* (New York: HarperCollins, 1993), 343. This chapter's title signifies on Jerry Lewis, dir., *The Nutty Professor* (New York: Jerry Lewis Entrprises, 1963).

1 In *African Americans and the Culture of Pain*, Debra Walker King theorizes "racial hurt" as racialized violence that poses an existential threat to its victim. She writes, "Pain is a personal experience, a feeling that is uniquely our own. . . . Racial hurt, however, is not something we own. Racial hurt owns us. It, not pain, attacks the soul and renders its victims wounded or worse—soul murdered" ([Charlottesville: University of Virginia Press, 2008], 39).

2 Bessie's remains are carted out as evidence in the trial for Mary's murder, but no trial is convened to pursue justice for Bessie's murder. Alas, Bessie is a poor black woman whose death and life are treated as inconsequential and contemptible—not meriting a trial or redress—by an antiblack legal system.

3 Wright, *Native Son*, 343.

4 Wright, *Native Son*, 342.

5 Wright, *Native Son*, 344.

6 This "balmy" man would find powerful alibi in St. Clair Drake and Horace Cayton's monumental 1945 study, *Black Metropolis: A Study of Negro Life in a Northern City* (Chicago: University of Chicago Press, 1993). Based on research conducted in 1930s Chicago, *Black Metropolis* exposes a city structured by de facto segregation and infrastructural antiblackness. For a study examining the racial inequity in contemporary Chicago, see Natalie Moore, *The South Side: A Portrait of Chicago and American Segregation* (New York: St. Martin's, 2017).

7 Ida B. Wells-Barnett, "Lynch Law in America," *The Arena* 23 (January 1900), https://www.blackpast.org/african-american-history/1900-ida-b-wells-lynch-law-america/.

8 Wright, *Native Son*, 344.

9 Hortense Spillers, "Mama's Baby, Papa's Maybe: An American Grammar Book," *Diacritics* 17, no. 2 (summer 1987): 72.

10 Regarding "critical fabulation," see Saidiya Hartman, "Venus in Two Acts," *Small Axe* 12, no. 2 (2008): 10–14.

11 Matt Ford, "America's Largest Mental Hospital Is a Jail," *Atlantic*, June 8, 2015, https://www.theatlantic.com/politics/archive/2015/06/americas-largest-mental -hospital-is-a-jail/395012/.

12 In this disclosure of "madness," I am especially influenced by and indebted to disclosures of "madness" (whether medicalized or not) in Patricia J. Williams, *The Alchemy of Race and Rights: Diary of a Law Professor* (Cambridge, MA: Harvard University Press, 1991); Ann Cvetkovich, *Depression: A Public Feeling* (Durham, NC: Duke University Press, 2012); PhebeAnn Marjory Wolframe, "The Mad-woman in the Academy, or, Revealing the Invisible Straightjacket: Theorizing and Teaching Saneism and Sane Privilege," *Disability Studies Quarterly* 33, no. 1 (2013), https://dsq-sds.org/article/view/3425/3200; and Keguro Macharia, "On Quitting," *The New Inquiry*, September 19, 2018, https://thenewinquiry.com /on-quitting. I am also emboldened by Margaret Price's book-length study of "madness" in academic discourses and spaces, *Mad at School Rhetorics of Mental Disability and Academic Life* (Ann Arbor: University of Michigan Press, 2011).

13 Jack Nicholson won the 1998 Academy Award for Best Actor for playing a comi-cally insufferable obsessive compulsive author in the romantic comedy *As Good as It Gets*. Nicolas Cage earned great acclaim for playing an obsessive compulsive con man in the 2003 heist comedy, *Matchstick Men*. In television, Tony Shal-houb won three Primetime Emmys for Lead Actor in a Comedy Series for his portrayal of an obsessive compulsive detective in the comedic crime procedural, *Monk*, which ran from 2002 to 2009.

14 Christina Sharpe proposes "black redaction," a practice of concealing visual and textual artifacts of black life in order to thwart regimes of hypervisibility and refuse the spectacularization of black abjection. See Sharpe, *In the Wake: On Blackness and Being* (Durham, NC: Duke University Press, 2016), 113–19.

15 Frantz Fanon, *Black Skin, White Masks*, trans. Charles Lam Markmann (London: Pluto Press, 1986), 206.

16 Martha Graham, qtd. in Agnes de Mille, *Martha: The Life and Work of Martha Graham* (New York: Random House, 1991), 264.

17 In this passage, Frantz Fanon is referring to his mentor: the Martinican states-man, Negritude vanguardist, and mad poet Aimé Césaire. After describing black Afro-Caribbeans who internalize white supremacist sensibilities—including bilious contempt for Africa and native Africans—Fanon describes Césaire as an iconoclast who loved Africa and adored his blackness. See Fanon, *Toward the African Revolution: Political Essays*, trans. Haakon Chevalier (New York: Grove Press, 1988), 26. Césaire expressed his own investment in radical madness, touting "the madness that remembers, the madness that howls, the madness that sees, the madness that is unleashed" in his *Notebook of a Return to the Native Land*, trans. Clayton Eshleman (Middletown, CT: Wesleyan University Press, 2001), 18.

18 Michel Foucault, *Madness and Civilization: A History of Insanity in the Age of Reason*, trans. Richard Howard (New York: Vintage, 1988), 11.

19 Natasha Trethewey, "Calling His Children Home," *Callaloo* 19, no. 2 (1996): 351.

20 Frank Ocean, "Wither," *Endless* (New York: Def Jam, 2016).

21 My references to "Nothingness" and "Infinity" are inspired by a poignant passage in Fanon's *Black Skin, White Masks*. Unfurling a phenomenology of existential turmoil amid antiblackness, Fanon writes, "I feel my soul as vast as the world, truly as deep as the deepest of rivers; my chest has the power to expand to infinity. I was made to give and they prescribe for me the humility of the cripple. When I opened my eyes yesterday, I saw the sky in total revulsion. I tried to get up but the eviscerated silence surged toward me with paralyzed wings. Not responsible for my acts, at the crossroads between Nothingness and Infinity, I began to weep" (119).

BIBLIOGRAPHY

Abdur-Rahman, Aliyyah I. *Against the Closet: Black Political Longing and the Erotics of Race*. Durham, NC: Duke University Press, 2012.

Abraham, Adam Everette, ed. *Sun Ra: Collected Works Vol. 1—Immeasurable Equation*. Chandler, AZ: Phaelos Books and Mediawerks, 2005.

Abrutyn, Seth B. "Positivism." In *Oxford Bibliographies in Sociology*. Oxford: Oxford University Press, 2013.

Aeschylus. *The Oresteia: Agamemnon; The Libation Bearers; The Eumenides*. Translated by Robert Fagles. New York: Penguin Books, 1984.

Ahad, Badia Sahar. "Introduction." In *Freud Upside Down: African American Literature and Psychoanalytic Culture*. Champaign: University of Illinois Press, 2010.

Aho, Tanja, Liat Ben-Moshe, and Leon J. Hilton. "Mad Futures: Affect/Theory/Violence." *American Quarterly* 69, no. 2 (2017): 291–302. https://doi.org/10.1353/aq.2017.0023.

Akomfrah, John, dir. *Precarity*. London: Smoking Dog Films, 2018.

Albertson, Chris. *Bessie*. Revised and expanded edition. New Haven, CT: Yale University Press, 2003.

"Alcoholic Indulgence Converts Negro Patient into a Dangerous Man." *The Daily States*, March 28, 1906.

Alexander, Elizabeth. *The Black Interior*. Minneapolis: Graywolf Press, 2004.

Alexander, Elizabeth. "'Can You Be BLACK and Look at This?': Reading the Rodney King Video(s)." *Public Culture* (fall 1994).

Alexander, Michelle. *The New Jim Crow: Mass Incarceration in the Age of Colorblindness*. New York: The New Press, 2012.

Allen, Donia Elizabeth. "The Role of the Blues in Gayl Jones's 'Corregidora.'" *Callaloo* 25, no. 1 (2002).

Althusser, Louis. "Ideology and Ideological State Apparatuses (Notes towards an Investigation)." 1970. In *Cultural Theory: An Anthology*, edited by Imre Szeman and Timothy Kaposy. Oxford: Wiley-Blackwell, 2010.

Armstrong, Louis. "Black and Blue." *Satch Plays Fats: The Music of Fats Waller*. New York: Columbia, 1955.

Avilez, GerShun. *Radical Aesthetics and Modern Black Nationalism*. Champaign: University of Illinois Press, 2016.

Awkward, Michael. *African American Literary Theory*. New York: New York University Press, 2000.

Badu, Erykah. "Out My Mind, Just In Time." *New Amerykah Part Two (Return of the Ankh)*. Universal Motown, 2010. CD.

Baker, Kelly. *Disturbers of the Peace: Representations of Madness in Anglophone Caribbean Literature*. Charlottesville: University of Virginia Press, 2013.

Bakhtin, Mikhail. *Rabelais and His World*. Bloomington: Indiana University Press, 1984.

Bao, Chiwen. "Haunted: Dave Chappelle's Radical Racial Politics in the Context of Co-Opted Blackness." In *The Comedy of Dave Chappelle*, edited by Kevin Wisniewski. Jefferson, NC: McFarland, 2009.

Baraka, Amiri. *The LeRoi Jones/Amiri Baraka Reader*. Edited by William J. Harris. New York: Basic Books, 1999.

Barker, Danny. *Buddy Bolden and the Last Days of Storyville*. London: Cassell, 1998.

Barrett, Robert J. "The 'Schizophrenic' and the Liminal Persona in Modern Society." *Culture, Medicine and Psychiatry* 22, no. 4 (December 1998).

Barshad, Amos. "On the Skit That 'Killed' Chappelle's Show." *The Fader*, July 29, 2016. https://www.thefader.com/2016/07/29/skit-that-killed-chappelles-show.

Basu, Biman. "Public and Private Discourses and the Black Female Subject: Gayl Jones' 'Eva's Man.'" *Callaloo* 19, no. 1 (winter 1996).

Bayer, Ronald. *Homosexuality and American Psychiatry: The Politics of Diagnosis: With a New Afterword on AIDS and Homosexuality*. Princeton, NJ: Princeton University Press, 1987.

Baynton, Douglas C. "Disability and the Justification of Inequality in American History." In *The Disability Studies Reader*, edited by Lennard J. Davis. 2nd ed. New York: Routledge, 2006.

Bechet, Sidney. *Treat It Gentle: An Autobiography*. 1960. New York: Da Capo Press, 2002.

Bell, Christopher. "Introducing White Disability Studies: A Modest Proposal." In *The Disability Studies Reader*, edited by Lennard J. Davis. 2nd ed. New York: Routledge, 2006.

Bell, Emma. "Imagine Madness: Madness, Revolution, Ressentiment and Critical Theory." Inter-disciplinary. Net 1st Global Conference. Madness: Probing the Boundaries. Unpublished. Oxford: Mansfield College, 2008.

Benjamin, Walter. "Theses on the Philosophy of History." 1942. In *Illuminations*. New York: Harcourt, Brace, Jovanovich, 1968.

Bersani, Leo. *Is the Rectum a Grave? And Other Essays*. Chicago: University of Chicago Press, 2010.

"The Best of 1998 Music." *Time*, December 21, 1998.

Bethell, Tom. "The Legend of Buddy Bolden." *National Review* 31, no. 3 (January 1979). Hogan Jazz Archive, Tulane University, New Orleans.

Blacktainment. "Lauryn Hill Defensively Tells Fan Why She Was Late for UK Concert." YouTube video, 4:01. October 3, 2014. https://www.youtube.com/watch?v=QAnelMUofS4.

Blyden, Nemata. *African Americans and Africa: A New History*. New Haven, CT: Yale University Press, 2019.

Bohman, James, and William Rehg. *Deliberative Democracy: Essays on Reason and Politics*. Cambridge, MA: MIT Press, 1999.

"Bolden: Calling His Children Home: 1877–1931." New Orleans Jazz. National Park Service. http://www.nps.gov/jazz/historyculture/bolden.htm.

"Bolden: The Story Behind the Movie: How the 'Inventor of Jazz' Was Brought to Life Onscreen." *JazzTimes*, April 26, 2019. https://jazztimes.com/features/profiles /bolden-the-story-behind-the-movie/.

Bonney, Joseph. "Jazz Great Buddy Bolden Could Be Heard a Mile Away." *New Orleans Times-Picayune*, May 1, 1978. Hogan Jazz Archive, Tulane University, New Orleans.

Boone, Christian. "Who Was Anthony Hill? Figure in DeKalb Police Shooting Case Suffered from Mental Illness." *Atlanta Journal-Constitution*, January 22, 2016.

Bor, Jacob, Atheendar S. Venkataramani, David R. Williams, and Alexander C. Tsai. "Police Killings and Their Spillover Effects on the Mental Health of Black Americans: A Population-Based, Quasi-Experimental Study." *The Lancet* 392, no. 10144 (2018): 302–10. https://doi.org/10.1016/s0140-6736(18)31130-9.

Bourne, Jenny. "Slavery in the United States." *EH.Net Encyclopedia*. March 26, 2008. http://eh.net/encyclopedia/slavery-in-the-united-states.

Brekke, John S., Cathy Prindle, Sung Woo Bae, and Jeffrey D. Long. "Risks for Individuals with Schizophrenia Who Are Living in the Community." *Psychiatric Services* 52, no. 10 (2001).

Breton, André. "First Surrealist Manifesto." *Surrealism*. 1924. Edited by Patrick Waldberg. New York: McGraw-Hill, 1971.

Breton, André. "Manifesto of Surrealism." 1924. In *Manifestoes of Surrealism*. Translated by Richard Seaver and Helen R. Lane. Ann Arbor: University of Michigan Press, 1969.

Brody, Jennifer Devere. *Impossible Purities*. Durham, NC: Duke University Press, 1998.

Bromberg, Walter, and Franck Simon. "The 'Protest' Psychosis: A Special Type of Reactive Psychosis." *Archives of General Psychiatry* 19, no. 2 (1968): 155–60.

Brooks, Daphne. *Bodies in Dissent: Spectacular Performances of Race and Freedom, 1850–1910*. Durham, NC: Duke University Press, 2006.

Brooks, Daphne. "'Bring the Pain': Post-Soul Memory, Neo-Soul Affect and Lauryn Hill in the Black Public Sphere." Conversations Lecture Series at the Institute for Research in African-American Studies at Columbia University. New York, December 4, 2009.

Brooks, Daphne. "A New Voice of the Blues." In *A New Literary History of America*, ed. Greil Marcus and Werner Sollors. Cambridge, MA: Harvard University Press, 2012.

Brooks, Daphne. "Nina Simone's Triple Play." *Callaloo* 34, no. 1 (2011): 176–97. https://doi.org/10.1353/cal.2011.0036.

Browne, David. "Review: Lauryn Hill's 'Unplugged' Draining." *Entertainment Weekly*, May 8, 2002.

Browning, Barbara. *Infectious Rhythm: Metaphors of Contagion and the Spread of African Culture*. New York: Routledge, 1998.

Bruce, La Marr Jurelle. "Shore, Unsure: Loitering as a Way of Life." *GLQ: A Journal of Lesbian and Gay Studies* 25, no. 2 (2019): 352–61. https://doi.org/10.1215 /10642684-7367824.

Bruggen, Madeleine van der, and Amy Grubb. "A Review of the Literature Relating to Rape Victim Blaming: An Analysis of the Impact of Observer and Victim Characteristics on Attribution of Blame in Rape Cases." *Aggression and Violent Behavior* 19, no. 5 (2014): 523–31. https://doi.org/10.1016/j.avb.2014.07.008.

Buehler, James W. "Racial/Ethnic Disparities in the Use of Lethal Force by US Police, 2010–2014." *American Journal of Public Health* 107, no. 2 (2017): 295–97. https:// doi.org/10.2105/ajph.2016.303575.

Burns, Sarah. *The Central Park Five: The Untold Story behind One of New York City's Most Infamous Crimes*. New York: Knopf, 2011.

Burton, Neel. "When Homosexuality Stopped Being a Mental Disorder: Not until 1987 Did Homosexuality Completely Fall out of the DSM." *Psychology Today*, September 18, 2015. https://www.psychologytoday.com/us/blog/hide-and-seek /201509/when-homosexuality-stopped-being-mental-disorder.

Caminero-Santangelo, Marta. *The Madwoman Can't Speak, or, Why Insanity Is Not Subversive*. Ithaca, NY: Cornell University Press, 1998.

Campbell, Bebe Moore. *Your Blues Ain't Like Mine*. New York: Random House, 1992.

Carby, Hazel V. "Policing the Black Woman's Body in an Urban Context." *Critical Inquiry* 18, no. 4 (1992): 738–55. https://doi.org/10.1086/448654.

Carpio, Glenda. *Laughing Fit to Kill: Black Humor in the Fictions of Slavery*. New York: Oxford University Press, 2008.

Carter, Dan T. *Scottsboro: A Tragedy of the American South*. Baton Rouge: Lousiana State University Press, 2007.

Cartwright, Samuel. "Diseases and Peculiarities of the Negro Race." *DeBow's Review: Southern and Western States*, volume 9, 1851.

Caruth, Cathy. *Unclaimed Experience: Trauma, Narrative, and History*. Baltimore: Johns Hopkins University Press, 1996.

Casper, Monica. "On Race, Trauma, and 'Strange Fruit.'" *The Feminist Wire*, April 7, 2012.

Catholic League. "Lauryn Hill Flips Her Lid." CatholicLeague.org. January 22, 2004.

Cervenak, Sarah. Introduction to *Wandering: Philosophical Performances of Racial and Sexual Freedom*. Durham, NC: Duke University Press, 2014.

Césaire, Aimé. *Notebook of a Return to My Native Land*. Middletown, CT: Wesleyan University Press, 2001.

Césaire, Suzanne. "The Domain of the Marvelous." *Surrealist Women: An International Anthology*, ed. Penelope Rosemont. Austin: University of Texas Press, 1998.

Cganemccalla. "Top 5 Black Comic Meltdowns: Dave Chappelle Goes to Africa," *NewsOne*, November 17, 2008. https://newsone.com/40592/top-5-black-comic -meltdowns/.

Chace, Zoe. "The Many Voices of Lauryn Hill." *NPR: Music*, June 28, 2010.

Chan, Sylvia. "On the Verge: *Unplugged* Captures Lauryn Hill Unwound." *San Francisco Bay Guardian*, June 12, 2002. http://www.sfbg.com/36/37/art_music_lauryn.html.

Chappelle, Dave. "Chappelle's Story." Interview by Oprah Winfrey. *The Oprah Winfrey Show* (2006).

Chappelle, Dave. "A Conversation with Dave Chappelle." Interview by Charlie Rose. (2004).

Chappelle, Dave. "Dave Chappelle." *Anderson Cooper 360*, July 11, 2006.

Chappelle, Dave. "Dave Chappelle: Inside the Actor's Studio." Interview by James Lipton. *Inside the Actor's Studio* (2006). DVD.

Chappelle, Dave. "Why Comedian Dave Chappelle Walked Away from $50 Million | The Oprah Winfrey Show | OWN." February 2, 2006.

Chappelle, Dave, and Charlie Rose. "Dave Chappelle Discusses Culture and 'Chappelle's Show.'" *The Charlie Rose Show*. April 28, 2004, https://charlierose.com/videos/5454.

Chappelle's Show—The Lost Episodes (Uncensored). Comedy Central (2006). DVD.

Chappelle's Show—Season 1 (Uncensored). Written by Dave Chappelle and Neal Brennan. Comedy Central (2004). DVD.

Chappelle's Show—Season 2 (Uncensored). Written by Dave Chappelle and Neal Brennan. Comedy Central (2005). DVD.

Cheng, Anne Anlin. *The Melancholy of Race: Psychoanalysis, Assimilation, and Hidden Grief*. New York: Oxford University Press, 2001.

Chesler, Phyllis. *Women and Madness*. New York: Doubleday, 1972.

Christgau, Robert. "Not Hop, Stomp." *The Village Voice*, April 22, 2003. https://www.villagevoice.com/2003/04/22/not-hop-stomp/.

Christian, Barbara. "The Race for Theory." *Cultural Critique*, no. 6 (1987): 51. https://doi.org/10.2307/1354255.

Chude-Sokei, Louis. *The Last "Darky": Bert Williams, Black-on-Black Minstrelsy, and the African Diaspora*. Durham, NC: Duke University Press, 2006.

Clabough, Casey. *Gayl Jones: The Language of Voice and Freedom in Her Writings*. Jefferson, NC: McFarland, 2008.

Clabough, Casey. "Toward an All-Inclusive Structure: The Early Fiction of Gayl Jones." *Callaloo* 29, no. 2 (spring 2006): 634–57.

Cleage, Pearl. "Looking for Lauryn." *Essence*, July 2002. http://findarticles.com/p/articles/mi_m1264/is_3_33/ai_87741110.

Cognard-Black, Jennifer. "'I Said Nothing': The Rhetoric of Silence and Gayl Jones's 'Corregidora.'" *NWSA Journal* 13, no. 1 (2001): 40–60.

Cohen, Cathy J. "Deviance as Resistance: A New Research Agenda for the Study of Black Politics." *Du Bois Review: Social Science Research on Race* 1, no. 1 (2004).

Cohodas, Nadine. *Princess Noire: The Tumultuous Reign of Nina Simone*. New York: Pantheon, 2010.

Colbert, Soyica Diggs. *Black Movements: Performance and Cultural Politics*. New Brunswick, NJ: Rutgers University Press, 2017.

Colbert, Soyica Diggs. "'When I Die, I Won't Stay Dead': The Future of the Human in Suzan-Lori Parks's *The Death of the Last Black Man in the Whole Entire World*." *Boundary 2* 39, no. 3 (2012): 191–220. https://doi.org/10.1215/01903659-1730671.

Collins, Dan. "VH1 Offers Best Album List." CBS News, January 4, 2001. https://www.cbsnews.com/news/vh1-offers-best-album-list.

Collins, Patricia Hill. *Black Feminist Thought: Knowledge, Consciousness, and the Politics of Empowerment*. New York: Routledge, 2000.

Coney, John, dir. *Sun Ra—Space Is the Place*. 1974. Barbara Deloney, Sun Ra, Raymond Johnson, Erika Leder, Christopher Brooks. Plexifilm, 2003. DVD.

Conquergood, Dwight. "Performance Studies: Interventions and Radical Research." *The Performance Studies Reader*, ed. Henry Bial and Richard Schechner. New York: Routledge, 2004.

Cooke, Anne, and British Psychological Society. *Understanding Psychosis and Schizophrenia*. Revised edition. Leicester: The British Psychological Society, 2017.

Cooper, Brittney. *Eloquent Rage: A Black Feminist Discovers Her Superpower*. New York: St. Martin's Press, 2018.

Cooper, David. *Psychiatry and Anti-Psychiatry*. London: Granada/Paladin, 1970.

Corcoran, Mary E., and Ajay Chaudry. "The Dynamics of Childhood Poverty." *The Future of Children* 7, no. 2, Children and Poverty (summer–autumn 1997).

Coscarelli, Joe. "Kanye West Is Hospitalized for 'Psychiatric Emergency' Hours after Canceling Tour." *The New York Times*, November 21, 2016. https://www.nytimes.com/2016/11/21/arts/music/kanye-west-hospitalized-exhaustion.html.

Crawford, Margo. *Dilution Anxiety and the Black Phallus*. Columbus: Ohio State University Press, 2008.

Crockett, I'Nasah. "'Raving Amazons': Antiblackness and Misogynoir in Social Media." *Model View Culture*, June 30, 2014. https://modelviewculture.com/pieces/raving-amazons-antiblackness-and-misogynoir-in-social-media.

Crouch, Stanley. *Kansas City Lightning: The Rise and Times of Charlie Parker*. New York: HarperCollins, 2013.

Cvetkovich, Ann. *Depression: A Public Feeling*. Durham, NC: Duke University Press, 2012.

D'Andrea, Niki. "DMX Moved to Mental-Health Unit at Arizona State Prison Complex." *Phoenix New Times*, December 27, 2010. Blog.

Davis, Angela Y. *Blues Legacies and Black Feminism: Gertrude "Ma" Rainey, Bessie Smith, and Billie Holiday*. New York: Pantheon Books, 1998.

Davison, Carol Margaret. "'Love 'em and Lynch 'em': The Castration Motif in Gayl Jones's Eva's Man." *African American Review* 29, no. 3 (autumn 1995).

Dawson, Michael. *Black Visions: The Roots of Contemporary African-American Political Ideologies*. Chicago: University of Chicago Press, 2003.

Degruy, Joy. *Post Traumatic Slave Syndrome: America's Legacy of Enduring Injury and Healing*. Milwaukee: Uptone Press, 2005.

Deleuze, Gilles, and Félix Guattari. *Anti-Oedipus: Capitalism and Schizophrenia*. 1972. Minneapolis: University of Minnesota Press, 1983.

Derrida, Jacques. *Of Grammatology*. Translated by Gayatri Spivak. Baltimore: Johns Hopkins University Press, 1976.

Dhejne, Cecilia, Roy Van Vlerken, Gunter Heylens, and Jon Arcelus. "Mental Health and Gender Dysphoria: A Review of the Literature." *International Review of Psychiatry* 28, no. 1 (2016). https://doi.org/10.3109/09540261.2015.1115753.

Diagnostic and Statistical Manual of Mental Disorders, Fourth Edition: DSM-IV-TR. Arlington, VA: American Psychiatric Association, 2000.

Diagnostic and Statistical Manual of Mental Disorders, Fifth Edition: DSM-V. Arlington, VA: American Psychiatric Association, 2013.

Diedrich, Maria, and Henry Louis Gates Jr., eds. *Black Imagination and the Middle Passage*. New York: Oxford University Press, 1999.

Dinshaw, Carolyn, Lee Edelman, Roderick A. Ferguson, Carla Freccero, Elizabeth Freeman, Judith Halberstam, Annamarie Jagose, Christopher Nealon, and Nguyen Tan Hoang. "Theorizing Queer Temporalities: A Roundtable Discussion." *GLQ: A Journal of Lesbian and Gay Studies* 13, nos. 2–3 (2007).

Dixon, Melvin. "Singing a Deep Song: Language as Evidence in the Novels of Gayl Jones." *A Melvin Dixon Critical Reader*, ed. Justin A. Joyce and Dwight A. McBride. Jackson: University Press of Mississippi, 2006.

DMX, "Party Up (Up in Here)." *. . . And Then There Was X*. New York: Def Jam, 1999.

"DMX Proves 'Grand Champ' On Album Chart." *Billboard*, September 24, 2003. https://www.billboard.com/articles/news/68953/dmx-proves-grand-champ-on-album-chart.

Donaldson, Elizabeth J. "The Corpus of the Madwoman: Toward a Feminist Disability Studies Theory of Embodiment and Mental Illness." *NWSA Journal* (Special Issue: Feminist Disability Studies) 14, no. 3 (autumn 2002).

Douglass, Frederick. *Narrative of the Life of Frederick Douglass, An American Slave: Written By Himself*. 1845. New Haven: Yale University Press, 2001.

Downs, Kenya. "When Black Death Goes Viral, It Can Trigger PTSD-like Trauma." *PBS News Hour*, July 22, 2016. https://www.pbs.org/newshour/nation/black-pain-gone-viral-racism-graphic-videos-can-create-ptsd-like-trauma.

Drake, St. Clair, and Horace Cayton. *Black Metropolis: A Study of Negro Life in a Northern City*. 1945. Chicago: University of Chicago Press, 1993.

"A Dream Comes True for John Legend." *PRNewswire*, August 23, 2005.

Drescher, Jack. "Out of DSM: Depathologizing Homosexuality." *Behavioral Sciences* 5, no. 4 (2015): 565–75. https://doi.org/10.3390/bs5040565.

Dubey, Madhu. "Gayl Jones and the Matrilineal Metaphor of Tradition." *Signs: Journal of Women in Culture and Society* 20, no. 21 (1995).

Du Bois, W. E. B. *The Souls of Black Folk*. 1903. New York: Signet Classic, 1995.

DuMonthier, Asha, Chandra Childers, and Jessica Milli. *The Status of Black Women in the United States*. Washington, DC: Institute for Women's Policy Research, 2017.

Eckhoff, Sally. "The Terrible Mystery of Gayl Jones." Salon.com. February 26, 1998.

Edwards, Brent Hayes. *The Practice of Diaspora: Literature, Translation, and the Rise of Black Internationalism*. Cambridge, MA: Harvard University Press, 2003.

Effiong, Phillip U. *In Search of a Model for African-American Drama: A Study of Selected Plays by Lorraine Hansberry, Amiri Baraka, and Ntozake Shange*. Lanham, MD: University Press of America, 2000.

Elam, Harry. *The Past as Present in the Drama of August Wilson*. Ann Arbor: University of Michigan Press, 2004.

Elbogen, Eric B., and Sally C. Johnson. "The Intricate Link Between Violence and Mental Disorder: Results From the National Epidemiologic Survey on Alcohol and Related Conditions." *Archives of General Psychiatry* 66, no. 2 (2009).

Ellison, Ralph. *Invisible Man*. 1952. New York: Random House, 1995.

Eng, David, and Shinhee Han. "A Dialogue on Racial Melancholia." *Loss: The Politics of Mourning*, ed. David Eng and David Kazanjian. Berkeley: University of California Press, 2002.

Eng, David, and Shinhee Han. *Racial Melancholia, Racial Dissociation: On the Social and Psychic Lives of Asian Americans*. Durham, NC: Duke University Press, 2019.

Epstein, Steven. *Impure Science: AIDS, Activism, and the Politics of Knowledge*. Berkeley: University of California Press, 1996.

Erb, Cynthia. "'Have You Ever Seen the Inside of One of Those Places?': *Psycho*, Foucault, and the Postwar Context of Madness." *Cinema Journal* 45, no. 4 (summer 2006).

Erevelles, Nirmala, and Andrea Minear. "Unspeakable Offenses: Untangling Race and Disability in Discourses of Intersectionality." *Journal of Literary and Cultural Disability Studies* 4, no. 2 (2010): 127–45. https://doi.org/10.3828/jlcds.2010.11.

Eversley, Shelly. "The Lunatic's Fancy and the Work of Art." *American Literary History* 13, no. 3 (autumn 2001).

Eze, Emmanuel Chukwudi, ed. *Race and the Enlightenment: A Reader*. Malden, MA: Blackwell, 1997.

Fanon, Frantz. *Black Skin, White Masks*. 1952. Translated by Charles Lam Markmann. London: Pluto Press, 1986.

Fanon, Frantz. *Toward the African Revolution: Political Essays*. 1964. Translated by Haakon Chevalier. New York: Grove Press, 1988.

Fanon, Frantz. *The Wretched of the Earth*. 1961. Translated by Constance Farrington. New York: Grove Press, 1963.

Farley, Christopher John. "Dave Speaks." *Time*, May 14, 2005.

Farley, Christopher John. "On the Beach with Dave Chappelle." *Time*, May 15, 2005.

Farley, Christopher John. "Songs in the Key of Lauryn Hill." *Time*, September 7, 1998.

Fausset, Richard. "Police Killing of Unarmed Georgia Man Leaves Another Town in Disbelief." *New York Times*, March 11, 2015.

Felluga, Dino Franco. *Critical Theory: The Key Concepts*. New York: Routledge, 2015.

Felski, Rita. "Suspicious Minds." *Poetics Today* 32, no. 2, Narrative and the Emotions (II) (summer 2011).

"Findings." Stanford Open Policing Project, 2020. https://openpolicing.stanford.edu/.

Fisher, Dexter, and Robert Stepto. "Introduction." *Afro-American Literature: The Reconstruction of Instruction*. New York: Modern Language Association of America, 1979.

Fitzgerald, Ella. "All the Things You Are." *Ella Fitzgerald Sings the Jerome Kern Song Book*. New York: Verve, 1963.

Flaherty, Anne. "Trump's Diagnosis for Critics: 'Trump Derangement Syndrome.'" *Associated Press News*, July 18, 2018. https://apnews.com/48225d1360864dcb861b 12e5cda12a32.

Fleetwood, Nicole. *Marking Time: Art in the Age of Mass Incarceration*. Cambridge, MA: Harvard University Press, 2020.

Fleetwood, Nicole. *Troubling Vision: Performance, Visuality, and Blackness*. Chicago: University of Chicago Press, 2011.

Fleming, Victor, dir. *Gone with the Wind*. Beverly Hills: Metro-Goldwyn-Mayer, 1939.

Foege, Alec. "Fugees: Leaders of the New Cool." *Rolling Stone*, September 5, 1996.

Ford, Matt. "America's Largest Mental Hospital Is a Jail." *Atlantic*, June 8, 2015. https://www.theatlantic.com/politics/archive/2015/06/americas-largest-mental-hospital -is-a-jail/395012/.

Foucault, Michel. *The History of Sexuality: An Introduction: Volume I*. 1976. Translated by Robert Hurley. New York: Vintage Books, 1990.

Foucault, Michel. *Madness: The Invention of an Idea*. Previously published as *Mental Illness and Psychology*. 1962. New York: Harper Perennial, 2011.

Foucault, Michel. *Madness and Civilization: A History of Insanity in the Age of Reason*. 1961. New York: Vintage, 1998.

Fox, Joe, Adrian Blanco, Jennifer Jenkins, Julie Tate, and Wesley Lowery. "What We've Learned about Police Shootings 5 Years after Ferguson." *Washington Post*, August 9, 2019. https://www.washingtonpost.com/nation/2019/08/09/what-weve -learned-about-police-shootings-years-after-ferguson/?arc404=true.

Fraser, Nancy. "Rethinking the Public Sphere: A Contribution to the Critique of Actually Existing Democracy." *Social Text*, nos. 25–26 (1990).

Frazier, E. Franklin. *Black Bourgeoisie: The Book That Brought the Shock of Self-Revelation to Middle-Class Blacks in America*. New York: The Free Press, 1957.

Freeman, Elizabeth. *Time Binds: Queer Temporalities, Queer Histories*. Durham, NC: Duke University Press, 2010.

Freud, Sigmund. "The Aetiology of Hysteria," "An Autobiographical Study," "Beyond the Pleasure Principle," "Civilization and Its Discontents," "The Ego and the Id," "Leonardo Da Vinci and a Memory of His Childhood," "Mourning and Melancholia." *The Freud Reader*. Edited by Peter Gay. New York: W. W. Norton, 1989.

Freud, Sigmund. *Jokes and Their Relation to the Unconscious*. 1905. Edited by Peter Gay. Translated by James Strachey. New York: W. W. Norton, 1990.

Freud, Sigmund. "Medusa's Head." In *Sexuality and the Psychology of Love*. 1922. New York: Touchstone, 1997.

Friedman, Roger. "Lauryn Hill: Brainwashed?" FoxNews.com. June 11, 2002. http://www.foxnews.com/story/0,2933,54993,00.html.

The Fugees. "Outro/Manifest." *The Score*. Columbia/Ruffhouse, 1996. CD.

Fuller, Doris A., H. Richard Lamb, Michael Biasotti, and John Snook. "Overlooked in the Undercounted: The Role of Mental Illness in Fatal Law Enforcement Encounters." *Treatment Advocacy Center*. TACReports.org. 2015.

Gabbard, Krin. *Hotter than That: The Trumpet, Jazz, and American Culture*. New York: Faber and Faber, 2008.

Gaines, Malik. "The Quadruple-Consciousness of Nina Simone." *Women and Performance: A Journal of Feminist Theory* 23, no. 2 (2013).

Gale, Alex. "On My Own: The Best Solo Breakouts." Bet.com. October 2012.

Garber, Marjorie, and Nancy J. Vickers, eds. *The Medusa Reader*. New York: Routledge, 2003.

Garbus, Liz, dir. *What Happened, Miss Simone?* Netflix and Radical Media, 2015.

Garland-Thomson, Rosemarie. "Feminist Disability Studies." *Signs* 30, no. 2 (2005) 1557–87.

Garner, Dwight. "Under a Strange, Soulful Spell." *New York Times*, February 18, 2010.

Gates, Henry Louis, Jr. *The Signifyin' Monkey: A Theory of African-American Literary Criticism*. New York: Oxford University Press, 1988.

Gelly, Dave. *Being Prez: The Life and Music of Lester Young*. New York: Oxford University Press, 2007.

Gemes, Ken. "Freud and Nietzsche on Sublimation." *The Journal of Nietzsche Studies*, no. 38 (autumn 2009).

George, William H., and Lorraine J. Martínez. "Victim Blaming in Rape: Effects of Victim and Perpetrator Race, Type of Rape, and Participant Racism." *Psychology of Women Quarterly* 26, no. 2 (2002). https://doi.org/10.1111/1471-6402.00049.

Giles, Jeff. "Songs in the Key of Strife: Lauryn Hill Comes Unplugged." *Newsweek*, May 13, 2002. http://www.newsweek.com/id/64512.

Gilman, Sander. *Difference and Pathology: Stereotypes of Sexuality, Race, and Madness*. Ithaca, NY: Cornell University Press, 1985.

Gilmore, Glenda. *Defying Dixie: The Radical Roots of Civil Rights, 1919–1950*. New York: W. W. Norton, 2008.

Gilroy, Paul. *The Black Atlantic: Modernity and Double Consciousness*. Cambridge, MA: Harvard University Press, 1992.

Gilroy, Paul. "Living Memory: A Meeting with Toni Morrison." *Small Acts*. Essex, UK: Serpent's Tail, 1993.

Giorgis, Hannah. "The Complicated Female Genius of Lauryn Hill." *The Atlantic*, August 27, 2018. https://www.theatlantic.com/entertainment/archive/2018/08/the-complicated-female-genius-of-lauryn-hill/568612/.

Glissant, Édouard. *The Collected Poems of Édouard Glissant*. Minneapolis: University of Minnesota Press, 2005.

Glissant, Édouard. *Poetics of Relation*. 1990. Translated by Betsy Wang. Ann Arbor: University of Michigan Press, 1997.

Goffman, Erving. *Asylums: Essays on the Social Situation of Mental Patients and Other Inmates*. New York: Anchor Books, 1961.

Gold, Joel, dir. *Nina Simone: A Historical Perspective*. New York: Cinemagic, 1970.

Goldsby, Jacqueline. *A Spectacular Secret: Lynching in American Life and Literature*. Chicago: University of Chicago Press, 2006.

Goldsmith, Barton. "Intimacy and Vulnerability: Can You Have One without the Other?" *Psychology Today*, April 2, 2010.

Goldstein, Joseph, and James C. McKinley Jr. "Police Sergeant Acquitted in Killing of Mentally Ill Woman." *New York Times*, February 15, 2018.

Goodman, John, and Sy Johnson. *Mingus Speaks*. Berkeley: University of California Press, 2013.

Gordon, Avery. *Ghostly Matters: Haunting and the Sociological Imagination*. Minneapolis: University of Minnesota Press, 2008.

Gordon, Devin. "Fears of a Clown." *Newsweek*, May 15, 2005. https://www.newsweek.com/fears-clown-118667.

Graff, Gary. "Wynton Marsalis on Bringing the Story of Jazz Originator Buddy Bolden to the Big Screen." *Billboard*, April 23, 2019. https://www.billboard.com/articles/news/8508244/wynton-marsalis-buddy-bolden-movie.

Gray, Richard J., and Michael Putnam. "Exploring Niggerdom: Racial Inversion and Language Taboos." In *The Comedy of Dave Chappelle: Critical Essays*, ed. K. A. Wisniewski. Jefferson, NC: McFarland.

Gray, Thomas R. "The Confessions of Nat Turner, the Leader of the Late Insurrection in Southhampton, Va., as fully and voluntarily made to Thomas R. Gray." In *Slave Narratives*, ed. William L. Andrews and Henry Louis Gates Jr. New York: Library of America, 2000.

Green, Anthony. "Dark Man X: The Resurrection," *GQ*, September 23, 2019, https://www.gq.com/story/dmx-the-resurrection.

Grier, William H., and Price M. Cobbs. *Black Rage*. New York: Basic Books, 1968.

Griffin, Farah Jasmine. *If You Can't Be Free, Be a Mystery: In Search of Billie Holiday*. New York: One World/Ballantine, 2002.

Griffin, Farah Jasmine. "That the Mothers May Soar and the Daughters May Know Their Names: A Retrospective of Black Feminist Literary Criticism." *Signs* 32, no. 2 (winter 2007).

Grunitzky, Claude. "The Prophet: Lauryn Hill." *Trace Magazine*, July 2005. http://webuser.fh-furtwangen.de/~krapf/fugees-online/special_interview_trace.htm.

Gundersen, Edna. "Lauryn Hill's Debut Smashes Record." *USA Today*, September 3, 1998.

Gussow, Adam. "'Shoot Myself a Cop': Mamie Smith's 'Crazy Blues' as Social Text." *Callaloo* 25, no. 1 (2002): 8–44. https://doi.org/10.1353/cal.2002.0017.

Hacking, Ian. *Mad Travelers: Reflections on the Reality of Transient Mental Illnesses*. Cambridge, MA: Harvard University Press, 2002.

Haegele, Justin Anthony, and Samuel Hodge. "Disability Discourse: Overview and Critiques of the Medical and Social Models." *Quest* 68, no. 2 (2016): 193–206. https://doi.org/10.1080/00336297.2016.1143849.

Haggins, Bambi. *Laughing Mad: The Black Comic Persona in Post-Soul America*. New Brunswick, NJ: Rutgers University Press, 2007.

Halberstam, Jack. *Female Masculinity*. Durham, NC: Duke University Press, 2019.

Hall, Stuart. "The Rediscovery of 'Ideology': Return of the Repressed in Media Studies." *Cultural Theory and Popular Culture: A Reader*, ed. John Story. 4th ed. Essex, UK: Pearson Education Limited, 2009.

Hanchard, Michael. "Afro-Modernity: Temporality, Politics, and the African Diaspora." *Public Culture* 11, no. 1 (1999).

Hansen, Helena, Philippe Bourgois, and Ernest Drucker. "Pathologizing Poverty: New Forms of Diagnosis, Disability, and Structural Stigma under Welfare Reform." *Social Science and Medicine* 103 (2014): 76–83. https://doi.org/10.1016/j.socscimed.2013.06.033.

Hardy, Ernest. "Fugee-L.A." *L.A. Weekly*, February 10, 2006. http://www.laweekly.com/index.php?option=com_lawcontent&task=view&id=12609&Itemid=125.

Harris, Keith M. "'That Nigger's Crazy': Richard Pryor, Racial Performativity, Cultural Critique." *Richard Pryor: The Life and Legacy of a "Crazy" Black Man*. Edited by Audrey Thomas McCluskey. Bloomington: Indiana University Press, 2008.

Harris, William J., ed. *The LeRoi Jones/Amiri Baraka Reader*. New York: Basic Books, 1999.

Hartman, Saidiya. *Lose Your Mother: A Journey along the Atlantic Slave Route*. New York: Farrar, Straus and Giroux, 2007.

Hartman, Saidiya. *Scenes of Subjection: Terror, Slavery, and Self-Making in Nineteenth-Century America*. New York: Oxford University Press, 1997.

Hartman, Saidiya. "The Time of Slavery." *South Atlantic Quarterly* 101, no. 4 (2002): 757–77. https://doi.org/10.1215/00382876-101-4-757.

Hartman, Saidiya. "Venus in Two Acts." *Small Axe: A Caribbean Journal of Criticism* 12, no. 2 (2008): 1–14. https://doi.org/10.2979/sax.2008.-.26.1.

Hartman, Saidiya. *Wayward Lives, Beautiful Experiments: Intimate Histories of Social Upheaval*. New York: W. W. Norton, 2019.

Harvilla, Rob. "The Disorientation of Lauryn Hill." *Village Voice*, August 7, 2007. http://www.villagevoice.com/2007-08-07/music/the-disorientation-of-lauryn-hill/.

Hayes, Rebecca M., Katherine Lorenz, and Kristin A. Bell. "Victim Blaming Others: Rape Myth Acceptance and the Just World Belief." *Feminist Criminology* 8, no. 3 (2013).

Heard, Danielle C. "'Don't Let Me Be Misunderstood': Nina Simone's Theater of Invisibility." *Callaloo* 35, no. 4 (2012): 1056–84. https://doi.org/10.1353/cal.2013.0011.

Hegel, Georg Wilhelm Friedrich. *The Philosophy of History*. 1837. New York: Dover, 1956.

Henderson, Mae G. "Speaking in Tongues: Dialogics and Dialectics and the Black Woman Writer's Literary Tradition." In *Changing Our Own Words: Essays on Criticism, Theory, and Writing by Black Women*. Edited by Cheryl Wall. New Brunswick, NJ: Rutgers University Press, 1989.

Hiatt, Brian. "Wyclef Jean Q&A: How the Ex-Fugee Got His Groove Back." *Rolling Stone*, November 29, 2007. http://www.rollingstone.com/music/news/wyclef-jean-q-a-how-the-ex-fugee-got-his-groove-back-20071129.

Higginbotham, Evelyn Brooks. *Righteous Discontent: The Women's Movement in the Black Baptist Church, 1880–1920*. Cambridge, MA: Harvard University Press, 1993.

Hilburn, Robert. "Hill Continues Her Lofty Course." *Los Angeles Times*, July 15, 2002. http://articles.latimes.com/2002/jul/15/entertainment/et-hilburn15.

Hildebrand, Lee. "Late Start, New Approach Disappoint Lauryn Hill Fans at Oakland Concert." *San Francisco Chronicle*, June 29, 2007. http://www.sfgate.com/cgi-bin/article.cgi?f=/c/a/2007/06/29/HILL.TMP.

Hill, Lauryn. "Adam Lives in Theory." *MTV Unplugged No. 2.0*. Columbia/Sony, 2002. CD.

Hill, Lauryn. "Black Rage." Life Is Good/Black Rage Tour. October 31, 2012.

Hill, Lauryn. "The Conquering Lion." *MTV Unplugged No. 2.0*. Columbia/Sony, 2002. CD.

Hill, Lauryn. "Consumerism." New York: Sony/Columbia, 2013.

Hill, Lauryn. "Doo Wop (That Thing)." *The Miseducation of Lauryn Hill*. Ruffhouse/Columbia, 1998.

Hill, Lauryn. "I Find It Hard to Say (Rebel)." *MTV Unplugged No. 2.0*. Columbia/Sony, 2002. CD.

Hill, Lauryn. "I Get Out." *MTV Unplugged No. 2.0*. Columbia/Sony, 2002. CD.

Hill, Lauryn. "I Gotta Find Peace of Mind." *MTV Unplugged No. 2.0*. Columbia/Sony, 2002. CD.

Hill, Lauryn. "Interlude 3." *MTV Unplugged No. 2.0*. Columbia/Sony, 2002. CD.

Hill, Lauryn. Interviewed by Peter Spirer, dir. *Rhyme & Reason*. Los Angeles: Miramax, 1997.

Hill, Lauryn. "Intro." *MTV Unplugged No. 2.0*. Columbia/Sony, 2002. CD.

Hill, Lauryn. "Lauryn Hill: Redemption Song." Interview by Sway. *MTVNews.com*.

Hill, Lauryn. "Looking for Lauryn." Interview by Pearl Cleage. *Essence*, July 2002.

Hill, Lauryn. "The Mystery of Iniquity." *MTV Unplugged No. 2.0*. Columbia/Sony, 2002. CD.

Hill, Lauryn. "Oh, Jerusalem." *MTV Unplugged No. 2.0*. Columbia/Sony, 2002. CD.

Hill, Lauryn. "The Prophet: Lauryn Hill." Interview by Claude Grunitzky. *Trace Magazine*. July 2005.

Hill, Lauryn. "They Call Me Ms. Hill." Interview with Joan Morgan. *Essence*, January 2006.

Hine, Darlene Clark. "Rape and the Inner Lives of Black Women in the Middle West." *Signs: Journal of Women in Culture and Society* 14, no. 4 (1989): 912–20. https://doi.org/10.1086/494552.

Hip Hop Library. "Nina Simone—Mississippi Goddam (Live in Netherlands)." YouTube video, 5:27. December 19, 2015. https://www.youtube.com/watch?v=ghhaREDM3X8.

Hobson, Janell, and R. Dianne Bartlow. "Introduction: Representin': Women, Hip-Hop, and Popular Music." *Meridians* 8, no. 1, Representin': Women, Hip-Hop, and Popular Music (2008).

Hobson, Vic. "Buddy Bolden's Blues." *The Jazz Archivist: A Newsletter of the William Ransom Hogan Jazz Archive* 21 (2008).

Hodes, Martha. "The Sexualization of Reconstruction Politics: White Women and Black Men in the South after the Civil War." *Journal of the History of Sexuality* 3, no. 3 (1993).

Hoffman, Miles. *The NPR Classical Music Companion: An Essential Guide for Enlightened Listening.* New York: Houghton Mifflin, 1997.

Holiday, Billie. "Strange Fruit." Commodore Records, 1938.

hooks, bell. "The Oppositional Gaze: Black Female Spectators." In *Black Looks: Race and Representation.* New York: Routledge Press, 1992.

Horton, Alex. "A Deputy in Houston Shot and Killed an Unarmed Black Man—Days after Stephon Clark's Death." *The Washington Post,* March 24, 2018.

Hughes, Langston. "Harlem." In *Montage of a Dream Deferred.* New York: Holt, 1951.

Hume, David. "Of National Characters." 1742. *Race and the Enlightenment: A Reader,* ed. Emmanuel Chukwudi Eze. Malden, MA: Blackwell Publishers, 1997.

Hunter, Dianne. "Hysteria, Psychoanalysis, and Feminism: The Case of Anna O." *Feminist Studies* 9, no. 3 (1983).

Ingham, John M. *Psychological Anthropology Reconsidered.* Cambridge: Cambridge University Press, 1996.

Jackson, Derrick Z. "Opinion: The N-Word and Richard Pryor." *New York Times,* December 15, 2005. https://www.nytimes.com/2005/12/15/opinion/the-nwordand-richard-pryor.html.

Jackson, John L. *Racial Paranoia: The Unintended Consequences of Political Correctness.* New York: Basic Civitas Books, 2010.

Jackson, Lawrence. *Ralph Ellison: Emergence of Genius.* Athens: University of Georgia Press, 2007.

James, Frank. "The Malcolm X Factor." *The Chicago Tribune,* November 8, 1991.

"Jazz Is Not an Illness." *New Orleans Times-Picayune,* July 14, 2001. Hogan Jazz Archives, Tulane University, New Orleans.

Jean, Wyclef, and Anthony Bozza. *Purpose: An Immigrant Story.* New York: HarperCollins, 2012.

Jefferson, Thomas. "Notes on the State of Virginia." 1785. *Race and the Enlightenment: A Reader,* ed. Emmanuel Chukwudi Eze. Malden, MA: Blackwell Publishers, 1997.

Jelly Roll Morton Collection, 1938 (AFS 1658 A-B), Archive of Folk Culture, American Folklife Center, Library of Congress, Washington, DC.

Jenkins, Candice M. *Private Lives, Proper Relations: Regulating Black Intimacy.* Minneapolis: University of Minnesota Press, 2007.

Johnson, Walter. "Possible Pasts: Some Speculations on Time, Temporality, and the History of Atlantic." *Amerikastudien/American Studies* 45, no. 4 (2000): 485–99.

Jones, Gayl. "Asylum." In *White Rat.* 1977. New York: Harlem Moon Press, 2006.

Jones, Gayl. *The Healing, Corregidora, Eva's Man.* New York: Quality Paperback Bookclub (Griot Editions), 1998. Originally published as *Corregidora,* New York: Random House, 1975, and as *Eva's Man,* New York: Random House, 1976.

Jones, LeRoi. *Dutchman; and, the Slave: Two Plays.* New York: Morrow, 1966.

Jones, LeRoi. "Revolutionary Theater." *Home: Social Essays.* New York: Morrow, 1966.

Jordan, June. "All About Eva: Eva's Man." *New York Times Book Review*, May 16, 1976.

Kafer, Alison. *Feminist Queer Crip*. Bloomington: Indiana University Press, 2013.

Kafer, Alison. "Health Rebels: A Crip Manifesto for Social Justice," YouTube video, 1:07:22, April 6, 2017. https://www.youtube.com/watch?v=YqcOUD1pBKw.

Kant, Immanuel. "Of National Characteristics, so far as They Depend upon the Distinct Feeling of the Beautiful and Sublime." 1764. *Race and the Enlightenment: A Reader*. Edited by Emmanuel Chukwudi Eze. Malden, MA: Blackwell Publishers, 1997.

Kanter, Arlene S. *The Development of Disability Rights Under International Law: From Charity to Human Rights*. New York: Routledge, 2015.

"Kanye West Stirs Up TMZ Newsroom Over Trump, Slavery, Free Thought." *TMZ*, May 1, 2018. https://www.tmz.com/2018/05/01/kanye-west-tmz-live-slavery-trump.

Kaplan, E. Ann. *Trauma Culture: The Politics of Terror and Loss in Media and Literature*. New Brunswick, NJ: Rutgers University Press, 2005.

Kaplan, Sara Clarke. "Souls at the Crossroads, Africans on the Water: The Politics of Diasporic Melancholia." *Callaloo* 30, no. 2 (2007): 511–26.

Karrer, Wolfgang. "Gayl Jones: Asylum." In *The African American Short Story 1970 to 1990: A Collection of Critical Essays*, edited by Wolfgang Karrer and Barbara Puschmann-Nalenz. Trier, Germany: Wissenschaftlicher Verlag Trier, 1993.

Karst, James. "A Newly Discovered Account of Jazz Legend Buddy Bolden's Mental Decline." *Nola.com*. January, 6 2019.

Keim, Curtis, and Carolyn Somerville. *Mistaking Africa: Curiosities and Inventions of the American Mind*, 4th ed. New York: Routledge, 2018.

Kelley, Robin D. G. *Freedom Dreams: The Black Radical Imagination*. New York: Beacon Press, 2003.

Kelley, Robin D. G. *Thelonious Monk: The Life and Times of an American Original*. New York: Free Press, 2009.

"Kendrick Lamar Talks About 'u,' His Depression & Suicidal Thoughts (Pt. 2) | MTV News." YouTube video, 10:39. April 1, 2015. https://www.youtube.com/watch?v=Hu4Pz9PjolI.

Kennedy, Adrienne. *Funnyhouse of a Negro: A Play in One Act*. New York: Samuel French, 1969.

Kennedy, Gerrick D. "Nas, Ms. Lauryn Hill Announce Joint Fall Tour." *Los Angeles Times*, September 19, 2012.

Kerby, Sophia. "The Top 10 Most Startling Facts about People of Color and Criminal Justice in the United States: A Look at the Racial Disparities Inherent in Our Nation's Criminal-Justice System." AmericanProgress.org. Washington, DC: Center for American Progress, March 13, 2012.

Kern, Jerome (music), and Oscar Hammerstein, II (lyrics). "All the Things You Are." 1939. *All the Things You Are—Music of Jerome Kern*. Audiophile, 1999. CD.

Keyes, Cheryl L. "Empowering Self, Making Choices, Creating Spaces: Black Female Identity via Rap Music Performance." *The Journal of American Folklore* 113, no. 449 (summer 2000).

King, Debra Walker. *African Americans and the Culture of Pain*. Charlottesville, VA: University of Virginia Press, 2008.

King, Martin Luther, Jr. "Letter from Birmingham Jail," April 16, 1963. In Martin Luther King Jr., *Why We Can't Wait*. New York: Signet Classics, 2000.

King, Martin Luther, Jr. "September 27, 1966: MLK—A Riot Is the Language of the Unheard," YouTube video, Interview with Mike Wallace, *60 Minutes*, 1966. https://www.youtube.com/watch?v=_K0BWXjJv5s.

King, Shaun. "Danny Ray Thomas Was a Broken Man Who Needed Help. Instead He Was Gunned Down by a Cop in Broad Daylight." *The Intercept*, March 30, 2018.

King, Shaun. "If You Are Black and in a Mental Health Crisis, 911 Can Be a Death Sentence." September 29, 2019. https://theintercept.com/2019/09/29/police-shootings-mental-health/.

King James Version of the Holy Bible. http://www.kingjamesbibleonline.org/.

Klein, Herbert S., Stanley L. Engerman, Robin Haines, and Ralph Shlomowitz. "Transoceanic Mortality: The Slave Trade in Comparative Perspective." *The William and Mary Quarterly* 58, no. 1, New Perspectives on the Transatlantic Slave Trade (January 2001).

Lackey, Michael. "Redeeming the Post-Metaphysical Promise of J. Saunders Redding's 'America.'" *CR: The New Centennial Review* 12, no. 3 (2012): 217–43. https://doi.org/10.1353/ncr.2012.0046.

Lamar, Kendrick. "The Blacker the Berry." *To Pimp a Butterfly*. Carson, CA: Top Dawg/Interscope Records, 2015.

Landau, Emily Epstein. *Spectacular Wickedness: Sex, Race, and Memory in Storyville, New Orleans*. Baton Rouge: Louisiana State University Press, 2013.

Lang, Steven. "Disorderly Conduct." *People*, May 12, 1997.

Latham, Stan, dir. *Dave Chappelle: Killin' Them Softly*. HBO Box Office, 2000.

Laub, Dori. "Bearing Witness or the Vicissitudes of Listening." In *Testimony: Crises of Witnessing in Literature, Psychoanalysis, and History*. New York: Routledge, 1991.

"Lauryn Hill Has Completely Lost Her Mind!" perezhilton.com. July 26, 2007.

"Lauryn Hill—Howard Stern Interview 1996." RAINFALL. YouTube.com. October 23, 2007.

"Lauryn Hill in Houston Texas oct 31 2012 live new sing Black Rage/and Explain [*sic*]." MCOAST. YouTube.com. November 1, 2012.

"Lauryn Hill Is a Song Thief!" perezhilton.com. July 31, 2007.

"Lauryn Hill Is the Flyest MC Ever." *The Source*, September 1998.

"Lauryn Hill—Shows Up LATE for Concert Then Lectures Fan on Respect!" *TMZ*, July 23, 2014. https://www.tmz.com/2014/07/23/lauryn-hill-concert-video-rant-disrespectful-fan-house-of-blues/.

"Lauryn Hill Speaks Out against Abusive Priests in the Church." *Jet*, January 12, 2004.

"Lauryn Hill Speaks Out on How Motherhood Made Her Sexy and Why She's Not a Diva." *Jet Magazine*, February 8, 1999.

LaValle, Victor. *The Ecstatic*. New York: Vintage, 2003.

Layton, Joe, dir. *Richard Pryor: Live on the Sunset Strip*. Los Angeles: Columbia Pictures, 1982.

Lee, Bandy X., ed. *The Dangerous Case of Donald Trump: 27 Psychiatrists and Mental Health Experts Assess a President.* New York: St. Martin's Press, 2017.

LeFrançois, Brenda A., Robert Menzies, and Geoffrey Reaume, eds. "Introducing Mad Studies." In *Mad Matters: A Critical Reader in Canadian Mad Studies.* Toronto: Canadian Scholars' Press, 2013.

Legend, John, featuring Lauryn Hill. "So High (Cloud 9 Remix)." Getting Out Our Dreams/Sony Urban Music/Columbia, 2005. CD.

Lettow, Susanne. "Feminism and the Enlightenment." *The Routledge Companion to Feminist Philosophy*, edited by Ann Garry, Serene J. Khader, and Alison Stone. Abingdon, VA: Routledge, 2017.

Lewis, Miles Marshall. "Reality Soundbites: Lauryn Hill's *MTV Unplugged 2.0.*" July 3–9, 2002. http://www.villagevoice.com/music/0227,lewis,36173,22.html.

Lewis, R. L'Heureux. "Racial Conspiracy and Research." *The Search for the Legacy of the USPHS Syphilis Study at Tuskegee*, ed. Ralph V. Katz and Rueben Warren. Lanham, MD: Lexington Books, 2011.

Lhamon, W. T. *Raising Cain: Blackface Performance from Jim Crow to Hip Hop.* Cambridge, MA: Harvard University Press, 2000.

Loewald, Hans. "Some Considerations on Repetition and Repetition Compulsion." *International Journal of Psychoanalysis* 52 (1971): 59–66.

Loewald, Hans. *Sublimation: Inquires into Theoretical Psychoanalysis.* New Haven, CT: Yale University Press, 1988.

Logan, Rayford W. *The Negro in American Life and Thought: The Nadir, 1877–1901.* New York: Dial Press, 1954.

Lomax, Alan. "Alan Lomax Collection." Library of Congress, Washington, DC, May–December 1938, 1658B.

Lomax, Alan. *Mister Jelly Roll: The Fortunes of Jelly Roll Morton, New Orleans Creole and "Inventor of Jazz."* Berkeley: University of California Press, 2001.

Long, Alecia P. *The Great Southern Babylon: Sex, Race, and Respectability in New Orleans, 1865–1920.* Baton Rouge: Louisiana State University Press, 2004.

Lorde, Audre. "Eva's Man." 1976. *I Am Your Sister: Collected and Unpublished Writings of Audre Lorde*, ed. Rudolph Byrd, Johnnetta Betsch Cole, and Beverly Guy-Sheftall. New York: Oxford University Press, 2009.

Lorde, Audre. "The Transformation of Silence into Language and Action." *Sister Outsider: Essays and Speeches.* Berkeley: Crossing Press, 1984.

Lorde, Audre. "The Uses of Anger: Women Responding to Racism." In *Sister Outsider: Essays and Speeches.* Berkeley: Crossing Press, 1984.

Lott, Eric. *Love and Theft: Blackface Minstrelsy and the American Working Class.* New York: Oxford University Press, 1993.

Love, Heather. *Feeling Backward: Loss and the Politics of Queer History.* Cambridge, MA: Harvard University Press, 2007.

Luhrmann, Tanya Marie, and Jocelyn Marrow. *Our Most Troubling Madness: Case Studies in Schizophrenia across Cultures.* Oakland: University of California Press, 2016.

Lyons, Brenda. "Interview with Ntozake Shange." *Massachusetts Review* 28, no. 4 (winter 1987).

MacArthur Research Network on Mental Health and the Law. "The MacArthur Violence Risk Assessment Study: September 2005 Update of the Executive Summary." May 2019. http://www.macarthur.virginia.edu/risk.html.

Macharia, Keguro. "On Quitting." *The New Inquiry*, September 19, 2018. https://thenewinquiry.com/on-quitting.

Mackey, Nathaniel. *Bedouin Hornbook*. Los Angeles: Sun and Moon Press, 1997.

MacKinnon, Catharine. *Feminism Unmodified: Discourse on Life and Law*. Cambridge, MA: Harvard University Press, 1987.

Magubane, Bernard Makhosezwe. *The Ties That Bind: African-American Consciousness of Africa*. 2nd ed. Trenton, NJ: African World Press, 1987.

Mahdani, Mahmood. *Citizen and Subject: Contemporary Africa and the Legacy of Late Colonialism*. Princeton, NJ: Princeton University Press, 1996.

Maher, Winifred B., and Brendan Maher. "The Ship of Fools: Stultifera Navis or Ignis Fatuus?" *American Psychologist* 37, no. 7 (July 1982).

Manning, Patrick, and William S. Griffiths. "Divining the Unprovable: Simulating the Demography of African Slavery." *The Journal of Interdisciplinary History* 19, no. 2 (autumn 1988).

Manso, Peter. "Chronicle of a Tragedy Foretold." *New York Times Magazine*, July 19, 1998.

Marquis, Donald M. *In Search of Buddy Bolden: First Man of Jazz*. 1978. Baton Rouge: Louisiana State University Press, 2005.

Marx, Karl. *A Contribution to the Critique of Political Economy*. 1859. International Books, 1979.

Marx, Karl. *Surveys from Exile: Political Writing Vol. 2*. Edited by David Fernbach. London: Penguin Books, 1973.

"Mauled His Mother-In-Law." *The Daily Picayune*, March 27, 1906.

Maxson, J. David. "Burying the King Again: Buddy Bolden's Jazz Funeral and Defleshed Memory." *Rhetoric Society Quarterly* 48, no. 5 (2018): 516–36. https://doi.org/10.1080/02773945.2018.1444194.

Mbembe, Achille. "Necropolitics." Translated by Libby Meintjes. *Public Culture* 15 (winter 2003).

Mbembe, Achille. *Necropolitics*. Durham, NC: Duke University Press, 2019.

McCall, Nathan. *Makes Me Wanna Holler: A Young Black Man in America*. New York: Vintage, 1994.

McCarthy, Michael. *Dark Continent: Africa as Seen by Americans*. Westport, CT: Greenwood Press, 1983.

McCluskey, Audrey Thomas. "Introduction: Richard Pryor: Comic Genius, Tortured Soul." *Richard Pryor: The Life and Legacy of a "Crazy" Black Man*. Edited by Audrey Thomas McCluskey. Bloomington: Indiana University Press, 2008.

McCusker, John. *Creole Trombone: Kid Ory and the Early Years of Jazz*. Jackson: University Press of Mississippi, 2012.

McDowell, Deborah E. "New Directions for Black Feminist Criticism." *Black American Literature Forum* 14, no. 4 (1980): 153. https://doi.org/10.2307/2904407.

McGeachan, Cheryl. "'The World Is Full of Big Bad Wolves': Investigating the Experimental Therapeutic Spaces of R. D. Laing and Aaron Esterson." *History of Psychiatry* 25, no. 3 (2014): 283–98.

McGee, Tiffany, and Alex Tresniowski. "What Ever Happened to . . . Lauryn Hill?" *People Magazine*, August 18, 2008. http://www.people.com/people/archive/article/0,,20221692,00.html.

McGuire, Danielle L. *At the Dark End of the Street: Black Women, Rape, and Resistance—A New History of the Civil Rights Movement from Rosa Parks to the Rise of Black Power*. New York: Vintage Books, 2010.

McGuire, Danielle L. "'It Was Like All of Us Had Been Raped': Sexual Violence, Community Mobilization, and the African American Freedom Struggle." *Journal of American History* (December 2004).

McIntosh, Kriston, Emily Moss, Ryan Nunn, and Jay Shambaugh. "Examining the Black-White Wealth Gap." *The Brookings Institution*, February 27, 2020. https://www.brookings.edu/blog/up-front/2020/02/27/examining-the-black-white-wealth-gap/.

McQueeny, Kevin. "Playing with Jim Crow: African American Private Parks in Early Twentieth Century New Orleans." MA thesis, University of New Orleans, 2005.

McRuer, Robert. "Compulsory Able-Bodiedness and Queer/Disabled Existence." In *Disability Studies: Enabling the Humanities*, edited by Sharon L. Snyder, Brenda Jo Brueggemann, and Rosemarie Garland-Thomson. New York: MLA, 2002.

Metzl, Jonathan. *The Protest Psychosis: How Schizophrenia Became a Black Disease*. Boston: Beacon Press, 2010.

Michel, Sia. "Dream-Girl Disenfranchised." *Village Voice*, September 1, 1998.

Mille, Agnes de. *Martha: The Life and Work of Martha Graham*. New York: Random House, 1991.

Miller, D. Scott. "Afrosurrealist Manifesto: Black Is the New Black—A 21st Century Manifesto." *D. Scott Miller: AfroSurreal Generation*. http://dscotmiller.blogspot.com/2009/05/afrosurreal.html.

Mills, Charles. "The Chronopolitics of Racial Time." *Time and Society* 29, no. 2 (2020), 297–317.

Mingus, Charles. "All the Things You Could Be by Now If Sigmund Freud's Wife Was Your Mother." *Charles Mingus Presents Charles Mingus*. Candid Records, 1961.

Mingus, Charles. *Beneath the Underdog: His World as Composed by Mingus*. New York: Knopf, 1971.

"Missouri Police Still Disproportionately Stop Black Drivers." *USNews*, May 29, 2020. https://www.usnews.com/news/best-states/missouri/articles/2020-05-29/missouri-police-still-disproportionately-stop-black-drivers.

Mitchell, Margaret. *Gone with the Wind*. New York: Macmillan, 1936.

Mlynar, Phillip. "Lauryn Hill's Top 5 Career-Torpedoing Tendencies." *L.A. Weekly*, February 14, 2012. https://www.laweekly.com/lauryn-hills-top-5-career-torpedoing-tendencies/.

Monahan, John, Henry J. Steadman, Eric Silver, Paul S. Appelbaum, Pamela Clark Robbins, Edward P. Mulvey, Loren H. Roth, Thomas Grisso, and Steven M.

Banks. *Rethinking Risk Assessment: The MacArthur Study of Mental Disorder and Violence*. Oxford: Oxford University Press, 2001.

Moore, Natalie. *The South Side: A Portrait of Chicago and American Segregation*. New York: St. Martin's Press, 2017.

Morgan, Joan. "Fly-Girls, Bitches, and Hoes: Notes of a Hip-Hop Feminist." *Social Text*, no. 45 (winter 1995).

Morgan, Joan. *She Begat This: 20 Years of The Miseducation of Lauryn Hill*. New York: Atria, 2018.

Morgan, Joan. "They Call Me Ms. Hill." *Essence*, January 2006. http://www.essence .com/essence/themix/entertainment/0,16109,1149478,00.html.

Morgan, TaNoah. "Malcolm X Gets Stamp of Approval; Leader Honored on King's Birthday by Government He Faulted." *Baltimore Sun*, January 16, 1999.

Morrison, Toni. *Beloved*. New York: Alfred A. Knopf, 1987.

Morrison, Toni. "Novelist Toni Morrison Looks Back on Her Youth and Family and Presents Her Newest Book, 'Jazz.'" Interview by Charlie Rose. *The Charlie Rose Show*, PBS, May 7, 1993. https://charlierose.com/episodes/18778.

Morrison, Toni. *Playing in the Dark: Whiteness and the Literary Imagination*. New York: Vintage Books, 1993.

Morrison, Toni. *Sula*. New York: Alfred A. Knopf, 1973.

Morton, Jelly Roll. "I Thought I Heard Buddy Bolden Say" (1988 Remastered). RCA Bluebird (BMG) 1988. CD.

Moten, Fred. "The Case of Blackness." *Criticism* 50, no. 2 (2008).

Moten, Fred. "An Interview with Fred Moten, Part I," by Adam Fitzgerald. *Literary Hub*, August 5, 2015.

Moten, Fred. *In the Break: The Aesthetics of the Black Radical Tradition*. Minneapolis: University of Minnesota Press, 2003.

"Ms Lauryn Hill." June 8, 2012. https://mslaurynhill.com/.

Mudimbe, V. Y. *The Idea of Africa*. Bloomington: Indiana University Press, 1994.

Mulvey, Laura. "Visual Pleasure and Narrative Cinema." In *Feminism and Film Theory*, ed. Constance Penley. New York: Routledge, Chapman, and Hall, 1988.

Muñoz, José Esteban. *Cruising Utopia: The Then and There of Queer Futurity*. New York: New York University Press, 2009.

Murphy, Keith. "7 Ways Lauryn Hill Can Make Us Forget a Decade of Crazy." Vibe .com. July 10, 2010.

"Music: The Best of 1998 Music." *Time*, December 21, 1998. http://www.time.com /time/magazine/article/0,9171,989884,00.html.

Musser, Amber. *Sensual Excess: Queer Femininity and Brown Jouissance*. New York: New York University Press, 2018.

Nashrulla, Tasneem. "An Unarmed Teen Was Running around Naked in an Oklahoma Neighborhood. Then Police Shot And Killed Him." *BuzzfeedNews*, May 2, 2019.

National Institute of Mental Health. "Mental Illness." NIH.gov, February 2019. https:// www.nimh.nih.gov/health/statistics/mental-illness.shtml#part_154788.

Neal, Mark Anthony. *Soul Babies: Black Popular Culture and the Post-Soul Aesthetic*. New York: Routledge, 2002.

"The New Classics: Music." *Entertainment Weekly*, June 20, 2008.

Nietzsche, Frederich. *Daybreak: Thoughts on the Prejudices of Morality*. 1881. Translated by R. J. Hollingdale. Cambridge: Cambridge University Press, 1997.

"Nina Simone—The Legend." Dir. Frank Lords. Perf. Nina Simone. London: BBC, 1992; Quantum Video, 1992. DVD.

Nyong'o, Tavia. *Afro-Fabulations: The Queer Drama of Black Life*. New York: New York University Press, 2018.

Ocean, Frank. "Bad Religion." On *Channel Orange*. New York: Def Jam, 2012.

Ocean, Frank. "thank you's." https://frankocean.tumblr.com/post/26473798723.

Ocean, Frank. "Wither." On *Endless*. New York: Def Jam, 2016.

Okoampa-Ahoofe, Kwame, Jr. "The Creative Genius of Lauryn Hill." *New York Amsterdam News*, February 23, 2000.

Olbermann, Keith. *Trump Is F*cking Crazy*. New York: Penguin, 2017.

Oliver, Paul. "Smith (née Robinson), Mamie." *The New Grove Dictionary of Jazz*, 2nd ed. New York: Oxford University Press, 2003.

Olsson, Göran Hugo, and Rachel Segal Hamilton. "'Concerning Violence' Is a New Meditation on Africa's Struggle for Freedom." *Vice*, November 24, 2014. https://www.vice.com/en_us/article/jmb47p/concerning-violence-rachel-segal-hamilton-310

Ondaajte, Michael. *Coming through Slaughter*. New York: Vintage, 1996.

Ovid. *Metamorphoses*. Translated by Anthony S. Kline. http://etext.lib.virginia.edu/latin/ovid/trans/Ovhome.htm.

Painter, Nell Irvin. "Soul-Murder and Slavery: Toward a Fully Loaded Cost Accounting." In *Southern History across the Color Line*. Chapel Hill: University of North Carolina Press, 2002.

Pajot, S. "Lauryn Hill, Charlie Wilson, and Bobby Brown at Jazz in the Gardens, March 19." *Miami New Times*, March 20, 2011. https://www.miaminewtimes.com/music/lauryn-hill-charlie-wilson-and-bobby-brown-at-jazz-in-the-gardens-march-19-6438468.

Pape, Carina. "'Race,' 'Sex,' and 'Gender': Intersections, Naturalistic Fallacies, and the Age of Reason." In *Thinking about the Enlightenment: Modernity and Its Ramifications*, ed. Martin L. Davies. London: Routledge, 2016.

Parks, Suzan-Lori. "The Death of the Last Black Man in the Whole Entire World." *Theater* 21, no. 3 (1990): 81–94. https://doi.org/10.1215/01610775-21-3-81.

Parks, Suzan-Lori, and Han Ong. "Suzan-Lori Parks by Han Ong." *BOMB Magazine*, April 1, 1994.

Patterson, Orlando. *Slavery and Social Death: A Comparative Study*. Cambridge, MA: Harvard University Press, 1982.

Perry, Imani. *Prophets of the Hood: Politics and Poetics in Hip Hop*. Durham, NC: Duke University Press, 2004.

Perry, John Weir. *Trials of the Visionary Mind: Spiritual Emergency and the Renewal Process*. Albany: State University of New York Press, 1998.

Pickens, Therí. *Black Madness :: Mad Blackness*. Durham, NC: Duke University Press, 2019.

Plato. *Phaedrus*. Translated by Benjamin Jowett. Mineola, NY: Dover, 2012.

Poe, Edgar Allan. *Edgar Allan Poe: Complete Tales and Poems*. Edison, NJ: Castle Books, 2002.

Poussaint, Alvin F. "Is Extreme Racism a Mental Illness?" *Western Journal of Medicine* 176, no. 1 (January 2002).

Powell, Fred. "Civil Society History IV: Enlightenment." In *International Encyclopedia of Civil Society*, edited by Helmut Anheier and Stefan Toepler. New York: Springer, 2010.

Powers, Ann. "Crossing Back Over from Profane to Sacred." *New York Times*, August 23, 1998. http://www.nytimes.com/1998/08/23/arts/pop-jazz-crossing -back-over-from-profane-to-sacred.html?src=pm.

Price, Margaret. "The Bodymind Problem and the Possibilities of Pain." *Hypatia* 30, no. 1 (2014): 268–84. https://doi.org/10.1111/hypa.12127.

Price, Margaret. *Mad at School: Rhetorics of Mental Disability and Academic Life*. Ann Arbor: University of Michigan Press, 2011.

Pritzker, Daniel, dir. *Bolden*. New York: Abramorama, 2019.

"Profiles in Courage: Toilet Pioneer." *Chappelle's Show—Season Two*, Episode 13, aired April 14, 2004. Written by Dave Chappelle and Neal Brennan. Comedy Central (2005). DVD.

Pryor, Rain. *Jokes My Father Never Taught Me: Life, Love, and Loss with Richard Pryor*. New York: HarperCollins, 2006.

Pryor, Richard. *Pryor Convictions*. New York: Knopf, 1995.

Quashie, Kevin. *The Sovereignty of Quiet: Beyond Resistance in Black Culture*. New Brunswick, NJ: Rutgers University Press, 2012.

Ramas, Maria. "Freud's Dora, Dora's Hysteria: The Negation of a Woman's Rebellion." *Feminist Studies* 6, no. 3 (1980).

Ramirez, Margaret. "Comedian Martin Lawrence Runs into Street, Yells at Cars." *Los Angeles Times*, May 8, 1996.

Ramsey, Guthrie. *The Amazing Bud Powell: Black Genius, Jazz History, and the Challenge of Bebop*. Berkeley: University of California Press, 2013.

Rankin, Kenrya. "NYPD Officer Kills Deborah Danner, Mentally Ill Black Woman." *Colorlines*, October 19, 2016.

Rebhorn, Matthew. "Flaying Dutchman: Masochism, Minstrelsy, and the Gender Politics of Amiri Baraka's "Dutchman." *Callaloo* 26, no. 3 (2003).

Rediker, Marcus. *The Slave Ship: A Human History*. Harmondsworth, UK: Penguin, 2011.

Reed, Anthony. *Freedom Time: The Poetics and Politics of Black Experimental Writing*. Baltimore: Johns Hopkins University Press, 2014.

Reed, Ishmael. *Conversations with Ishmael Reed*, ed. Bruce Dick and Amritjit Singh. Jackson: University Press of Mississippi, 1995.

Reichman, Thomas, dir. *Mingus: Charles Mingus*. Inlet Films, 1968.

Reiss, Benjamin. *Theaters of Madness: Insane Asylums and Nineteenth-Century American Culture*. Chicago: University of Chicago Press, 2008.

"Report: California Cops More Likely to Stop Black Drivers." January 2, 2020. https:// www.usnews.com/news/best-states/california/articles/2020-01-02/report -california-cops-more-likely-to-stop-black-drivers.

"Report: Dave Chappelle in a Mental Health Facility." *Associated Press*, May 11, 2005. https://www.today.com/popculture/report-chappelle-mental-health-facility-wbna7821711.

Richard Pryor: Live in Concert. Jeff Margolis, dir. MPI Home Video, 1979. DVD.

Richards, Chris. "Lauryn Hill Moves Her R&B toward Progressive Rock." *The Washington Post*, March 1, 2012. https://www.washingtonpost.com/lifestyle/style/lauryn-hill-moves-her-randb-toward-progressive-rock/2012/03/01/gIQAYkzMlR_story.html.

Richards, Sandra. "What Is to Be Remembered? Tourism to Ghana's Slave Castle-Dungeons." *Critical Theory and Performance*, rev. and enlarged ed., ed. Janelle Reinelt and Joseph R. Roach. Ann Arbor: University of Michigan Press, 2007.

Ricoeur, Paul. *Freud and Philosophy: An Essay on Interpretation*. 1965. New Haven, CT: Yale University Press, 1970.

Roach, Joseph. *Cities of the Dead: Circum-Atlantic Performance*. New York: Columbia University Press, 1996.

Robinson, Cedric J., and Robin D. G. Kelley. *Black Marxism: The Making of the Black Radical Tradition*. 2nd ed. Chapel Hill: University of North Carolina Press, 2000.

Rodgers, Richard (music), and Oscar Hammerstein II (lyrics). "My Favorite Things." *The Sound of Music* (film soundtrack). 1965. RCA Victor, 2000. CD.

Rodis, Peter, dir. *Nina Simone: A Historical Perspective*. 1970.

"*Rolling Stone* 1998 Critics." http://www.rocklistmusic.co.uk/rolling.htm#98.

Ross, Marlon. *Manning the Race: Reforming Black Men in the Jim Crow Era*. New York: New York University Press, 2004.

Rowell, Charles H. "An Interview with Gayl Jones." *Callaloo* 16 (1982): 32–53.

Rowley, Hazel. *Richard Wright: The Life and Times*. New York: Henry Holt, 2001.

Rubin, Jeffrey B. *The Good Life: Psychoanalytic Reflections on Love, Ethics, Creativity, and Spirituality*. Albany: State University of New York Press, 2004.

Russell, Dick. "How a West African Shaman Helped My Schizophrenic Son in a Way Western Medicine Couldn't." *Washington Post*, March 24, 2015. https://www.washingtonpost.com/posteverything/wp/2015/03/24/how-a-west-african-shaman-helped-my-schizophrenic-son-in-a-way-western-medicine-couldnt/.

Rustin, Nichole, and Sherrie Tucker, eds. *Big Ears: Listening for Gender in Jazz Studies*. Durham, NC: Duke University Press, 2008.

Samuels, Ellen. "Six Ways of Looking at Crip Time." *Disability Studies Quarterly* 37, no. 3 (2017).

Scaggs, Austin. "Kanye West: No Kicks from Champagne." *Rolling Stone*, December 30, 2004. https://www.rollingstone.com/music/news/kanye-west-no-kicks-from-champagne-20041230.

Schalk, Sami. *Bodyminds Reimagined: (Dis)Ability, Race, and Gender in Black Women's Speculative Fiction*. Durham, NC: Duke University Press, 2018.

Schalk, Sami. "Reevaluating the Supercrip." *Journal of Literary and Cultural Disability Studies* 10, no. 1 (2016): 71–86.

Schapira, Laurie Layton. *The Cassandra Complex: Living with Disbelief: A Modern Perspective on Hysteria*. Charleston, SC: Booksurge, 1988.

Schneider, V. B. "What Is It to Be Rational?" *Philosophy Now* 1 (1991).

Schwartz, Robert C., and David M Blankenship. "Racial Disparities in Psychotic Disorder Diagnosis: A Review of Empirical Literature." *World Journal of Psychiatry* 4, no. 4 (2014): 135.

Scott, James C. *Domination and the Arts of Resistance: Hidden Transcripts*. New Haven, CT: Yale University Press, 1990.

Sedgwick, Eve Kosofsky. "Paranoid Reading and Reparative Reading, or, You're So Paranoid, You Probably Think This Essay Is about You." In *Touching Feeling: Affect, Pedagogy, Performativity*. Durham, NC: Duke University Press, 2003.

The Sentencing Project. "Racial Disparity in Sentencing: A Review of the Literature." SentencingProject.org. Washington, DC: The Sentencing Project, 2005.

Shakespeare, Tom. "The Social Model of Disability." In *The Disability Studies Reader*. 2nd ed. Edited by Lennard J. Davis. New York: Routledge, 2006.

Shakespeare, William. *Hamlet* (Folger Shakespeare Library). New York: Simon and Schuster, 2003.

Shange, Ntozake. *Liliane: Resurrection of the Daughter*. New York: Picador, 1994.

Shange, Ntozake. *Sassafras, Cypress, and Indigo*. New York: Picador, 1996.

Shange, Ntozake. "Spell #7." *Three Pieces*. New York: St. Martin's Press, 1992.

Shapiro, Nat, and Nat Hentoff, eds. *Hear Me Talkin' to Ya: The Story of Jazz as Told by the Men Who Made It*. Mineola, NY: Dover, 1966.

Sharpe, Christina. *In the Wake: On Blackness and Being*. Durham, NC: Duke University Press, 2016.

Sharpe, Christina. *Monstrous Intimacies: Making Post-Slavery Subjects*. Durham, NC: Duke University Press, 2010.

Showalter, Elaine. *The Female Malady: Women, Madness, and English Culture, 1890–1980*. New York: Penguin Books, 1987.

Silsby, Gilien. "People with Schizophrenia Are Often Targets for Criminals." *USC News*, October 22, 2001. https://news.usc.edu/4303/People-With-Schizophrenia-Are-Often-Targets-for-Criminals/.

Simone, Nina. "Hey Buddy Bolden." *Nina Simone Sings Ellington*. Colpix Records, 1962. CD.

Simone, Nina. "Mississippi Goddam." *Nina Simone in Concert*. Philips Records, 1964.

Simone, Nina. "Simone Says." Interview by Brantley Bardin. *Details*, January 1997. http://brantleybardin.com/_articles/hits_nina_simone.html.

Simone, Nina. "To Love Somebody." New York: RCA Victor, 1969.

Simone, Nina. "Who Knows Where the Time Goes?" *Black Gold*. New York: RCA Records, 1970.

Simone, Nina. "Why? (The King of Love Is Dead)." *'Nuff Said!* RCA Victor, 1968.

Simone, Nina, and Stephen Cleary. *I Put a Spell on You: The Autobiography of Nina Simone*. New York: Pantheon Books, 1992.

Simpson, Tyrone R. "When Keeping It Real Goes Wrong: Pryor, Chappelle, and the Comedic Politics of Post-Soul." *Richard Pryor: The Life and Legacy of a "Crazy"*

Black Man. Edited by Audrey Thomas McCluskey. Bloomington: Indiana University Press, 2008.

Siskel, Gene. "Richard Pryor Comes Clean in Harrowing Recap of Life." *Chicago Tribune*, May 4, 1986.

Smith, Barbara. "Toward a Black Feminist Criticism." *Women's Studies International Quarterly* 2, no. 2 (January 1978): 183–94. https://doi.org/10.1016/s0148-0685(79)91780-9.

Smith, Mamie. "Crazy Blues." 1920. *Crazy Blues: The Best of Mamie Smith*. Sony Records, 2004. CD.

Snyder, Terri L. *The Power to Die: Slavery and Suicide in British North America*. Chicago: University of Chicago Press, 2015.

Solange. "Mad." *A Seat at the Table*. Saint/Columbia, 2016.

Sontag, Susan. *On Photography*. New York: Penguin Books, 2010.

Spence, Sean. "Dementia Praecox and the Birth of Jazz." Abstract. Hogan Jazz Archives, Tulane University, New Orleans.

Spillers, Hortense J. "'All the Things You Could Be by Now, if Sigmund Freud's Wife Was Your Mother': Psychoanalysis and Race." *boundary 2* 23, no. 3 (1996).

Spillers, Hortense J. Interview by Tim Haslett. February 4, 1998. BlackCulturalStudies.org.

Spillers, Hortense J. "Mama's Baby, Papa's Maybe: An American Grammar Book." *Diacritics* 17, no. 2 (Culture and Countermemory: The "American" Connection) (summer 1987).

Spillers, Hortense J. "Peter's Pans: Eating in the Diaspora." *Black, White, and in Color: Essays on American Literature and Culture*. Chicago: University of Chicago Press, 2003.

Spillers, Hortense, Saidiya Hartman, Farah Jasmine Griffin, Shelly Eversley, and Jennifer L. Morgan. "'Whatcha Gonna Do?': Revisiting 'Mama's Baby, Papa's Maybe: An American Grammar Book': A Conversation with Hortense Spillers, Saidiya Hartman, Farah Jasmine Griffin, Shelly Eversley, and Jennifer L. Morgan." *Women's Studies Quarterly* 35, nos. 1–2 (April 1, 2007): 299–309. http://www.jstor.org/stable/27649677.

"*Spin* Albums of the Year 1998." http://www.rocklistmusic.co.uk/spinend.htm.

Stallings, L. H. *Funk the Erotic: Transaesthetics and Black Sexual Cultures*. Champaign: University of Illinois Press, 2015.

Stanghellini, Giovanni, Massimo Ballerini, Simona Presenza, Milena Mancini, Andrea Raballo, Stefano Blasi, and John Cutting. "Psychopathology of Lived Time: Abnormal Time Experience in Persons with Schizophrenia." *Schizophrenia Bulletin* 42, no. 1 (2016). https://doi.org/10.1093/schbul/sbv052.

Stephens, Michelle Ann. *Skin Acts: Race, Psychoanalysis, and the Black Male Performer*. Durham, NC: Duke University Press, 2014.

Stewart, Sara. "What Are You Laughing At? Back from Africa, Back on Film, Dave Chappelle Won't Back Down." *New York Post*, February 16, 2006. https://nypost.com/2006/02/19/what-are-you-laughing-at-back-from-africa-back-on-film-dave-chappelle-wont-back-down/.

"Strikes Mother with Water Pitcher." *The New Orleans Item*, March 28, 1906.

Susman, Gary. "New 'Chappelle' DVD Is Fastest-Selling TV Disc Ever." *Entertainment Weekly*, June 1, 2005. https://ew.com/article/2005/06/01/new-chappelle-dvd-fastest-selling-tv-disc-ever/.

Szasz, Thomas. *The Ethics of Psychoanalysis: The Theory and Method of Autonomous Psychotherapy*. New York: Basic Books, 1965.

Szwed, John. *Space Is the Place: The Lives and Times of Sun Ra*. New York: Da Capo Press, 1998.

Tandon, Ajay, Christopher Murray, Jeremy Lauer, and David Evans. "Measuring Overall Health System Performance for 191 Countries." *Geneva, World Health Organization*, 2000. https://www.who.int/healthinfo/paper30.pdf.

Tate, Claudia C. "An Interview with Gayl Jones." *Black American Literature Forum* 13, no. 4 (1979).

Tate, Claudia C. *Psychoanalysis and Black Novels: Desire and the Protocols of Race*. New York: Oxford University Press, 1998.

Teplin, Linda A., Gary M. McClelland, Karen M. Abram, and Dana A. Weiner. "Crime Victimization in Adults with Severe Mental Illness: Comparison with the National Crime Victimization Survey." *Archives of General Psychiatry* 62, no. 8 (2005). doi:10.1001/archpsyc.62.8.911.

Tettenborn, Éva. "Melancholia as Resistance in Contemporary African American Literature." *MELUS* 31, no. 3 (2006): 101–21.

Tighe, Janet A. "'What's in a Name?'" *Journal of the American Academy of Psychiatry and the Law Online* 33, no. 2 (2005): 252. http://www.jaapl.org/content/33/2/252.abstract.

Tillet, Salamishah. "In the Shadow of the Castle: (Trans)Nationalism, African American Tourism and Gorée Island." *Research in African Literatures* 40, no. 4 (2009), 122–41.

Torrey, E. Fuller, Aaron Kennard, Don Eslinger, Richard Lamb, and James Pavle. "More Mentally Ill Persons Are in Jails and Prisons Than Hospitals: A Survey of the States." Arlington, VA: Treatment Advocacy Center, 2010.

Touré. "The Mystery of Lauryn Hill." *Rolling Stone*, October 30, 2003. http://www.rollingstone.com/news/story/5940100/the_mystery_of_lauryn_hill.

Trethewey, Natasha. "Calling His Children Home." *Callaloo* 19, no. 2 (spring 1996).

Tucker, Sherrie. "Big Ears: Listening for Gender in Jazz Studies." *Current Musicology*, nos. 71–73 (spring 2001–2002).

Tucker, Sherrie. *Swing Shift: "All-Girl" Bands of the 1940s*. Durham, NC: Duke University Press, 2000.

Turk, Edward Baron. "Comedy and Psychoanalysis: The Verbal Component." *Philosophy and Rhetoric* 12, no. 2 (spring 1979).

Tyrangiel, Josh. "Unplugged and Unglued." *Time*, May 13, 2002. http://www.time.com/time/magazine/article/0,9171,1002421,00.html.

Vaish, Amrisha, Tobias Grossmann, and Amanda Woodward. "Not All Emotions Are Created Equal: The Negativity Bias in Social-Emotional Development." *Psychological Bulletin* 134, no. 3 (2008): 383–403. https://doi.org/10.1037/0033-2909.134.3.383.

Vance, Carol, ed. *Pleasure and Danger: Exploring Female Sexuality*. Boston: Routledge and Kegan Paul, 1984.

Walcott, Rinaldo. *Black Like Who? Writing Black Canada*. 2nd ed. London, Ontario: Insomniac Press, 2003.

Walker, Alice. "In Search of Our Mother's Gardens." *In Search of Our Mother's Gardens: Womanist Prose*. San Diego: Harcourt and Brace, 1983.

Wall, Cheryl. "Trouble in Mind: Blues and History in *Corregidora*." In *Worrying the Line: Black Women Writers, Lineage, and Literary Tradition*. Chapel Hill: University of North Carolina Press, 2005.

Wallace, Amy. "Amen! (D'Angelo's Back)." *GQ*, June 2012.

Warren, Calvin. "Black Time: Slavery, Metaphysics, and the Logic of Wellness." In *The Psychic Hold of Slavery: Legacies in American Expressive Culture*, edited by Soyica Diggs Colbert, Robert J. Patterson, Aida Levy-Hussen. New Brunswick, NJ: Rutgers University Press, 2016.

Washington, Salim. "All the Things You Could Be by Now: *Charles Mingus Presents Charles Mingus* and the Limits of Avant-Garde Jazz." *Uptown Conversation: The New Jazz Studies*, ed. Robert O'Meally, Brent Hayes Edwards, and Farah Jasmine Griffin. New York: Columbia University Press, 2004.

Waters, Anita M. "Conspiracy Theories as Ethnosociologies: Explanation and Intention in African American Political Culture." *Journal of Black Studies* 28 (September 1997).

Watson, Elijah J. "'Don't Waste Your Money on Her': Lauryn Hill Angers Toronto Fans for Late Performance." *OkayPlayer*, July 2018. https://www.okayplayer.com/music/lauryn-hill-angers-toronto-fans-for-late-performance.html.

Waxman, Sharon. "The Tragedy of the Comic." *Washington Post*, June 24, 1997. https://www.washingtonpost.com/wpsrv/style/longterm/movies/review97/fmartinlawrence.htm.

Weaver, Vesla Mae. "Why White People Keep Calling the Cops on Black Americans." *Vox*, May 29, 2018. https://www.vox.com/first-person/2018/5/17/17362100/starbucks-racial-profiling-yale-airbnb-911.

Weheliye, Alexander. *Habeas Viscus: Racializing Assemblages, Biopolitics, and Black Feminist Theories of the Human*. Durham, NC: Duke University Press, 2014.

Wehring, Heidi J., and William T. Carpenter. "Violence and Schizophrenia." *Schizophrenia Bulletin* 37, no. 1 (2011).

Wells-Barnett, Ida B. "Lynch Law in America." *The Arena*, January 23, 1900. https://www.blackpast.org/african-american-history/1900-ida-b-wells-lynch-law-america/.

West, Cornel. "The Making of an American Radical Democrat of African Descent." *The Cornel West Reader*. New York: Basic Civitas Books, 2000.

West, Cornel. "The Political Intellectual." *The Cornel West Reader*. New York: Basic Civitas Books, 2000.

West, Kanye. "All Falls Down." *Freshman Adjustment*. Chicago: Chi Town Gettin' Down Inc., 2004.

West, Kanye. "Kanye West/Charlemagne Interview." Interviewed by Charlemagne. YouTube video, 1:45:05. May 2018. https://youtu.be/zxwfDlhJIpw.

West, Kanye. "Yikes." *Ye*. New York: GOOD Music/Def Jam, 2018.

West, Kanye (@kanyewest). "my point is for us to have stayed in that position even though the numbers were on our side means that we were mentally enslaved." Twitter, May 1, 2018. https://twitter.com/kanyewest/status/991459400018624512.

West, Kanye (@kanyewest). "The reason why I brought up the 400 years point is because we can't be mentally imprisoned for another 400 years. We need free thought now. Even the statement was an example of free thought[.] It was just an idea." Twitter, May 1, 2018.

West, Kanye (@kanyewest). "to make myself clear. of course I know that slaves did not get shackled and put on a boat by free will." Twitter, May 1, 2018.

West, Kanye (@kanyewest). "You don't have to agree with trump but the mob can't make me not love him. We are both dragon energy. He is my brother. I love everyone. I don't agree with everything anyone does. That's what makes us individuals. And we have the right to independent thought." Twitter, April 25, 2018. https://twitter.com/kanyewest/status/989179757651574784?s=20.

Wicker, Jewel. "Concert Review: Lauryn Hill Shows Up More than 2 Hours Late to Atlanta Show." *Atlanta Journal-Constitution*, May 7, 2016. https://www.ajc.com/blog/music/concert-review-lauryn-hill-shows-more-than-hours-late-atlanta-show/kkFJSBQjLkeWlKGiyXOU7O.

Wilderson, Frank B., III. "Blacks and the Slave/Master Relation." In *Afro-pessimism: An Introduction*, by C. S. Soong. KPFA Radio, 2015, 2017.

Wilderson, Frank B., III. *Red, White & Black: Cinema and the Structure of U.S. Antagonisms*. Durham, NC: Duke University Press, 2010.

Williams, Patricia J. *The Alchemy of Race and Rights*. Cambridge, MA: Harvard University Press, 1991.

Williams, Patricia J. "Gathering the Ghosts." *The A-Line*, August 30, 2018. https://alinejournal.com/vol-1-no-3-4/gathering-the-ghosts/.

Williams-Forson, Psyche. *Building Houses Out of Chicken Legs: Black Women, Food, and Power*. Chapel Hill: University of North Carolina Press, 2006.

Williams-Forson, Psyche. "The Future of Food Studies—Intersectionality." *Notes on the Field* (Graduate Association for Food Studies) 6, no. 1 (2019). https://doi.org/10.21428/92775833.c8830e27.

Williams-Washington, Kristin N., and Chmaika P. Mills. "African American Historical Trauma: Creating an Inclusive Measure." *Journal of Multicultural Counseling and Development* 46, no. 4 (2018): 246–63. https://doi.org/10.1002/jmcd.12113.

Willis, Kiersten. "Lauryn Hill Fans Trash Singer after She Showed Up Late Again to Concert." *Atlanta Black Star*, July 20, 2018. https://atlantablackstar.com/2018/07/20/lauryn-hill-fans-trash-singer-after-she-showed-up-late-again-to-concert/.

Wilson, August. *Seven Guitars*. 1995. Electronic edition. Alexander Street Press, 2013.

Wilson, Eric G. *Everyone Loves a Good Train Wreck—Why We Can't Look Away*. New York: Farrar, Straus and Giroux, 2013.

Wilson, Michael. "When Mental Illness Meets Police Firepower; Shift in Training for Officers Reflects Lessons of Encounters Gone Awry." *New York Times*, December 28, 2003.

Winant, Howard. *Racial Conditions: Politics, Theory, Comparisons*. Minneapolis: University of Minnesota Press, 1994.

Witter, Simon. "Lauryn Hill: 'I'm not afraid to be the person I am.'" *The Guardian*, August 21, 2013. https://www.theguardian.com/music/2013/aug/21/rocks-back-pages-lauryn-hill.

Wolf, James, and Hartmut Geerken, eds. *Sun Ra: The Immeasurable Equation—The Collected Prose and Poetry*. Wartaweil, Germany: Waitawhile Press, 2006.

Wolfe, George C. *The Colored Museum*. London: Metheun, 1987.

Wolframe, PhebeAnn Marjory. "The Madwoman in the Academy, or, Revealing the Invisible Straightjacket: Theorizing and Teaching Saneism and Sane Privilege." *Disability Studies Quarterly* 33, no. 1 (2012). https://doi.org/10.18061/dsq.v33i1.3425.

Wolk, Josh. "Chappelle's No Show." *Entertainment Weekly*, May 11, 2005. https://ew.com/article/2005/05/11/chappelles-no-show/.

Wood, Robert W. *Memorial of Edward Jarvis, M.D.* Boston: American Statistical Association, 1885.

Woodson, Carter G. *The Mis-education of the Negro*. 1933. New York: Tribeca Books, 2013.

Woolf, Virginia. *A Room of One's Own*. 1929. Annotations by Susan Grubar. Orlando: Harcourt, 2005.

Wright, Richard. *Native Son*. 1940. New York: HarperCollins, 1993.

Young, Dannagal Goldthwaite. *Irony and Outrage: The Polarized Landscape of Rage, Fear, and Laughter in the United States*. New York: Oxford University Press, 2019.

Young, Harvey. *Embodying Black Experience: Stillness, Critical Memory, and the Black Body*. Ann Arbor: University of Michigan Press, 2010.

Yuan, Jada. "Lauryn Hill: Not Crazy After All These Years?" *New York Magazine*, October 26, 2006. http://nymag.com/daily/intel/2006/10/lauryn_hill_not_crazy_after_al.html.

"Yvonne Seon." *The History Makers: The Nation's Largest African-American Video Oral History Collection*. https://www.thehistorymakers.org/biography/yvonne-seon-39.

Zafar, Aylin. "In Defense of Lauryn Hill." *The Atlantic*, September 1, 2010. https://www.theatlantic.com/entertainment/archive/2010/09/in-defense-of-lauryn-hill/62343/.

INDEX

Abdur-Rahman, Aliyyah, 92–93
ableism, 180
Aeschylus, 152
Africa, 184–87
Afro-alienation act, 154, 156, 162
Afro-ambivalent, 187
Afrofuturism, 62–63, 202
Afro-pessimism 3, 239n4, 246n68
"Afrosurreal Manifesto" (Miller), 11
Agamemnon (Aeschylus), 152
Alabama, 61
Alexander, Elizabeth, 141
"All Falls Down" (West), 163
"All the Things You Are" (Kern and
    Hammerstein II), 208–9
"All the Things You Could Be by Now
    If Sigmund Freud's Wife Was Your
    Mother" (Mingus), 67, 208–10
"All the Things You Could Be by Now
    If Sigmund Freud's Wife Was Your
    Mother: Psychoanalysis and Race"
    (Spillers), 23–24
American English, 135–36, 157
American Picture Book, 33
American Psychiatric Association, 62, 66,
    213
American Score, 33
Amsterdam, Netherlands, 160
antiblackness: antiblack psychopathology/
    psychiatry and, 17–18, 25–26, 28–29,
    45–47, 66–67; black people internal-
    izing antiblackness and, 195; causing

different modes of madness, 33–34,
136–37; coding blackness as excess, 44,
161; coding black people as mad, 4–5,
12–13, 16, 25–26, 67, 73, 206; conspir-
ing against black freedom and, 17–18,
247nn70–71; of the English language,
135, 156–57; framing antiblack racism
as mental illness, 27–29; hiding under
white liberalism, 126; images and sounds
of, 33; insistence that black people get
over racial hurt and, 213; is madness,
223; madness sharpening an opposition
to, 52; modern governance and, 109;
murder in response to, 131; paranoia in
response to, 73–74, 192–93; presidential antiblackness and, 165; producing
a bleak black now, 218; rage and, 24,
33; Reason and, 19, 26, 47; structural
antiblackness in Chicago, 232; terrorism
and, 201; in the US criminal justice
system, 189–91. *See also* blackness; colorism; race; white supremacy
anticolonial violence, 72, 159
antipornography feminists, 112–13
antipsychiatry movement, 24–25, 248n95
antiwhiteness, 26
Armstrong, Louis, 55–56
asylum, the, 16–17, 39, 130–31, 133, 246n64
"Asylum" (Jones), 104–7. *See also* Jones,
    Gayl
Atlantic, The, 212
autobiography, 64

avant-garde black performance, 156
Avilez, Gershun, 12

"Bad Religion" (Ocean), 228–29
Badu, Erykah, 229
bag lady, 160–61. *See also* women
Bakhtin, Mikhail, 39, 95, 161, 181
Banjo (McKay), 122
Baraka, Amiri, 71–72, 74, 213–14
Barrett, Robert, 15
Basu, Biman, 104
Bellevue Psychiatric Hospital, 66–67, 208
Beloved (Morrison), 19
Beneath the Underdog: His World as Composed by Mingus (Mingus), 63–64
Benjamin, Walter, 107
"Beyond the Pleasure Principle" (essay, Freud), 86
Bible, the, 95–96, 124
biomedical psychiatry, 14
bipolar disorder, 163, 167–68, 203
bitchiness, 126
Black, 5–6
Black Arts Movement, 74
Black Bourgeoisie (Frazier), 119
black common sense, 193–94
black countercriminology, 190–91
"Blacker the Berry, The" (Lamar), 221–23
blackface, 132, 172–74
Black Lives Matter Movement, 221
blackness: Afro-ambivalence toward Africa, 187; ambivalence and, 23–24; black middle class and, 119, 129–30, 132, 269n4, 281n87; black queer love and, 229; black rage as madness and, 7–8; conflating black literature with writer's biography and, 107; degrading names and, 156–57; diaspora and, 183; forging lives in offbeats and, 206; hair and, 130–31, 150; incarceration and, 234, 260n105; insurgent blackness and, 21–22; internalizing antiblackness, 195; police violence and, 34, 69, 178, 197, 250n114; racist medicine and, 268n93;

on *The Real World*, 181, 183; Reason and, 15, 190; respectability and, 24, 110–11, 118–19, 173, 269n4; retooling psy sciences to address, 23–25, 73; richness of possibility in, 3, 6; schizophrenia and, 25, 45–46; silence and, 93, 266n49; slavery and, 4, 17, 246n68; stereotypes of, 25–26, 71, 101, 126, 140, 172–73, 182, 219, 232–33; success by neoliberal standards and, 163–64; therapeutic efficacy of violence and, 72, 74; unwanted touch and, 157–58; white supremacy's fear of black radical planning, 233. *See also* antiblackness; black women; colorism; crazy nigger
black paranoia, 67, 191–94
Black Power, 24
Black Power Movement, 74
Black Pride, 130
black radical creativity, 6, 11–12, 60, 70, 140
Black Rage (Cobbs and Grier), 24
"Black Rage" (Hill), 158–60
Black Skin, White Masks (Fanon), 23, 73, 237
black sociality, 70
black studies scholarship, 11–12, 22
black time, 206
black women: black feminism and, 150; black feminist literary critics and, 112; blues music and, 87; as incapable of genius, 274n7, 278n47; mad black women in literature, 77–79, 107, 111, 113, 131, 133; mastering the voices and, 170; pain of, 141, 146; paranoia and, 193; patriarchal prerogative over, 119–20, 127, 271; performers who died young and, 170; psychopathologizing, 25–26; racism and sexism impacting, 77–78, 98, 111, 113, 118, 170, 262n16; resonant crack in black women's aural art and, 155–56; strategies of survival and, 18; susceptibility to being labeled crazy and, 162; talent of black women overshadowed

by their sorrow, 141; US black women's literature and, 112; utilizing rage, 159; visible seam in black women's visual art, 155; vulnerability if viewed as crazy and, 149. *See also* blackness; blueswoman; *Eva's Man* (Jones); Hill, Lauryn Ms.; *Liliane: Resurrection of the Daughter* (Shange); women

"Blind Supremacy" (Chappelle), 181

Blount, Herman Poole, 60

blues aesthetics, 88–89

blues music, 70, 75–77, 86–87. *See also* music

blues ritual, 87–88, 264n28

blueswoman, 87. *See also* black women

Bodies in Dissent (Brooks), 11

bohemianism, 161

Bolden, Charles (Buddy Bolden): in an asylum, 45–48, 59; background of, 41; Bolden effect and, 39–40, 43, 70; in *Coming through Slaughter,* 56–59; in "Funky Butt Blues," 48–49, 59; as the inventor of jazz, 36, 41–42, 251n1; Louis Armstrong and, 55–56; madness and music and, 45; madtime and, 206–7; mythic afterlife of, 37–40, 48; Nina Simone and, 50–51; queer domesticity and, 255n29; in *Seven Guitars,* 52–56; sexual reputation of, 37–38, 253n16; supposed mental breakdown of, 44, 58–59, 206–7; uncertainty and, 32–33, 45, 50; volume of, 37, 42–44, 51, 69, 254n25. *See also* "Calling His Children Home" (Trethewey); *Coming through Slaughter* (Ondaatje); jazz; music; *Seven Guitars* (play, Wilson)

Brennan, Neal, 194–95

Bromberg, Walter, 25–26

Brooks, Daphne, 11, 154

Brooklyn, New York, 153

Buddy Bolden Band, 253n15

"Buddy Bolden's Blues" (Bolden or Cornish). *See* "Funky Butt Blues" (Bolden or Cornish)

Bush, George W., 164–65

Calhoun, John C., 18, 247n70

"Calling His Children Home" (Trethewey), 36–39, 46, 49–50, 59

Caminero-Santangelo, Marta, 81

Campbell, Tisha, 196

capitalism, 151, 155–56, 174, 198, 213, 218

carceral time, 210–11

Carey, Mariah, 195

carnivalesque humor, 181

Cartwright, Samuel, 17–18, 25–26, 46

Caruth, Cathy, 146

Cassandra, 152–53

castration anxiety, 101, 103

Catholic Church, 152

Catholic League, 152

"Celebrity Trial Jury Selection" (Chappelle), 189–90

Cervenak, Sarah, 11–12

Césaire, Aimé, 23

Césaire, Suzanne Roussy, 22

Channel Orange (album, Ocean), 228

Chappelle, Dave: anti-Africa prejudice and, 185–86; cracking truth to power, 178, 181; cutting loose and, 178–80; departure from *Chappelle's Show* of, 174; flees to South Africa and, 174, 183–86; living under pressure and, 178–80; mad methodology and, 175; madness and, 174–79, 191–92; Ms. Lauryn Hill and, 199–200; paranoia and, 191–95; racial carnivalesque and, 181; Richard Pryor and, 187–88; to snap/click and, 172–74, 183; upbringing of, 175–76; US criminal justice system and, 189–91. *See also* performance; Pryor, Richard

Chappelle, William David, III, 176

Chappelle's Show, 172, 179–80, 189, 194, 198

Charles Mingus Presents Charles Mingus (album, Mingus), 67, 208

Cheng, Anne, 224

Chicago, 232

Christ, 124

Civilization and Its Discontents (Freud), 72

civil rights, 24, 140, 175, 201–2

madness (continued)

12; excess and, 44, 161, 183; exclamation and, 72, 74, 77, 108; feminized madness and, 131; genius and, 20–21, 139–40, 163; grotesque forms and, 39, 161–62; as historical formation, 14; idioms of madness and, 9, 71–72, 107, 126, 134, 177–78, 221; jazz and, 59–60, 68–69, 76, 207–8; in *Liliane: Resurrection of the Daughter,* 111, 126, 129, 131, 133–34, 136–37; literature and, 30–31, 56–59, 81; mad black creativity and, 2, 5, 12, 162, 177; mad black scholar and, 231–32, 234; mad black women in literature and, 77–79, 107, 111, 113, 131, 133; maddening of black genius and, 140, 199; mad studies and, 13–14; messiness of, 9; metaphor and, 72, 77, 142; murder and, 72, 74, 77, 113; music and, 29–30, 45, 50, 142, 203–4; narrative efficacy in, 81; performance and, 31, 51–57, 59, 142, 145, 203, 219–20; as place, 183, 186–87; potential of, 9, 12, 23, 126, 161, 170, 189, 198, 207, 224–25, 229–30, 248n85, 262n5; privacy through, 149; prophecy and, 20–21, 54, 139, 152–53; psychic life of black madness and, 179; Reason and, 4–5, 8, 20; romanticizing, 15, 168; sharpening one's opposition to antiblackness, 52; slavery and, 4–5, 18; as a strategy for survival, 18, 61, 192–93, 289n76; sublimation and, 72–73, 77, 111, 129; theory of racial madness, 34; uncertainty of, 11, 32; used to punish people who transgress social norms, 166–67; of the US pop culture industry, 184; visuality of Ms. Lauryn Hill's madness and, 160. *See also* crazy nigger; mad methodology; madtime; medicalized madness; mental illness; phenomenal madness; psychosocial madness; rage

Madness and Civilization: A History of Insanity in the Age of Reason (Foucault), 1

Madness: The Invention of an Idea (Foucault), 69

"Mad Real World, The" (Chappelle), 181–82

mad studies, 13–14

madtime: in black expressive culture, 206; black liberation struggles and, 207, 229–30; Buddy Bolden and, 206–7; defining, 32; depressive time and, 212–17; manic time and, 204, 208–12; melancholic time and, 224–29; metaphysical syncopation and, 205; schizophrenic time and, 217–23; Western Standard time, 204. *See also* madness

Malcolm X, 248n93

male gaze, 101–2

"Mama's Baby, Papa's Maybe: An American Grammar Book" (Spillers), 1–3, 33, 135, 157

mania, 208

manic depressive order, 50

manic time, 204, 208–12

"Manifest/Outro" (Fugees), 150

Ma Rainey. *See* Rainey, Ma

Marley, Rohan, 277n35

Marquis, Donald, 46, 56–57

Marriott, David, 28–29

Martin (show), 196

Martin, Trayvon, 221

material violence, 75, 109

Mbembe, Achille, 4–5, 109, 269n104

McCluskey, Audrey, 188

McKay, Claude, 122

Mecca, Saudi Arabia, 174

medicalized madness: antiblackness and, 34; Dave Chappelle and, 174–75; definition of, 7; in *Eva's Man,* 81; intersecting with other modes of madness, 8–9, 144; Kanye West and, 168; in *Liliane: Resurrection of the Daughter,* 111, 137; in *Native Son,* 233; Nina Simone and, 203; potential in, 9–10; schizophrenia as, 144; in *Seven Guitars,* 53. *See also* madness; mental illness

medical model of disability, 13

Medusa, 99–101

"Medusa's Head" (essay, Freud), 101

melancholia, 224–29

melancholic time, 224–29

memory, 82

menses, 80, 124

mental illness: bad behavior as, 28; degradation of persons with, 137; deinstitutionalization and, 176, 260n105; framing antiblack racism as, 27–29; impact on "Mississippi Goddam," 203; incarceration and, 234, 260n105; Nathaniel Turner and, 20; as a risk factor for police violence, 34, 69, 178, 250n113; as a sham, 25; as a social construction, 7, 14; stigma and, 25, 196, 235. *See also* madness; medicalized madness; phenomenal madness; psychosocial madness

Menzies, Robert, 13–14

metaphysical syncopation, 205–6

Middle Passage, 3–4, 16, 24. *See also* slavery

Miller, Scott D., 11

Mingus, Charles, 33, 59, 63, 208–10, 258n87. *See also* jazz

Mingus trio, 65

miscegenated psychoanalysis, 68

Miseducation of Lauryn Hill, The (album, Hill), 139, 141–43, 149, 154, 162

"Mississippi Goddam" (Simone), 159, 201–2, 208

Mitchell, Margaret, 123

modernity, 5, 49

Morgan, Joan, 170

Morrison, Toni, 18–19, 27, 222, 224, 241n18, 271n30, 289n76

Morton, Ferdinand (Jelly Roll), 42–44, 48–49, 69

Moten, Fred, 11, 39, 41

motherhood, 124–25, 153, 278n53

MTV, 181

MTV Times Square studios, 143

MTV Unplugged No. 2.0 (album/performance, Hill), 140, 143–47, 151, 225–26, 277n35

mule of the world, 170

murder: as both a physical and discursive act, 74, 97; in *Dutchman,* 71; in *Eva's Man,* 77–79, 91–92, 94, 96–98, 109; madness and, 72, 74, 77, 113; as the outcome of regimes of violence, 78, 98, 131, 134, 136; sublimation and, 129; symbolic murder and, 120

music: black protest music, 50–51, 74–75, 141–42, 156, 159, 201, 215; black women musicians in public pain and, 141; madness and, 29–30, 45, 50, 142, 203–4; pop music, 139; racial capitalism in, 156; relation between homicide and, 75. *See also* blues music; Bolden, Charles (Buddy Bolden); Hill, Lauryn, Ms.; hip-hop; jazz

"Mystery of Iniquity" (Hill), 163

Name of the Father, 125

Narrative of the Life of Frederick Douglass (Douglass), 80

Native Son (Wright), 231–34

Naylor, Gloria, 250n110, 270n4

Neal, Mark Anthony, 175

necropolitics, 109, 269n104

necropower, 109

Négritude, 22–23

New Orleans, 37, 41, 44, 55–56, 164

Newton, Huey, 250n110

Newsweek, 226

New York (magazine), 161

New York Philharmonic Hall, 215

Nietzsche, Friedrich, 12, 21

"Niggar Family, The" (Chappelle), 179, 181

Nina Simone Sings Ellington (album, Simone), 50

Notebook of a Return to the Native Land (Césaire), 23

obsessive compulsion, 132

obsessive compulsive disorder, 235–36

Ocean, Frank, 226–29

Ohio, 176

Olsson, Göran Hugo, 159

Ondaatje, Michael, 56–59

race: racial capitalism and, 153, 155–56, 162, 175, 198, 213; racial inversions and, 181; racialized reason and, 189–91; racial madness and, 34; racial paranoia and, 191–93; racial profiling and, 285n31; racial satire and, 172; racism is killing me inside and, 179; racist medicine and, 106, 268n93; racists hating themselves and, 222. *See also* antiblackness; blackness

Radical Aesthetics and Modern Black Nationalism (Avilez), 12

radical anachronism, 60

radical compassion, 10, 29, 40, 81, 97, 99, 109, 168, 234, 243n33

rage: antiblackness and, 24, 33; black rage as madness and, 7–8; black women utilizing, 159; Dave Chappelle and, 174 75; in *Eva's Man,* 81, 94; intersecting with other modes of madness, 8–9; Kanye West and, 168; in *Liliane: Resurrection of the Daughter,* 111, 126–29, 137; as a mode of madness, 7–8; Ms. Lauryn Hill and, 140, 158–59; in *Native Son,* 233; Nina Simone and, 202–3; potential in, 9–10, 24, 75, 126, 129, 136, 159; in *Seven Guitars,* 53. *See also* madness; mental illness

Rainey, Ma, 87

rationalist readers, 15, 34, 64, 84, 94

reading upside down, 107, 181, 286n38

"Ready or Not" (Fugees), 142

Reaganomics, 175

Real World, The, 181, 183

reason, 4, 190–91

Reason: Africa as unReason, 184; antiblackness and, 18–20, 26, 47; blackness and, 15, 190; capitalism and, 151; defining, 4; defying, 16, 23; as good, 29; law enforcement and, 34; manic time and, 208; ostracizing and, 8; parapositivism and, 70; Reasonable historiography and, 57; in standard social realist protest novels, 86; violence of, 9, 15, 81, 98, 135, 196

Reaume, Geoffrey, 13–14

Reed, Ishmael, 188

religious rites, 96

repetition compulsion, 82–85, 124

representational violence, 74–75, 100

repression, 123, 148

resonant crack, 155

respectability, 24, 110–11, 118–19, 122, 131, 141, 149, 173, 269n4

Ricoeur, Paul, 193

ritual logic, 96–97

Roach, Joseph, 39–40

Rolling Stone, 151

Rose, Charlie, 27, 194, 222

Rowell, Charles, 86

"Saint Pablo" (West), 167

Samuels, Ellen, 205

San Francisco Bay Guardian, 151

San Francisco Chronicle, 160

satire, 182–83

schizophrenia: blackness and, 25, 45–46; Charles Mingus and, 66; as medicalized madness, 144; Nina Simone and, 50, 203; phenomenological account of, 69, 217; potential in, 12, 218; as the result of violence, 217–18; schizophrenic time, 217–23; as a social construction, 7; stigma and, 15, 211, 222–23, 235

scholar-activist, 233

Score, The (album, the Fugees), 142, 150

Sedgwick, Eve, 193

"See See Rider" (Ma Rainey), 87

self-saboteur disorder, 216

Seon, Yvonne, 175–76

settler colonialism, 98, 108, 127

Seven Guitars (play, Wilson), 51–56, 256n52. *See also* Bolden, Charles (Buddy Bolden)

sex-positive feminism, 112–13

sexual immorality, 107

sexual symbolism, 37

sexual violence, 80, 83–84, 92, 99–100, 102–5

Trump, Donald J., 27–29, 164, 249n107
Trump Derangement Syndrome, 249n107
Turner, Nathaniel, 20–21
Tuskegee Syphilis Experiments, 106
Twenty-Fifth Annual Martin Luther
    King Jr. Concert Series, 153–54
twitch, 149

unreliable narration, 82–86
"Uses of Anger, The" (essay, Lorde), 159

vagabond lover of life, 122
Vatican, the, 152
Viacom, 181
Vibe, 151
victim-blaming, 99–100
View, 22
Village Voice, 143, 153–54, 226
violence: anticolonial violence and, 72,
    159; contextualizing individual violence
    in the context of regimes of, 81–82, 98,
    107–9; material violence and, 75, 109;
    in the modern West, 108; murder as the
    outcome of regimes of, 78, 98, 131, 134,
    136; police and, 34, 178; of Reason, 9, 81,
    98, 135; Reason and, 196; representational
    violence, 74–75, 100; schizophrenia and,
    217–18; sexual violence and, 80, 83–84, 92,
    99–100, 102–5; symbolic violence, 108–9;
    therapeutic efficacy of, 72, 74; wrought by
    empathy, 243n33. *See also* trauma
visible seam, 155

Walker, Alice, 110, 118
Walker, Kara, 250n110
Walker, Minnie, 118
Wallace, Amy, 216
Wandering (Cervenak), 11–12
Warren, Calvin, 206
Washington, Salim, 41
Washington, DC, 176
Washington Post, The, 196, 212
We Insist! Max Roach's Freedom Now Suite
    (album, Max Roach Quintet), 156

Wells, Ida B., 233
West, Cornel, 152, 281n87
West, Kanye, 140, 162–68, 198
West, the: anti-Africa logics in, 184–87;
    binaries structuring, 241n18; disability in,
    13; insanity and, 16; madness and creativ-
    ity in, 12; philosophy in, 4; psychiatric
    science in, 13–14; regimes of violence in,
    108. *See also* Enlightenment; Euromo-
    dernity; Western Standard Time
Western normativity, 62
Western philosophy, 4
Western Standard Time, 204, 207–8, 213,
    218. *See also* Enlightenment; Euromo-
    dernity; West, the
white anxiety, 225
white femininity, 123
white liberalism, 126, 201–2
whiteness, 22, 26, 182
White Rat (Jones), 104–7
white supremacy, 5, 26, 89–90, 101, 159, 198,
    202, 222, 233. *See also* antiblackness
"Who Knows Where the Time Goes?"
    (Simone), 214–15
Wilderson, Frank, 28–29, 246n68
Williams, Monnica, 34
Williams, Patricia J., 10, 243n35
Wilson, August, 51–57, 256n52
Winfrey, Oprah, 174, 185–86
"Wither" (Ocean), 227, 229
women, 94, 100–101, 113, 124–25, 131, 146,
    160, 260n104. *See also* bag lady; black
    women; feminism
Wolfe, George C., 250n110
Woolf, Virginia, 110
Wretched of the Earth (Fanon), 72, 159
Wright, Richard, 192, 231

Ye (album, West), 167
Yellow Springs, 176
"Yikes" (West), 167
You So Crazy (standup, Lawrence), 196

Zimmerman, George, 221